taschen's
1000
favorite websites

WITHDRAWN

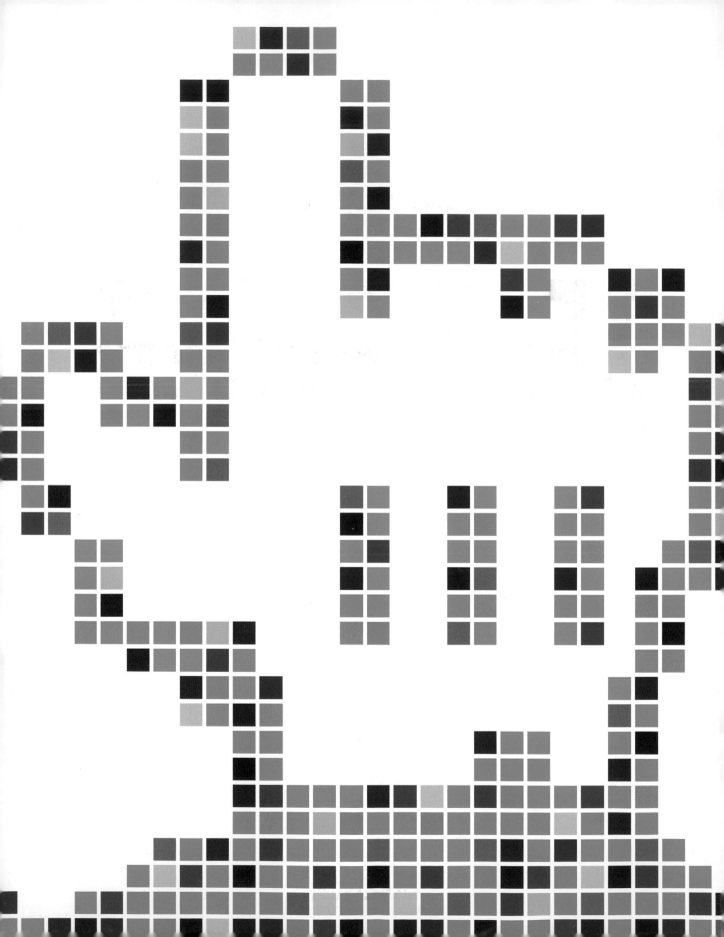

taschen's

TASCHEN
KÖLN LONDON LOS ANGELES MADRID PARIS TOKYO

contents

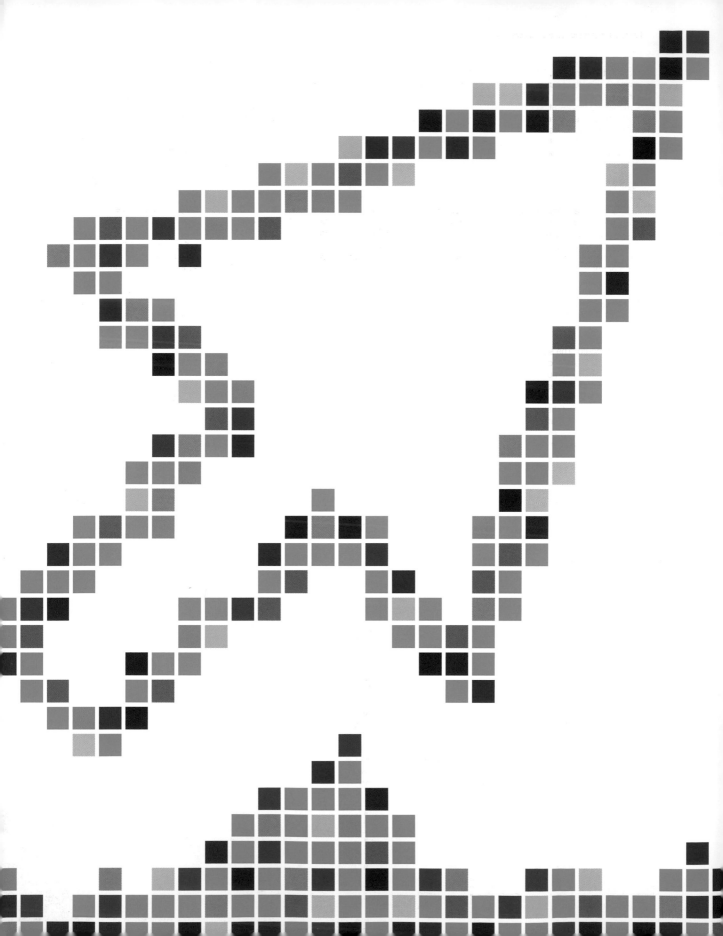

Just a click away. That's the distance that separates us today from most of the surprises, information, solutions, contacts and experiences in this life of ours. And this simple click is in fact the path to our new e-lifestyle on the World Wide Web. After its initial development as a military communication resource, the web has grown and undergone numerous phases. In terms of design standards, the pages were at first constructed using nothing more than html. This was then followed by the script phase, during which people also discovered gif animations. This brought movement and visual dynamism to the web. Although they were sometimes annoying and took their time to download, gifs added a great deal of fun to the web. This innovation is now becoming the cult part on the web. Further experimentation centered on Flash, and it is still with us and getting stronger by the day, particularly for creative professionals who make their sites their window to the outside world. This phase started almost simultaneously with Shockwave, adding the possibility of interaction online, which has taken us to the phase in which we are now, where all these resources with moreover the addition of movies and sound are making the www even better than ever.

It terms of communications media, the Web has also gone though a lot of stages. The first could be defined as the curiosity stage. Few people had access at first and even fewer had pages. Things were happening very fast, but we could only get the necessary information from a very small handful of publications or from what we heard by word of mouth. The second phase was the informative stage, which was still not really about information-providing on the large scale, because it all took much too much time and required real professionals to make the pages. The corporations and website pioneers put in a great deal of work to get things to this point, and yet it was still only the beginning. But the seed had been planted and was growing. The third stage was about information proper, and now on a grand scale. Thanks to massive investments made by media corporations, not to mention the loss of billions of dollars, these companies started to transfer their material to the web, where they could now enjoy spectacular speed and quality. But the best thing was that this was all being made available for free on the net. Nobody could have imagined that such a flow of information would ever come and grow so rapidly. Corporations and governments joined forces and added a whole new world of online services. From e-commerce to government tax forms, users began to see the new possibilities of the massive move from offline to online service accessibility and exploit it.

The next step was interaction, the point when millions were joining the web revolution every day and wanted and needed to get more instantaneous feedback. Interactivity itself was no longer a question of technology, it was a change in people's way of thinking. Of course it was all sped on by the popularization of programming languages, new resources, and tons of relevant publications. Not to mention the exchange of information online. More services offering instant feedback now added to both the happiness of the users and the benefit of the companies. It is from this point that the net has evolved to where it is today, or at least to where we are now going: the entertainment era. Time, money and sweat have always been needed, but the entertainment aspect requires that all the previous phases are properly working before it can really function as it should. Better lines, large numbers of people accessing and demanding services, plus large commercial interest, are all needed. But we are getting there. A lot of movies are already online and huge numbers of sites on music, games, animation, and interaction are popping up every day. No matter what you do, whether you buy a book or you play games online, the focus now is on the experience you should be getting and how it compares to "real life". The big breakthrough for this was the creation

of broad public access to high-speed lines such as isdn and DSL. The investments are proving their worth and the increase of people's "pleasure" while navigating the web is highly significant.

By this stage it no longer matters what we call it – the net, www, web, online page, home page, or whatever – definitions of the particulars have lost their importance. The main thing now is the change it has produced in our lives and the expectations it creates for the world to come. As we have seen, the web has achieved a point where anyone can and should do something. Although it is also true that the speed at which it has grown has created difficulties in creating international standards, this can in fact be seen as a real challenge. And this challenge is one of the reasons behind this book. At least when it comes to the parameters of beauty, navigation, creativity, attractiveness and artistry that are relevant to the areas in which TASCHEN publishes. And the medium has by no means reached its final form(impossible for a medium that grows by millions of pages a day…), for on the contrary it is just beginning for those who are searching for new, thrilling solutions. This book is divided into a number of chapters representing genuinely creative areas on the web, such as advertising, art, architecture, movies, fashion, photography, illustration, design, and eroticism. That's not to say that the examples serve simply to illustrate these fields. On the contrary, versatility online consists in extracting the best of what it is offered and applying it to any field one wishes.

The icons give you a quick idea of what to look for, i.e. whether you will find animations, sounds, downloadable material, or whatever. This publication is a compilation of 1000 pages that will shorten your path to finding great solutions online and give you millions of fresh insights. You can pick and choose from these 1000 great starting points and find the best to optimize your personal navigation time. Have a nice trip!

THE DVD
This book comes with a DVD. You can play it both on your computer and your DVD player. It contains 6 interviews done with 6 different creatives from 6 different countries, each talking about different topics. They will show you how they use the net to maximize production, get inspiration, find technical support, help clients, provide better service, exchange ideas, stay plugged to the latest news, and put their creativity to its best use. No software installation is needed, just the DVD player. The DVD is code 0, which means that it is compatible with all DVD players.

- Country
- Contains Flash
- Contains Movies
- Web Page with Sound
- Contains Shockwave
- Download Possible
- Downloadable Software
- Free Material
- Information Web Page
- Corporate Web Page
- Personal Web Page
- Cool Links in the Site

Un clic de souris. C'est la distance qui nous sépare aujourd'hui de la plupart des surprises, des informations, des solutions, des contacts et des expériences de notre vie. Ce simple clic nous conduit en fait vers notre nouveau mode de vie électronique sur le World Wide Web. Après avoir été développé initialement comme ressource de communication militaire, le web s'est transformé en passant par différentes phases. En termes de design, les pages étaient tout d'abord développées en HTML. La phase de script a suivi, pendant laquelle les gens ont découvert les images gif animées. Elle a apporté du mouvement et du dynamisme visuel au web. Bien qu'elles étaient quelques fois agaçantes et prenaient du temps à télécharger, les images gif ont ajouté beaucoup d'amusement au web. Cette innovation est depuis devenue un aspect culte du web. D'autres expérimentations centrées sur Flash ont pris la relève. Elles sont encore d'actualité et s'imposent jour après jour, plus particulièrement pour les professionnels de la création qui font de leur site une fenêtre vers le monde extérieur. Cette phase a démarré presque simultanément avec Shockwave, avec en plus la possibilité d'interagir en ligne, ce qui nous conduit à la phase dans la quelle nous sommes aujourd'hui, où toutes ces ressources, avec l'ajout de séquences vidéo et de sons, améliorent le web plus que jamais auparavant.

En termes de supports de communication, le web a également traversé de nombreuses étapes. La première peut être définie comme l'étape de curiosité. Quelques personnes avaient accès à Internet, encore moins disposaient de pages. Les choses évoluaient très rapidement, mais il n'était possible d'obtenir les informations requises qu'à partir de quelques publications ou par le bouche à oreille. La seconde étape était l'étape de l'information, qui ne fournissait cependant pas encore d'information à grande échelle, car il fallait de véritables professionnels pour créer les pages et cela prenait encore beaucoup trop de temps. Les entreprises et les pionniers du web ont travaillé d'arrache-pied pour faire évoluer les choses, mais elles n'en étaient encore qu'à leur début. Toutefois, l'idée était lancée et ne demandait qu'à se concrétiser. La troisième étape était véritablement celle de l'information à grande échelle. Grâce à des investissements massifs effectués par des entreprises de l'industrie des médias, sans oublier les milliards de dollars perdus, ces entreprises ont commencé à transférer leurs propriétés sur le web, où il pouvaient désormais constater une qualité et une vitesse incroyables. Chose encore plus intéressante, tout cela était disponible gratuitement sur le net. Personne ne pouvait imaginer qu'un tel flux d'information pouvait exister et croître aussi rapidement. Les entreprises et les gouvernements se sont associés pour créer un nouvel ensemble de services en ligne. Que ce soit au travers de sites de commerce électronique ou de formulaires d'imposition en ligne, les utilisateurs ont commencé à entrevoir les nouvelles possibilités liées à l'accessibilité des services et à les exploiter.

L'étape suivante fut l'interaction, le point où chaque jour, des millions d'individus rejoignaient la révolution web et souhaitaient obtenir des informations instantanément. L'interactivité elle-même n'était plus tant une question de technologie, mais un changement dans la façon de penser des individus. Bien sûr, tout ceci fut accéléré par la popularisation des langages de programmation, des nouvelles ressources, et de milliers de publications pertinentes, sans oublier l'échange d'information en ligne. De nouveaux services offrant des informations instantanées s'ajoutaient à l'engouement des utilisateurs et au bénéfice des entreprises. C'est à partir de ce moment que le net a évolué vers ce qu'il est devenu aujourd'hui, ou au moins ce vers quoi nous nous dirigeons : l'ère des loisirs. Le temps, l'argent et la sueur, ont toujours été des composants requis, mais l'aspect loisir exige que toutes les phases précédentes fonctionnent correctement avant de pouvoir réellement jouer le rôle qu'on attend de lui. De meilleures infrastructures, plus d'individus accédant au net et souhaitant des services, des intérêts commerciaux plus importants – tous ces composants sont requis et nous avons presque atteint cet objectif. Un grand nombre de films sont déjà mis en ligne, et de très nombreux sites musicaux, de jeux, d'animation et d'interaction naissent chaque jour. Quoi que vous fassiez, que vous achetiez un livre ou jouiez à des jeux en ligne, l'accent est maintenant mis sur l'expérience que vous devriez vivre et sa

comparaison avec la « vraie vie. » La percée majeure dans ce domaine a été la mise à disposition de connexions haut débit telles qu'ISDN et DSL à un plus large public. Les investissements ont porté leurs fruits, et l'augmentation du « plaisir » éprouvé à surfer le web est très significative.

La manière dont nous nommons cette étape n'a plus d'importance – le net, www, le web, les pages en ligne, la page d'accueil, etc. – la définition des détails a perdu de son importance. Ce qui compte maintenant est le changement produit dans nos vies et nos attentes quant au monde à venir. Comme nous l'avons vu, le web a atteint un point où chacun peut et devrait faire quelque chose, bien qu'il est vrai qu'à la vitesse où le web a évolué, les difficultés à le rendre pleinement international sont de taille. Cette problématique est une des raisons qui ont conduit à cet ouvrage, au moins en ce qui concerne les paramètres de beauté, de navigation, de créativité, d'attraction et de qualité artistique chers aux domaines de prédilection de TASCHEN. Le web est très loin d'avoir atteint sa forme finale (ce qui est impossible pour un support qui grandit à raison de plusieurs millions de page chaque jour…) ; au contraire, ce n'est encore que le début pour ceux qui recherchent des nouvelles solutions. Cet ouvrage est divisé en plusieurs chapitres représentant différents domaines créatifs du web, tels que la publicité, l'art, l'architecture, le cinéma, la mode, la photographie, l'illustration, le design et l'érotisme. Il va sans dire que ces exemples ne servent simplement qu'à illustrer ces domaines. La versatilité du web consiste à extraire le meilleur de ce qui est offert pour l'appliquer à n'importe quel autre domaine.

Les icônes vous donnent un aperçu rapide de ce que vous trouverez sur les sites, que ce soient des animations, des sons, des contenus téléchargeables, etc. Cet ouvrage est une compilation de 1 000 pages qui facilitera votre recherche des meilleures solutions en ligne et vous apportera des millions de nouvelles inspirations. Vous pouvez choisir parmi ces 1 000 bases de départ celles qui optimiseront votre recherche personnelle. Bon voyage !

Le DVD
Cet ouvrage est fourni avec un DVD. Vous pouvez le lire sur votre ordinateur ou votre lecteur DVD de salon. Il contient 6 interviews de 6 créatifs de 6 pays différents, chacun s'exprimant sur des sujets différents. Ils vous montreront comment ils utilisent le net pour maximiser leur production, s'inspirer, trouver du support technique, aider leurs clients, fournir un meilleur service, échanger des idées, se tenir au courant des dernières nouveautés, et mettre leur créativité à bon escient. Le DVD est encodé pour la région 0, ce qui signifie qu'il est compatible avec tous les lecteurs.

- Pays
- Contient du Flash
- Contient des animations
- Site avec son
- Contient du Shockwave
- Téléchargement possible
- Logiciel à télécharger
- Contenus gratuits
- Site d'information
- Site institutionnel
- Page personnelle
- Liens intéressants dans le site

Nur ein Mausklick trennt uns heute von den vielfältigen Überraschungen, Informationen, Lösungen, Kontakten und Erfahrungen, die das moderne Leben zu bieten hat. Und dieser simple Mausklick führt uns zum neuen „E-Lifestyle", dem elektronischen Lebensstil im World Wide Web. Ursprünglich als militärisches Kommunikationssystem geplant, ist das Web seither ständig gewachsen und hat inzwischen viele Stadien durchlaufen. Die Gestaltung der Sites beschränkte sich anfangs auf die reine Seitenbeschreibungssprache HTML (Hypertext Markup Language). Als Nächstes folgte die Script-Phase, in der man auch die bewegten Bilder (Animated GIFs) entdeckte. Die animierten Grafiken brachten Bewegung und visuelle Dynamik ins Web. Obwohl diese GIF-Bilder manchmal nervten und das Herunterladen eine ganze Weile dauerte, vergrößerten sie den Spaß-Faktor enorm. Heute hat das bislang meistbenutzte Grafikformat im Internet bereits Kultstatus erreicht. Weiteres Experimentieren bescherte uns Flash (??); davon profitieren wir noch heute, und Flash wird von Tag zu Tag bedeutender, vor allem für die so genannten Kreativen, die ihre Website als Fenster zur Außenwelt gestalten. Diese Phase begann fast zeitgleich mit Shockwave, was uns die Möglichkeiten der Online-Interaktion eröffnete und uns in das aktuelle Stadium hinüberleitete, in dem alle diese Mittel und Möglichkeiten und speziell die Video- und Audiowiedergabe das World Wide Web noch weiter verbesserten.

Auch als Kommunikationsmittel hat das Web eine Vielzahl von Phasen durchlaufen. Zuerst war es Neugier. Nur wenige hatten anfangs Zugang zum Web und kaum einer hatte eine eigene Homepage. Die Entwicklung verlief rasant, doch die nötigen Informationen musste man sich mühsam zusammensuchen oder war auf Mundpropaganda angewiesen. Danach folgte die Phase der Information, die allerdings nicht wirklich informativ war, denn das Erstellen der Seiten dauerte viel zu lange und erforderte echtes Profi-Wissen. Die Firmen und Website-Pioniere steckten sehr viel Arbeit hinein, und doch stand man erst am Anfang. Aber die Saat war aufgegangen. In der dritten Phase ging es um echte Informationen im großen Stil. Dank enormer Investitionen von Medienunternehmen, nicht zu vergessen Dollar-Verluste in Milliardenhöhe, begannen diese Firmen, ihr Datenmaterial ins Netz zu stellen, das jetzt zur Freude seiner Nutzer mit rasantem Tempo und hoher Qualität aufwartete. Doch das Beste daran war die kostenlose Nutzung all dieser Informationen im Web. Niemand hätte sich vorstellen können, dass je eine solche Informationsflut entstehen und so rasch anwachsen würde. Unternehmen und Regierungen taten sich zusammen und erschufen fast eine neue Welt von Online-Diensten. Ob E-Commerce oder Steuerformulare – die Nutzer entdeckten nach und nach die neuen Möglichkeiten, die der Wechsel von offline zu online bot, und nahmen diese Angebote und Dienste reichlich in Anspruch.
Der nächste Schritt war Interaktion: Millionen Nutzer täglich entfesselten die Web-Revolution, indem sie ein unmittelbares Feedback einforderten und auch benötigten. Interaktivität war nicht länger eine Frage der Technik, vielmehr hatte sich das Denken der Menschen gewandelt. Natürlich wurde das Ganze beschleunigt durch die Verbreitung von Programmiersprachen, durch neue Möglichkeiten und tonnenweise Fachliteratur, nicht zu vergessen der Austausch von Informationen online. Immer mehr Dienste mit direktem Feedback mehrten sowohl die Freude der Nutzer als auch den Profit der Firmen. Von da an entwickelte sich das Web zu dem, was es heute ist, oder war zumindest auf dem besten Wege dorthin: zu einem Medium der puren Unterhaltung. Zeit, Geld und Schweiß hat es immer gekostet, doch für den Unterhaltungsaspekt müssen erst all die vorherigen Phasen richtig laufen, damit es optimal funktioniert. Bessere Verbindungen, eine Vielzahl von Menschen, die Dienste anbieten und in Anspruch nehmen, sowie ein großes wirtschaftliches Interesse, all das wird benötigt. Doch wir sind auf dem besten Weg dorthin. Es laufen bereits viele Filme online, und täglich kommen jede Menge Web-Angebote zu Musik, Spielen, Animation und Interaktion dazu. Was man tut, ob man ein Buch kauft oder sich online an einem Computerspiel beteiligt, heute geht es im Wesentlichen um die dabei zu machende Erfahrung und wie sie sich zum „richtigen Leben" verhält. Der große Durchbruch gelang mit dem breiten öffentlichen Zugang zu High-Speed-Verbindungen wie ISDN und DSL. Die Investitionen haben sich gelohnt, und es ist erstaunlich, wie viel mehr Spaß das Surfen im Internet heute macht.

Da spielt es keine Rolle mehr, wie wir dieses Medium nennen: Internet, Web, WWW, World Wide Web, Online-Betrieb, Homepage oder dergleichen. Die einzelnen Definitionen haben ihre Bedeutung verloren. Was wirklich zählt, ist die Veränderung, die es in unserem Leben bewirkt hat, und die Erwartungen, die es für die Zukunft weckt. Das Internet hat inzwischen einen Stand erreicht, auf dem jeder etwas tun kann und sollte. Zugegebenermaßen hat das Tempo, mit dem diese Entwicklung vonstatten ging, Probleme beim Festlegen internationaler Standards aufgeworfen, doch sollte dies als echte Herausforderung gesehen werden. Diese Herausforderung war mit ein Grund für dieses Buch, zumindest wenn Parameter wie Schönheit, Navigation, Kreativität, Attraktivität und Kunst gefragt sind – Größen, die für das Verlagsprogramm von Taschen von Bedeutung sind. Dabei hat das Medium Internet noch längst nicht seine endgültige Form erreicht (unmöglich für ein Medium, das täglich um Millionen Sites anwächst ...), ganz im Gegenteil: es formt sich gerade erst für diejenigen, die nach neuen, aufregenden Lösungen suchen.
Das vorliegende Buch gliedert sich in verschiedene Kapitel zu wirklich kreativen Bereichen im Internet, z.B. Werbung, Kunst, Architektur, Film, Mode, Fotografie, Illustration, Design und Erotik. Das heißt aber nicht, dass die Beispiele nur für diese Bereiche gelten. Ganz im Gegenteil, die Vielseitigkeit im Web besteht ja gerade darin, das Beste aus dem großen Angebot herauszusuchen und es auf jeden gewünschten Bereich anzuwenden. Die Icons (Bildsymbole) helfen gezielt beim Suchen, z.B. nach Animationen, Sounds, Material zum Herunterladen und vielem mehr. Das 1000 Seiten starke Buch verkürzt die Online-Suche nach großartigen Lösungen und gewährt unendlich viele, neue Einblicke. Der Leser kann sich aus der Fülle der Informationen die besten herauspicken, um damit das Surfen im World Wide Web zu optimieren. In diesem Sinne – eine angenehme Datenreise!

Das Buch erscheint inklusive einer DVD. Diese DVD ist sowohl auf dem Computer als auch auf dem DVD-Player abspielbar. Sie enthält sechs Interviews zu diversen Themen mit sechs verschiedenen so genannten Kreativen aus sechs verschiedenen Ländern. Diese sechs Personen zeigen, wie sie die Möglichkeiten des Internets für sich nutzen, z.B. zur Produktionssteigerung, zur Inspiration, für technische Unterstützung, für den Kundendienst, für den Austausch von Ideen, für die Versorgung mit den neuesten Nachrichten und für den optimalen Einsatz ihrer Kreativität. Es muss keine extra Software installiert werden. Die DVD hat die Kennung 0, das heißt, ihr Code ist mit allen DVD-Playern kompatibel.

- USA Land
- F Enthält Flash
- Enthält Filme (Videos?)
- Website mit Sound
- SW Enthält Shockwave
- Download möglich
- Software zum Herunterladen
- Kostenloses Datenmaterial
- I Information Site
- C Corporate Website
- P Homepage
- Interessante Links auf der Site

Eén muisklik, dat is hoever u verwijderd bent van verrassingen, kennis, oplossingen en persoonlijke contacten, kortom van alle menselijke ervaringen. Die ene muisklik is de poort naar de nieuwe e-lifestyle op het world wide web. Wat ooit begon als een militair communicatiemiddel is na enkele technologische stadia te hebben doorlopen, uitgegroeid tot het omvangrijke internet zoals we dat nu kennen. Aanvankelijk werden internetpagina's gemaakt met alleen HTML, maar al snel kwam de script-fase, de tijd waarin ook de zogenoemde GIF-animaties werden ontwikkeld. Met GIF als bestandstype deden beweging en visuele dynamiek hun intrede op internet. Hoewel ze soms van slechte kwaliteit waren en het lang duurde om ze te laden, maakten animaties internet wel veel aantrekkelijker. Webanimaties zijn nu al zo populair dat ze een ware cult zijn geworden. Na verdere ontwikkelingen deed Flash geleidelijk zijn intrede. Het bleek een succes, want tegenwoordig wordt het veel door professionele ontwerpers gebruikt, die met hun site het contact met de buitenwereld leggen. Tegelijk met Flash begonnen ook de ontwikkelingen van Shockwave, dat uiteindelijk goede on line interactie mogelijk maakte. Het huidige stadium brak aan: het tijdperk waarin de combinatie van de eerste ervaringen met de nieuwe aspecten van film en geluid zullen leiden tot een professioneel en snel internet.

Ook in termen van communicatiemedia heeft internet vele stadia doorlopen. Het eerste stadium kan worden omschreven als het stadium van nieuwsgierigheid. Toen internet pas was opgezet hadden slechts enkelen toegang en nog minder hadden een eigen website. De ontwikkelingen gingen snel, maar voor nieuwe kennis konden programmeurs slechts putten uit een handvol publicaties of een beroep doen op collega's. Het tweede stadium behelsde het informatietijdperk, hoewel er zeker nog geen sprake was van informatievoorziening en –verspreiding op grote schaal. Alle ontwikkelingen kostten veel tijd en goede sites niet konden worden gemaakt zonder de kennis van professionals. De internetbedrijven en websitepioniers hebben er veel energie in gestoken om te komen waar we nu zijn, en toch is dit nog maar het begin. Het zal nog wel een tijd duren voordat we er echt de vruchten van kunnen plukken. Ook in het derde stadium werd de informatieverspreiding verder ontwikkeld, en nu ook op grote schaal. Dankzij de grote investeringen van mediabedrijven konden programmeurs hun toepassingen plaatsen op een snel en hoogwaardig internet, hoewel ook veel geld in verloren projecten werd gestoken. Misschien wel het beste gevolg van de ontwikkelingen is dat veel informatie kosteloos beschikbaar werd. Niemand kan ooit hebben voorspeld dat de stroom informatie zo omvangrijk zou worden en zo snel zou groeien. Bedrijven en overheden hebben de handen ineengeslagen en een heel nieuw gebied van on line services opgezet. Van e-commerce tot belastingformulieren, gebruikers raakten bekend met de voordelen van de on line services en gingen er gebruik van maken.

Het volgende stadium was gericht op interactiviteit, een fase waarin elke dag zich vele nieuwe gebruikers aansloten bij de internetrevolutie en waarin zij verlangden naar directere reacties en feedback. Interactiviteit was niet langer een vraag van technologie, maar het was een verandering in de denkwijze van de betrokkenen. Natuurlijk hielp de technologie wel de snelheid van de interactie te vergroten door de ontwikkeling van nieuwe programmeertalen, nieuwe bronnen en stapels goede publicaties, en niet te vergeten de informatie-uitwisseling on line. De services die snel konden reageren op acties van gebruikers waren behalve in het voordeel van de gebruikers ook in het voordeel van bedrijven. Vanaf dat moment begon internet zich te ontwikkelen tot waar we nu zijn of ten minste, waar we nu naar toe gaan: het tijdperk van entertainment. Tijd, geld en inspanning zijn altijd al nodig geweest, maar de opkomst van on line entertainment vereist dat alle voorgaande stadia goed zijn doorlopen voordat het kan

werken zoals het zou moeten. Betere verbindingen, grote aantallen gebruikers die toegang en services verlangen, en bovenal grote commerciële belangen zijn alle nodig. Toch is het slechts een kwestie van tijd: op dit moment zijn al veel films on line te bekijken en komen er elke dag nieuwe sites over muziek, games, animatie en interactiviteit bij. Wat je ook doet op het net, of je nu een boek koopt of een on line game speelt, de nadruk ligt op hoe de gebruiker de interactie ervaart en hoe internet zich verhoudt tot het 'echte leven'. Van grote invloed hierop was de ontwikkeling van snelle internetverbindingen voor het grote publiek, zoals ISDN en ADSL. De investeringen blijken het nu al waard geweest te zijn, want het genoegen waarmee gebruikers momenteel van internetdiensten gebruikmaken, is zichtbaar gegroeid.

Op dit moment maakt het niet meer uit hoe we het noemen -– het net, web, www, internet, on line services – het belang van benaming is ondergeschikt. Waar het om gaat, is de verandering die het heeft teweeggebracht in de maatschappij en de verwachtingen die het schept voor toekomstige ontwikkelingen. Internet heeft het punt bereikt waarop iedereen iets kan en zou moeten doen. Het verschil tussen de snelheid waarmee internet groeit en de snelheid waarmee internationale standaarden worden ontwikkeld heeft wel voor enkele problemen gezorgd, maar die kunnen we ook zien als een nieuwe uitdaging. En deze uitdaging is een van de redenen voor dit boek, want de maatstaven voor esthetiek, navigatie, originaliteit, aantrekkelijkheid en kunstzinnigheid zijn veelal onderwerp van de publicaties van TASCHEN. Internet als medium heeft nog lang niet zijn definitieve vorm gekregen. Wellicht zal het medium dat met vele nieuwe websites per dag uitdijt dat punt nooit bereiken, want voor degenen die zoeken naar nieuwe, opwindende vormen is het pas begonnen. Dit boek is verdeeld in hoofdstukken over zuiver creatieve gebieden van internet, zoals advertenties, kunst, architectuur, films, mode, fotografie, illustraties, vormgeving en erotiek. De vele voorbeelden in dit boek zijn niet slechts bedoeld als illustratie: internet wordt veelzijdig door van elke site de beste ideeën te gebruiken en die te combineren op de manier zoals u wilt.

Door de pictogrammen is snel opzoeken mogelijk, of u nu zoekt naar animaties, geluid, materiaal dat u kunt downloaden of wat dan ook. Dit boek is een verzameling van 1000 websites; het zal de weg naar goede on line services gemakkelijker maken en vele nieuwe verfrissende ideeën geven. Zoek tussen de 1000 startpunten en haal het beste eruit voor een goede, persoonlijke navigatie. Een goede reis!

De dvd
Dit boek wordt geleverd met een dvd, die zowel met een dvd-speler als een computer is af te spelen. De dvd bevat zes interviews met zes verschillende ontwerpers uit zes verschillende landen, elk met een ander thema. In deze interviews vertellen de ontwerpers hoe zij internet gebruiken om hun productiviteit te maximaliseren, inspiratie op te doen, technische hulp te vinden en opdrachtgevers helpen betere diensten te verlenen. Verder lichten ze toe hoe ze ideeën uitwisselen, op de hoogte blijven van het laatste nieuws en hun creativiteit uiten. Er is geen extra software nodig, slechts de dvd-speler. De dvd heeft code 0, wat betekent dat hij compatible is met elke speler.

- 🇺🇸 Land
- 🅵 Website met Flash
- ▱ Website met film
- 🅚 Website met geluid
- 🆂🆆 Website met Shockwave
- ⬛ Downloaden mogelijk
- ▣ Software te downloaden
- ☺ Gratis materiaal
- 🅸 Informatie over website
- 🅲 Website van bedrijf
- 🅿 Website van persoon
- 🔗 Website met nuttige links

Un clic. Eso es todo lo que nos separa hoy en día de infinidad de sorpresas, información, soluciones, contactos y experiencias vitales. Un simple clic que, en realidad, constituye la puerta de acceso a un estilo de vida radicalmente nuevo: una vida electrónica en la World Wide Web. Desde su concepción original como recurso de comunicación militar, Internet ha ido creciendo y atravesando numerosas fases. En términos de diseño, en un primer momento las páginas se construían exclusivamente en html. A esta etapa le sucedió la fase de los scripts, durante la cual los usuarios descubrieron los gifs animados, que otorgaban movimiento y dinamismo visual y, aunque en ocasiones podían resultar molestos y tardar en descargarse, lo cierto es que convirtieron Internet en un mundo mucho más ameno. Es precisamente esta innovación la que se está perfilando como el objeto de culto de Internet. La experimentación en este campo se realiza básicamente en Flash y está cobrando cada vez más fuerza, sobre todo entre los profesionales creativos, para quienes su página web constituye una ventana al mundo exterior. El inicio de esta fase corrió paralelo a la aparición de Shockwave, gracias al cual fue posible la interacción online que nos ha conducido al punto en el que nos encontramos hoy: un estadio en el que todos estos recursos, con la adición de películas y sonido, están haciendo la www más compleja e interesante que nunca.

En cuanto a su papel como medio de comunicación, Internet también ha atravesado múltiples etapas, la primera de las cuales podría definirse como la de la curiosidad. En un primer momento, pocas personas tenían acceso a Internet y muchas menos poseían una página web propia. El medio avanzaba a una velocidad asombrosa, pero tan sólo era posible consultar información en un puñado de publicaciones y páginas cuya existencia se había difundido por el boca a boca. Después de ésta vino la que se ha llamado fase informativa, pese a no entrañar todavía una difusión de información a gran escala, ya que la navegación era muy lenta y para la elaboración de las páginas se requerían auténticos profesionales. Las empresas y los sitios web pioneros hicieron un gran esfuerzo por alcanzar este punto, y sin embargo aquello no era más que el principio. Pero la semilla estaba plantada e iba creciendo. La tercera fase fue la de la información a gran escala. Los medios de comunicación efectuaron inversiones ingentes (que en ocasiones supusieron pérdidas de miles de millones de dólares) para transferir su material a la web, un entorno que les permitía disfrutar de una velocidad y una calidad espectaculares. Pero lo mejor de todo era que Internet ponía aquella información al alcance de todos de forma gratuita. Nadie podía haber imaginado que aquel flujo de información crecería a tal velocidad. Empresas y gobiernos aunaron fuerzas y ofrecieron un nuevo mundo de servicios online: desde el comercio electrónico a la cumplimentación de documentos fiscales a través de Internet, los usuarios empezaron a apreciar las ventajas de aquella importantísima transición de los servicios offline a los online.

El siguiente paso fue la interacción: millones de personas participaban ya de la revolución internauta y cada vez querían respuestas más rápidas. La interactividad dejó de ser una cuestión tecnológica y cambió la mentalidad de la gente. Sin duda, todo ello se debió a la popularización de los lenguajes de programación, a los nuevos recursos y a toneladas de publicaciones especializadas, sin olvidar el intercambio de información online. Surgieron así nuevos servicios que ofrecían respuestas inmediatas, para satisfacción de los usuarios y beneficio de las empresas. A partir de aquel punto la Red evolucionó hasta alcanzar su estadio actual, o al menos el período al que nos dirigimos: la era del ocio. Aparte de dedicar el tiempo, el capital y los esfuerzos ineludibles, para que Internet satisfaga las necesidades de ocio, las fases previas deben funcionar perfectamente. Y para ello se requieren líneas mejores, el acceso y solicitud de servicios de muchas personas y un gran interés comercial. Pero lo estamos consiguiendo. Ya hay un sinnúmero de películas online e incontables sitios web de música, juegos, animación e interacción. Y el número se multiplica día tras día. Al margen de para qué se utilice Internet, ya sea para comprar un libro o para participar en juegos online, lo importante ahora es la experiencia

del internauta y su comparación con la «vida real». El gran avance lo ha propiciado la aparición de las líneas de alta velocidad, como ISDN o ADSL, que ponen a disposición de los usuarios un acceso mucho más veloz. Las inversiones están dando su fruto, como demuestra el número creciente de usuarios que navegan «por placer».

En esta etapa de Internet, la www, la Red, la Web o como queramos llamarla, las definiciones de particulares han perdido toda relevancia. Lo importante ahora es el cambio que Internet ha producido en nuestras vidas y las expectativas que crea para el futuro. Como hemos visto, Internet se encuentra en un punto en el que todo el mundo puede y debería hacer algo. Y aunque es cierto que la velocidad a la que ha evolucionado ha planteado dificultades a la hora de definir estándares internacionales, este aspecto constituye en realidad todo un desafío. Y ese desafío es una de las razones por las que existe este libro, al menos en lo que concierne a los parámetros de estética, navegación, creatividad, atractivo y calidad artística relevantes para la línea editorial de TASCHEN. El medio no ha adquirido su forma definitiva (ni previsiblemente podrá hacerlo, ya que cada día se suman millones de páginas nuevas). Por el contrario, para quienes buscan soluciones innovadoras, esto no ha hecho más que empezar. Este volumen se divide en varios capítulos correspondientes a las áreas creativas de Internet: publicidad, arte, arquitectura, películas, moda, fotografía, ilustración, diseño y erotismo. Los ejemplos no deben tomarse como una mera ilustración de estos campos, sino como una muestra de la versatilidad del medio, que permite extraer lo mejor de cada sitio y aplicarlo a las necesidades propias.

Los iconos permiten hacerse una idea rápida de qué buscar: animaciones, sonidos, material descargable... Esta publicación es en realidad una recopilación de 1.000 páginas que le facilitarán el camino para hallar ideas frescas y grandes soluciones online. Visite estos fantásticos 1.000 puntos de partida y descubra cómo sacar el máximo partido a su navegación. ¡Buen viaje!

EL DVD
El libro incluye un DVD, que puede ver tanto en su ordenador como en su reproductor de DVD. El DVD contiene seis entrevistas a seis creativos de seis países distintos, en cada una de las cuales se abordan temas diferentes. Los creativos explican cómo utilizan Internet para mejorar su producción, inspirarse, hallar asistencia técnica, ofrecer soluciones a sus clientes, proveerles de un servicio mejor, intercambiar ideas, estar al corriente de las últimas noticias y extraer el máximo provecho de su creatividad. No requiere la instalación de ningún software. El DVD está programado en código 0 y es compatible con todos los reproductores.

País
Contiene Flash
Contiene películas
Página web con sonido
Contiene Shockwave
Descargas disponibles
Descarga de software
Material gratuito
Página informativa
Página comercial
Página personal
Vínculos de interés

introduzione

A solo un clic. È la distanza che ci separa oggi da mille sorprese, soluzioni, informazioni, contatti ed esperienze. Un semplice clic ci apre infatti le porte di un nuovo stile di vita elettronico nel World Wide Web. Dopo il suo iniziale sviluppo come strumento di comunicazione militare, la Rete è cresciuta ed ha attraversato differenti fasi. Per quel che riguarda il disegno, al principio le pagine web venivano realizzate solo in Html; poi venne la fase degli Script, durante la quale gli utenti scoprirono anche le animazioni Gif che apportavano movimento e dinamicità visiva al Web. Anche se a volte era esasperante aspettare che apparissero, le Gif hanno dato alla Rete una buona dose di allegria e attualmente sono molto di moda. Poi si è passati al formato Flash, ancora oggi presente in Rete e sempre più richiesto, specialmente dai professionisti creativi che fanno del loro sito una finestra aperta al mondo. Quasi simultaneamente nasceva la tecnologia Shockwave, che forniva la possibilità di interagire online, arrivando così alla fase attuale in cui questi strumenti, con l'aggiunta di filmati e suoni, ci offrono un Web più grande che mai.

Anche come mezzo di comunicazione, Internet ha attraversato molte fasi. La prima potremmo definirla la fase della curiosità. Al principio erano in pochi a poter accedervi ed ancor meno ad avere una pagina web. La Rete cresceva rapidamente, ma potevamo ottenere le informazioni necessarie solo attraverso una manciata di pubblicazioni o tramite passaparola. La seconda fu la fase dell'informazione, ma non si trattava realmente di un servizio informativo su grande scala, perché richiedeva troppo tempo e dei veri professionisti per realizzare le pagine web. Le imprese e i pionieri dei siti web dovettero fare grandi sforzi per ottenere tali risultati, e tuttavia era solo l'inizio. Ma il seme era stato piantato e le radici crescevano. La terza fase riguardava l'informazione vera e propria, e stavolta su grande scala. Grazie ai grandi investimenti da parte dell'industria della comunicazione, senza citare le perdite miliardarie, queste compagnie iniziarono a trasferire il loro materiale al Web, che offriva una velocità ed una qualità spettacolari. Ma la cosa migliore era che tutto veniva messo a disposizione in forma gratuita. Nessuno avrebbe mai potuto immaginare la creazione di un tale flusso di informazioni, né che sarebbe poi cresciuto così rapidamente. Le imprese e i governi si unirono per offrire un nuovo mondo di servizi online, dall'e-commerce ai moduli per la denuncia dei redditi, e gli utenti iniziarono così a scoprire e a sfruttare queste nuove possibilità.

Il passo seguente fu l'interazione. Milioni di persone si univano ogni giorno alla rivoluzione informatica, desiderando e necessitando un maggior feedback in tempo reale. L'interazione stessa non era più una questione di tecnologia ma di un nuovo modo di pensare della gente. Chiaro che la popolarizzazione dei linguaggi di programmazione, i nuovi strumenti e un'ondata di pubblicazioni sul tema, per non parlare dello scambio di informazioni online, contribuirono ad accelerare il processo. I nuovi servizi interattivi facevano aumentare, così, tanto l'allegria degli utenti quanto i proventi delle compagnie. Di qui la Rete si è sviluppata fino al punto in cui si trova attualmente, o almeno fino alla fase verso cui ci dirigiamo: l'era del divertimento. Tempo, denaro e sudore sono sempre stati necessari, ma il successo di questa nuova fase si basa sul perfetto funzionamento delle precedenti: linee migliorate, un gran numero di persone che richiedono e accedono ai servizi e un forte interesse da parte del mondo del commercio. E ci siamo quasi. Ci sono già moltissimi film disponibili online e un numero incredibile di siti su musica, giochi, animazione e interazione che spuntano come funghi. Non importa cosa fai, se compri un libro o se giochi online, l'importante adesso è come ti viene presentato il tutto in comparazione alla vita reale. La grande rivoluzione in questo senso è stata possibile grazie alla creazione delle linee ad alta velocità come l'Isdn e l'Adsl. Gli investimenti sono risultati fruttuosi e il "piacere" di navigare in Rete è aumentato significativamente.

A questo punto non importa più come lo chiamiamo - Internet, Web, Rete, ecc. - definire i particolari non è più importante. L'importante oggi è il cambiamento che ha prodotto nella nostra vita e le aspettative per il futuro. Come abbiamo visto, il Web è arrivato a uno stadio in cui ognuno di noi può e deve fare qualcosa, ma è anche vero che la velocità con cui è cresciuto ha reso difficile creare degli standard internazionali. È una vera e propria sfida e una delle ragioni per cui abbiamo creato questo libro, almeno per quel che riguarda l'estetica, la navigazione, la creatività, l'attrattiva e l'arte, che sono i soggetti principali delle pubblicazioni della TASCHEN. Internet non ha affatto raggiunto il suo stadio finale (impossibile per un mezzo che cresce al ritmo di milioni di pagine al giorno...), e anzi, è solo agli inizi per coloro che cercano soluzioni nuove ed emozionanti. Il libro è diviso in vari capitoli che rappresentano differenti spazi creativi nel Web, come la pubblicità, l'arte, l'architettura, il cinema, la moda, la fotografia, l'illustrazione, il design e l'erotismo. Ciò non vuol dire che gli esempi servono semplicemente ad illustrare questi campi, anzi, la versatilità online consiste nell'estrarre il meglio da quel che ci viene offerto ed applicarlo al tema che ci interessa.

Le icone danno un'idea generale sulla ricerca da eseguire, ad esempio: animazioni, suoni, materiale scaricabile o altro. Il libro è una raccolta di 1000 pagine che abbreviano il cammino per trovare grandi soluzioni online, offrendo descrizioni dettagliate e amene. Si può scegliere tra questi 1000 grandi punti di partenza per cercare il modo migliore di sfruttare la navigazione. Buon viaggio!

IL DVD
Il libro è accompagnato da un DVD che si può utilizzare sia su computer che con un riproduttore DVD. Contiene 6 interviste realizzate a 6 creativi provenienti da 6 diversi paesi e ognuno di loro affronta un tema differente. Analizzano l'uso della Rete per ottimizzare la produzione, trovare ispirazione e supporto tecnico, aiutare i clienti, fornire un miglior servizio, scambiare idee, essere al corrente delle ultime notizie e sfruttare al meglio la loro creatività. Non è necessario nessun software di installazione, solo un riproduttore per DVD. Il DVD è a codice 0 ed è quindi compatibile con tutti i riproduttori.

- USA Nazione
- F Contenuto Flash
- Contenuto Video
- Pagina Web con Audio
- SW Contenuto Shockwave
- Trasferimento Possibile
- Software Scaricabile
- Materiale Gratuito
- I Pagina Web di Informazione
- C Pagina Web Commerciale
- P Pagina Web Personale
- Link nel Sito

À distância de um clique. Esta é a distância que hoje nos separa da maior parte das surpresas, informações, soluções, contactos e experiências da nossa vida. E, na verdade, este simples clique constitui o caminho para o nosso novo estilo de vida electrónico na World Wide Web. Após o desenvolvimento inicial como um meio de comunicação militar, a web cresceu e passou por inúmeras fases. Em termos de padrões de design, as páginas eram inicialmente desenhadas utilizando apenas html; seguiu-se depois uma fase de script, durante a qual foram também descobertas as animações gif. Estes desenvolvimentos trouxeram movimento e dinamismo visual à web. Apesar destas animações gif serem, por vezes, fastidiosas e de requererem um certo tempo para serem carregadas, proporcionavam uma boa dose de divertimento à web. Esta inovação está a tornar-se no culto da web. As experiências posteriores concentradas no Flash, que actualmente não só continua a existir como se tem tornando mais forte dia após dia, especialmente para os profissionais criativos que fazem dos seus sites a sua janela para o mundo exterior. Esta fase iniciou-se quase simultaneamente com o Shockwave, acrescentando a possibilidade de interactividade on-line, e conduziu-nos à fase onde nos encontramos hoje e na qual todos estes recursos, em conjunto com os filmes e som, fazem com que a www seja hoje melhor do que nunca.

Relativamente aos meios de comunicação, a web passou também por várias fases. A primeira poderia ser definida como a fase da curiosidade. No princípio, poucas pessoas tinham acesso à web e ainda menos pessoas possuíam as suas próprias páginas web. Os acontecimentos sucediam-se muito rapidamente mas apenas era possível obter as informações necessárias a partir de uma quantidade muito reduzida de publicações ou a partir das informações transmitidas oralmente. A segunda fase constitui a fase informativa, que ainda não se centrava verdadeiramente no fornecimento de informações em grande escala, uma vez que esse processo requeria demasiado tempo e necessitava dos serviços de verdadeiros profissionais para a concepção das páginas web. As empresas e os pioneiros de websites dedicaram grande parte do seu trabalho para que as coisas chegassem a esse ponto mas, apesar disso, este era apenas o início. No entanto, a semente tinha sido plantada e estava a crescer. A terceira fase tratava da informação propriamente dita e agora em grande escala. Graças aos enormes investimentos feitos por empresas de media, sem mencionar as perdas de milhões de dólares, essas empresas começaram a transferir o seu material para a web, onde podiam agora usufruir de velocidade e qualidade espectaculares. O melhor de tudo é que todo este material estava a ser disponibilizado gratuitamente na Internet. Ninguém poderia imaginar que um tal fluxo de informação poderia, alguma vez, ter lugar e crescer de forma tão rápida. As empresas e os governos uniram esforços a tornaram possível todo um mundo novo de serviços on-line. Desde o e-commerce aos formulários governamentais para impostos, os utilizadores começaram a descobrir e explorar as novas possibilidades proporcionadas pela passagem em massa da acessibilidade a serviços off-line para on-line.

O passo seguinte foi a interactividade, o ponto em que milhões de pessoas se uniam diariamente à revolução da web e exigiam e necessitavam de respostas mais imediatas. A própria interactividade já não era uma questão de tecnologia, tratava-se de uma mudança na forma de pensar das pessoas. Claro que tudo isto se acelerou com a popularização das linguagens de programação, dos novos recursos e de uma imensa quantidade de publicações relevantes, sem mencionar o intercâmbio de informações on-line. Mais serviços que ofereciam respostas imediatas juntavam-se à satisfação dos utilizadores e à vantagem das empresas. É a partir deste ponto que a Internet evoluiu até ao estado em que se encontra hoje ou, pelo menos, até onde nos dirigimos actualmente: a era do lazer. O tempo, dinheiro e suor foram sempre necessários, contudo, o aspecto do lazer requer que todas as fases anteriores funcionem adequadamente. São necessárias melhores linhas, um grande número de pessoas acedendo e solicitando serviços, além de um enorme interesse comercial. Mas estamos a chegar a esse ponto. Existem já muitos filmes on-line e uma enorme

quantidade de sites de música, jogos, animação e interactividade aparece diariamente. Independentemente do que faz, quer compre um livro ou jogue on-line, a atenção incide agora na experiência que deve obter e da maneira como esta se compara à "vida real". A grande conquista neste campo foi a criação de um vasto acesso público a linhas de alta velocidade como ISDN e ADSL. Os investimentos estão a provar o seu valor e o aumento da "satisfação" das pessoas que navegam pela web é extremamente significativo.

Nesta fase, já não interessa como lhe chamamos – Internet, www, web, página on-line, página principal ou qualquer outra designação – as definições específicas já não têm importância. O tema fulcral neste momento é a mudança que provocou nas nossas vidas e as expectativas que cria para o futuro. Tal como vimos, a web atingiu um estado no qual qualquer pessoa poderá e deverá fazer alguma coisa, embora seja igualmente verdade que a velocidade à qual todo este processo ocorreu criou certas dificuldades no estabelecimento de padrões internacionais e esse facto pode ser visto como um verdadeiro desafio. E este desafio é uma das razões que está na origem da publicação deste livro. Pelo menos, no que se refere aos parâmetros de beleza, navegação, criatividade, atracção e capacidades artísticas, que são os factores relevantes para as áreas sobre os quais a TASCHEN publica. E o meio não atingiu, de forma alguma, o seu estado final (impossível, considerando que este meio cresce ao ritmo de milhões de novas páginas por dia…), antes pelo contrário, está apenas a começar para aqueles que procuram soluções novas e excitantes. Este livro está dividido em vários capítulos que representam áreas genuinamente criativas na web, tais como publicidade, arte, arquitectura, filmes, moda, fotografia, ilustração, design e erotismo. Não se pretende dizer com isto que os exemplos servem apenas para ilustrar estes campos de actividade. Pelo contrário, a versatilidade on-line consiste em extrair o melhor do que se oferece e em aplicá-lo a qualquer campo que se deseje.

Os ícones dão uma ideia rápida sobre o que consultar, quer se procure informação sobre animações, som, material para descarregar ou qualquer outro tema. Esta publicação é uma compilação de 1000 páginas que tornarão mais curto o seu caminho para a descoberta de magníficas soluções on-line e que lhe proporcionarão milhões de novas informações. Poderá escolher a partir destes 1000 excelentes pontos de partida e encontrar a melhor maneira de optimizar o seu tempo de navegação pessoal. Tenha uma boa viagem!

O DVD
Este livro vem acompanhado de um DVD. Poderá reproduzi-lo no seu computador ou no seu leitor do DVD. Contém 6 entrevistas a 6 criadores de 6 países diferentes, cada um abordando tópicos diferentes. Estes 6 criadores mostrar-lhe-ão como utilizam a Internet para maximizar a produção, obter inspiração, encontrar apoio técnico, ajudar clientes, proporcionar um melhor serviço, trocar ideias, manter-se informados sobre as últimas novidades e utilizar a sua criatividade da melhor maneira possível. Não é necessária a instalação de qualquer software, apenas um leitor de DVD. O código do DVD é 0, o que significa que é compatível com todos os leitores de DVD.

- País
- Contém Flash
- Contém Filmes
- Página web com som
- Contém Shockwave
- Descarga possível
- Software descarregável
- Material grátis
- Página web de informação
- Página web de empresa
- Página web pessoal
- Links interessantes no site

クリックしてサイトを行き来すること。それだけのことで、ふだんの生活にあるような、驚き、情報、ソリューション、コンタクト、経験からは、引き離されるほどの距離を移動することになる。クリックという簡単な操作をするだけで、ワールド・ワイド・ウェブ上で、Eスタイルという新しい生活への道が開かれるのだ。もともと、ウェブは、軍事上の通信手段として開発され、成長したものだが、多くの段階を経てきた。デザイン標準の点からいえば、ウェブ・ページは最初、HTMLだけで書かれていたが、やがてスクリプトによって代用され、同じ頃GIF動画も開発された。このおかげで、ウェブには視覚的な力強さが生まれた。GIFはダウンロードに時間がかかるし、面倒なものであったが、ウェブの楽しさは倍加した。その斬新さは今やウェブの中では熱狂的に支持される部分ともなっている。フラッシュを中心とし、とりわけ、外部世界への窓となるものをサイトにつくっているクリエイティブな専門家のために、さらなる研究が進められ、日に日に身近でより確実なものになっている。この段階は、ショックウェーブと同時に始まり、オンラインでの双方向性の可能性を高めている。こうしたすべての素材に動画や音声が追加され、ワールド・ワイド・ウェブはこれまで以上によいかたちに整い、現在の段階に至ったのだ。

コミュニケーションのメディアという点で、ウェブは多くの段階を通過してきた。その第一は、好奇心の段階と定義できるだろう。当初は、ウェブ・ページにアクセスする人も、ウェブ・ページを持っている人もほとんどいなかった。事態は急速に変わったが、ひとにぎりの本からの知識やクチコミで伝え聞いたことが情報源となっているだけだった。第二の段階は説明の段階で、あまりにも時間がかかり、ウェブ・ページをつくるには正真正銘の専門家が必要で、大規模な情報提供をするまでには至っていなかった。企業とウェブサイトの開発者はこの段階にたどりつくまでに、大量の仕事をこなさなくてはならなかったが、それも端緒が開かれたばかりだった。しかし、種は蒔かれ、実っていった。第三の段階は、情報の妥当さが問われる段階で、これは現在も大きな範囲で行われている。数十億ドルもの損失が出たとはいえ、メディア関連企業が膨大な投資をし、各企業も資財をウェブに移動し始め、目を見張るスピードとクオリティを達成することができた。幸いなことに、こうしたものすべてがネットでは無料で利用できるようになりつつある。これほどの情報量がこれほど短い期間に拡大するとは、誰が予想し得たであろうか？ 官民一体となって新しいオンラインサービスの世界を作り上げたのだ。Eコマースから納税申告書まで、ユーザーは、オフィスからオンラインサービスにアクセスする方向への大きな動きを目にし、また利用もしている。

次の段階は対話であり、そこでは数百万の人々が、日々ウェブ革命に参加し、より多くのフィードバックを手軽に得たいと思い、またそうする必要があると思っている。双方向性はもはや技術的な問題ではなく、われわれの思考様式がどう変わるかにかかっている。もちろん、新しい資源ともいうべき、プログラム言語の普及や数トンになろうかという関連書籍はこの変化に拍車をかけた。オンラインでの情報の交換はいうまでもない。即時性のフィードバックをもたらすたくさんのサービスが増え、ユーザーを満足させ、企業の利益にも供している。この点ゆえに、ネットが今日のような発展を遂げ、あるいは、少なくとも、現在行われているエンターテイメントの時代が到来するまでになったのだ。時間、資金、労力はつねに求められるものだが、エンターテイメントの部分については、既に述べたことすべてが確実にうまくいっていなければ、本来の姿で役割を果たすことはできない。よりよい通信網、多くの利用者のアクセスに対応するサービス、さらに、通商上の利益、これらすべてが今求められている。今、われわれは、そういう点に到達しつつある。すでにオンラインにアップされた映画は多い。大量の音楽、ゲーム、動画、相互作用が毎日ひっきりなしに登場している。あなたが何をしようと、本を買おうと、オンラインのゲームをし

ようと、そうした経験のあり方や、どこまで「現実の生活」に近づくかが重要だ。この課題の大きな突破口は、広く一般の人がアクセスできるISDNやDSLなどの高速通信網をつくることにかかっている。この部門への投資は、それに見合う価値があるものだということがわかってきたし、インターネットをしながら「娯楽」を楽しむ人は著しく増えている。

この段階に至る以前に、いわゆるネット、ウェブ、オンラインページ、ホームページ等々という言葉はもう問題ではなくなり、細かい定義も重要ではなくなっている。大切なことは、インターネットがわれわれの生活にもたらした変化、そして、それが来るべき世界にそなえて生みだした可能性である。すでに見てきたように、ウェブがあれば、誰でもが何かすることができるし、また、何かすべきだという段階にわれわれは到達しているのだ。ウェブが発達して来たのと同じスピードで、国際標準の上での困難もまた生じてきたのは事実だが、これはさし迫った問題であろう。この問題は、本書が書かれた動機のひとつともなっている。少なくとも、美的要素については、創造性、魅力、芸術的成果などに関わり、これは弊社が刊行している出版物のジャンルに重なる。このメディアはまだまだ、その最終的な形式をとる状態には至っていない（一日に数百万もアップされるページとともに膨張するメディアにとって、それは不可能である……）。逆に、新しいものやぞくぞくするようなソリューションを求める人たちにとっては、まだ初期段階のメディアにとどまっているともいえる。本書は、ウェブに関して、広告、アート、建築、映画、ファッション、写真、イラスト、デザイン、エロティシズムなど純粋にクリエイティブな領域ごとの章立てになっている。掲げられた具体例によって、そのジャンルを説明しているだけではない。むしろ、オンラインの多様性は、そこに提供されたものが最良のものを引き出し、ユーザーの希望するどんなジャンルにでも充てられることにある。

アイコンをみれば、動画、音声、ダウンロードできる素材でもなんでも、探しているものが一目でわかる。本書は、オンライン上で最高のソリューションを見つけ、最先端の現場を知るための最短ルートを千ページにまとめたものだ。読者は、これら千の出発点から自由に項目を選んで、ネット航海を最大限に活かすことができる。それでは、よいご旅行を！

DVD
本書にはDVDがついている。コンピュータでも、DVDプレイヤーでも使用できる。内容は、6カ国、6人のクリエイティブたちとのインタビューで、それぞれ異なったテーマについて語ってもらったもの。彼らがどのようにネットを活用し、最大限の効果を引き出し、情報を手に入れ、技術的なサポートを得て、クライアントに奉仕し、よりよいサービスを提供し、アイディアを交換し、最新のニュースに接続し続け、自分たちのクリエイティビティーを最大に生かしているのかを知ることができる。DVDプレイヤーなら、ソフトをインストールする必要はなく、DVDの地域コードがゼロなら、すべてのプレイヤーで使用可能である。

USA	国
F	フラッシュを含む
▭	ムービーを含む
◁	サウンドを含む
SD	ショックウェーブをを含む
▾	ダウンロード可能
▣	ソフトウェアのダウンロード可能
☺	フリー素材
I	ウェブ・ページ情報
C	企業用ウェブ・ページ
P	個人用ウェブ・ページ
▦	サイトのクールなリンク

들어가며

오늘날 우리는 단 한 번의 클릭으로 실제 삶에서 일어나는 놀라운 사건들, 정보, 해결 방법과 만남, 경험 등을 맛볼 수 있게 되었다. 단순한 클릭 한 번이 인터넷 상에서는 우리를 새로운 e-라이프스타일로 이끄는 길이 되는 것이다. 초기에 군사 통신을 목적으로 개발된 웹은 이후 다양한 단계를 거치며 발전해 왔다. 디자인의 측면에서 보자면, 처음에 웹 페이지는 html로만 구성되어 있다가 스크립트 단계로 발전했으며 그러는 동안에 gif 애니메이션도 개발되어 웹에 움직임과 시각적인 역동성이 생겨났다. 물론 그래서 가끔 성가실 때도 있고 다운로드에 시간도 걸리지만, 움직이는 gif로 인해 웹이 훨씬 재미있어진 셈이다. 이러한 혁신적인 변화는 웹 상에서 하나의 컬트로 자리잡았으며, 한 걸음 더 나아가 Flash에 더 많은 실험들이 행해졌다. 이는 지금도 계속되고 있고 하루가 다르게 발전하고 있는데, 특히 웹 사이트를 제작하는 웹 디자이너들에게서 두드러진다. 이 단계는 Shockwave와 거의 동시에 진행되고 있으며, 온라인에서 상호 작용의 가능성을 더욱 높여 주었다. 상호 작용을 통해 우리는 지금의 단계에 이르렀으며, 이제 영상과 소리까지 더해진 이 모든 자원들은 www을 예전보다 훨씬 근사한 것으로 만들어 주고 있다.

커뮤니케이션 매체로도 웹은 많은 단계를 거쳐 왔다. 제일 처음은 호기심의 단계였다고 할 수 있다. 처음엔 접속하는 사람도 별로 없었고, 홈페이지를 가진 사람은 더더욱 드물었다. 상황은 빠르게 전개되는데, 필요한 정보들을 얻는 방법은 얼마 되지 않는 웹 관련 출판물을 뒤적이거나 말로 전해 듣는 게 고작이었다. 그 다음은 정보 제공의 단계이다. 웹 페이지를 만드는 데에는 정말 많은 시간과 진짜 전문가가 필요했기 때문에 그 규모는 여전히 작았다. 기업과 초기 웹 전문가들이 많은 노력을 기울인 덕분에 여기까지 다다르긴 했지만, 여전히 시작 단계에 불과했던 것이다. 그러나 그들의 노력은 서서히 결실을 맺기 시작했다.

이어 적합한 정보들이 큰 규모로 존재하는 세 번째 단계에 이르게 된다. 여기엔 미디어 회사들이 수십 억 달러의 손해를 감수하면서까지 대규모 투자를 한 덕이 크다. 이들은 자기네 정보 자료를 웹에서 공유하기 시작했고, 이제 웹 상에서 빠른 속도와 질을 누릴 수 있게 되었다. 그러나 무엇보다 가장 좋은 점은 웹에서 이러한 정보를 무료로 얻을 수 있게 되었다는 섬이다. 이와 같은 정부의 흐름이 가능해지고 또 그렇게 빠른 속도로 성장하리라고는 누구도 상상할 수 없었다. 기업과 정부가 협력해 온라인 서비스라는 전혀 새로운 세계를 만들었다. 전자상거래에서 세무 서식에 이르기까지, 이용자들은 오프라인이 온라인으로 바뀌는 대세의 가능성을 목격했으며, 거기에 동참하기 시작했다.

다음은 상호 작용의 단계이다. 매일 수백만 명이 웹의 혁명에 동참하고 즉각적인 피드백을 요구하게 된 단계이다. 상호 활동은 더 이상 기술적인 문제가 아니라, 사람들의 사고 방식의 변화 그 자체였다. 정보 교환은 물론, 대중화된 프로그래밍 언어, 새로운 정보, 넘쳐나는 관련 출판물들이 이를 더욱 가속화했다. 이제 즉각적인 피드백을 제공하는 보다 많은 서비스로 이용자들은 더욱 즐거워졌고 회사는 더 큰 혜택을 누릴 수 있게 되었다. 통신망이 오늘과 같이 그리고 지금도 계속해서 발전함으로써 오락의 시대를 여는 게 가능해졌다. 다른 일과 마찬가지로 시간이 걸리고 많은 돈과 노력이 투자되어야 하는 것도 중요하지만, 오락의 측면이 제 기능을 발휘하기 위해서는 이전의 단계들이 제 역할을 하고 있어야 한다. 인터넷 회선이 빨라지고 많은 사람들이 접속해서 서비스를 이용해야 하며 상업적인 흥미도 크게 유발되어야 하는데, 이 모든 게 거의 이루어져 가고 있다. 이미 많은 영화들이 인터넷에 올라와 있으며 음악, 게임, 애니메이션과 상호 교류를 제공하는 어마어마한 수의 사이트들이 매일 쏟아져 나오고 있다. 책을 사거나 게임을 하거나 온라인에서 뭘 하든 상관없이, 핵심은 이용자가 얻게 되는 경험들에 있으며, 그것을 '현실 세계'에 어떻게 대입하느냐에 있다. 이나 DSL과 같은 초고속 망에 많은 이용자들이 접속하게 되면서 커다란 도약이

이루어졌다. 투자 가치가 입증되고 있고, 웹 항해의 중요성 못지 않게 사람들의 讀膏탓蓼이 커지는 것이 확인되고 있다.

통신, www, 웹, 온라인 페이지, 홈페이지… 이제 우리가 무엇이라고 부르든 상관없는 단계가 되었으며, 세부적인 것의 정의는 중요하지 않게 되었다. 보다 중요한 것은 그것이 우리 삶에 가져 온 변화이고 앞으로 다가올 미래에 대한 기대치이다. 웹은 누구나 무언가를 할 수 있고 해야 하는 지점에 이르렀다. 워낙 성장 속도가 빨라 국제적인 표준을 만들기 어려웠던 것이 사실이지만, 그만큼 하나의 도전으로 남겨져 있다. 이는 이 책을 만든 이유 중의 하나이다. 적어도 TASCHEN이 출판해 온 영역들과 관련 있는 아름다움, 항해, 독창성, 매혹 그리고 예술성이라는 범주의 문제에 있어서는 그러하다. 또한 하루에도 수백만 페이지가 새로 생겨나는 웹이라는 매체가 최종적인 형태를 갖게 되는 건 불가능하다. 오히려 새롭고 신나는 솔루션들을 찾고 있는 사람들에겐 단지 시작일 뿐이기 때문이다. 이 책은 여러 장으로 구성되어 있는데, 각 장은 광고, 예술, 건축, 영화, 패션, 사진, 일러스트레이션, 디자인, 에로티시즘과 같은 분야처럼 웹에서 지정 창조적인 분야들을 대표한다. 이 예들이 단순히 이 분야들에 관한 웹 페이지를 보여 주기만 하는 것은 아니다. 온라인의 융통성이라는 것은 주어진 것 중 최고를 골라내 그것을 원하는 어떤 분야에나 적용하는 데 있기 때문이다.

아이콘은 애니메이션, 사운드, 다운로드할 수 있는 자료 등 찾고자 하는 분야를 빨리 찾을 수 있게 도와 준다. 1000개의 웹 페이지로 이루어저 있는 이 책의 각 페이지들은 독자들이 온라인에서 마땅한 해답을 찾기 위해 들여야 하는 수고를 덜어줄 것이며 수많은 새로운 통찰을 제공할 것이다. 이 1000가지 중에 골라서 시작할 수 있으며, 자신의 개인적인 항해에 맞는 가장 좋은 것을 발견할 수 있다. 부디 좋은 여행이 되기를.

DVD

이 책에는 DVD가 포함되어 있다. DVD에는 창의적인 활동을 하고 있는 각기 다른 국적의 여섯 명과의 인터뷰 여섯 개가 담겨 있다. 각기 다른 주제들로 전개되며, 그들이 인터넷을 어떻게 이용하는지 보여 줄 것이다. 그들은 인터넷을 통해서 생산을 극대화하고 영감을 얻고 기술적인 지원을 찾고 고객을 돕고 더 나은 서비스를 제공하고 아이디어를 교환하고 힝싱 최근의 뉴스들을 접하며 그들이 가진 창의성을 잘 활용하고 있다. 본 DVD는 컴퓨터와 DVD 플레이어에서 모두 볼 수 있으며, 다른 소프트웨어를 인스톨할 필요가 없다. DVD 코드는 제로( )이다. 이는 곧 모든 플레이어에 맞는다는 것을 뜻한다.

- **USA** 국가
- **F** 플래시 사용
- ▢ 영화 포함
- **K** 사운드가 있는 웹 페이지
- **SD** Shockwave 사용
- ▥ 다운로드 가능
- ▣ 다운로드할 수 있는 소프트웨어
- ☺ 무료 자료
- **I** 정보 제공 웹 페이지
- **C** 기업 웹 페이지
- **P** 개인 웹 페이지
- ▦ 유용한 링크 포함

前言

滑鼠點選一下，這就是我們和生活中大多數令人驚喜的事物、資訊、解決問題的方法、聯絡以及經驗的距離。這麼簡單的一按，就是通往全球資訊網（World Wide Web）上我們嶄新的e生活風格的途徑。原本應軍事通訊需要而生的全球資訊網後來日漸茁壯，並歷經無數的發展階段。就設計標準而言，網頁構成最初使用的不過是html格式，之後則添加了script；而與script同時，人們也開始運用gif網路動畫，為網頁增添了動作與視覺動態效果。儘管這種動畫有時挺煩人的，下載也很耗時，但它們卻能為網頁添加許多趣味。這種當時的創舉如今在網路上受到狂熱擁護。接下來的實驗以Flash這種網路檔案影像格式為主，直到今日，Flash仍然廣獲使用，並且日益壯大，更是專業設計人員用來讓他們所設計的網頁成為通往外界窗口的重要工具。幾乎與這個階段同時，Shockwave也開始興起，更增加了線上互動的可能性。正是這種互動將全球資訊網帶到今日我們所處的發展階段，所有資訊都添加了影音效果，使全球資訊網變得比以往更多采多姿。

作為傳播媒體，網路也經歷了幾個不同的階段。第一個階段可稱之為好奇階段，當時僅有少數人才能上網，而擁有自己網頁者更是鳳毛麟角。事物瞬息萬變，而當時的人卻僅能從少之又少的出版品或經由口傳耳聞來獲得所需的網路知識。第二個階段是資訊供給期，但此時還談不上是大規模的訊息供應，因為依然十分耗時，而網頁的製作也必須仰賴真正的專業人士。儘管如此，一些公司與網站拓荒者依舊對此耗費無數的心血與努力，然而這還只是個開頭。所幸播下的種子日益成長，第三個階段則是真正的資訊供應階段，同時規模龐大。多虧媒體業者的巨額投資——更別提其中數十億美元的損失了——這些公司開始將自己的訊息傳輸上網，如今，它們已能享受網路驚人的速度與品質了；而最好的是，這些在網路上都可以免費使用。從前沒有人料想得到，像這樣的資訊流居然會有到來的一天，而且成長如此快速。企業與政府更是攜手合作，為線上服務開拓了全新的世界，從電子商務到政府稅務表格等各種運用，使用者也開始發現了從「離線」轉向「線上服務」這種大幅變動的優點，並加以利用。

下一步則是互動。當每天都有數百萬人參與這場網路革命，希望、同時也需要獲得更多的即時回應時，互動就應運而生了。此時互動本身已非技術層面的問題，而在於人類思考方式的改變。當然，程式語言的普及、新資源的興起以及大量的相關出版品，遑論線上資訊的交換等都加速了網路互動化的發展。如今，許多服務都提供即時回應，不僅增添了使用者的樂趣，對公司也大有裨益。正是由於這個因素，網路才能發展成今日的面貌，或者至少是我們正要抵達的：娛樂的階段！時間、金錢、汗水固然一直都不可或缺，但唯有在前面幾個階段都能完美運作之後，我們才能達到這個階段：而更好更快的線路、為數極多的人上網並需要各種服務、此外豐厚的經濟效益等也都缺一不可。如今我們正朝此目標邁進，許多影片已經在網路上播放，每天都有大量的音樂、遊戲、動畫及互動性的網站冒出來；不管你在網路上做什麼，是在買書或玩線上遊戲，重點在於能給你什麼樣的體驗與感受，以及這種體驗與感受和「真實生活」相較之下如何。促成這種發展的大突破是大眾化的高速通信網，如ISDN及DSL等的興起，如今證明了高速通信網的投資確實值得，同時也大大提昇了悠遊網路的「樂趣」。到了這個階段，我們如何稱呼它——無論是叫它網路、www、web、網頁或是其他名稱——這些定義和名詞都已無關緊要，重要的是網路對我們生活所帶來的變化以及網路所引發的我們對未來世界的期待。顯而易見的是，網路已經發展到

了讓每個人都能、但同時也應該參與的階段。誠然，網路的成長速度確實使得制定國際通用的標準益發困難，但事實上，我們可將此視為是一種真正的挑戰，而這種挑戰正是我們出版這本書的動機之一。至少在涉及到與我們TASCHEN出版社出版領域相關網頁之美觀、網路「導航安排」、創意、魅力及藝術表現等時。網路這種媒介絕對還沒有達到它的最終型態（這對一個每天增加數百萬網頁的媒體而言也是不可能的）；相反地，對那些始終在尋找新、炫的呈現方式者還算是方興未艾呢！本書分成許多篇章介紹創意行業的傑出網頁，諸如廣告、藝術、建築、電影、流行時尚、攝影、插畫、設計與情色等等；這並不表示這些例子只是為了要呈現這些行業，恰好相反，網路之所以多采多姿，在於能萃取精華，隨心所欲地運用在任何一個領域上。

本書的圖示能讓你很快得知網頁的特色，例如在哪裡可以找到動畫、音效呈現、可下載的資訊等。本書總共搜羅了1000個網頁，能縮短你找到傑出網頁的途徑，並提供你數以百萬計的新靈感。你可以從這1000個絕妙的起點著手，找出最好的以減少你的搜尋時間。祝你旅途愉快！

DVD

本書也附有DVD，可以在電腦上或DVD播放機上觀賞。這片DVD收有與六名來自六個不同國家的創作者的六篇訪談，每名受訪者談論的主題各不相同。他們會說明，他們如何運用網路以完善生產過程、汲取靈感、尋求技術支援、協助客戶、提供更完善的服務、交換意見、隨時獲得最新資訊，充分發揮自己的創意。觀賞這片DVD時，不需安裝其他軟體，只要有DVD播放機就行了。這片DVD並無區碼限制，與所有DVD播放機都相容。

- USA 國家
- F 含Flash
- 含影片
- 配有聲效
- SD 含Shockwave
- 可下載資料
- 可下載軟體
- 免費資訊
- I 資訊網頁
- C 企業網頁
- P 個人網頁
- 酷網鏈結

starting to
load now...

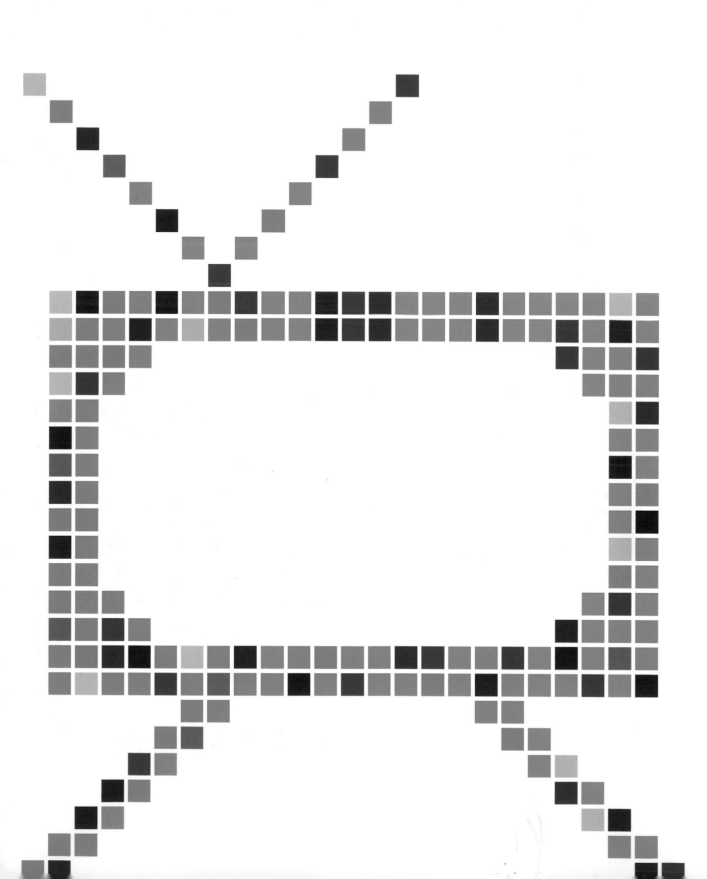

www.dieselmarketing.com

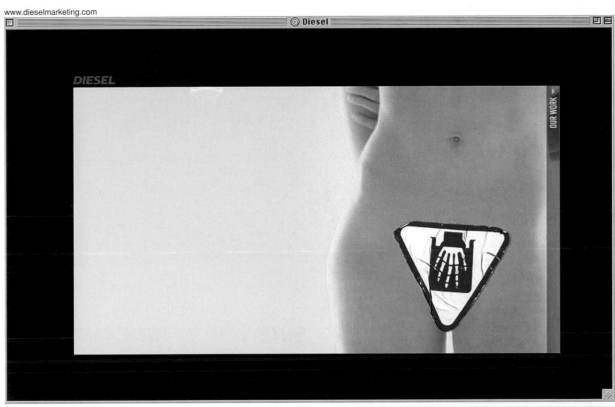

www.archermalmo.com

SE F C

www.breathewords.com

PT F ⏴ ⏴ P 🔄

www.h23.cl

CL F ⏴ ⏴ P 🔄

www.i-c-i.net

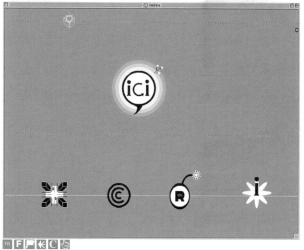

FR F ⏴ ⏴ C 🔄

www.brandstormconsulting.com

USA F C

www.lopeznegrete.com

USA F ⏴ ⏴ C

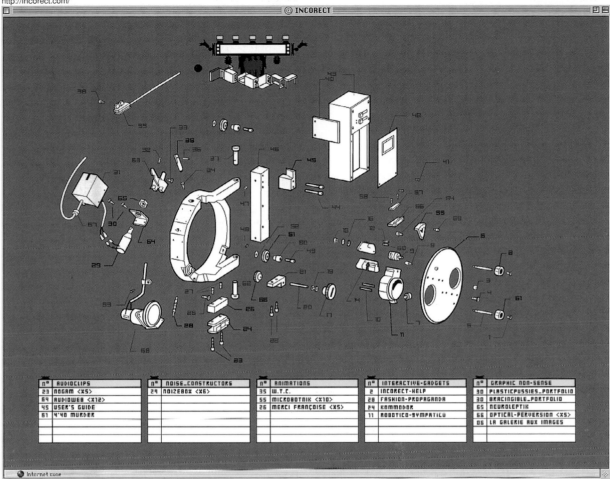

n°	AUDIOCLIPS
23	NOGAM <X5>
64	AUDIOWEB <X12>
45	USER'S GUIDE
61	4'40 MURDER

n°	NOISE_CONSTRUCTORS
29	NOIZEBOX <X6>

n°	ANIMATIONS
35	W.T.C.
55	MICROBOTNIK <X10>
26	MERCI FRANÇOISE <X5>

n°	INTERACTIVE-GADGETS
2	INCORECT-HELP
28	FASHION-PROPAGANDA
24	KOMMODOR
11	ROBOTICO-SYMPATICO

n°	GRAPHIC NON-SENSE
30	PLASTICPUSSIES_PORTFOLIO
30	BRACINGIBLE_PORTFOLIO
65	NEUROLEPTIK
66	OPTICAL-PERVERSION <X5>
05	LA GALERIE AUX IMAGES

[∨] CLICK ON THE INCORECT'S HEAD   DON'T FORGET TO GIVE US DOLLARDS [$]

1209000@INCORECT.COM   NOGAM@INCORECT.COM   YO60.0@INCORECT.COM

[>>] CONTACT@INCORECT.COM.........

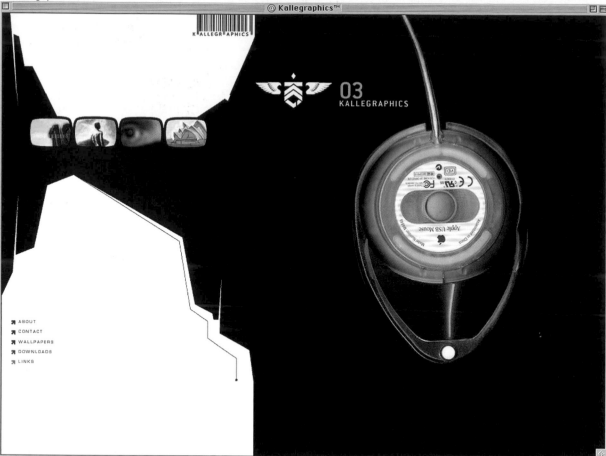

http://ElasticBrand.com

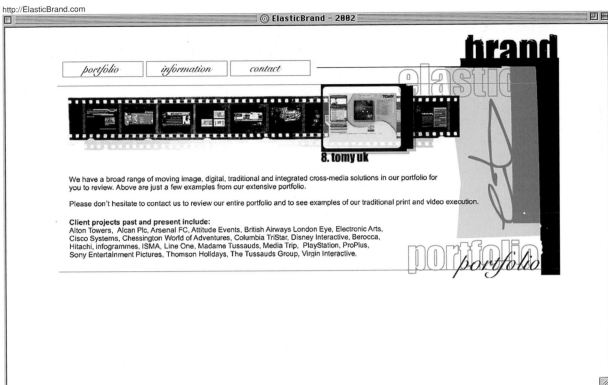

@ ElasticBrand - 2002

We have a broad range of moving image, digital, traditional and integrated cross-media solutions in our portfolio for you to review. Above are just a few examples from our extensive portfolio.

Please don't hesitate to contact us to review our entire portfolio and to see examples of our traditional print and video execution.

Client projects past and present include:
Alton Towers, Alcan Plc, Arsenal FC, Attitude Events, British Airways London Eye, Electronic Arts, Cisco Systems, Chessington World of Adventures, Columbia TriStar, Disney Interactive, Berocca, Hitachi, infogrammes, ISMA, Line One, Madame Tussauds, Media Trip, PlayStation, ProPlus, Sony Entertainment Pictures, Thomson Holidays, The Tussauds Group, Virgin Interactive.

www.manualdesign.no

@ Faro Manual design

MANUAL.DESIGN
GRAPHIC DESIGN FOR THE HOME ENTERTAINMENT BUSINESS AND THE FINE ART CULTURE

01 work | 02 clients | 03 services | 04 contact | 05 messageboard

GRAPHIC DESIGN FOR THE HOME ENTERTAINMENT BUSINESS AND FINE ART CULTURE.

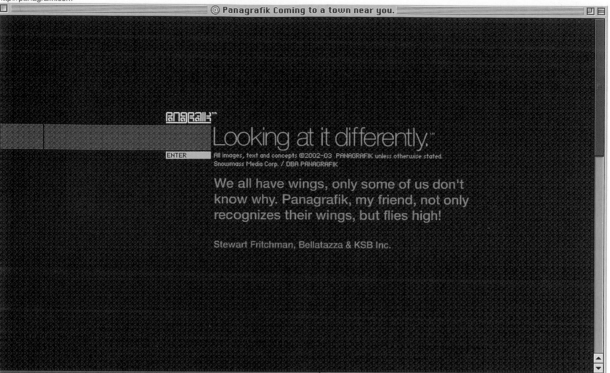

Looking at it differently.™

We all have wings, only some of us don't know why. Panagrafik, my friend, not only recognizes their wings, but flies high!

Stewart Fritchman, Bellatazza & KSB Inc.

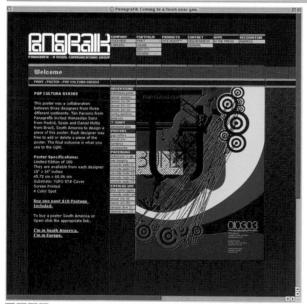

@ http://www.boulevart.biz/

BOULEVART
CREATIVE SOLUTIONS

onze diensten

HOME | PORTFOLIO | NIEUWS | PARTNERS | CONTACT

A creative intellectual is a person who has discovered something more interesting than sex.

1 | BOULEVART.BIZ

BoulevArt is een jong ontwerpbureau dat visuele communicatie verzorgt in de nieuwe media.

Met een gemotiveerd team, sterk onderlegd in de diverse disciplines van deze media gaan we voor niets minder dan een optimale gebruikservaring.

Kleine KMO of grote multi-national, BoulevArt beschikt over alle middelen om je project tot een succesvol einde te brengen.

Onze Diensten

- Web- & Graphical User Interface Design
- Multimedia & Flash MX
- Information Architecture
- Webmastering
- Back-End Solutions & Modules
- Branding & Concept
- Hosting & DNS Services
- Search Engine Optimalisation

2 | FOCUS

Compass Europe | Corporate website

In schril contrast tot onze snelle hightech economie waarin wij ons allemaal bevinden biedt Compass-Europe vanuit de ervaringsleermethode bewust de natuur aan als facilitaire ondersteuning van diverse bedrijfstrainingen.

Een 'outdoor' programma is geen survival, geen fysieke uitputtingsslag of waaghalzerij.
Lees meer...

Verder uitgewerkte cases kan je terugvinden in onze portfolio.

Datafiche

Periode
Februari 2003

Technologie
HTML
SQL
Prototyping
css
Javascript
ASP

Team
Sven Luyten
Hans Humblet

© 2003 BoulevArt nv | info@boulevart.biz | t ++32 (0)3 870 89 42 | f ++32 (0)3 871 99 51

www.linoleum-studio.com

www.hetstormtrotterdam.nl

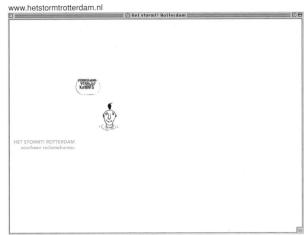

www.2voltad.com

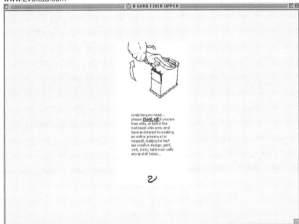

www.admt.jp

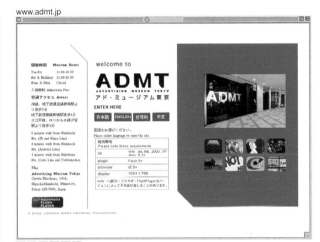

www.fitch.com

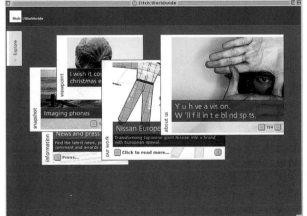

www.afg1.com

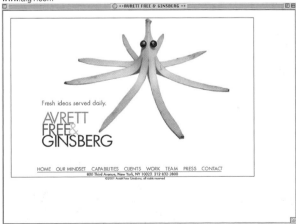

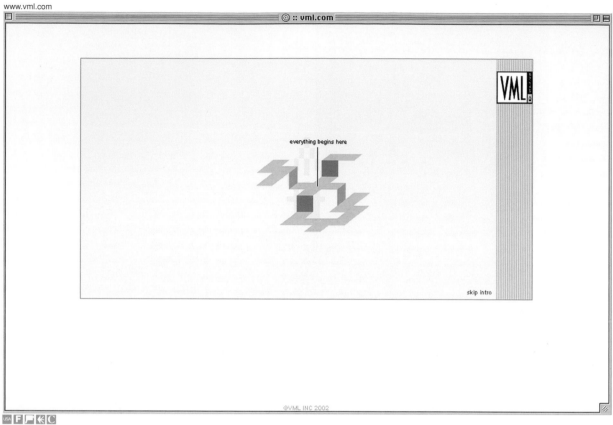

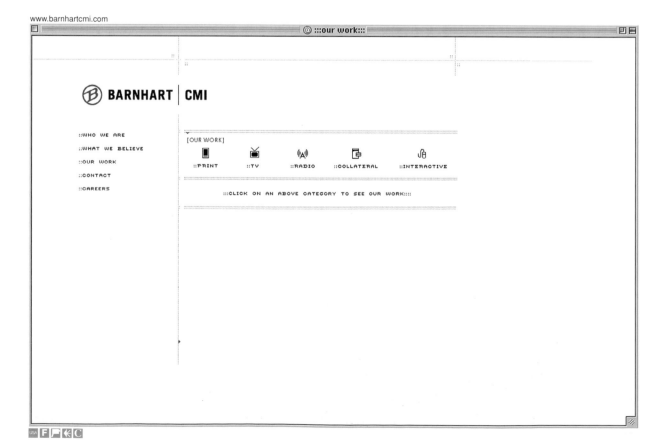

www.zimmerman.com

@ >>> the / zimmerman / agency >>>

music: on off

the / **zimmerman** / agency
an integrated marketing communications firm

USA F C

www.austinkelley.com

@ [AUSTIN KELLEY ADVERTISING]

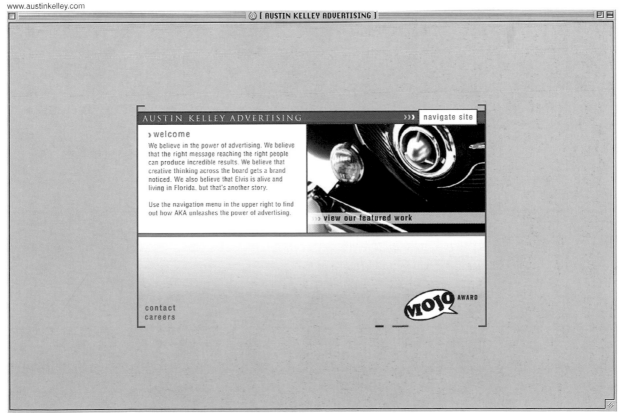

AUSTIN KELLEY ADVERTISING

>>> navigate site

> welcome

We believe in the power of advertising. We believe
that the right message reaching the right people
can produce incredible results. We believe that
creative thinking across the board gets a brand
noticed. We also believe that Elvis is alive and
living in Florida, but that's another story.

Use the navigation menu in the upper right to find
out how AKA unleashes the power of advertising.

>>> view our featured work

contact
careers

MOJO AWARD

USA F C

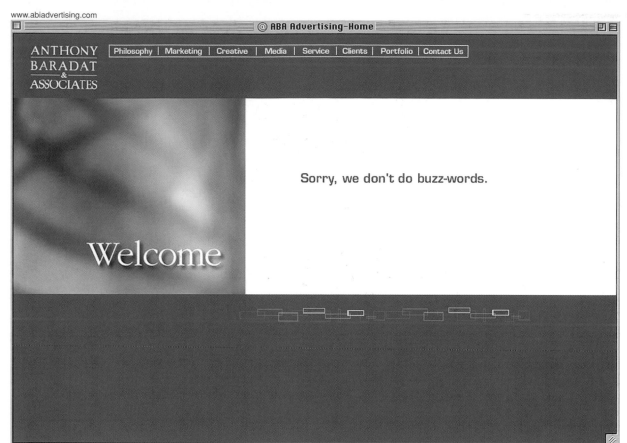

www.arnoldworldwide.com

www.baileylauerman.com

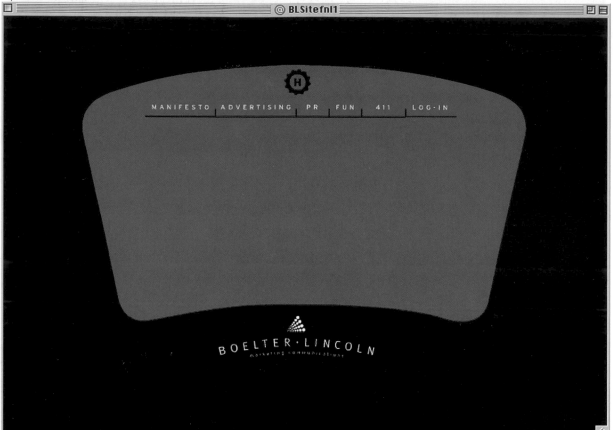

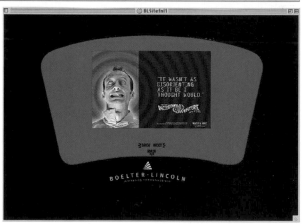

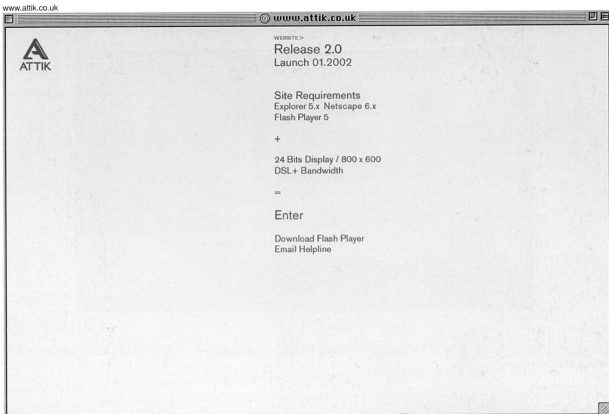

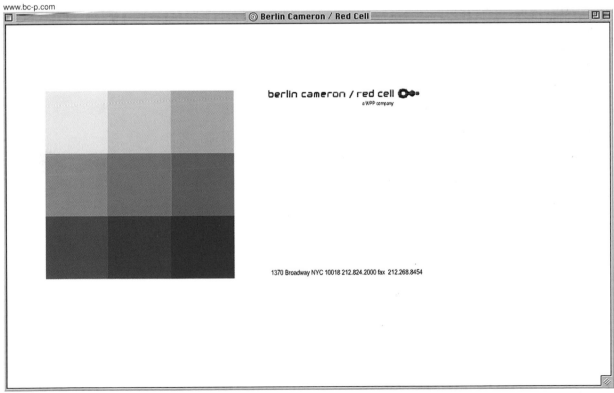

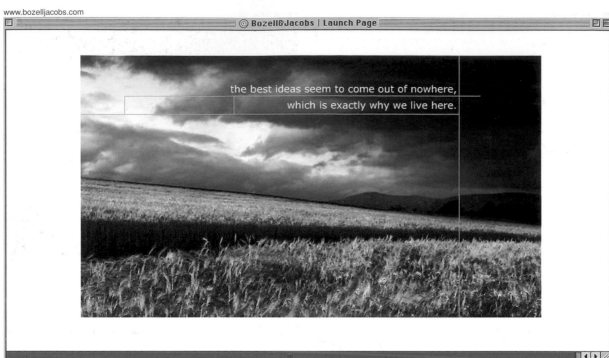

www.pulleyn.com

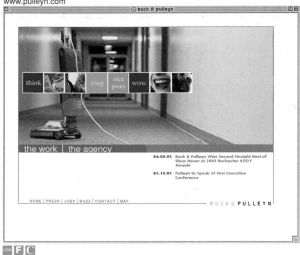

www.wambam.com

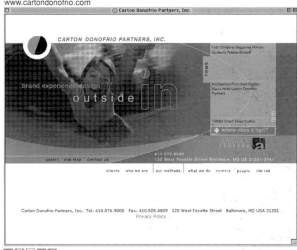

www.campbell-ewald.com

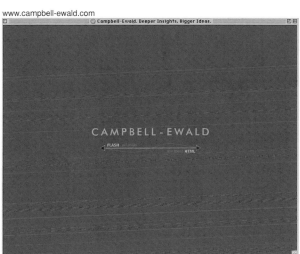

www.cartondonofrio.com

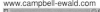

www.casanova.com

www.claritycoverdalefury.com

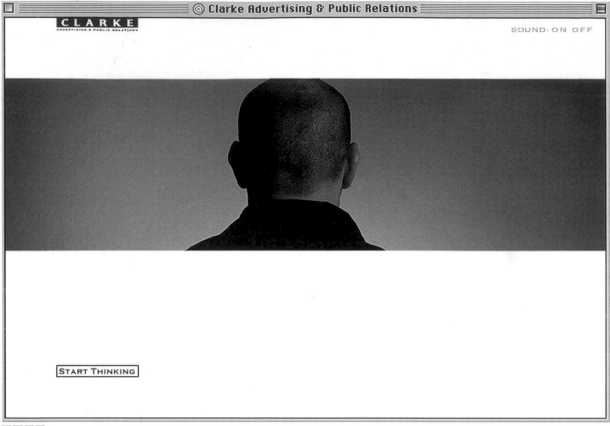

@ Clarke Advertising & Public Relations

CLARKE
ADVERTISING & PUBLIC RELATIONS

SOUND: ON OFF

START THINKING

USA F C

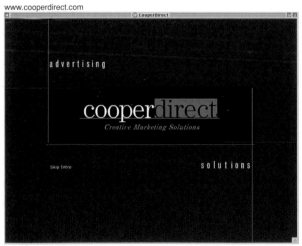

© CooperDirect

advertising

cooperdirect
Creative Marketing Solutions

Skip Intro

solutions

USA F C

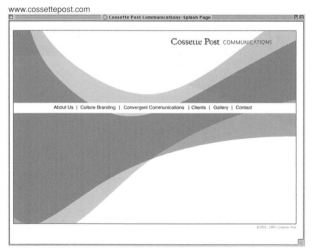

© Cossette Post Communications-Splash Page

Cossette Post COMMUNICATIONS

About Us | Culture Branding | Convergent Communications | Clients | Gallery | Contact

©2001-2002 Cossette Post

USA F C

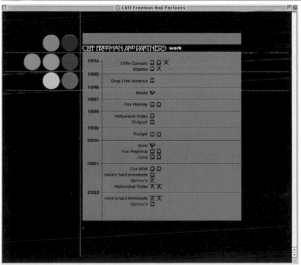

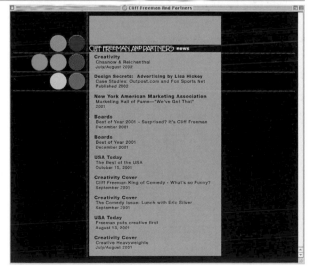

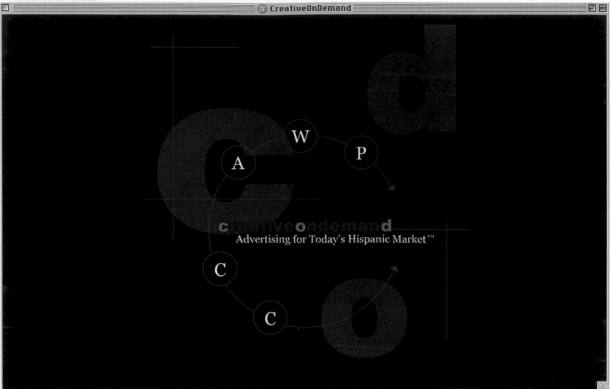

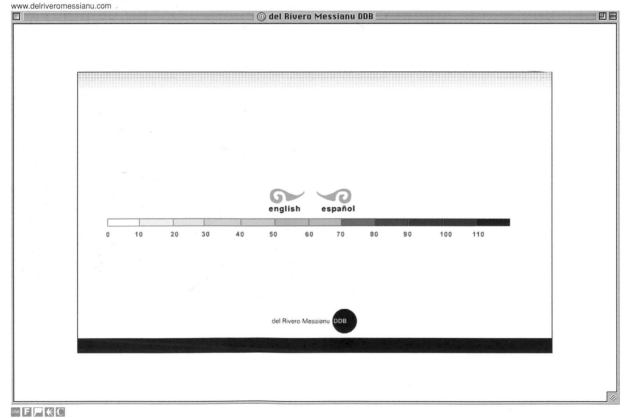

www.erwinpenland.com

www.fallon.com

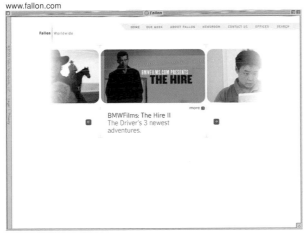

www.fkmagency.com

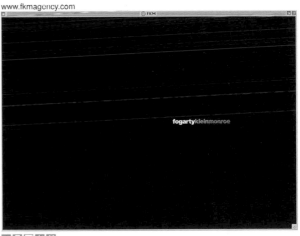

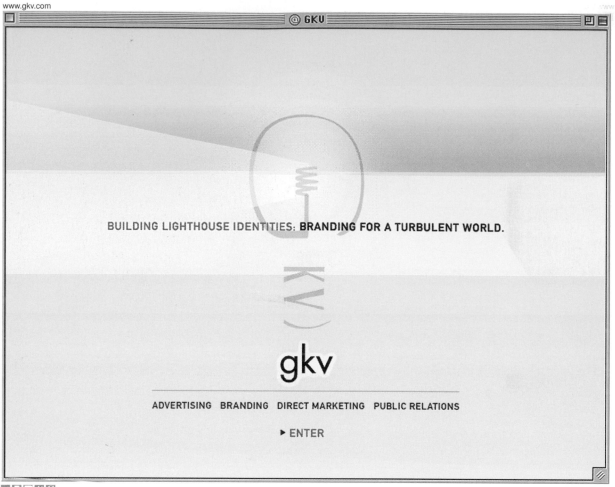

www.grantjacoby.com

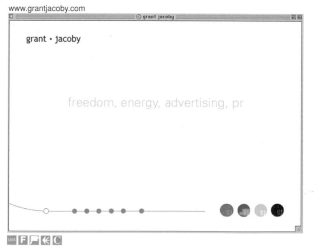

www.gardner-nelson.com

www.thecartel.com

www.marcusa.com

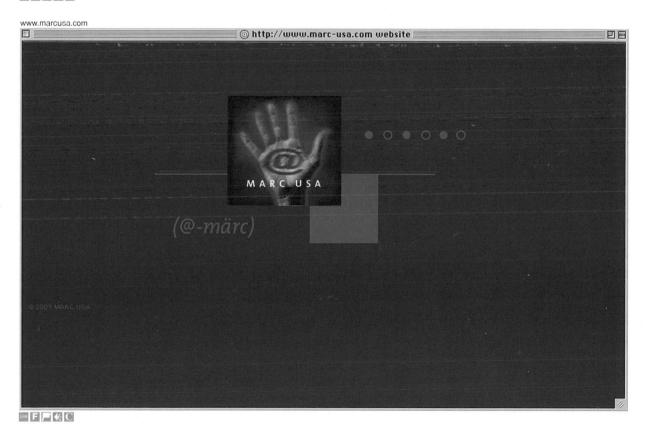

www.interlexlatino.com/

www.latinocreative.com

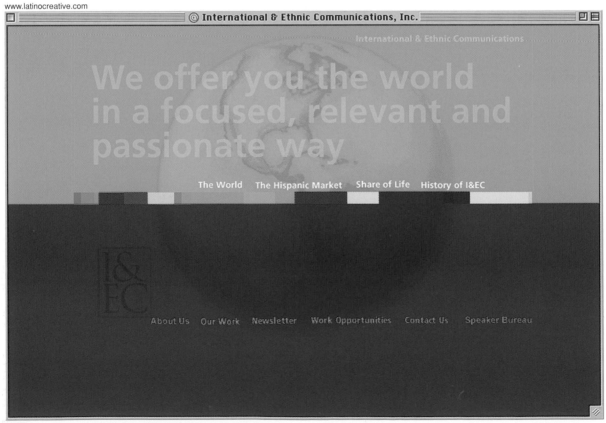

www.kilgannon.com

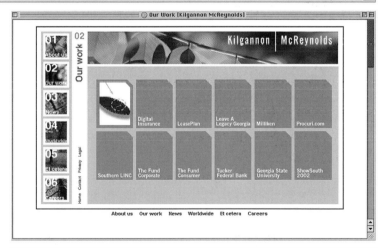

www.keatingmagee.com

www.kaplanthaler.com

www.laughlin.com

@ La Agencia

skip intro

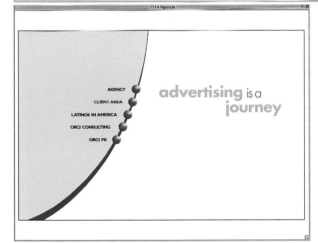

www.masius.com

@ Masius.com

We make the complex simple

masius

www.mcclainfinlon.com

@ McClain Finlon Advertising | Shocked!

MISSION

AT McCLAIN FINLON ADVERTISING, OUR MISSION IS TO CREATE EXTRAORDINARY COMMUNICATIONS THAT PRODUCE DRAMATIC RESULTS FOR AMERICA'S MOST AMBITIOUS BRANDS. TO INSPIRE US, WE'VE SURROUNDED OURSELVES WITH COLLECTIONS FROM ARCHITECTURE AND POPULAR CULTURE — LIKE OUR FAMOUS CHAIR COLLECTION. AND OUR DISPLAYS OF KEYS, SHOES, GUMBALL MACHINES, EYEGLASSES, AND DOORKNOBS. THEY SERVE TO REMIND US OF OUR ULTIMATE GOAL AS STEWARDS OF OUR CLIENTS' BRANDS: TO CONNECT CLASSIC IDEAS FROM THE PAST WITH OUR VISION OF WHERE COMMUNICATIONS IS GOING IN THE FUTURE; TO INSPIRE BOLD IDEAS AND, ULTIMATELY, ENDURING BRANDS.

ENTER

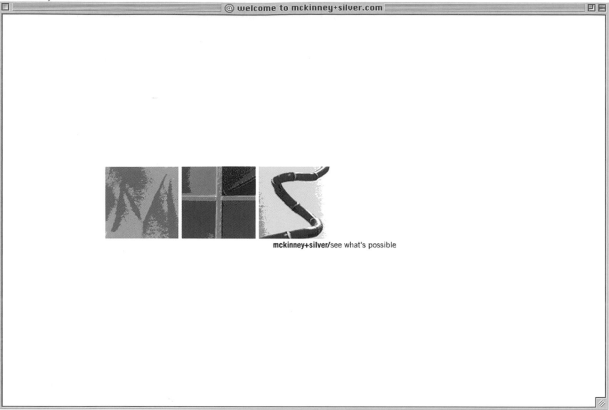

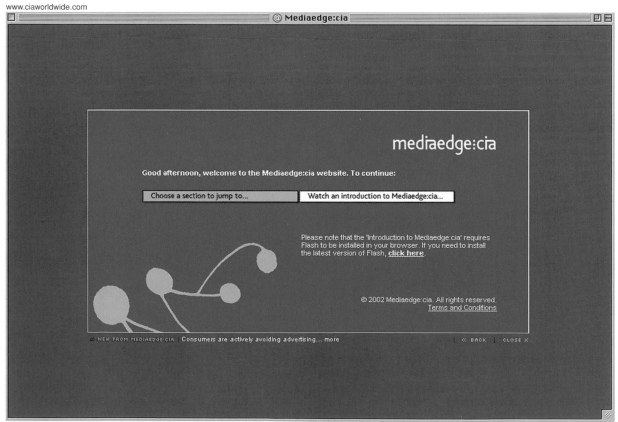

www.meyerwallis.com

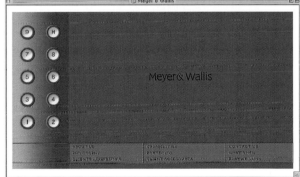

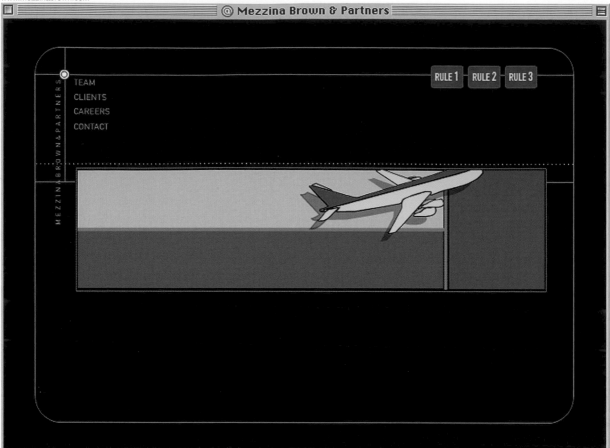

www.pbpb.com

www.publicissl.com

www.rpa.com

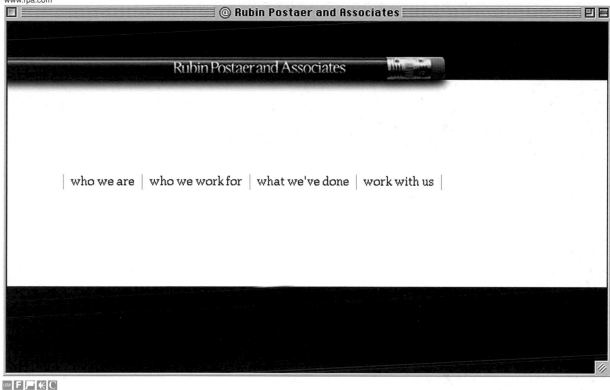

who we are | who we work for | what we've done | work with us

www.leoburnett.com

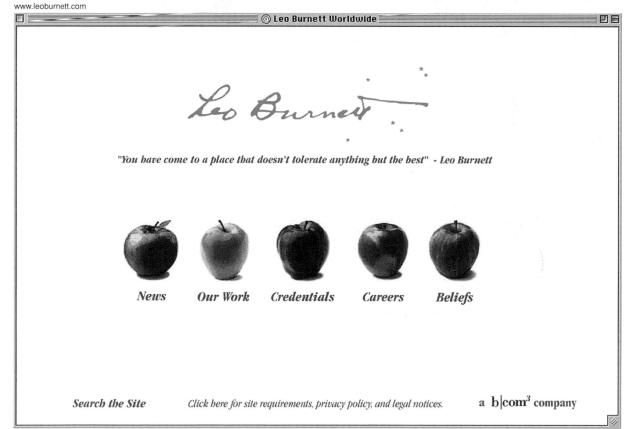

"You have come to a place that doesn't tolerate anything but the best" - Leo Burnett

News   Our Work   Credentials   Careers   Beliefs

Search the Site   Click here for site requirements, privacy policy, and legal notices.   a b|com³ company

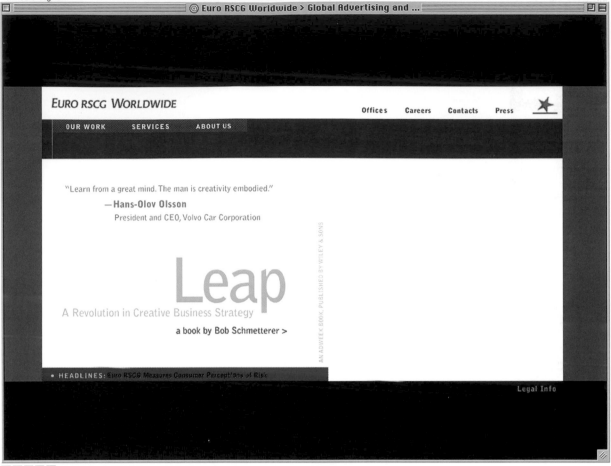

EURO RSCG WORLDWIDE

Offices   Careers   Contacts   Press

OUR WORK   SERVICES   ABOUT US

"Learn from a great mind. The man is creativity embodied."

—Hans-Olov Olsson

President and CEO, Volvo Car Corporation

Leap

A Revolution in Creative Business Strategy

a book by Bob Schmetterer >

AN ADWEEK BOOK, PUBLISHED BY WILEY & SONS

• HEADLINES: Euro RSCG Measures Consumer Perceptions of Risk

Legal Info

USA F K C

www.AlPunto.com

BEING HISPANIC IS NOT ABOUT A LANGUAGE OR A RACE;
IT'S ABOUT BEING A PART OF A CULTURE.

alpunto

Client Area   ©2002 al Punto Advertising, Inc.

USA F K C

www.ckideas.com

Who We Are

What We Do

Experience

cruz/kravetz:
IDEAS

News

- login

Links

Contact Us

USA F C

www.enlacecomm.com

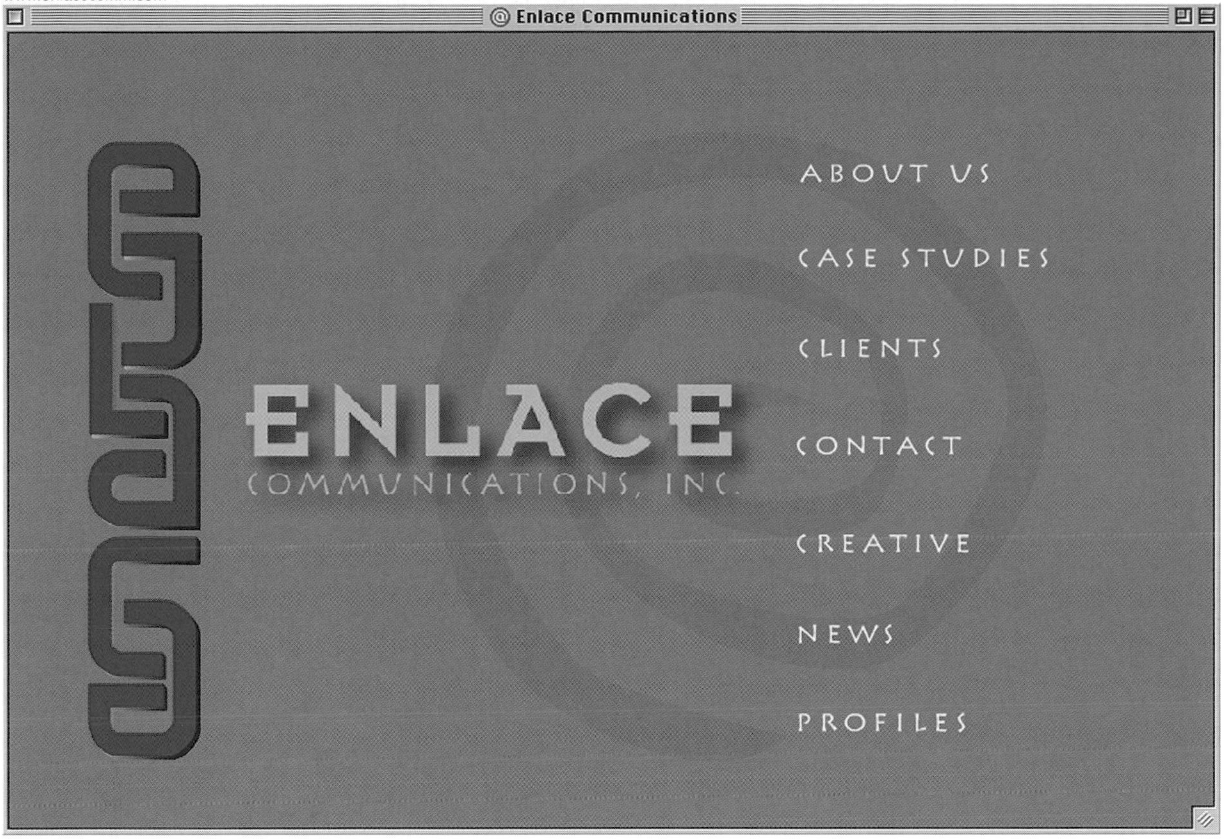
Enlace Communications
ABOUT US
CASE STUDIES
CLIENTS
ENLACE
COMMUNICATIONS, INC.
CONTACT
CREATIVE
NEWS
PROFILES

www.headquartersadv.com

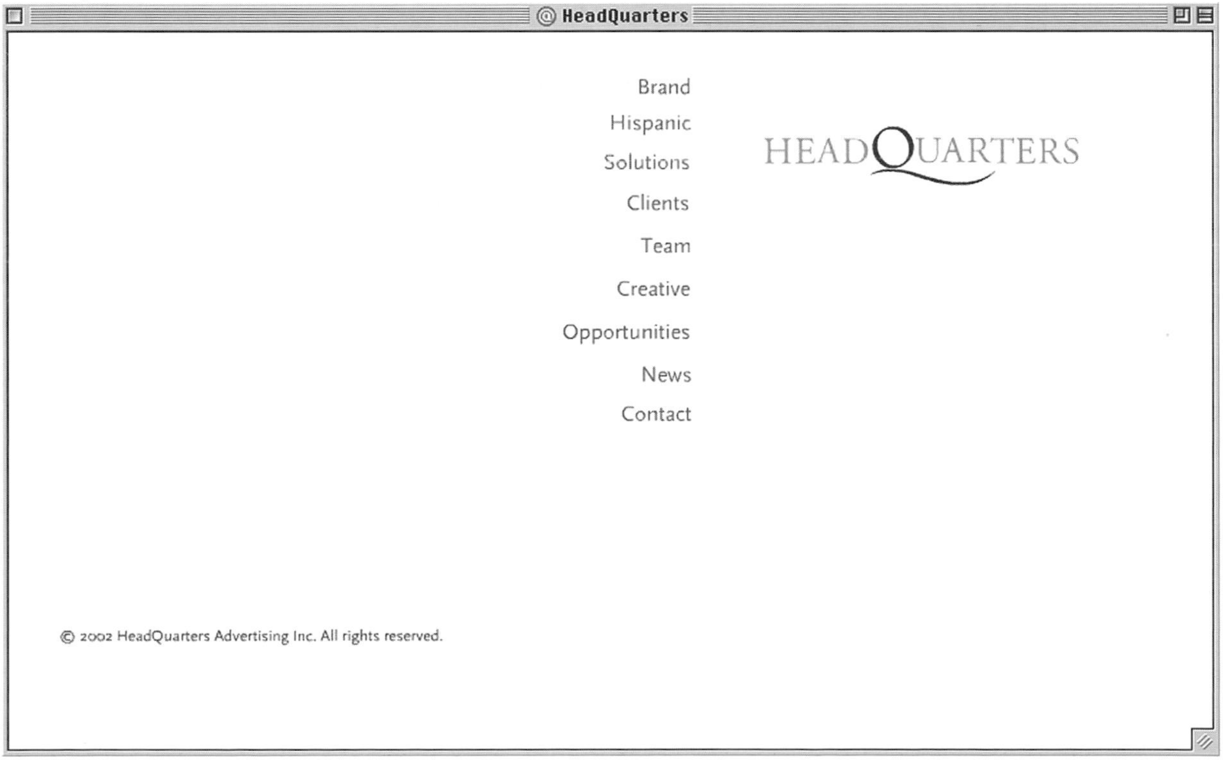
HeadQuarters
Brand
Hispanic
Solutions
Clients
Team
Creative
Opportunities
News
Contact
HEADQUARTERS
© 2002 HeadQuarters Advertising Inc. All rights reserved.

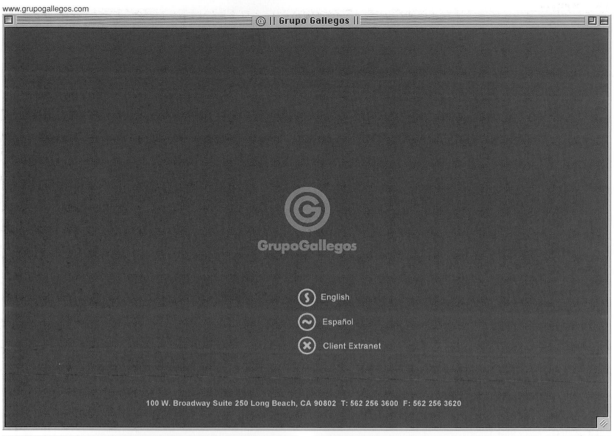

www.iacadgroup.com

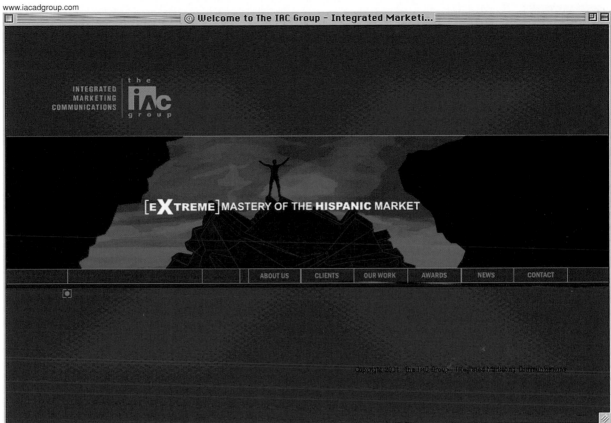

www.winglatino.com

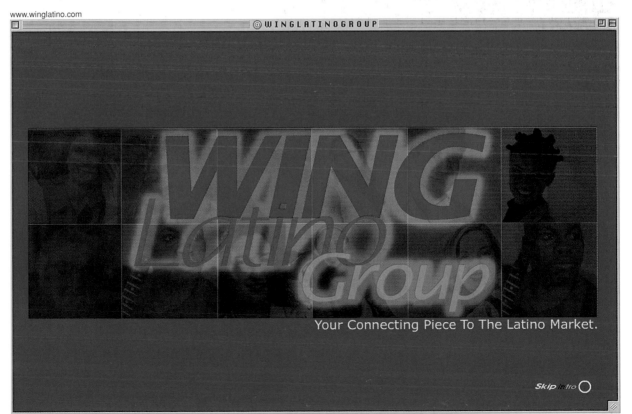

www.vidal-partnership.com

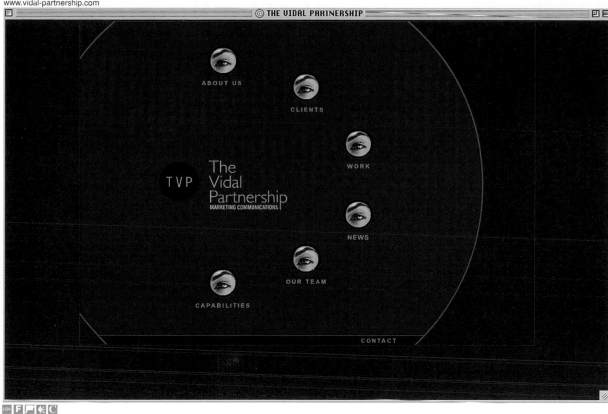

THE VIDAL PARTNERSHIP

ABOUT US

CLIENTS

WORK

TVP The Vidal Partnership
MARKETING COMMUNICATIONS

NEWS

OUR TEAM

CAPABILITIES

CONTACT

USA F C

www.jsmplus.com

@ welcome to jsm+ communications

JSM+

Welcome to JSM+ Communications
a full-service advertising agency

? ⚐ ⚒ 📁 ✉

DCA Advertising Renames West Coast Operation
Formerly JSM+ Communications, Los Angeles Office to operate as DCA Advertising
more

Watch our "bike-cam" virtual tour! **Watch** our "scooter-cam" virtual tour!

Copyright @2002 JSM+ Communications

USA F C

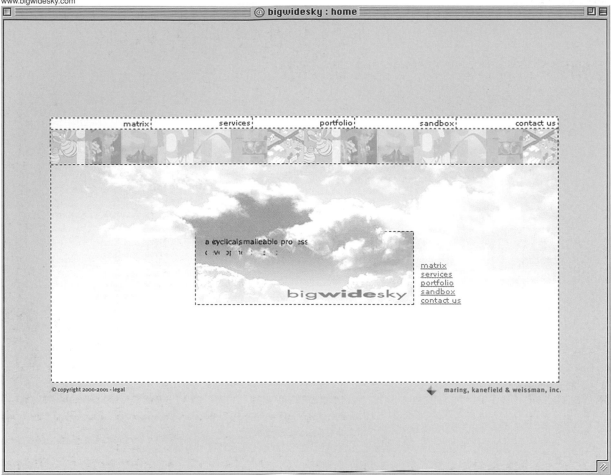

@ bigwidesky : home

matrix   services   portfolio   sandbox   contact us

a cyclicalsmalleable process

bigwidesky

matrix
services
portfolio
sandbox
contact us

© copyright 2000-2001 - legal

maring, kanefield & weissman, inc.

USA F C

www.buntingroup.com

@ http://www.buntingroup.com/Intro2.html

We are not a New York agency. We do not have offices on Michigan Avenue or Lakeshore Drive in Chicago. We're here in Nashville, Tennessee.

And while that may not be the place you'd expect to find an agency with our resources, our work or our **nationally recognized**, category-leading client roster, it has begun to make all the sense in the world. Thanks to the gradual turn of the marketplace toward an overwhelming need for advertising and communications resources that are **"consumer fluent."**

Because instead of viewing the lives of real Americans from the periphery of the country, we are an agency that **lives among them**, and speaks their language. Without any hint of false dialect or some ivory tower fantasy about **who real people are**, how they live, or what Madison Avenue thinks they need.

It is this intimate sense and **celebration of the mainstream** that, for the last three decades, has given us the insight to create some of the most unique, **relevant** and credible advertising in America.

ABOUT US | OUR FRIENDS AND PARTNERS | THE WORK | RECOGNITION | NEWS | CONTACT US

USA F C

www.teamoneadv.com

@ Team One Advertising

Looking for the best agency? You'll Find It Here.

PHONES JUST GOT FUN.

Ideas Are Bigger Than Ads.

We came to Lexus with a concept: create an entire Web site dedicated to Lexus safety. They loved the idea. And we drove people to the site with a campaign of 15-second TV spots. Today, LexusSafety.com is one of the most popular areas of the Lexus Web site. Hey, even we didn't see that one coming.

TeamOne
ADVERTISING

USA F C

www.reynardusandmoya.com

www.smmadagency.com

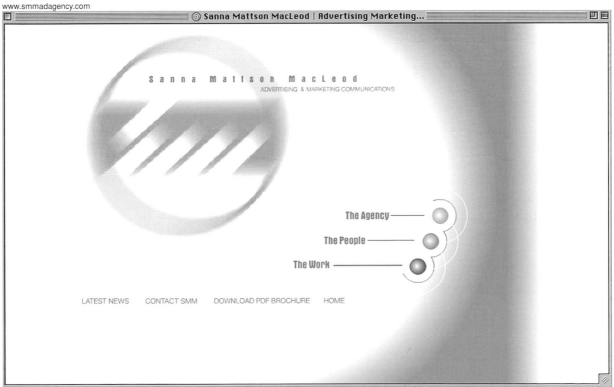

@ St. John & Partners

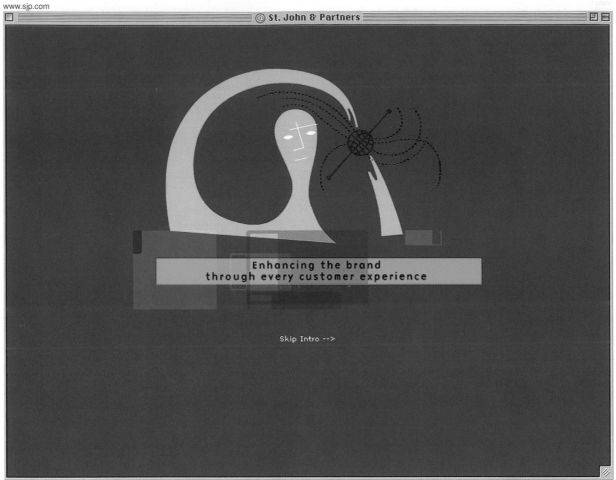

Enhancing the brand
through every customer experience

Skip Intro -->

The Brownstein Group

we never, ever stop thinking about your business. ever.

You | Us

THE BROWNSTEIN GROUP
DON'T BE JUST ANOTHER @®

todd taylor
senior art director

skip

The Dan Rosenthal Co. Web site

THE DAN ROSENTHAL CO.

Welcome to a unique ad agency with a reputation
for creating advertising that works. Here, everyone is creative.
Everyone develops ideas. ›

www.thecampbellgroup.com

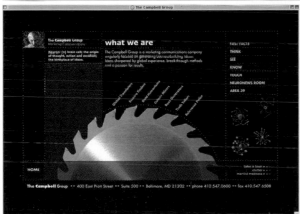

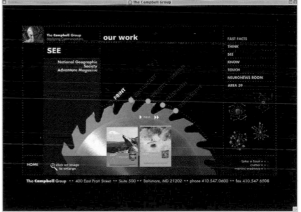

www.coxadvertising.com

www.fahlgren.com

www.trone.com

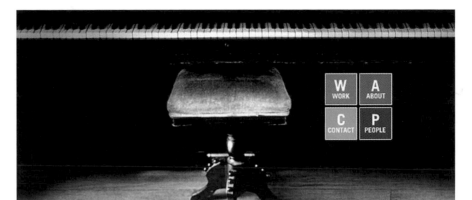

WHAT WE VALUE (3 OF 4):   TALENT   ▶ NEWS

www.bch.com

www.wyseadv.com

www.arch.iit.edu

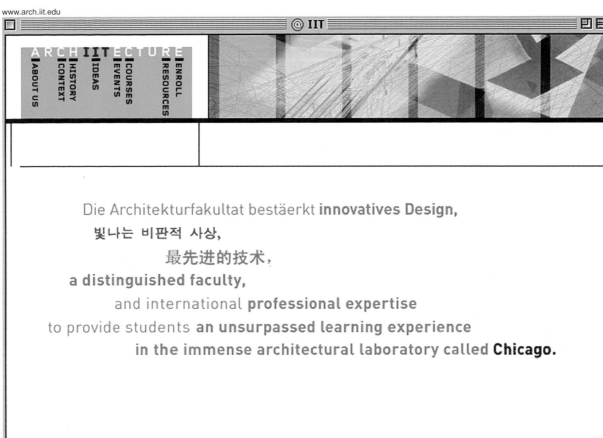

Die Architekturfakultat bestäerkt **innovatives Design,**

빛나는 비판적 사상,

最先进的技术,

a distinguished faculty,

and international **professional expertise**

to provide students **an unsurpassed learning experience**

in the immense architectural laboratory called **Chicago.**

EMAIL | HOME | College of Architecture

ILLINOIS INSTITUTE OF TECHNOLOGY

---

www.charlesmoore.org

the charles w. moore center *for* the study of place

enter

---

www.jkl.fi/kulttuur/aalto/

ALVAR AALTO

alvaraalto.fi

CV, BIBLIOGRAPHY...
CV, KIRJALLISUUS...

ALVAR AALTO'S LIFE
ALVAR AALLON ELÄMÄ

ARCHITECTURE
ARKKITEHTUURI

DESIGN
MUOTOILU

FOUNDATION SÄÄTIÖ
ACADEMY AKATEMIA
MUSEUM MUSEO
ARCHIVES ARKISTOT

Riihitie House · Riihitien talo

Muuratsalo Experimental House ·
Muuratsalon koetalo

ELEPHANT
& butterfly

HAE / SEARCH

CONTACTS YHTEYSTIEDOT

SITE MAP HAKEMISTO

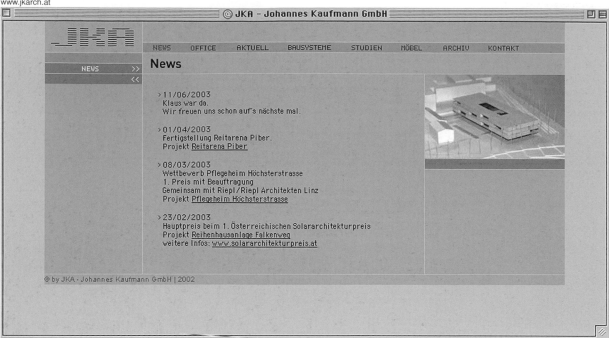

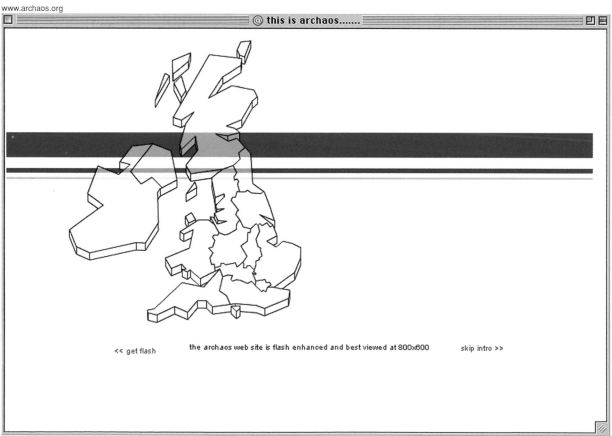

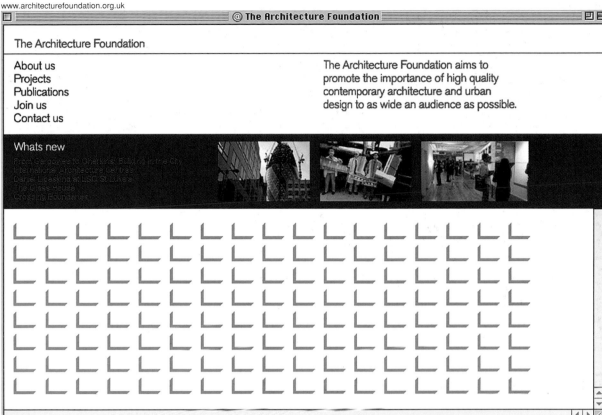

The Architecture Foundation

About us
Projects
Publications
Join us
Contact us

The Architecture Foundation aims to promote the importance of high quality contemporary architecture and urban design to as wide an audience as possible.

Whats new
From Gargoyles to Gherkins: Building in the City
International Architecture Centres
Daniel Libeskind at LSO St Luke's
The Glass House
Crossing Boundaries

www.hayesdavidson.com

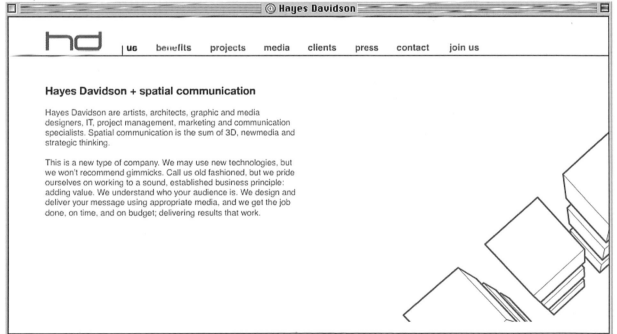

hd | us   benefits   projects   media   clients   press   contact   join us

Hayes Davidson + spatial communication

Hayes Davidson are artists, architects, graphic and media designers, IT, project management, marketing and communication specialists. Spatial communication is the sum of 3D, newmedia and strategic thinking.

This is a new type of company. We may use new technologies, but we won't recommend gimmicks. Call us old fashioned, but we pride ourselves on working to a sound, established business principle: adding value. We understand who your audience is. We design and deliver your message using appropriate media, and we get the job done, on time, and on budget; delivering results that work.

Home News Sitemap Kontakt Links

DATENFLUG

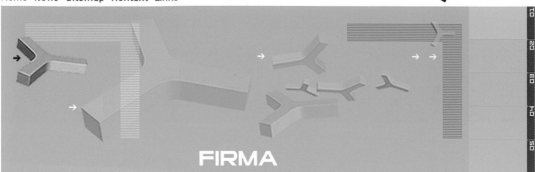

FIRMA

Datenflug Kompetenzen Produkte Projekte Referenzen   back

Datenflug

→ Firma
  Vision
  Network
  History
  Impressum

Firma

Datenflug wurde im Jahr 2000 als Agentur für virtuelle Architektur
und neue Medien von Rolf Kretschmer, Benedikta Scheibenzuber und
Jonas Schmidt in Berlin gegründet.
Im Januar 2001 wurde Datenflug in eine GmbH umgewandelt.

Geschäftsführung:

Dipl.-Ing. Benedikta Scheibenzuber → scheibenzuber@datenflug.de
Dipl.-Ing. Rolf Kretschmer   → kretschmer@datenflug.de
Dipl.-Ing. Jonas Schmidt   → schmidt@datenflug.de

top   back

DE F C S

www.murphyjahn.com

Murphy/Jahn
DIGITAL

ENGLISH   DEUTSCH

DE F P

www.hpp.com

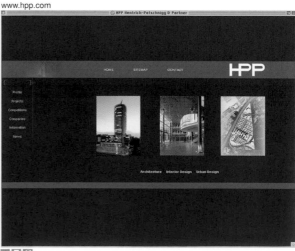

DE F C

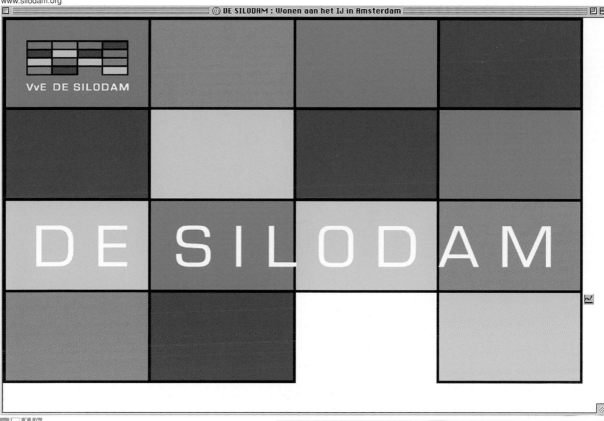

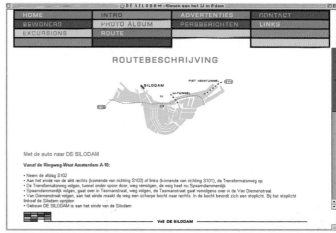

ROUTEBESCHRIJVING

Met de auto naar DE SILODAM

Vanaf de Ringweg-West Amsterdam A-10:

- Neem de afslag S102
- Aan het einde van de afrit rechts (komende van richting S103) of links (komende van richting S101), de Transformatorweg op
- De Transformatorweg volgen, tunnel onder spoor door, weg vervolgen, de weg heet nu Spaarndammerdijk
- Spaarndammerdijk volgen, gaat over in Tasmanstraat, weg volgen, de Tasmanstraat gaat vervolgens over in de Van Diemenstraat
- Van Diemenstraat volgen, aan het einde maakt de weg een scherpe bocht naar rechts. In de bocht bevindt zich een stoplicht. Bij het stoplicht linksaf de Silodam oprijden
- Gebouw DE SILODAM is aan het einde van de Silodam

ALLMANN SATTLER WAPPNER · ARCHITEKTEN

UPDATED 13.05.2003

AKTUELL BAUTEN WETTBEWERBE PUBLIKATIONEN BIOGRAPHIEN BÜRO LINKS

www.behnisch.com

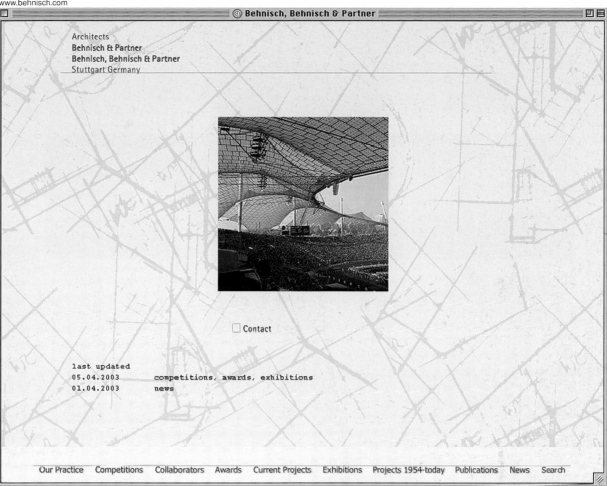

@ Behnisch, Behnisch & Partner

Architects
Behnisch & Partner
Behnisch, Behnisch & Partner
Stuttgart Germany

☐ Contact

last updated
05.04.2003   competitions, awards, exhibitions
01.04.2003   news

Our Practice   Competitions   Collaborators   Awards   Current Projects   Exhibitions   Projects 1954-today   Publications   News   Search

DE F C

www.juliesnowarchitects.com

USA F C

www.bcj.com

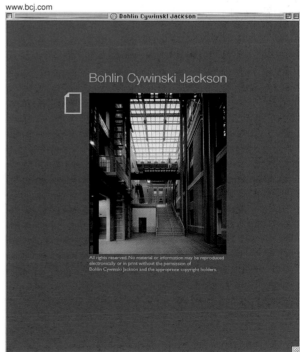

@ Bohlin Cywinski Jackson

Bohlin Cywinski Jackson

USA F C

.::Snøhetta – Snøhetta::.

SNØHETTA

PROJECTS   FACTS   CONTACT

| BIBLIOTHECA ALEXANDRINA | DEN NORSKE OPERA | TURNER MUSEET |

EVENTS AND INFORMATION

→ Tjuvholmen Competition
→ Snøhetta wins stoneprize
→ More News 2002

.::Snøhetta – Picture gallery::.

SNØHETTA

PROJECTS   FACTS   CONTACT

Snøhetta > Projects > Parks and Gardens > Toyen Culture Park > Picture gallery

related information:

→ Project description
→ Picture gallery

Picture gallery

.::Snøhetta – Projects::.

SNØHETTA

PROJECTS   FACTS   CONTACT

Snøhetta > Projects

Projects and casestudies

→ Cultural buildings
→ Bridges, Roads, Public Spaces
→ Parks and Gardens
→ Commercial buildings
→ Miscellaneous

Projects

CULTURAL BUILDINGS
Bibliotheca Alexandrina, New Opera house, Turner Museum, Cultural Centre Sandvika, Karmøy Fishing Museum, Kansai-Kan Library, Lillehammer Olympic Art Museum

BRIDGES, ROADS & PUBLIC SPACES
Olafiagangen, Oslo

PARKS & GARDENS
Toyen Culture Park

COMMERCIAL BUILDINGS
Norwegian Embassy in Berlin, Hamar Town Hall, Institut of Neurobiologie, Marseille

MISCELLANEOUS
Artesia, Sans, Zumtobel Staff Showroom

Search projects and project related material:

[   ] [Search]

▣ Harry Seidler and Associates . ARCHITECTS & P...

Harry Seidler and Associates
ARCHITECTS & PLANNERS

copyright:

enter site:
I agree to the copyright conditions above

a garyventerARCHITECT website

site revision 2.1

© Montalbetti+Campbell

AU F C

▣ Pugh + Scarpa Architecture

PUGH + SCARPA ARCHITECTURE PRESENTS

TO LIVE AND DRAW IN LA

ABOUT P+S   PORTFOLIO   FEATURES

NEWS   WEB DESIGN BY ARCHINECT   CURRENT FEATURE CREDITS

USA F C

@ Pei Partnership Architects

PEI PARTNERSHIP ARCHITECTS 257 Park Avenue South, NY, NY 10010-7304   Tel: 212 674 9000   Fax: 212 674 5900

about us   selected projects   clients   news

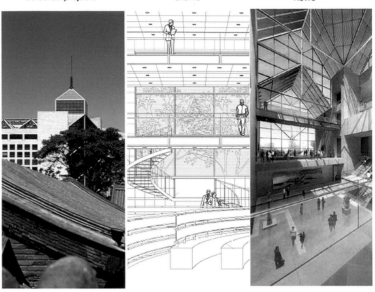

Left:
Bank of China Head Office Building
Beijing, China

Middle:
Opera of the Future
Massachussetts Institute of Technology
Cambridge, MA

Right:
Chengdu Museum
Chengdu, China

USA C

www.uniquenvironments.co.uk

@ uniquenvironments

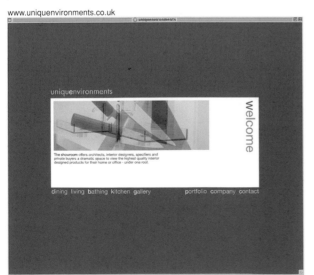

uniquenvironments

welcome

The showroom offers architects, interior designers, specifiers and
private buyers a dramatic space to view the highest quality interior
designed products for their home or office - under one roof.

dining living bathing kitchen gallery   portfolio company contact

UK F C

www.michaelwilford.com

@ Michael Wilford

MICHAEL WILFORD

Masterplanning
Theatres & Performing Arts
Museums & Art Galleries
Libraries & Archives
Academic
Civic & Government
Offices, HQs & Factories

Awards
Project List
Michael Wilford Profile
Articles & Publications
Michael Wilford + MUMA
Wilford Schupp GMBH
Contacts

office@michaelwilford.com

UK F C

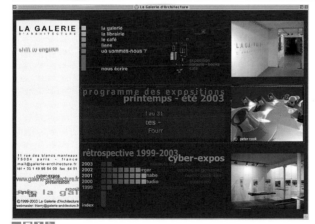

www.ac-plan.de

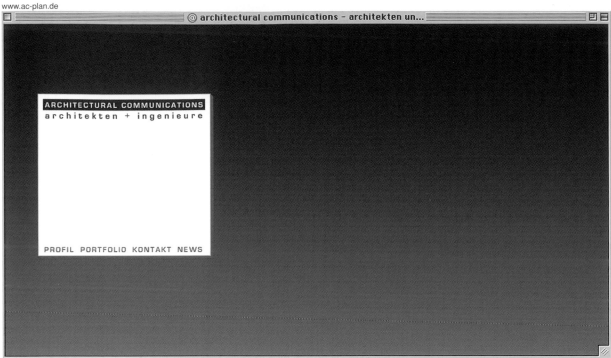

ARCHITECTURAL COMMUNICATIONS
architekten + ingenieure

PROFIL PORTFOLIO KONTAKT NEWS

DE F C

www.egidemeertens.be

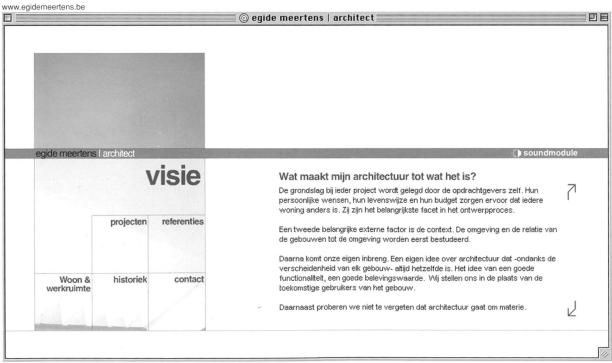

egide meertens | architect

soundmodule

visie

projecten   referenties

Woon &   historiek   contact
werkruimte

Wat maakt mijn architectuur tot wat het is?

De grondslag bij ieder project wordt gelegd door de opdrachtgevers zelf. Hun persoonlijke wensen, hun levenswijze en hun budget zorgen ervoor dat iedere woning anders is. Zij zijn het belangrijkste facet in het ontwerpproces.

Een tweede belangrijke externe factor is de context. De omgeving en de relatie van de gebouwen tot de omgeving worden eerst bestudeerd.

Daarna komt onze eigen inbreng. Een eigen idee over architectuur dat -ondanks de verscheidenheid van elk gebouw- altijd hetzelfde is. Het idee van een goede functionaliteit, een goede belevingswaarde. Wij stellen ons in de plaats van de toekomstige gebruikers van het gebouw.

Daarnaast proberen we niet te vergeten dat architectuur gaat om materie.

BE F P

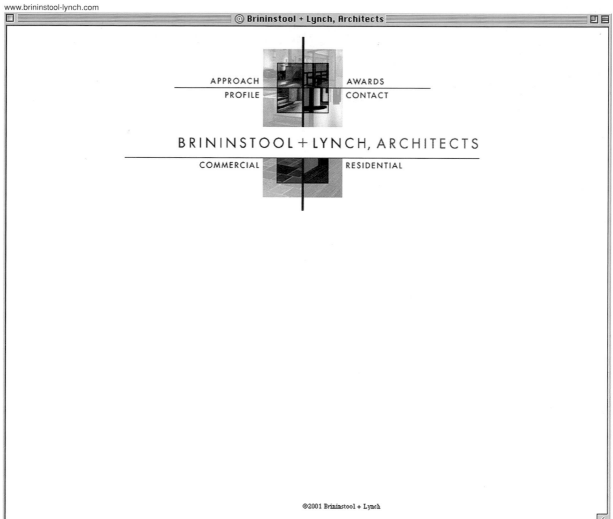

www.studiosarch.com

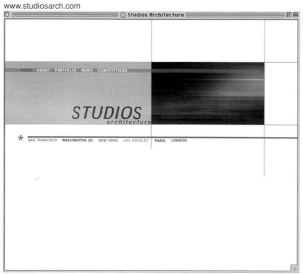

www.ghcp.com

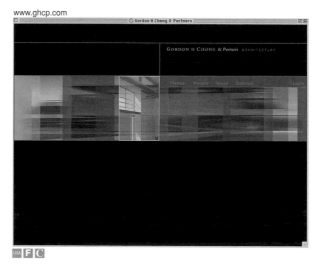

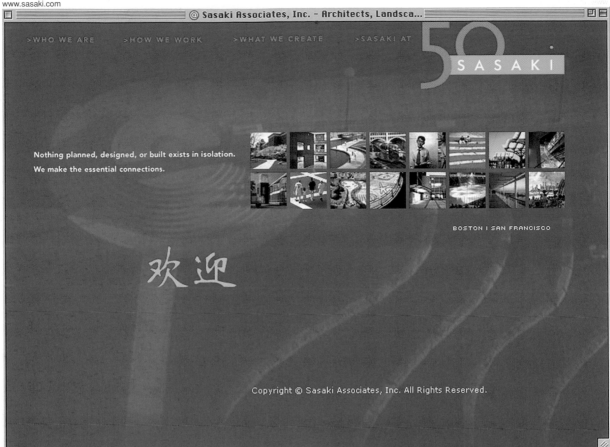

Nothing planned, designed, or built exists in isolation.
We make the essential connections.

BOSTON | SAN FRANCISCO

欢迎

People who are passionate about connection

Collaboration is our culture. Because Hideo Sasaki pioneered the multidisciplinary firm, we understand better than anyone how to bring multiple disciplines to bear to make the end result richer. We relish the opportunity to transform difficult assignments into breakthrough work for our clients.

More on Who We Are >>

A legacy of critical thinking and open inquiry Founded in 1953 by Hideo Sasaki, Sasaki Associates is an interdisciplinary firm of more than 270 professionals.

Planning and Urban Design
Landscape Architecture
Architecture
Interior Design
Civil Engineering
Graphic Design

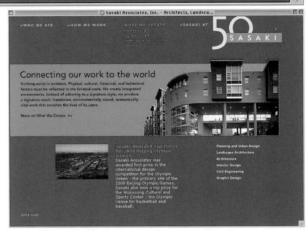

Connecting our work to the world

Nothing exists in isolation. Physical, cultural, historical, and behavioral factors must be reflected in the finished work. We create integrated environments. Instead of adhering to a signature style, we produce a signature result: handsome, environmentally sound, economically vital work that enriches the lives of its users.

More on What We Create >>

Sasaki Awarded Top Prizes for 2008 Beijing Olympic Games. Sasaki Associates was awarded first prize in the international design competition for the Olympic Green - the primary site of the 2008 Beijing Olympic Games. Sasaki also won a top prize for the Wukesong Cultural and Sports Center - the Olympic venue for basketball and baseball.

Planning and Urban Design
Landscape Architecture
Architecture
Interior Design
Civil Engineering
Graphic Design

USA F C

www.manciniduffy.com

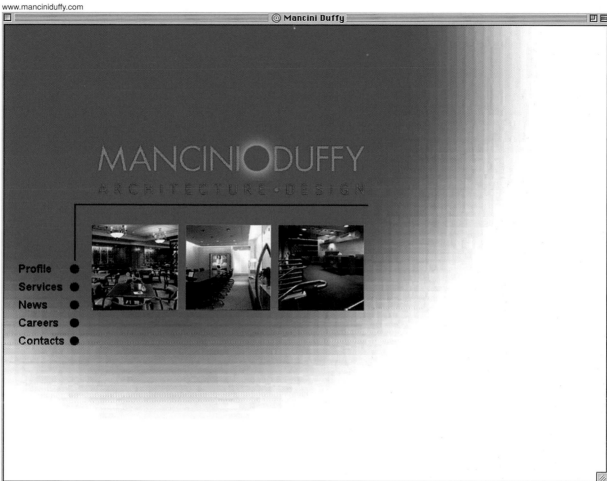

@ Mancini Duffy

MANCINIODUFFY
ARCHITECTURE · DESIGN

Profile ●
Services ●
News ●
Careers ●
Contacts ●

USA F C

www.perkinswill.com

Welcome To Perkins & Will

PERKINS
&WILL

OUR WORK   NEWS   CONTACT   CAREER

USA C

www.rmw.com

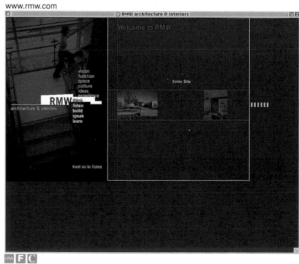

RMW architecture & interiors

Welcome to RMW

vision
function
space
culture
ideas
experience
think
listen
build
speak
learn

RMW
architecture & interiors

Enter Site

trust us to listen

USA F C

@ Scottish Architecture .com

www.scottisharchitecture.com

SEARCH

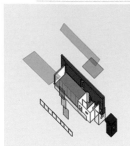

INTRODUCTION

EDUCATION

COMMUNITY

EXHIBITIONS AND TOURS

THE BUILT ENVIRONMENT

WHATS NEW

News Headlines: May 14, 2003

Back to the drawing board for Glasgow's brand new image
The launch of a new £2m brand for Glasgow has been shelved by the city's tourist board because of a failure to agree a design......

Solution toplanning fiasco liesin the past
Why do the most pleasing parts of Scotland's townscapes pre-date the arrival of municipal planning? Is Edinburgh's Georgian New Town so pleasing by accident...

RIAS BEST BUILDING AWARD
FULL DETAILS OF ALL FIVE SHORTLISTED

THE NATIONAL PROGRAMME
PART OF THE POLICY ON ARCHITECTURE

New on the site

Latest Additions:
- Featured Opinion: Andy McAvoy
- Student's Guide to Architecture
- Common-Place Exhibition

What's hot in the forums:
Rebuild or Renew? - The fire that recently raged through Edinburgh and has devastated part of the historic Old Town has engendered a huge sense of loss. However, it has also opened up an opportunity for Scotland's capital to demonstrate this country's contemporary architectural vision.

THE REGENERATION OF GLASGOWS CLYDE
REPORT ON RECENT CONFERENCE

STUDENTS GUIDE
STUDYING ARCHITECTURE IN SCOTLAND

MAILING LIST   EMAIL US   FEEDBACK   PRINT PAGE   SITE MAP

ARCHITECTURE   The Lighthouse

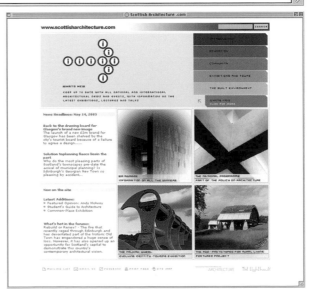

www.rias.org.uk

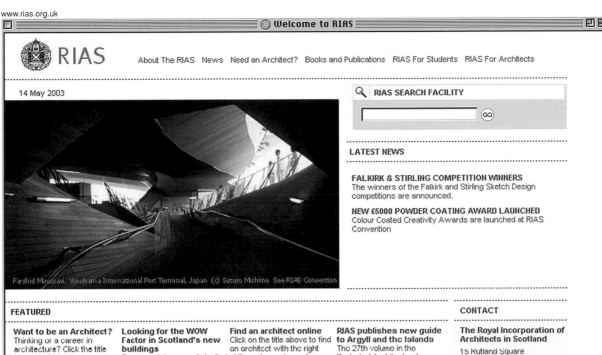

www.thelighthouse.co.uk

Richard Meier & Partners Architects

(Home)

Firm Profile

Projects

News

Press

Contact

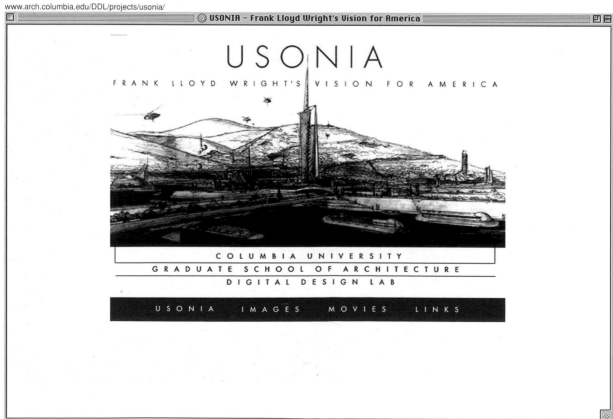

USONIA

FRANK LLOYD WRIGHT'S VISION FOR AMERICA

COLUMBIA UNIVERSITY
GRADUATE SCHOOL OF ARCHITECTURE
DIGITAL DESIGN LAB

USONIA   IMAGES   MOVIES   LINKS

www.richardrogers.co.uk

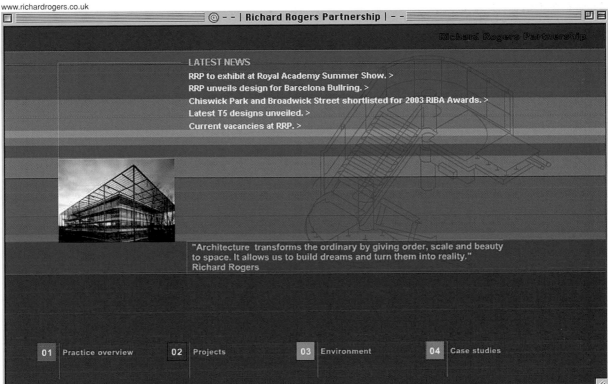

www.calatrava.com

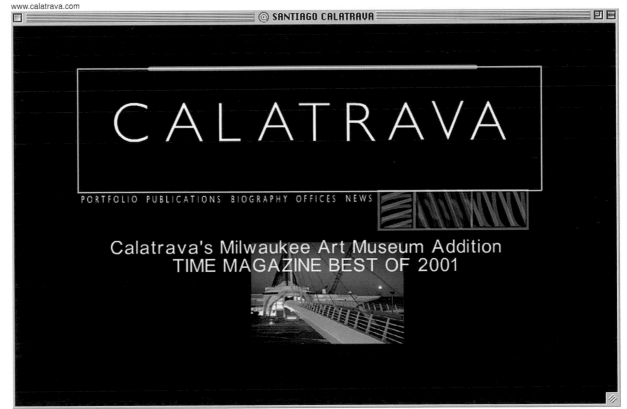

@ mario botta architetto

MARIO BOTTA ARCHITETTO

| ENGLISH | ITALIANO | GET FLASH |

mario botta architetto
via ciani 16   6904   lugano   switzerland

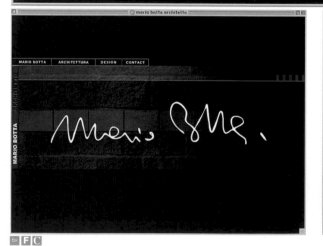

@ mario botta architetto

MARIO BOTTA | ARCHITETTURA | DESIGN | CONTACT

@ mario botta architetto

MARIO BOTTA | ARCHITETTURA | DESIGN | CONTACT

LAVORI RECENTI

spazi privati
spazi pubblici
spazi sacri
cronologia

Architectural Association School of Architecture

Important Information for Staff and Students
Severe Acute Respiratory Syndrome (SARS)
Guidance for Travellers

About the AA   Programmes   Events   Resources   Members   Email

RDON MATTA-CLA
SPACE BETWEE
KING THROUGH A
XHIBITION

© Architectural Association 2003 | If nothing appears in the main window download **Flash** | Alternatively go directly to **AA News** page
Important information for staff and students - Severe Acute Respiratory Syndrome (SARS) - Guidance for travellers.

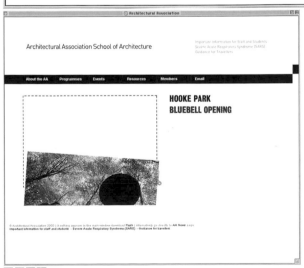

Architectural Association School of Architecture

Important Information for Staff and Students
Severe Acute Respiratory Syndrome (SARS)
Guidance for Travellers

About the AA   Programmes   Events   Resources   Members   Email

**HOOKE PARK
BLUEBELL OPENING**

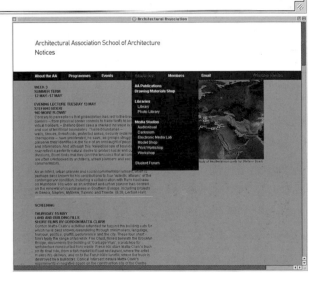

Architectural Association School of Architecture
Notices

About the AA   Programmes   Events   Resources   Members   Email

WEEK 3
SUMMER TERM
12 MAY–17 MAY

EVENING LECTURE TUESDAY 13 MAY
STEFANO BOERI
'NO MORE FLOWS'

AA Publications
Drawing Materials Shop

Libraries
Library
Photo Library

Media Studios
Audiovisual
Darkroom
Electronic Media Lab
Model Shop
Print Workshop
Workshop

Student Forum

SCREENING

THURSDAY 15 MAY
LAND AND BUILDING FILLS
SHORT FILMS BY GORDON MATTA-CLARK

@ HOUSING & URBANISM ARCHITECTURAL ASSOCIATION ...

Housing and Urbanism
Architectural Association School of Architecture

www.zaha-hadid.com

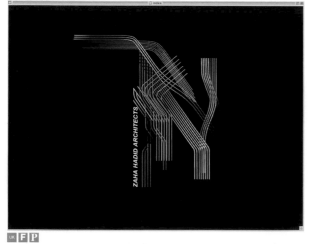

www.alsoparchitects.com

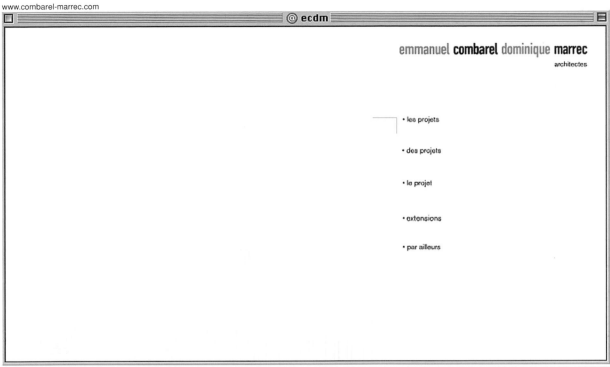

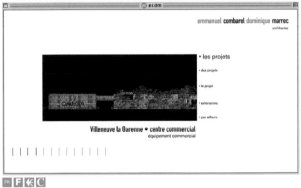

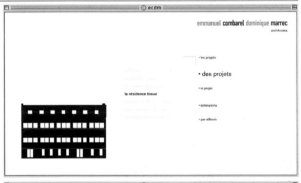

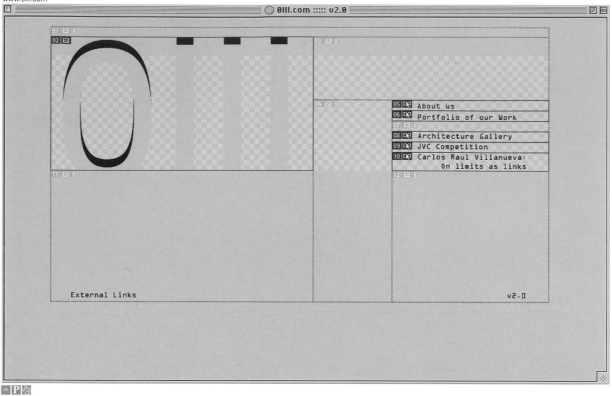

01
02
03
04
05 About us
06 Portfolio of our Work
07
08 Architecture Gallery
09 JVC Competition
10 Carlos Raul Villanueva:
   On limits as links
11
12

External Links

v2.0

DE P S

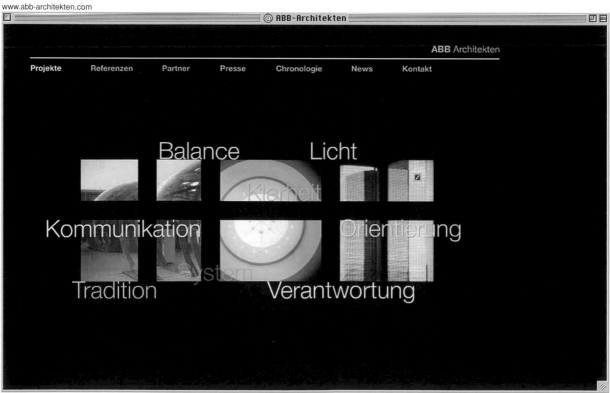

ABB Architekten

Projekte   Referenzen   Partner   Presse   Chronologie   News   Kontakt

Balance   Licht

Klarheit

Kommunikation   Orientierung

Tradition   System   Verantwortung

DE F C

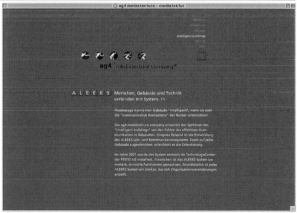

ag4 | mediatecture company®

HERZLICH WILLKOMMEN !

"Mediatektur" gestaltet Lebensräume kommunikativ, so dass die Raumstrukturen in unserer globalen Informationsgesellschaft wirklich "intelligent" werden.

Im Mittelpunkt der Arbeit steht die Integration von Medientechnik in die Architektur, die aktiv die Kommunikation von Mensch zu Mensch unterstützt und komplexere soziale Prozesse ermöglicht.

http://fanuelearchitecture.com

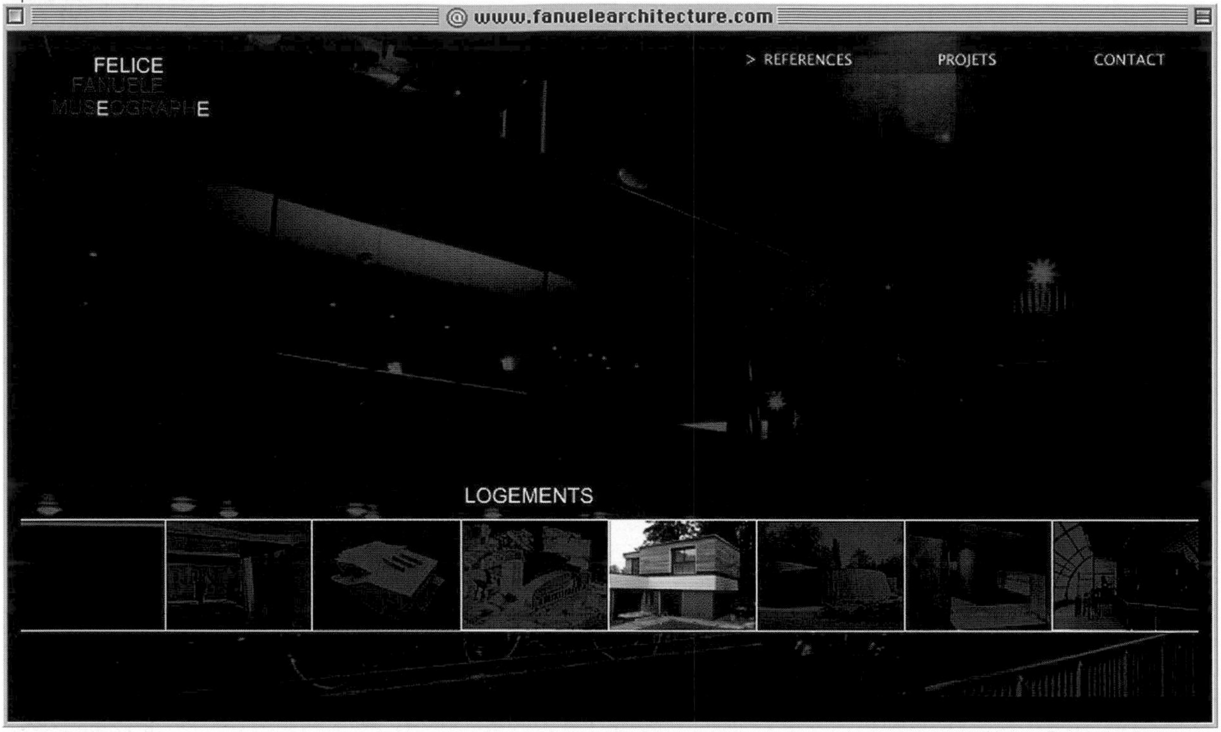
www.fanuelearchitecture.com
FELICE
FANUELE
MUSEOGRAPHIE
> REFERENCES
PROJETS
CONTACT
LOGEMENTS

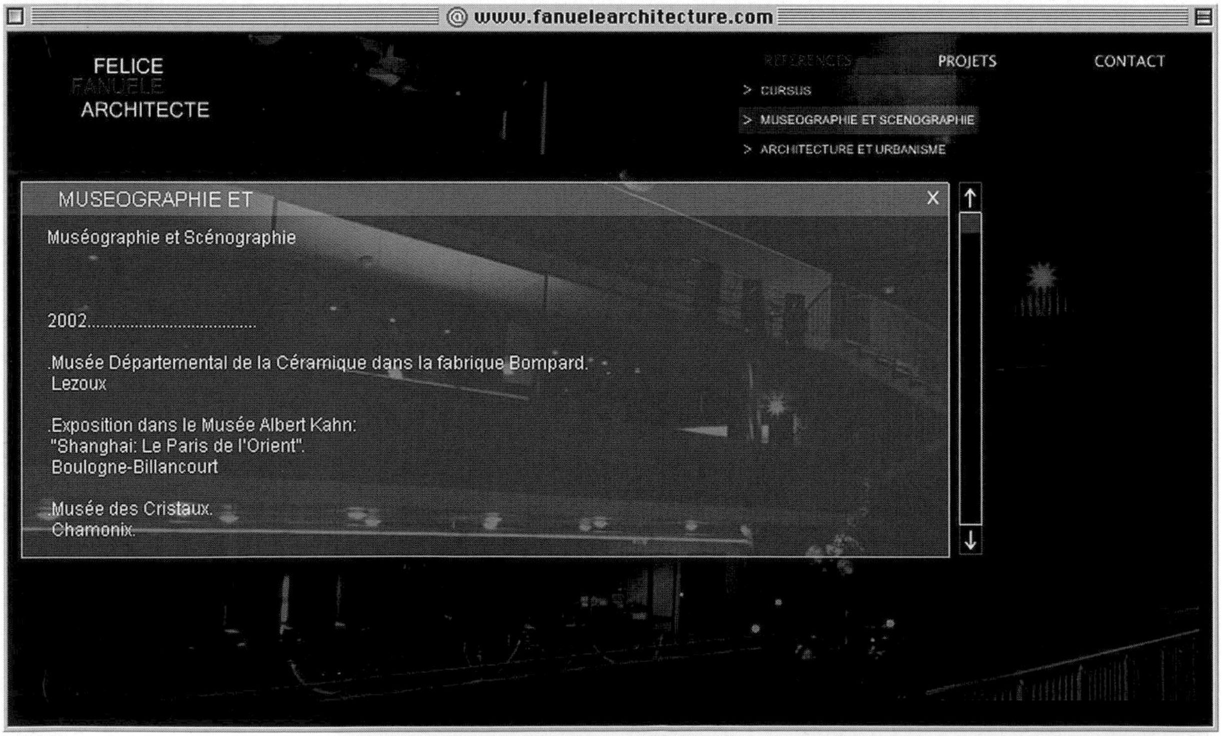
www.fanuelearchitecture.com
FELICE
FANUELE
ARCHITECTE
REFERENCES
PROJETS
CONTACT
> CURSUS
> MUSEOGRAPHIE ET SCENOGRAPHIE
> ARCHITECTURE ET URBANISME
MUSEOGRAPHIE ET
X
Muséographie et Scénographie
2002.....................................
.Musée Départemental de la Céramique dans la fabrique Bompard.
Lezoux
.Exposition dans le Musée Albert Kahn:
"Shanghai: Le Paris de l'Orient".
Boulogne-Billancourt
.Musée des Cristaux.
Chamonix.

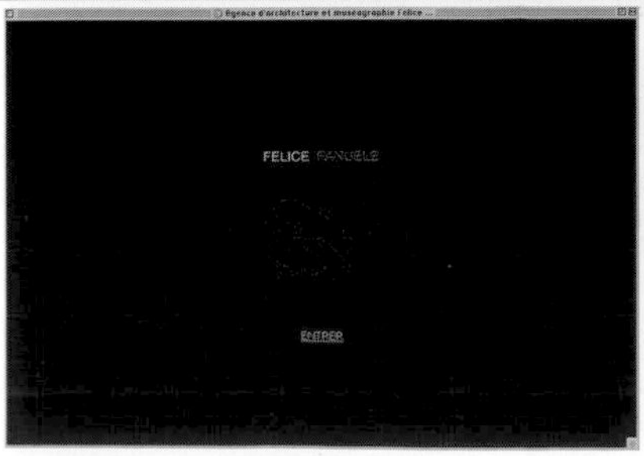
FELICE FANUELE
ENTRER

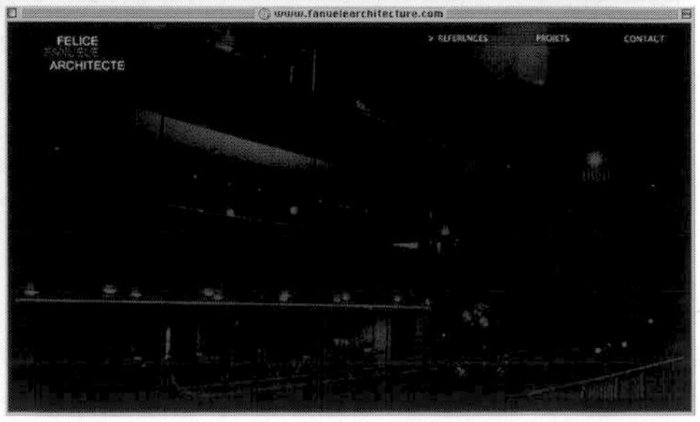
www.fanuelearchitecture.com
FELICE
FANUELE
ARCHITECTE
> REFERENCES
PROJETS
CONTACT

BERTHELIER FICHET TRIBOUILLET

SOPHIE BERTHELIER PHILIPPE FICHET BENOIT TRIBOUILLET

mise à jour : 11/03/2003
Best viewed in 1024*768
under IE5+ & NS6+

[English Version]

[Version Francaise]

© Lycée Rémi Belleau a nogent le rotrou

NOGENT LE ROTROU

Réalisation :
extension du lycée Rémi Belleau à Nogent le Rotrou

Maîtrise d'ouvrage :
Conseil Régional du Centre

Shon :
3100 m²

Coût des travaux :
2.6 M€ HT

Programme :
salles d'enseignement scolaire
informatique
salles banalisées

© Page Principale du site web bft-architectes b...

PRINCIPAL
SOMMAIRE
N O B
ACTUALITE
PROJETS
REMIBELLEAU
NICOLASROBERT
NOTREDAME
DEMIPENSION
AUDIVW
POINTINFO
IMMEUBLE
ATHISMONS
SAINTLUBIN
MAISONNEUDOR
HOTELIMPOTS
HOPITALLOCAL
CONCOURS
GYMNASE
SEMICHAGE
EN2002
EN2001
ANCIEN
AGENCE
PRESENTATION
PUBLICATIONS
EMAIL

EXPOSITION RUSHES 2 - IFA - INSTITUT FRANCAIS D'ARCHITECTURE - PARIS - 17 FEV
MAI 2000

BERTHELIER FICHET TRIBOUILLET

FR F C

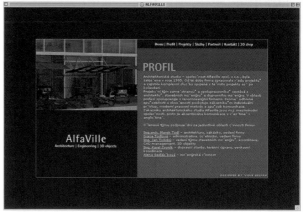

http://ama-a.com

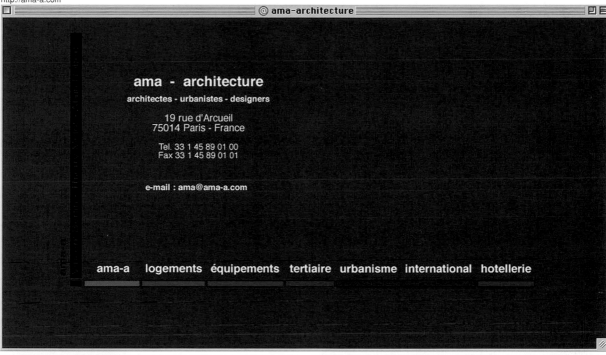

@ ama-architecture

ama - architecture

architectes - urbanistes - designers

19 rue d'Arcueil
75014 Paris - France

Tel. 33 1 45 89 01 00
Fax 33 1 45 89 01 01

e-mail : ama@ama-a.com

ama-a   logements   équipements   tertiaire   urbanisme   international   hotellerie

○ ama-architecture

1) Associés
Vincent Bertin   Président d'ama-a
Thierry Melot   Gestion et chantiers
Alain Robert   Architecte DPLG
                            Né le 14 Février 1961

2) Concept

3) Equipe

4) Agence

5) Infos

index   logements   équipements   tertiaire   urbanisme   international   hotellerie

○ ama-architecture

1) Associés
Vincent Bertin
Thierry Melot
Alain Robert

2) Concept

3) Equipe

4) Agence

5) Infos   Les locaux du 19 rue d'Arcueil, Paris 14ème

index   logements   équipements   tertiaire   urbanisme   international   hotellerie

○ ama-a / tertiaire et industriel

batiments tertiaires   programme / localité / surface / mission / maître d'ouvrage
et industriels
                                  • Siège Social Computer Associates Nanterre 12 000 m2 APS 1997
2002   CCPRIM (image)
2001   • Commissariat à l'Energie Atomique - Projet EVA Fontenay-aux-Roses
2000   18 000 m2 Concours CEA.
1997
1996
1995
1994
1993
1992
1991
1990
1988

ama-a   logements   équipements   index   urbanisme   international   hotellerie

○ ama-a / international

expérience   programme / localité / surface / mission / année / maître d'ouvrage
internationale
Algérie   • Quartier d'affaires et gare TGV-ICE Köln messe 200 000 m2 Concours 1999
Arabie Saoudite   Ville de Cologne
Allemagne   • La tour de la Poste Bonn 70 000 m2 Concours 1998
Cameroun   Deutsche Bundespost
Espagne   • Ville nouvelle de Layenhof - 12 000 habitants Mayence 246 ha Concours 1998
Etat de Bahrain   Ville de Mayence
Iles du Cap Vert   • Ministère des Transports Berlin 18 000 m2 Concours restreint 1996
Iran   Etat Allemand
Liban   • Université du Cinéma Potsdam-Babelsberg 12 000 m2 Concours 1996
Lybie   Land de Brandebourg
Maroc   • Le quartier de la gare Oldenbourg 15 ha Concours restreint 1996
Mauritanie   Land de Basse Saxe
République Dominicaine   • Le territoire de la gare Cologne 200 ha Concours (lauréat) 1995
Sénégal   Villes Européennes de la Grande Vitesse (image)
                                 • Centre d'affaires Düsseldorf 20 ha Plan masse 1992 Sari

ama-a   logements   équipements   tertiaire   urbanisme   index   hotellerie

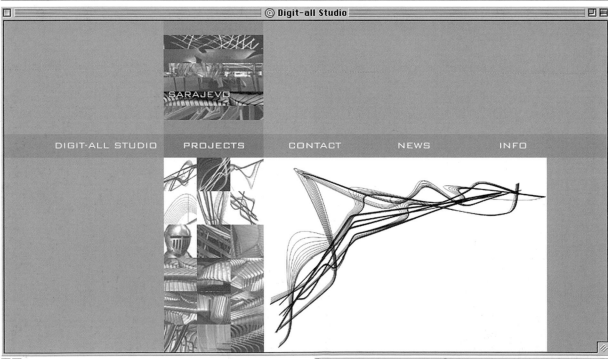

www.zz-berlin.de

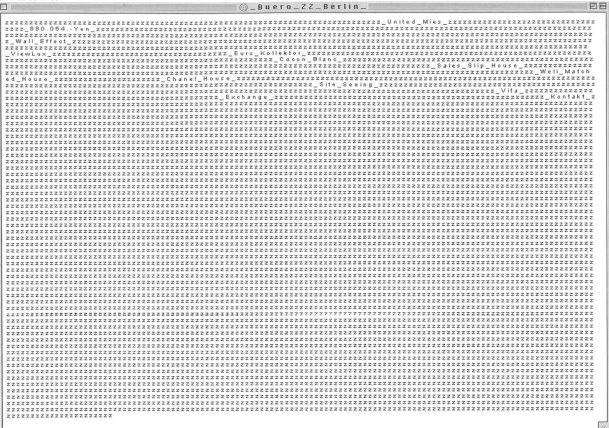

`@ _Buero_ZZ_Berlin_`

```
zzzzzzzzzzzzzzzzzzzzzzzzzzzzzzzzzzzzzzzzzzzzzzzzzzzzzzzzzzzzzzzz_United_Mies_zzzzzzzzzzzzzzzzzzzzzzzzzz
zzzz_880.064.·Yen_zzzzzzzzzzzzzzzzzzzzzzzzzzzzzzzzzzzzzzzzzzzzzzzzzzzzzzzzzzzzzzzzzzzzzzzzzzzzzzzzzzzzz
z_Wall_Effect_zzzzzzzzzzzzzzzzzzzzzzzzzzzzzzzzzzzzzzzzzzzzzzzzzzzzzzzzzzzzzzzzzzzzzzzzzzzzzzzzzzzzzzzzz
_ViewLux_zzzzzzzzzzzzzzzzzzzzzzzzzzzzzzzzz_Euro_Kollektor_zzzzzzzzzzzzzzzzzzzzzzzzzzzzzzzzzzzzzzzzzzzzz
zzzzzzzzzzzzzzzzzzzzzzzzzzzzzzzzzzzzzzzzzzzzzz_Cooon_Blanc_zzzzzzzzzzzzzzzzzzzzzzzzzzzzzzzzzzzzzzzzzzzz
zzzzzzzzzzzzzzzzzzzzzzzzzzzzzzzzzzzzzzzzzzzzzzzzzzzzzzzzzzzzzzzzzzz_Sales_Slip_House_zzzzzzzzzzzzzzzzzz
zzzzzzzzzzzzzzzzzzzzzzzzzzzzzzzzzzzzzzzzzzzzzzzzzzzzzzzzzzzzzzzzzzzzzzzzzzzzzzzzz_Well_Match
ed_House_zzzzzzzzzzzzzzzzzzzzzzz_Chanel_House_zzzzzzzzzzzzzzzzzzz_Site_Seeing_zzzzzzzzzzzzzzzzzzzzzzzzz
zzzzzzzzzzzzzzzzzzzzzzzzzzzzzzzzzzzzzzzzzzzzzzzzzzzzzzzzzzzzzzzzzzzzzzzzzzzzz_Vita_zzzzzzzzzzzzzz
zzzzzzzzzzzzzzzzzzzzzzzzzzz_Exchange_zzzzzzzzzzzzzzzzzzzzzzzzzzzzzzzzzzzzzzzzzzzzzzzz_Kontakt_z
```

www.archilab.it

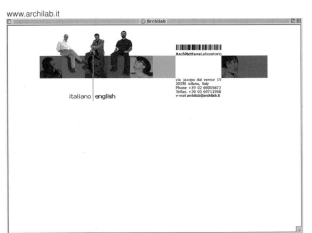

`@ Archilab`

ArchitetturaLaboratorio

via jacopo dal verme 15
20159 milano, Italy
Phone +39 02 69005672
Tel/fax. +39 02 69711958
e-mail archilab@archilab.it

italiano | english

www.architecture-studio.fr

`@ Architecture-Studio Paris`

ARCHITECTURE – STUDIO

@ **Archgroup Landskron**

ARCHGROUP
LANDSKRON

ARCHITEKTEN
+
ZIVILINGENIEURE FÜR
INNENARCHITEKTUR

unser produkt =
die erfüllung max. qualität in design, funktion, ökologie und ökonomie.

skip

© **Archgroup Landskron**

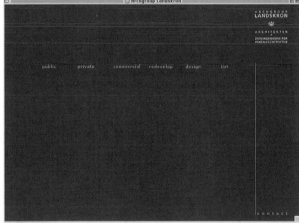

public   private   commercial   redevelop   design   list

contact

© **Archgroup Landskron**

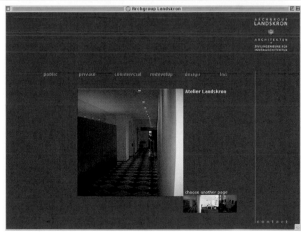

public   private   commercial   redevelop   design   list

Atelier Landskron

choose another page

contact

ARCHITECTURECAFE INTRODUCEERT UNIEK INTERNATIONAAL PROJECTENCENTRUM

Architecturecafe introduceert met trots hét uniek internationaal projectencentrum! De plaats waar architecten hun succesvolle projecten op nationaal én internationaal niveau kunnen etaleren. Wordt lid en voeg uw projecten toe. Laat zien wie er meetelt in de Nederlandse architectuur!

news features

Rotterdam krijgt extra bouwtoezicht may 13, 2003

De gemeente Rotterdam krijgt achttien extra voltijdbanen voor de uitvoering van het bouwtoezicht. Zo moet het tij worden gekeerd na een vernietigend rapport over de schaarse controles en het gebrek aan optreden bij misstanden. Het aantal controles in de havenstad is inmiddels opgevoerd. *read more at..*

courtesy: Martijn ten Napel

Eten bij de boer in een mobiele Maurer may 12, 2003

Voor de manifestatie '2003 - het Jaar van de Boerderij' is door Maurer United Architects [MUA] een mobiel restaurant ontwikkeld. Donderdag 8 mei zal op boerderij 'Het Meer' in Angeren, Gemeente Lingewaard te Gelderland de gecombineerde opening plaatsvinden van de Boerderij Estafette en het Jaar van de Boerderij in Gelderland. *read more at..*

courtesy: MUA

Serpentine Gallery Pavilion 2003, Oscar Niemeyer may 12, 2003

The Serpentine Gallery Pavilion 2003, now under construction in Hyde Park, is designed by Brazilian architect, Oscar Niemeyer. The pavilion is a temporary structure erected for special events on the gallery's lawn from June to September. This is the first structure in Britain by the 95-year-old Brazilian architect who designed Brasilia; his country's capital city. *read more at..*

courtesy: Arcspace

Netherlands
home

COUNTRY   LANGUAGE

tell a friend
sign in

membership

firms
consultants
presentation
organizations

projectcenter(new)
jobcenter

education
student organizations
students

museums
exhibitions
lectures

bookstore
publishers
journals

competitions
news features
famous architects
links

---

http://gasarchitektur.sil.at

www.scheicher.at

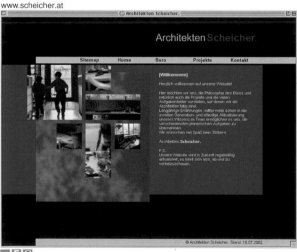

ARCHITEKTUR **alleine**
ist selten das,
was **BAUHERREN** benötigen.

SKIP INTRO

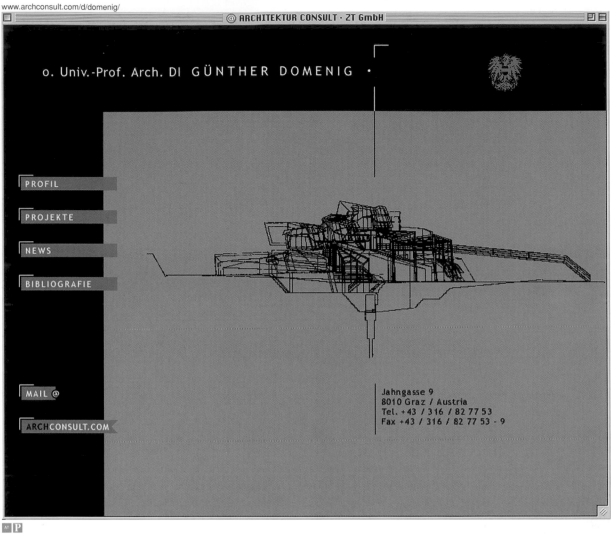

ARCHITEKTUR CONSULT · ZT GmbH

o. Univ.-Prof. Arch. DI GÜNTHER DOMENIG ·

PROFIL

PROJEKTE

NEWS

BIBLIOGRAFIE

MAIL @

ARCHCONSULT.COM

Jahngasse 9
8010 Graz / Austria
Tel. +43 / 316 / 82 77 53
Fax +43 / 316 / 82 77 53 - 9

AT P

architects FLN

arkkitehdit
.. L oy

FI C

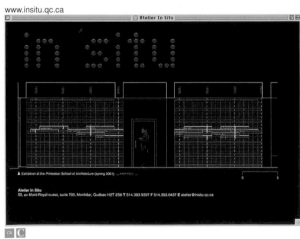

Atelier In Situ

▲ Exhibition at the Princeton School of Architecture (spring 2001) ...

Atelier In Situ
55, av Mont-Royal ouest, suite 700, Montréal, Québec H2T 2S6 T 514.393.9397 F 514.393.0437 E atelier@insitu.qc.ca

CA C

www.atelierbigcity.com

atelier Big City

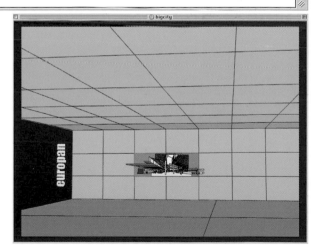

if you can't see the
animation on the left, then
download the Flash4
plugin **here**

- enter -

...bygger på erfaring

tegnestuen   institutioner   restaurering   konkurrencer   byggeri   design   aktuelt

Prison Island, Zanzibar

Prison Island er en meget lille ubeboet ø, beliggende ca. tre kilometer nordvest fra Stone Town. Fængslet blev bygget ca. 1837 var det første opholdssted for slaver der kom fra fastlandet, inden de blev bragt til markedet i Stone Town. Bag fængslet er der en atriumgård omgivet af en et-etagers bygning med fængselsceller og et cirkulært vandreservoir i midten til at opsamle drikkevand i. Bygningen er lavet af koralsten fra øen selv, og pudset med lermørtel og kalket.
Der har ikke været stor interesse i at bevare bygningen, da den repræsenterer et sort kapitel i lokalbefolkningens historie.
Nu, da bygningen er ved at forgå, vil man dog gerne have den registreret. Desuden har øen et enestående dyre- og fugleliv.

Projektperiode   1999-2000

tegnestuen   institutioner   restaurering   konkurrencer   byggeri   design   aktuelt

Specialfritidshjem

Københavns Kommune
B+ har projekteret et nyt specialfritidshjem til Strandparkskolen i København SV.
Fritidshjemmet er på knap 700 m2 med 5 grupper til børn med forskellige handicaps.
Der bliver 3 grupperum med birum til børn med vidtgående handicap, og 2 grupperum med birum til multihandicappede. Sidstnævnte bliver betjent med liftsystem ophængt i loft. Derudover bliver der 2 køkken/alrum, personalerum, depot og toiletrum. Fritidshjemmet etableres med nyeste ressourcebesparende teknik, bl.a. et hybrid ventilationssystem som kombinerer naturlig og mekanisk ventilation.
Fritidshjemmet projekteres til præfabrikeret udførelse.

Budgetoverslag   8,9 mill. kr.
Projektperiode   2001

tegnestuen   institutioner   restaurering   konkurrencer   byggeri   design   aktuelt

@ Berger+Parkkinen

BERGER + PARKKINEN Architekten

NEWS

Die Botschaften der Nordischen Länder in Berlin Tiergarten

Die fünf Nordischen Länder - Dänemark, Island, Finnland, Norwegen und Schweden- beschließen, auf einem Grundstück ihre Botschaften zu errichten.

Von außen sind die Gebäude durch das Kupferband verhüllt und verbunden. Die Hülle nimmt den Botschaften das konkret Gebäudehafte, und führt sie zur landschaftlichen Dimension des Tiergartens über: Der große Maßstab macht die Gruppe von sechs Gebäuden zu einem "landmark" im Herzen Berlins.

Tower 24 - Frankfurt, Bürohochhaus, geladener Wettbewerb, Ankauf

Durch eine Neuinterpretation des klassischen 3 Scheiben Hochhauses gelingt es, einen besonders schlank wirkenden Turm zu konzipieren, der dennoch die Annehmlichkeiten eines leistungsfähigen zentralen Kernes und großzügige offene Grundrisse bietet. Die 2 ineinander verschlungenen spiegelbildlichen Körper stellen eine offene Form dar.
Diese Offenheit ist Ausdruck der geplanten Flexibilität und Vielfältigkeit in der Nutzung des Turmes. Darüber hinaus strahlt dieser spezielle Körper eine integrative Kraft aus, die weit über die Grundgrenzen fühlbar ist.Der Turm ist nicht abgeschlossen, sondern richtet sich an seine Umgebung.Diese Idee findet sich auch in der technischen Lösung wieder. Die besondere Form erlaubt es, die Windenergie direkt für die Bewegung der Luft im Haus zu nutzen

Bahnhofszentrum Altona-Hamburg Wettbewerb 1.Preis

Das neue Bahnhofszentrum in Hamburg - Altona wird auf einen mehrschichtigen Verkehrsknotenpunkt errichtet.
Der Gebäudekomplex besteht aus dem Bahnhof, Handel, Büros und Serviceeinrichtungen.
Im vorhandenen, durch die Zeitgeschichte mit starken Kontrasten gezeichneten städtischen Gefüge kommt dem Neubau des Bahnhofszentrums eine wichtige Aufgabe zu: Der Neubau muß als integrierendes Element die ungelösten Spannungen des Quartiers aufnehmen und auflösen, und gleichzeitig einen neuen Maßstab für die weitere Entwicklung setzten.

DON GIL, Wettbewerb 1.Preis

Die Donna Gil-Filialen in Österreich bekommen ein neues Kleid. Das Leitmotiv des Entwurfes bildet das klassische Modeatlier oder auch der Maßsalon als Ort des individuellen Umgangs mit Mode, in der Atmosphäre eines anspruchsvollen Geschäfts, in dem die Rituale des Verhüllens und Verkleidens bequem und geschützt stattfinden können. Bereits im September sollen die beiden ersten Filialen in Wien in der Mariahilferstraße und am Graben eröffnet werden. Sechs weitere Filialen werden folgen.

Berger + Parkkinen Architekten GmbH

Im Frühjahr 2002 wurde das Büro Berger + Parkkinen Architekten von einer Personengesellschaft in eine GmbH übergeführt. Dieser Schritt entspricht der in den letzten Jahren erfolgten Entwicklung des Büros, und stellt für weitere zu erwartende Entwicklungen eine leistungsfähige und anpassungsfähige Struktur dar.

Neue Adresse

Das Wiener Büro wird im April dieses Jahres neue Räume in der Neubaugasse 40/5 ganz in der Nähe des bisherigen Büros beziehen.

Portfolio
Ausstellungen
Publikationen
Bürostruktur
Kontakt

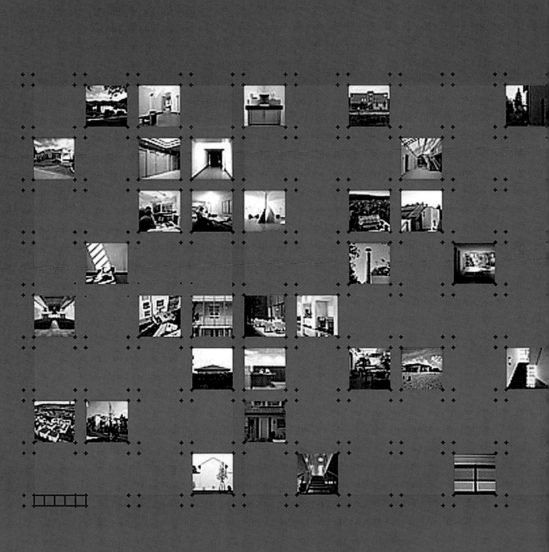

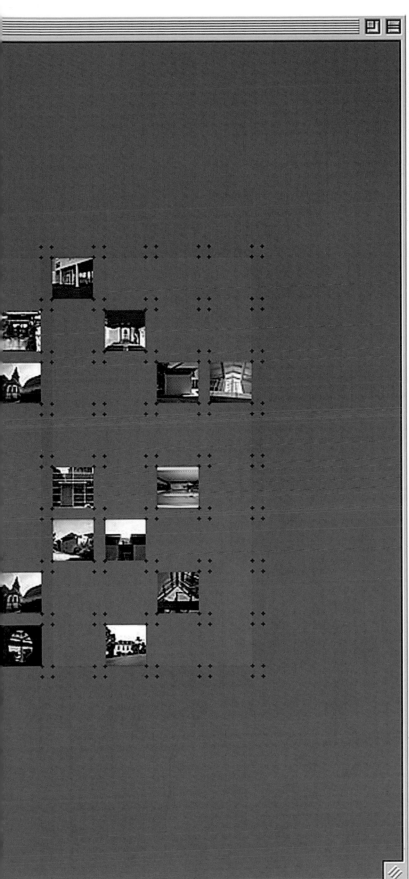

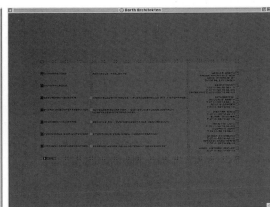

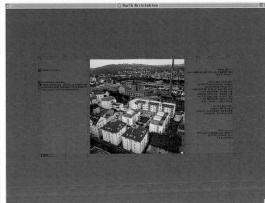

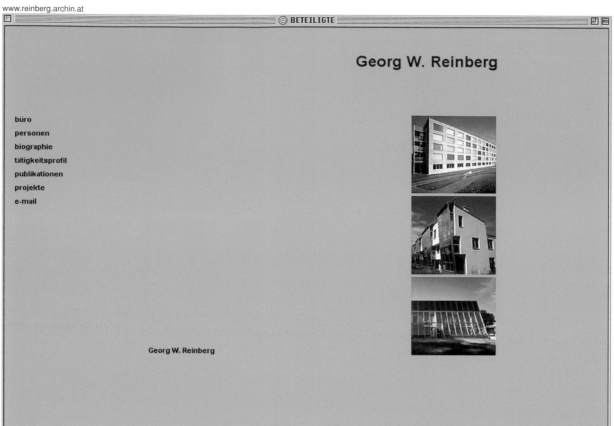

Georg W. Reinberg

büro

personen

biographie

tätigkeitsprofil

publikationen

projekte

e-mail

Georg W. Reinberg

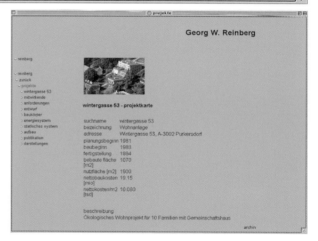

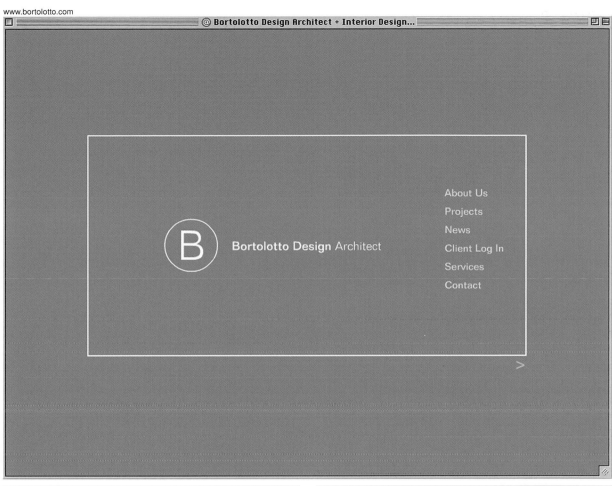

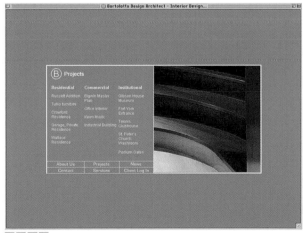

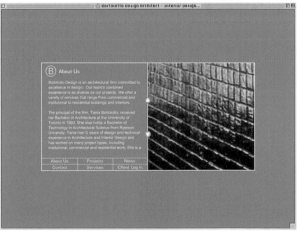

BANKWITZ ARCHITEKTEN
BANKWITZ BERATEN PLANEN

Kommentar

DE C

http://yototo.com/archi/

ARCHITEKTÖN -- Doru Bumbaru

ARCHITEKTÖN

Home
Reflections
Projects
Informations

Doru Bumbaru B.Arch., M.Sc.

Architect n[MF architecte, fr. L architectus, fr Gk architektōn master builder, fr archi- + tektōn builder, carpenter -- more at TECHNICAL] 1 : one who designs buildings and superintends their construction 2 : one who plans and achieves a difficult objective. "Webster's New Collegiate Dictionary"

"Or la tâche essentielle de l'état consiste bien en ceci : protéger l'individu, lui offrir la possibilité de se réaliser en tant que personne humaine et créatrice."
Albert Einstein

"Les excès du système de compétition et de spécialisation prématurée sous le fallacieux prétexte d'efficacité, assassinent l'esprit, interdisent toute vie culturelle et suppriment même les progrès dans les sciences d'avenir."
Albert Einstein

FR C

www.insanegrafix.com/

kinky side of architecture

NAVIGATEUR
_sparks
_nervous
_kinkys
_dispatch
_crib

BRAINWAVE
_arch
_web
_grafx
_maps
_misc

ARCHITECTUOUS
URBNGRFXSTUDIO

SHOWCASE
ON THE BOARDS

light fixture

art gallery

DISPLAY

Is MatrixReloaded really THIS bad? I'm gonna hold back a bit before I see this flix then. Keep yer expectation low, boys and girls!
posted by noel > on 5/18/2003 08:40:04 AM

Wanna start your own war? Go bomb any countries you want! THE WORLD WARS!
posted by noel > on 5/14/2003 11:01:22 AM

Check out the new ad from Honda, its just cool as hell! See the process of making this masterpiece here!
posted by noel > on 5/9/2003 02:51:23 PM

microbians - experimental arts media inspiration
posted by noel > on 5/8/2003 11:16:00 PM

oh...you just gotta love this! I just looove sketches collection! Sketchbook by Kevin Cornell is one of 'em!
posted by noel > on 5/8/2003 10:41:33 PM

Just finished watching MTVIcon:Metallica. It brought back some of the old memories when I was in a heavymetal band back in the early nineties. Damn we rocked! And I still am! The hell with it, I'm downloading Metallica's tune! :D
posted by noel > on 5/6/2003 11:43:26 PM

Put NBA and MLB aside for a while, its time for English Premier League. One of my favorite teams of all time, Manchester United has won 2002/2003 Barclaycard Premiership title! Wohooo!
posted by noel > on 5/4/2003 04:02:36 PM

Happy 2nd Anniversary godora.com!
posted by noel > on 5/2/2003 06:34:58 AM

POWERED BY:

USA I

© AA ::::::::: PROJECTS REVIEW 2000/2001

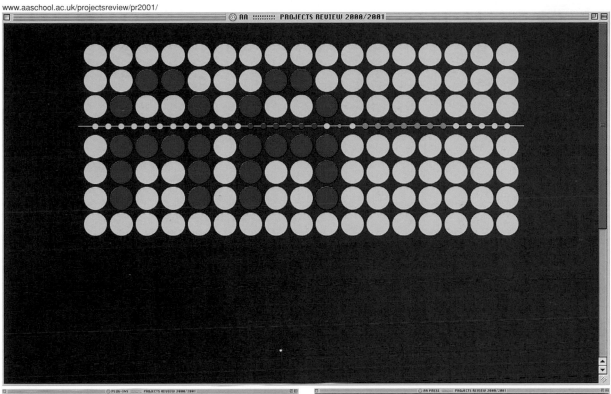

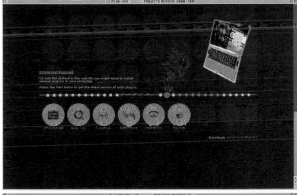

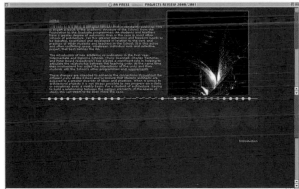

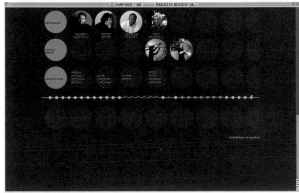

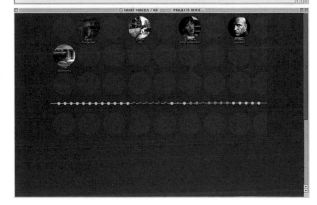

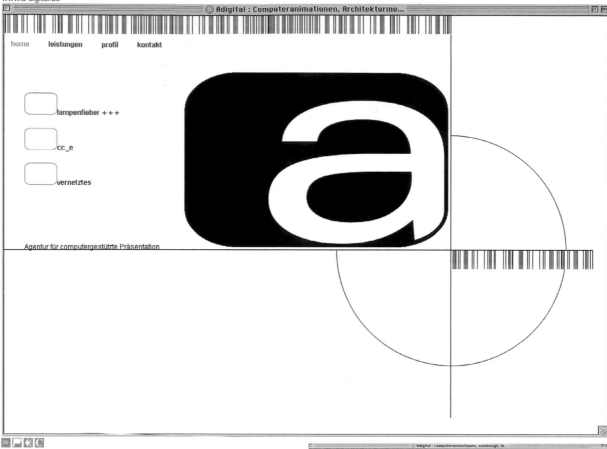

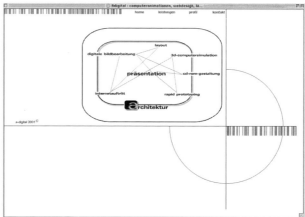

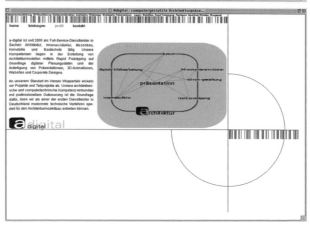

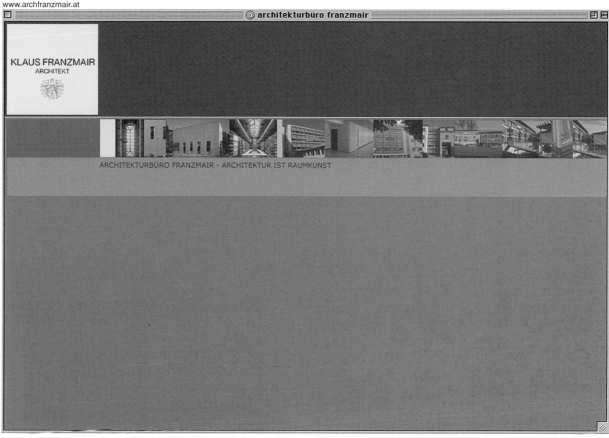

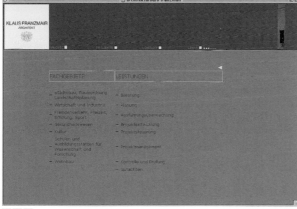

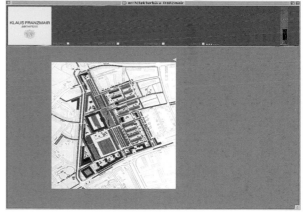

@ FUTURE SYSTEMS

F U T U R E   S Y S T E M S

projects

profile

publications

awards

people

location

recruitment

home

THE WAREHOUSE   20 VICTORIA GARDENS   LONDON   W11 3PE
T 020 7243 7670 F 020 7243 7690 email@future-systems.com www.future-systems.com

---

@ FUTURE SYSTEMS

F U T U R E   S Y S T E M S

221   Lords Media Centre   1994

projects
profile
publications
awards
people
location
recruitment
home

There exists at Lord's a tradition of patronage of innovative structures - the objective of the design has been to respect and savour the essential nature of Lord's while bringing to it a building that will herald the coming millennium and provide the most elegant and state-of-the-art media centre in the world. The NatWest Media Centre at Lord's will be one of the most innovative buildings this century. It will be the first all aluminium semi-monocoque building in the world. It represents a breakthrough, not just in the creation of a new three-dimensional aesthetic but in its method of construction; this building was built and fitted out not by the construction industry but by a boatyard, using the very latest advances in boat building technology. Raised 15m above the ground, the aerodynamic contours of the building reflect the sweep of the plan of the Ground with the enclosing skin formed by a smooth, white, seamless shell. The west facing glazing is inclined to avoid any glare or reflections while providing unobstructed views of the game for the world's media.

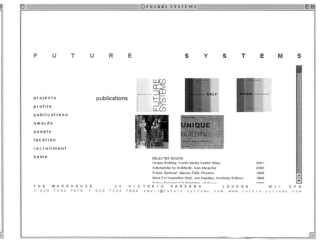

<<   >>

THE WAREHOUSE   20 VICTORIA GARDENS   LONDON   W11 3PE
T 020 7243 7670 F 020 7243 7690 email@future-systems.com www.future-systems.com

---

@ FUTURE SYSTEMS

F U T U R E   S Y S T E M S

projects   publications
profile
publications
awards
people
location
recruitment
home

SELECTED BOOKS
Unique Building, 'Lord's Media Centre' Wiley   2001
Automobiles by Architects, Ivan Margolius   2000
'Future Systems', Marcus Field, Phaidon   1999
'More For Inspiration Only', Jan Kaplicky, Academy Editions   1999

THE WAREHOUSE   20 VICTORIA GARDENS   LONDON   W11 3PE
T 020 7243 7670 F 020 7243 7690 email@future-systems.com www.future-systems.com

UK C

www.geocities.com/tornioff/

`@ blow up peter torniov blow up`

AT ▭ P ▣

http://dam.inm.de

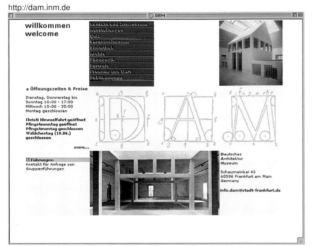

DE I ▣

www.carusostjohn.com

UN F C

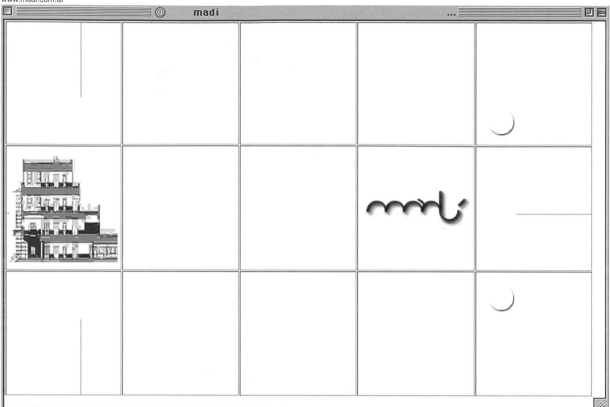

Es ist klar, daß auch wir nur wieder
it is clear that we too are only able

Fragmente setzen können, aber
to set fragments as well, but

vielleicht solche, die diese Tatsache
perhaps of a kind which do not

nicht zum Stil erheben.
raise this fact to a style

Riegler Riewe >>

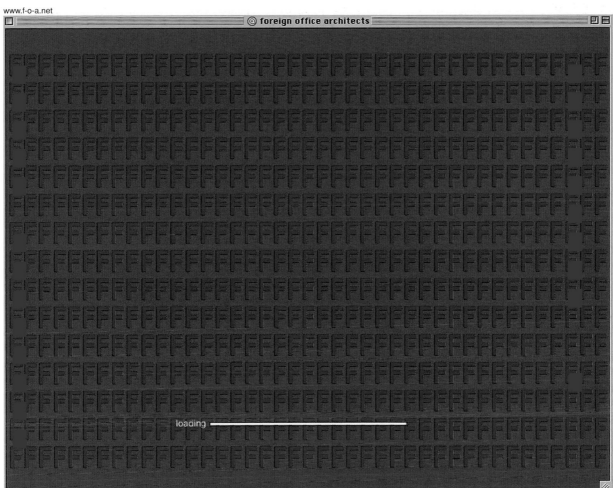

loading ━━━━━━━━━━━━━━━

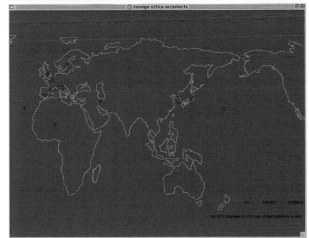

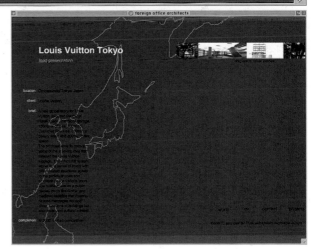

home   news   architecture   product design   studio pieces   biography   chronology   contact

PEDDLE THORP
Architects

| CLICK ON IMAGES TO CONTINUE |
Level 29 AMP Place . 10 Eagle St . Brisbane QLD 4000
ph +61 07 3226 6200 . fx +61 07 3226 6201
Peddle Thorp & Harvey Pty Ltd
Trading as Peddle Thorp Architects
ACN 010 699 573 ABN 19 010 699 573
Best viewed using Netscape Navigator or MS Explorer 3 or above, Arial Font
All content at www.peddlethorp.com.au remains the property of Peddle Thorp Architects and may not be reproduced without written
permission

ARCHITEKTUR CONSULT · ZT GmbH

DEUTSCH   ENGLISH

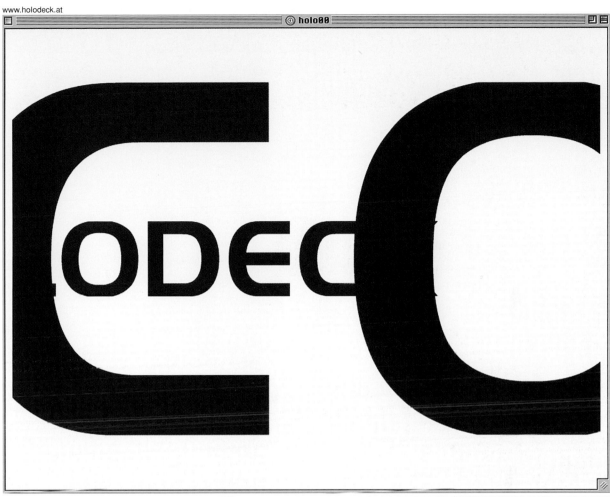

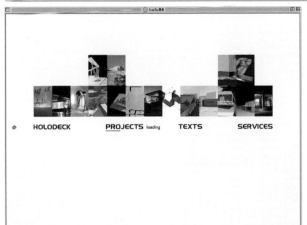

@   **HOLODECK**   <u>PROJECTS</u> loading   **TEXTS**   **SERVICES**

log. hospital
ozeanum stralsund
walk into rythm 357
connected with MAX
walking city
highriser 01

THINK TANKS   PUBLIC ENTITIES   PRIVATE UNITS   TEMPORARY SETTINGS   DOWNLOADS

@   **HOLODECK**   **PROJECTS**   **TEXTS**   **SERVICES**

project
function/type
program
location
design/construction
design
project value
construction costs

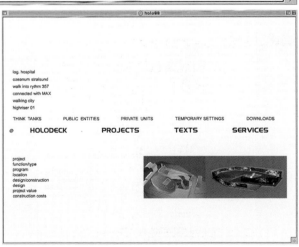

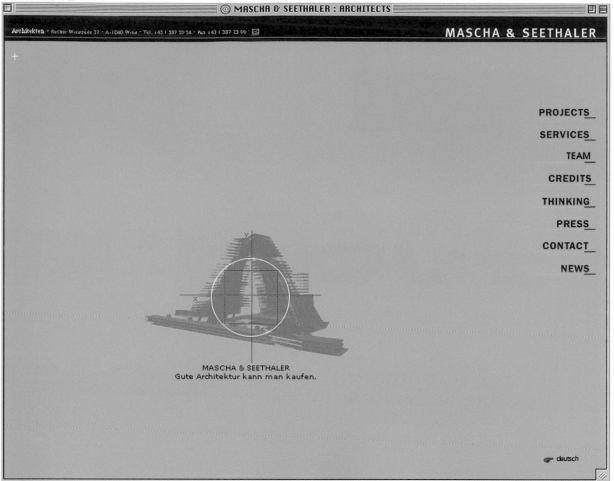

Architekten · Rechte Wiedzeile 37 · A-1040 Wien · Tel. +43 1 337 29 24 · Fax +43 1 337 23 99 ·

MASCHA & SEETHALER

PROJECTS

SERVICES

TEAM

CREDITS

THINKING

PRESS

CONTACT

NEWS

MASCHA & SEETHALER
Gute Architektur kann man kaufen.

deutsch

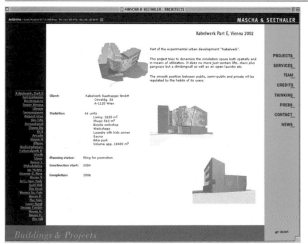

Kabelwerk Part E, Vienna 2002

Part of the experimental urban development "Kabelwerk".

This project tries to dynamize the circulation space both spatially and in means of utilization. It does no more just contain lifts, stairs plus gangways but a climbingwall as well as an open laundry etc.

The smooth position between public, semi-public and privates will be regulated by the habits of its users.

Client: Kabelwerk Bautraeger GmbH
               Osvaldg. 33
               A-1120 Wien

Statistics: 66 units
               Living: 2620 m²
               Shops 510 m²
               Bicycle workshop
               Workshops
               Laundry with kids corner
               Sauna
               Bike park
               Volume app. 19400 m³

Planning status: filing for promotion

Construction start: 2004

Completion: 2006

Buildings & Projects

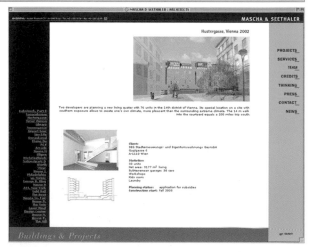

Hustergasse, Vienna 2002

Two developers are planning a new living quater with 76 units in the 14th district of Vienna. Its special location on a site with southern exposure allows to create one's own climate, more pleasant than the surrounding extreme climate. The 14 m walk into the courtyard equals a 200 miles trip south.

Client: DEG Stadterneuerungs- und Eigentumswohnungs GesmbH
               Gugigasse 6
               A-1110 Wien

Statistics: 33 units
               Net area: 3177 m² living
               Subterranean garage: 36 cars
               Workshops
               Kids room
               Laundry

Planning status: application for subsidies
Construction start: Fall 2003

Buildings & Projects

www.olk.cc

OSKAR LEO KAUFMANN

NEWS PRESS INC. WORK

© OLK 2003

A¹ P

www.lichtblauwagner.com

AT F C Ub

www.bolster.li

CH C

@ theunit

theunit | | | | |
architects

featured on BBC world

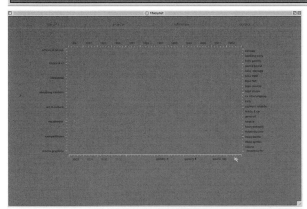

bathroom gablitz

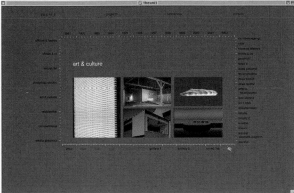

art & culture

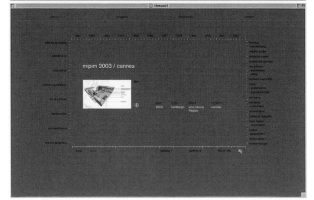

mipim 2003 / cannes

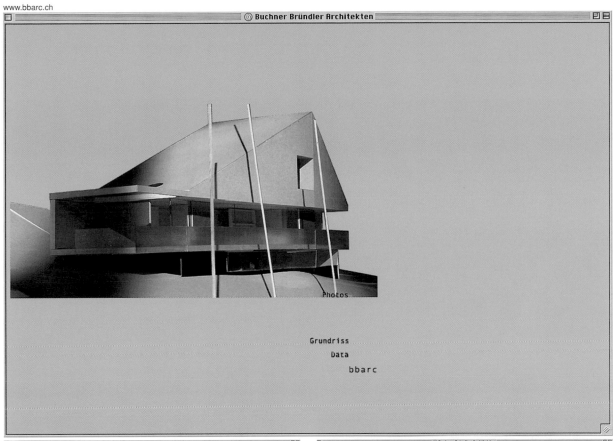

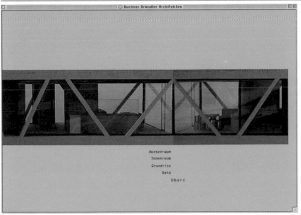

@ CMB DESIGN ARCHITECTURE & INTERIOR DESIGN

WELCOME TO THE CMB ARCHITECTURE & INTERIORS PAGE.

E F K C

www.metstudio.com

MET studio

ABOUT US   APPROACH   SERVICES   CLIENTS   PORTFOLIO   NEWS   AWARDS   CONTACT

The Lucent Centre of Excellence
The company's main executive briefing centre in Europe

NEWS

> February 2003: In response to an interesting brief by a leading German
...more

> February 2003: MET Studio Associate James Norton
...more

> January 2003: MET Studio Design has always been an international
...more

> December 2002: As well as being named a finalist
...more

PORTFOLIO

> A truly international portfolio.
...more

WASSER LAND

AWARDS

> Design Week Best Of Show 2000.
> Design Week Best Of Exhibition 2000.
> Best Exhibition DBA Design Effectiveness Awards 2000
...more

5 Maidstone Buildings Mews, 72-76 Borough High Street, London SE1 1GN.
Tel: +44 20 7378 7938. Fax: +44 20 7378 7339. e-mail: info@metstudio.com

Copyright

UK C

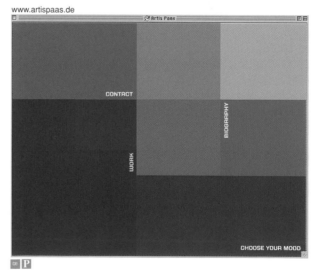

www.artispaas.de

Artis Pans

CONTACT

BIOGRAPHY

WORK

CHOOSE YOUR MOOD

DE P

www.grimshaw-architects.com

UK F C

www.groupe-e2.com

FR C

www.buro-interior.be

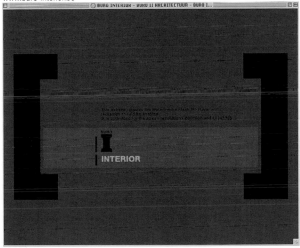

BE F C

www.kunz-av.de

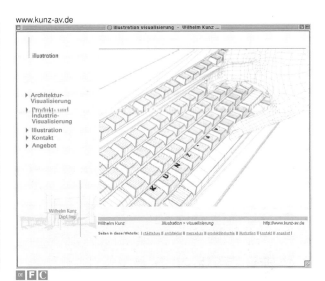

DE F C

www.entasis.dk

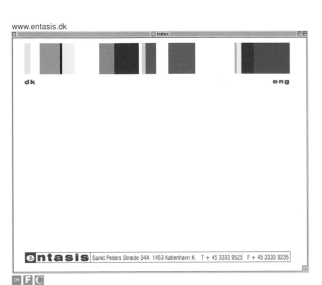

DK F C

www.kerteszepiteszstudio.hu

HU C

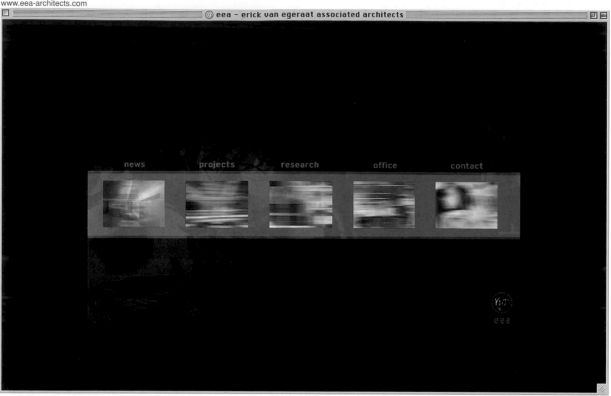

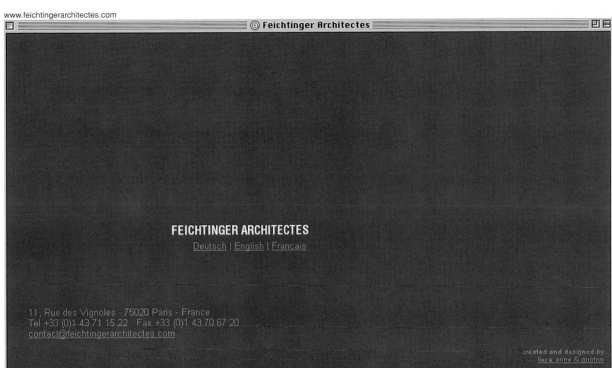

FEICHTINGER ARCHITECTES

Deutsch | English | Francais

11, Rue des Vignoles - 75020 Paris - France
Tel +33 (0)1 43 71 15 22   Fax +33 (0)1 43 70 67 20
contact@feichtingerarchitectes.com

created and designed by
liess, anne & gordon

11, Rue des Vignoles - 75020
Paris - France
Tel +33 (0)1 43 71 15 22
Fax +33 (0)1 43 70 67 20
contact@feichtingerarchitectes.com

FEICHTINGER ARCHITECTES
The Office | Projects | Project Search | News

career | collaborators | exhibitions | publications

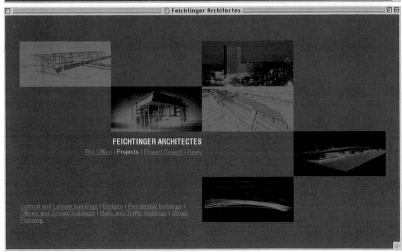

FEICHTINGER ARCHITECTES
The Office | Projects | Project Search | News

Cultural and Leisure buildings | Bridges | Residential buildings |
Offices and School buildings | Halls and Traffic buildings | Urban
Planning

@ Welcome

Dan S. Hanganu Architects

@ Main

PORTRAIT · PROJECTS AND BUILDINGS · AWARDS · PUBLICATIONS · CONTACT

Dan S. Hanganu Architects

www.jlp.ca

ACTUALITÉS   ORGANISATION   SERVICES   PORTFOLIO

3200 rue Rachel Est Montréal [Québec] Canada H1W 1A4
téléphone: (514) 527-8821 - fax: (514) 527-7548
[info@jlp.ca]

CA F C

www.joergbrune.de

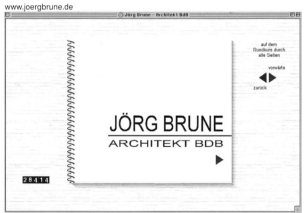

DE P

http://mei.dx0.de

DE P

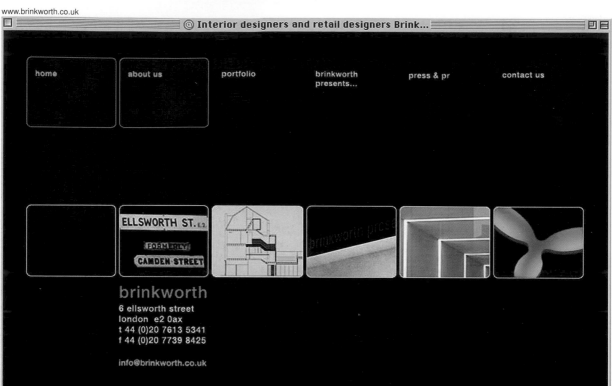

brinkworth

6 ellsworth street
london e2 0ax
t 44 (0)20 7613 5341
f 44 (0)20 7739 8425

info@brinkworth.co.uk

Diesel Buchanan St. Glasgow 1997   -1-2-

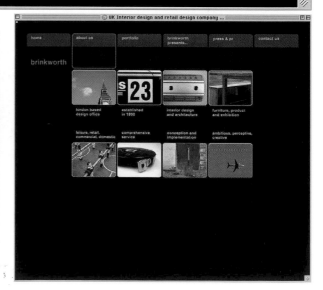

www.kmd.ie

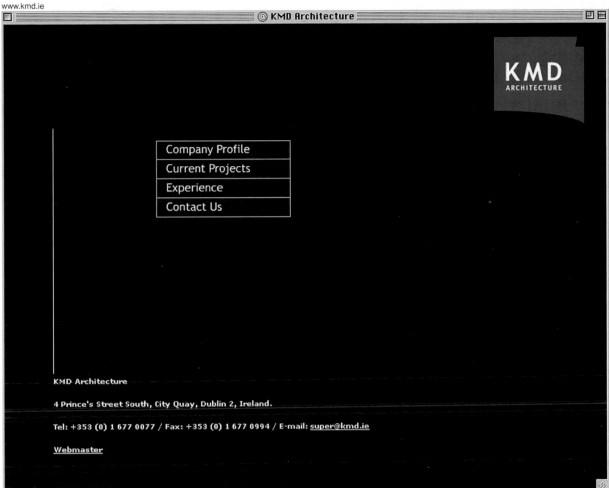

@ KMD Architecture

KMD
ARCHITECTURE

Company Profile
Current Projects
Experience
Contact Us

KMD Architecture

4 Prince's Street South, City Quay, Dublin 2, Ireland.

Tel: +353 (0) 1 677 0077 / Fax: +353 (0) 1 677 0994 / E-mail: super@kmd.ie

Webmaster

www.architekt-luft.de

Luft & Partner: Freie Architekten

PROFIL   MAS
PROJEKTE   FEEDBACK
ÖKOLOGIE   GASTEBUCH
INNOVATION   MAIL-SERVICE
PHILOSOPHIE

LUFT & PARTNER
Freie Architekten

ARCHITEKTURBÜRO LUFT & PARTNER · HÖRDENER STRASSE 1 · 76571 GAGGENAU
TELEFON: 0 72 24 / 93 90 10 · TELEFAX: 0 72 24 / 93 90 93 · WWW.ARCHITEKT-LUFT.DE

www.mbas.de

mbas

MBA / S

MATTHIAS BAUER ASSOCIATES

ARCHITECTURE URBANISM LANDSCAPE

contact   projects   office   portfolio   home

0/I lab

LAB[au] architecture and urbanism ©

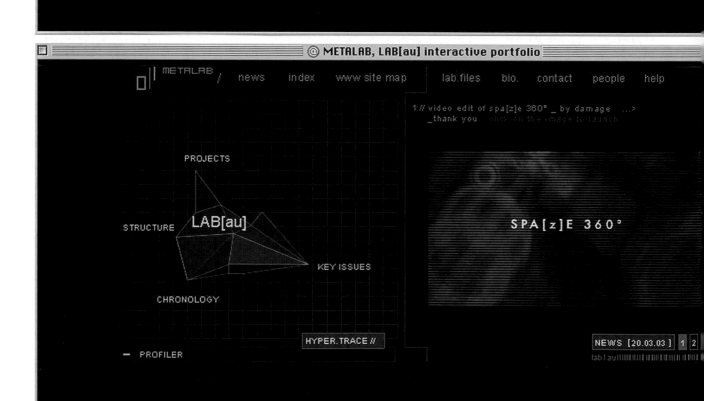

@ METALAB, LAB[au] interactive portfolio

METALAB / news index www site map lab.files bio. contact people help

1:// video edit of spa[z]e 360° _ by damage ...>
_thank you click on the image to launch

PROJECTS

STRUCTURE LAB[au]

KEY ISSUES

CHRONOLOGY

HYPER.TRACE //

— PROFILER

SPA[z]E 360°

NEWS [20.03.03] 1 2

lab[au

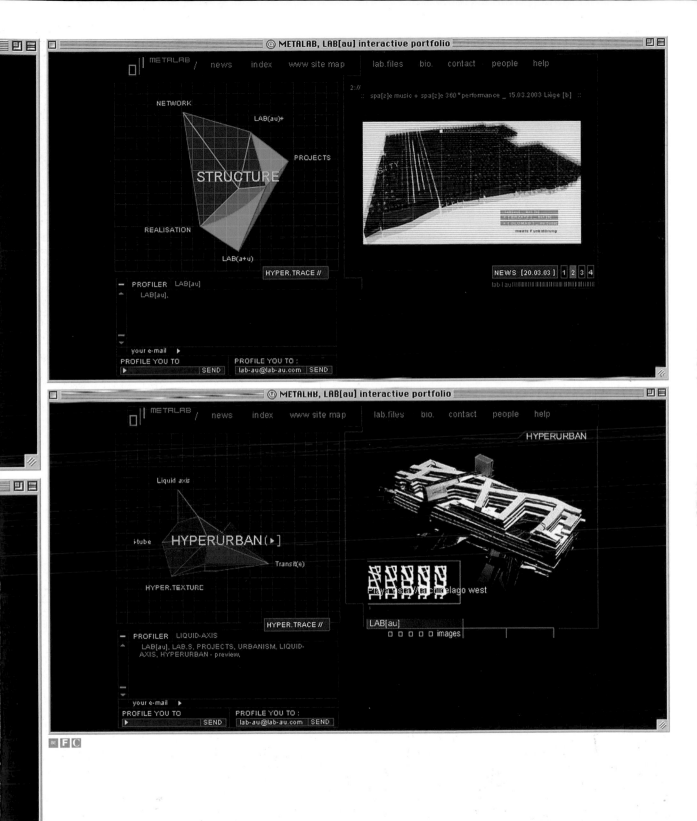

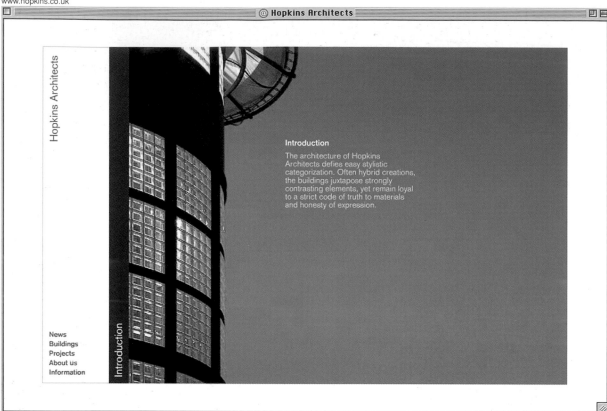

Hopkins Architects

@ Hopkins Architects

Introduction

The architecture of Hopkins
Architects defies easy stylistic
categorization. Often hybrid creations,
the buildings juxtapose strongly
contrasting elements, yet remain loyal
to a strict code of truth to materials
and honesty of expression.

News
Buildings
Projects
About us
Information

Introduction

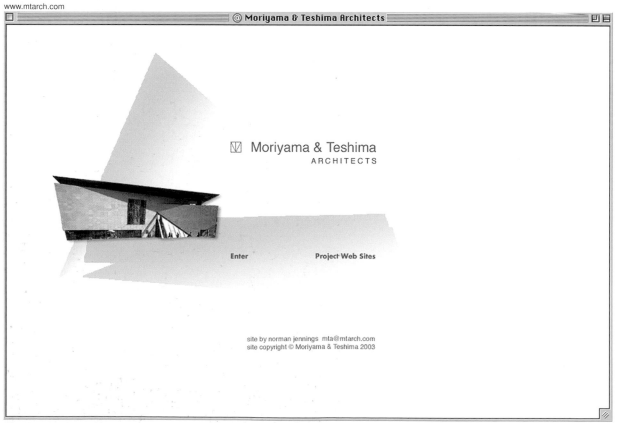

@ Moriyama & Teshima Architects

Moriyama & Teshima
ARCHITECTS

Enter   Project Web Sites

site by norman jennings mta@mtarch.com
site copyright © Moriyama & Teshima 2003

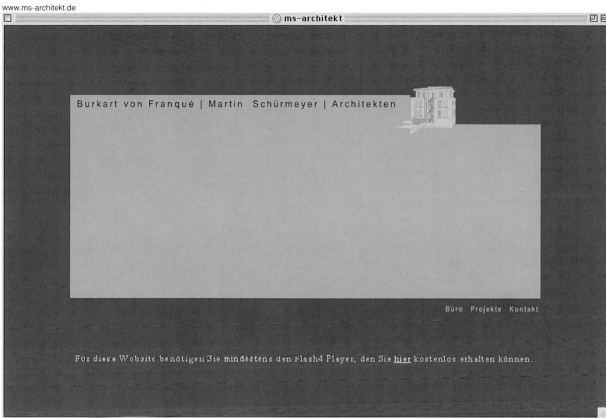

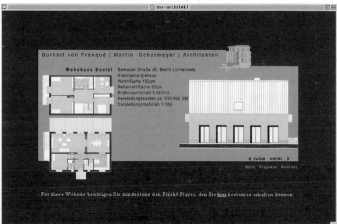

www.pthibault.com

@ Pierre Thibault, architecte

pierre **thibault**

i n t r o

INTRODUCTION
BIOGRAPHIE
ATELIER
PROJETS
EXPOSITIONS
PUBLICATIONS

ENGLISH

mail@pthibault.com

© pierre thibault,
architecte
06.01.2003
version 1.3

La pratique de Pierre Thibault architecte se distingue depuis 14 ans par les réponses sensibles apportées aux besoins des clients et au contexte environnemental. La qualité de son travail et de ses réalisations ainsi que la maturité de sa réflexion architecturale lui ont déjà valu plusieurs prix et mentions au Québec, au Canada, aux États-Unis et en Europe. Principal concepteur, Pierre Thibault s'appuie sur une équipe de professionnels composée d'architectes et de techniciens seniors à l'expérience et aux qualifications complémentaires dans le domaine de la conception, de la réalisation et de la gestion de projets architecturaux.

CA P

---

www.sophiehicks.com

Sophie Hicks, S.H.Ltd Architects, London | CO...

SOPHIE HICKS

ARCHITECTURE - RETAIL
ARCHITECTURE - RESIDENTIAL
DESIGN
PRESS
CV

HOME

S.H. LIMITED ARCHITECTS

16. POWIS MEWS, LONDON, W11 1JN, UK
TEL +44(0)2077922631   FAX +44(0)2072723328
e-mail: mail@sophiehicks.com

© SH LTD ARCHITECTS   SITE CREDITS

UK C

---

www.urban-environments.net

@ ue | architecture

urban environments

loading...
if you have a slow internet connection this might take a while. after loading, the whole page will work instantaneously - thank you for your patience.

DE SW C

http://www.skyscraper.org/timeformations/intro.html

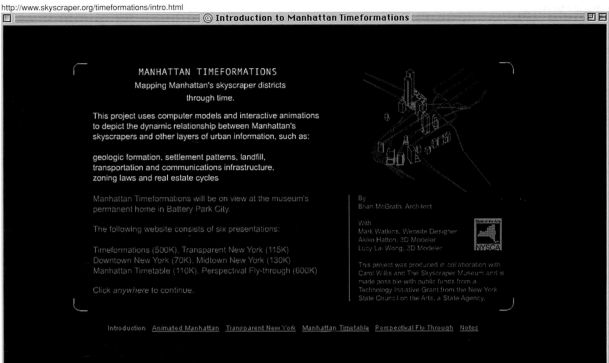

MANHATTAN TIMEFORMATIONS
Mapping Manhattan's skyscraper districts
through time.

This project uses computer models and interactive animations
to depict the dynamic relationship between Manhattan's
skyscrapers and other layers of urban information, such as:

geologic formation, settlement patterns, landfill,
transportation and communications infrastructure,
zoning laws and real estate cycles

Manhattan Timeformations will be on view at the museum's
permanent home in Battery Park City.

The following website consists of six presentations:

Timeformations (500K), Transparent New York (115K)
Downtown New York (70K), Midtown New York (130K)
Manhattan Timetable (110K), Perspectival Fly-through (600K)

Click *anywhere* to continue.

By
Brian McGrath, Architect

With
Mark Watkins, Website Designer
Akiko Hattori, 3D Modeler
Lucy Lai Wong, 3D Modeler

This project was produced in collaboration with
Carol Willis and The Skyscraper Museum and is
made possible with public funds from a
Technology Initiative Grant from the New York
State Council on the Arts, a State Agency.

Introduction   Animated Manhattan   Transparent New York   Manhattan Timetable   Perspectival Fly-Through   Notes

www.ruegemer.de

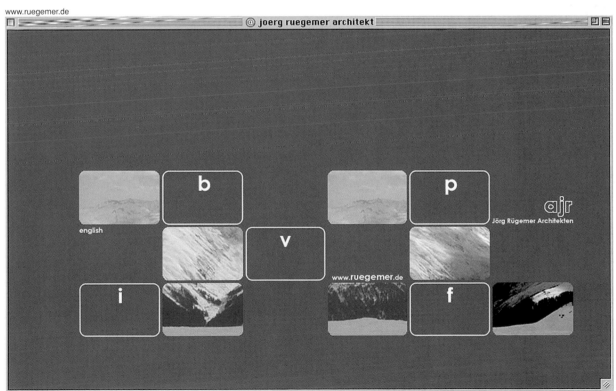

joerg ruegemer architekt

english

b

p

ajr
Jörg Rügemer Architekten

v

www.ruegemer.de

i

f

www.sauerbruchhutton.de

DE C

www.degrezero.com

USA F C

www.alleswirdgut.cc

Architektur ZT GmbH * Große Neugasse 27 * A-1040 Wien / Austria * T +43-1-9610437 * F +43-1-9610411 * awg@alleswirdgut.cc

AT F C

www.azw.at

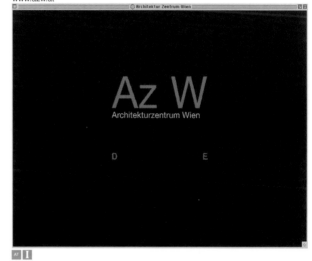

AT I

http://wilhelm-partner.com

DE F C

www.wischhusen-architektur.de

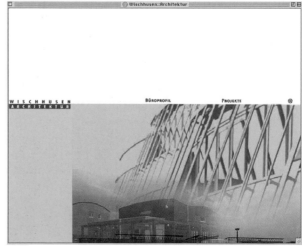

DE C

www.bartlett.ucl.ac.uk

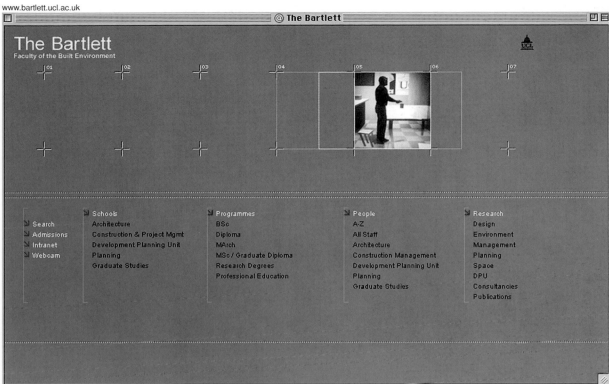

www2.parsons.edu/architecture

büro für architektur

bauten und projekte

buildings and projects

FR F C

USA F C

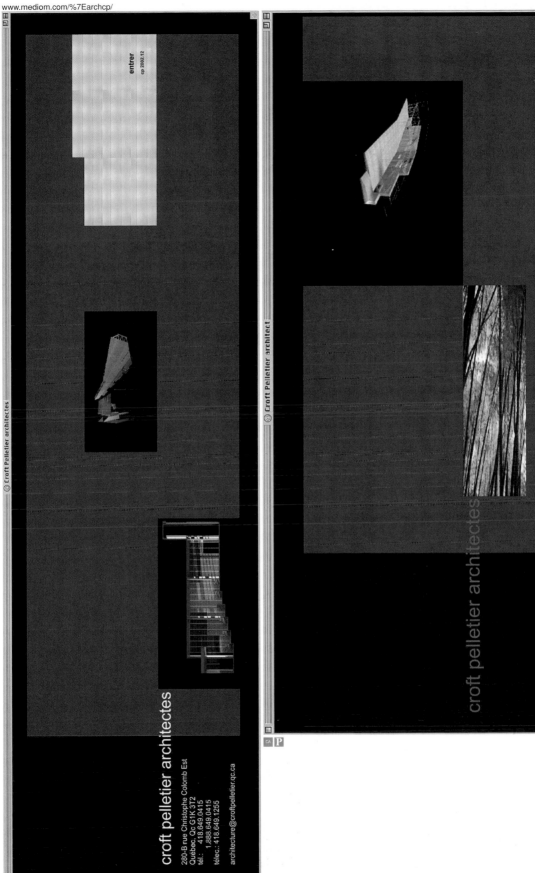

croft pelletier architectes

280-B rue Christophe Colomb Est
Québec, Qc G1K 3T2
tél.: 418.649.0415
1.888.649.0415
télec.: 418.649.1255

architecture@croftpelletier.qc.ca

SCHUSTER ARCHITEKTEN
DÜSSELDORF

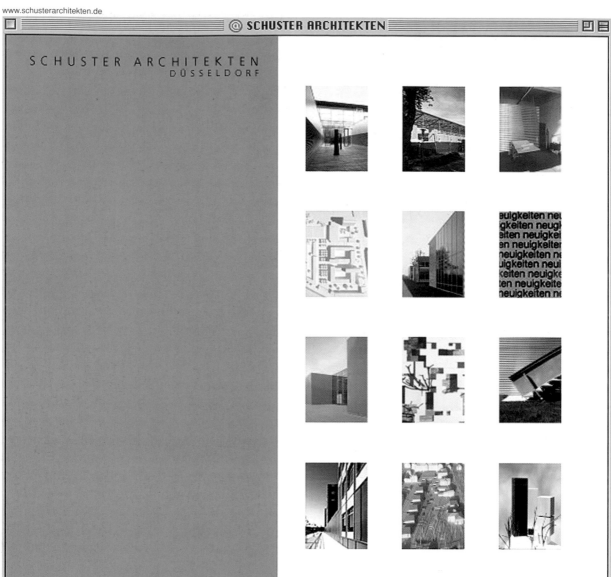

neuigkeiten neu
igkeiten neugk
eiten neuigkei
en neuigkeiten
neuigkeiten ne
uigkeiten neui
keiten neuigke
ten neuigkeiten
neuigkeiten ne

www.saucierperrotte.com

www.zechner.com/

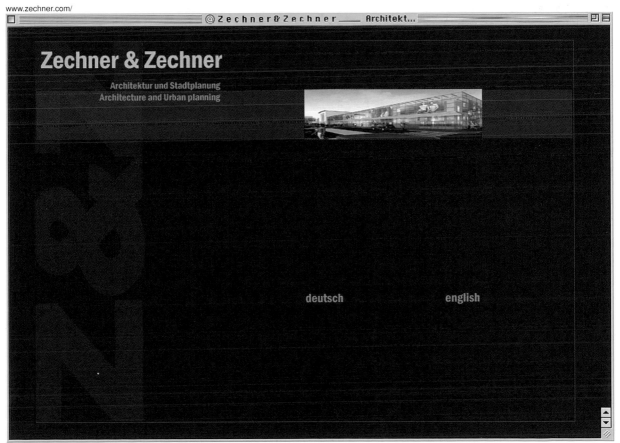

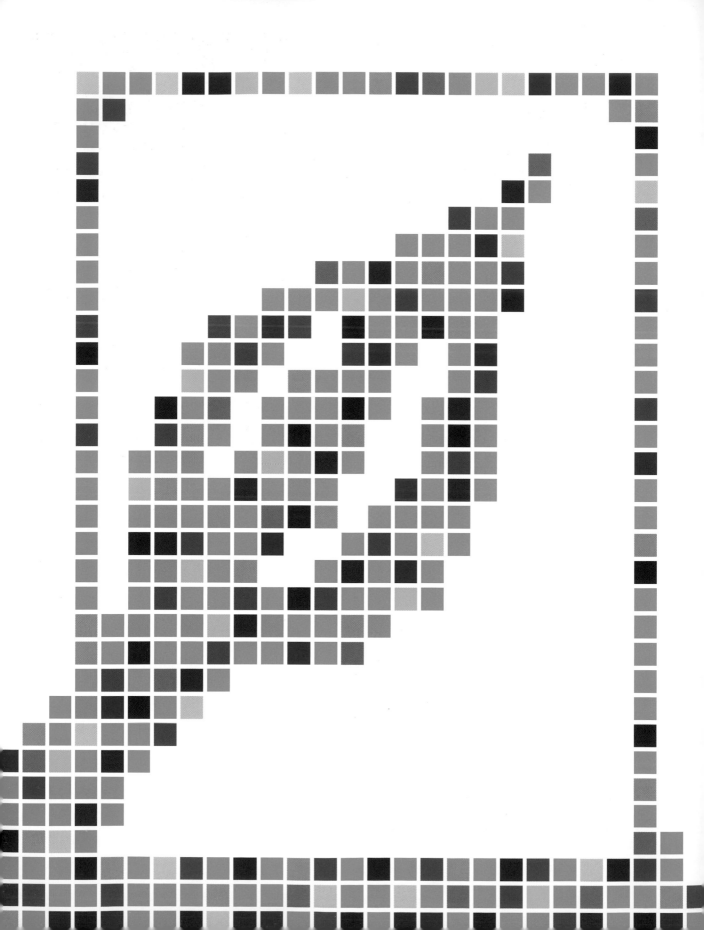

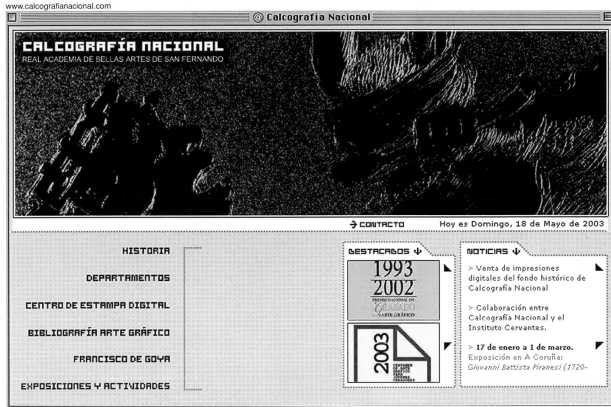

@ Calcografía Nacional

CALCOGRAFÍA NACIONAL
REAL ACADEMIA DE BELLAS ARTES DE SAN FERNANDO

→ CONTACTO — Hoy es Domingo, 18 de Mayo de 2003

HISTORIA

DEPARTAMENTOS

CENTRO DE ESTAMPA DIGITAL

BIBLIOGRAFÍA ARTE GRÁFICO

FRANCISCO DE GOYA

EXPOSICIONES Y ACTIVIDADES

DESTACADOS ↓

1993 2002
PREMIO NACIONAL DE GRABADO Y ARTE GRÁFICO
2003

NOTICIAS ↓

> Venta de impresiones digitales del fondo histórico de Calcografía Nacional

> Colaboración entre Calcografía Nacional y el Instituto Cervantes.

> **17 de enero a 1 de marzo.** Exposición en A Coruña: *Giovanni Battista Piranesi (1720-*

@ Calcografía Nacional

CALCOGRAFÍA NACIONAL — CENTRO DE ESTAMPA DIGITAL
REAL ACADEMIA DE BELLAS ARTES DE SAN FERNANDO

HISTORIA | DEPARTAMENTOS | ESTAMPA DIGITAL | BIBLIOGRAFÍA ARTE GRÁFICO | GOYA | EXPOSICIONES Y ACTIVIDADES

01. Qué es una estampa digital
02. Centro de nuevos lenguajes
03. Antecedentes
04. Proyectos del Centro
05. Conservación de obras de arte

PRESENTACIÓN

En otoño del año 2000 fue creado en el ámbito de la Calcografía Nacional el Centro de Investigación y Desarrollo de la estampa Digital.

A menudo, las nuevas tecnologías y las técnicas tradicionales de reproducción gráfica se consideran opuestas. Desde hace algunos años artistas de gran prestigio internacional vienen utilizando los nuevos recursos tecnológicos como herramientas en el proceso creativo de sus obras.

El uso de técnicas digitales en la creación de obras de arte ha originado una intensa controversia en el mundo de la estampa tradicional. Sin embargo, la impresión digital debe ser entendida como un conjunto de técnicas diferentes a los métodos convencionales de estampación mecánica y química, pero no como un procedimiento en competencia con dichos métodos. La nueva tecnología puede expandir el horizonte de las posibilidades creativas del artista

imágenes ↓

NOTICIAS ↑ | DESTACADOS ↑
» HOME

@ Calcografía Nacional

CALCOGRAFÍA NACIONAL — FRANCISCO DE GOYA
REAL ACADEMIA DE BELLAS ARTES DE SAN FERNANDO

HISTORIA | DEPARTAMENTOS | ESTAMPA DIGITAL | BIBLIOGRAFÍA ARTE GRÁFICO | GOYA | EXPOSICIONES Y ACTIVIDADES

01. Caprichos
02. Desastres de la Guerra
03. Tauromaquia
04. Disparates

PRESENTACIÓN

El principal tesoro conservado en la Calcografía Nacional son las láminas de cobre grabadas al aguafuerte por Francisco de Goya, obras cumbres de la historia universal del grabado.

El estudio, investigación y difusión de la obra de Goya ocupan un lugar destacado en las actuaciones de la institución.

La historia de la estampa moderna tiene su referente inicial en la producción gráfica de Francisco de Goya. Sus series gráficas -Caprichos, Desastres de la Guerra, Tauromaquia y Disparates-, constituyen el punto de inflexión entre la estampa de reproducción tradicional en talla dulce y el grabado de creación en sentido moderno.

La evolución de la técnica en el arte gráfico goyesco fue continua. Alcanzó un extraordinario dominio de los útiles y una perfecta combinación de los

imágenes ↓

NOTICIAS ↑ | DESTACADOS ↑
» HOME

ES F I

@ Calcografía Nacional

CALCOGRAFÍA NACIONAL — FRANCISCO DE GOYA
REAL ACADEMIA DE BELLAS ARTES DE SAN FERNANDO

HISTORIA | DEPARTAMENTOS | ESTAMPA DIGITAL | BIBLIOGRAFÍA ARTE GRÁFICO | GOYA | EXPOSICIONES Y ACTIVIDADES

01. Caprichos
02. Desastres de la Guerra
03. Tauromaquia
04. Disparates

TAUROMAQUIA

La construcción del mito romántico de Goya por los escritores franceses del siglo XIX, alimentado por los tópicos definidores del carácter nacional hispano -como su afición a las truculentas corridas de toros-, se encuentra en deuda con la *Tauromaquia*. El tema de los toros, por su aparente inmediatez y por la remisión a una realidad objetivable, enraizada popularmente y no exenta de connotaciones costumbristas, podría llevar a considerar la *Tauromaquia* de Goya como un conjunto de estampas carentes de la profundidad conceptual del resto de su producción gráfica. Un repaso a la fortuna de esta serie pone de manifiesto que no se ha librado de dicha consideración.

El artista comenzó a grabar las escenas taurinas probablemente al mismo tiempo, o incluso antes, de haber concluido los *Caprichos enfáticos*. Si se acepta que la*Tauromaquia* posee un carácter lúdico, cabría preguntarse cómo es posible que un individuo fuera

imágenes ↓

NOTICIAS ↑ | DESTACADOS ↑
» HOME

Abbot Hall
Art Gallery

The Gallery   Information   What's On   Education   Online Shop

● How to use this site

● Information for the press

LAKELANDARTSTRUST

UK C

http://are-f.com

:: ryan francesconi ::

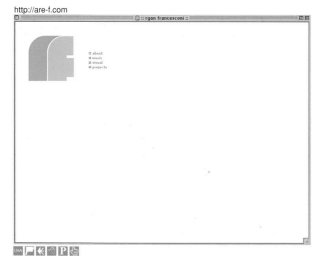

:: about
:: music
:: visual
:: projects

USA P

www.andrearosengallery.com

@ Andrea Rosen Gallery

Andrea Rosen Gallery   homegalleryartistsexhibitionscontactlinksgallery2

USA C

www.303gallery.com

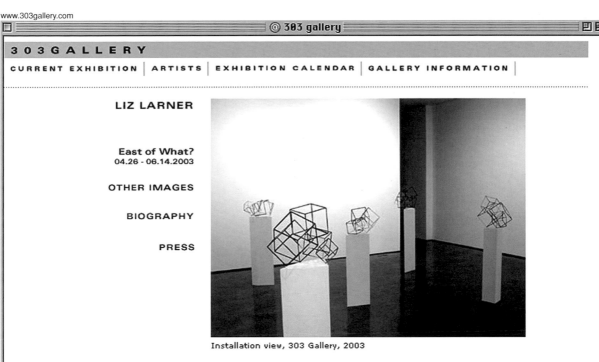

303 GALLERY

CURRENT EXHIBITION | ARTISTS | EXHIBITION CALENDAR | GALLERY INFORMATION

LIZ LARNER

East of What?
04.26 - 06.14.2003

OTHER IMAGES

BIOGRAPHY

PRESS

Installation view, 303 Gallery, 2003

USA C

www.absolutdigitalart.com

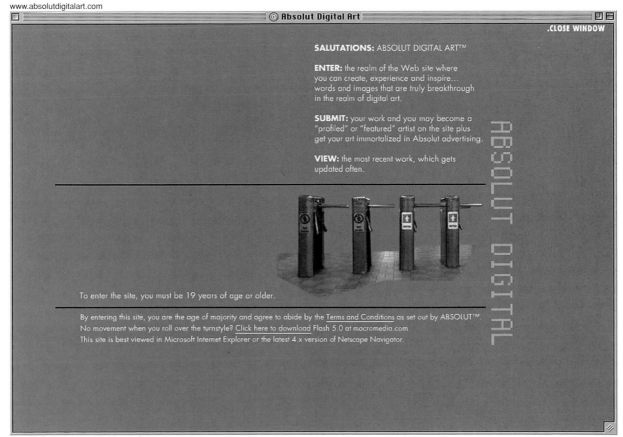

@ Absolut Digital Art

.CLOSE WINDOW

SALUTATIONS: ABSOLUT DIGITAL ART™

ENTER: the realm of the Web site where you can create, experience and inspire... words and images that are truly breakthrough in the realm of digital art.

SUBMIT: your work and you may become a "profiled" or "featured" artist on the site plus get your art immortalized in Absolut advertising.

VIEW: the most recent work, which gets updated often.

ABSOLUT DIGITAL

To enter the site, you must be 19 years of age or older.

By entering this site, you are the age of majority and agree to abide by the Terms and Conditions as set out by ABSOLUT™. No movement when you roll over the turnstyle? Click here to download Flash 5.0 at macromedia.com This site is best viewed in Microsoft Internet Explorer or the latest 4.x version of Netscape Navigator.

USA F I

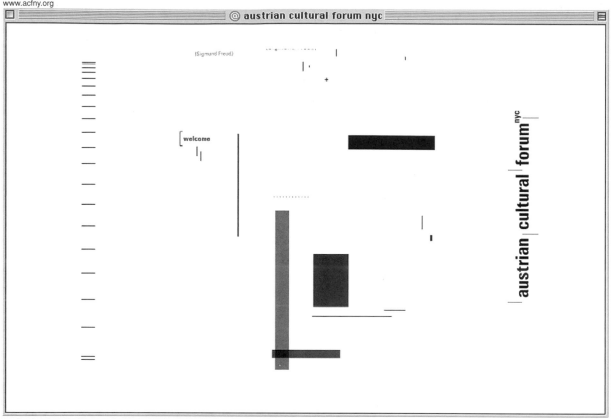

austrian | cultural | forum nyc

(Sigmund Freud)

welcome

archive

what
- Visual Arts
- New Media
- Architecture/Design
- Music
- Film
- Literature
- Performing Arts
- Interdisciplinary

when
from (mm/dd/yy)   to (mm/dd/yy)

where
ACF   New York   other

text search

> start search

program & events — featured events
calendar
subscribe
archive

austrian | cultural | forum nyc

@ tour

the building | the floors   credits

Welcome

Welcome to the virtual tour of the
Austrian Cultural Forum.

Click on **the building** to see the exterior
and click on **the floors** for interior details.
Let your mouse be the guide and scroll
over individual areas to zoom in.

North Facade

alan alborough

biography | contact

© alan alborough

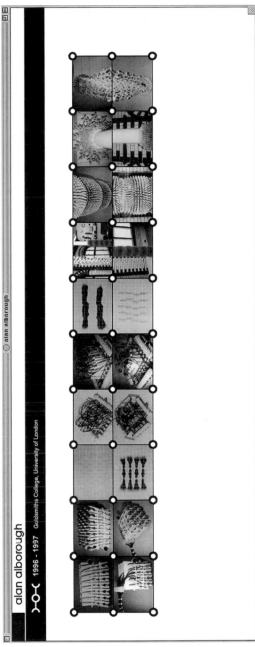

alan alborough

1996 - 1997   Goldsmiths College, University of London

© alan alborough

www.scherware.com

art

@scherware

scherware.com/structure

SINGLE SERVINGS   THE NEW LOOK OF TRAINING   AUDIO TEXT   ST

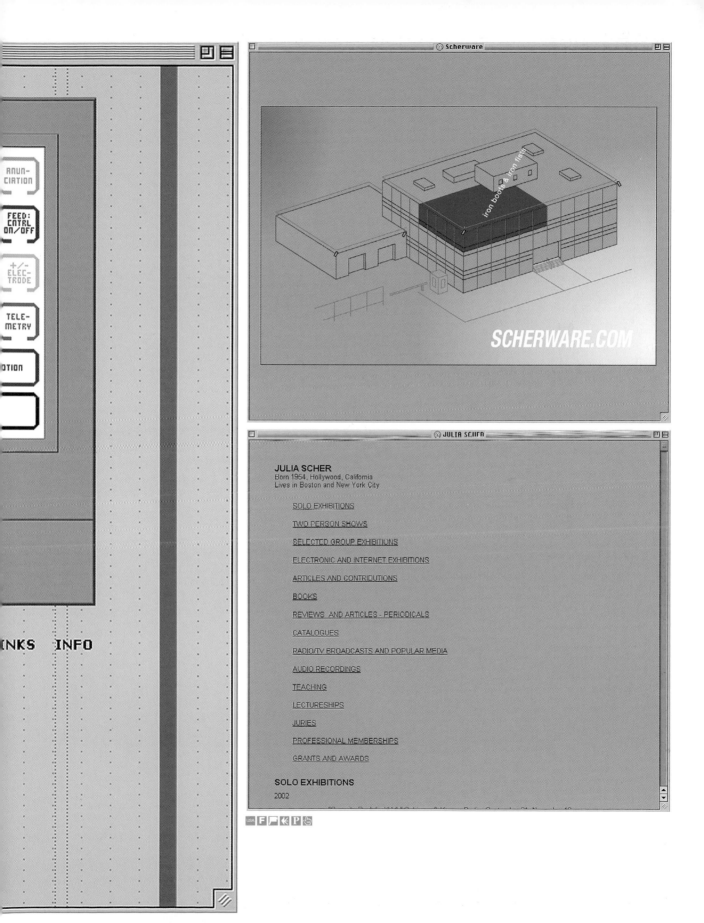

ANUN-
CIATION

FEED:
CNTRL
ON/OFF

+/-
ELEC-
TRODE

TELE-
METRY

OTION

INKS   INFO

Scherware

iron boots & iron fists

SCHERWARE.COM

JULIA SCHER

JULIA SCHER
Born 1954, Hollywood, California
Lives in Boston and New York City

SOLO EXHIBITIONS

TWO PERSON SHOWS

SELECTED GROUP EXHIBITIONS

ELECTRONIC AND INTERNET EXHIBITIONS

ARTICLES AND CONTRIBUTIONS

BOOKS

REVIEWS AND ARTICLES - PERIODICALS

CATALOGUES

RADIO/TV BROADCASTS AND POPULAR MEDIA

AUDIO RECORDINGS

TEACHING

LECTURESHIPS

JURIES

PROFESSIONAL MEMBERSHIPS

GRANTS AND AWARDS

SOLO EXHIBITIONS

2002

feature
DO IT
the tv, the museum &
the home version

ARKIPELAG TV
RealVideo clips

WHAT'S GOING ON
Moscow & London

THE QUEEN OF
MUD STRIKES
AGAIN

I LOVE YOU WITH
MY FORD

CURRENT MEDIA
PRAGMATISM

ART ORBIT

ISSUE #2
JUNE 1998

on the generation
of the tone-deaf

MARTIN BIGUM

do it tv

17 REAL VIDEO CLIPS WITH AMONG OTHERS
DAMIEN HIRST, DAVE STEWART, ILYA KABAKOV,
YOKO ONO, GILBERT & GEORGE & STEVEN PIPPIN

RUSSIAN SPRING

the factory of
found clothing

interviews
MARTIN BIGUM
The Generation of
the Tone-Deaf

RUSSIAN SPRING
St Petersburg;
Yegorova, Pershina-
Yakimanskaya,
Pilkin

snapshots
MAGNUS BÄRTÅS

editorial
ANNIKA HANSSON

art orbit #1
art orbit #3
art orbit #4

art orbit is produced by art node
in partnership with stockholm – cultural capital of europe '98

~ #2 CONTENT ~ BRIEFLY ~ SNAPSHOTS ~ ADS & MESSAGES ~ CONTRIBUTORS ~ CURRENT ISSUE ~ WHAT IS ART ORBIT ~

www.artpublic.ch

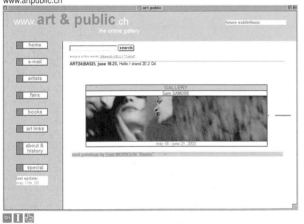

www.arts-reunion.com

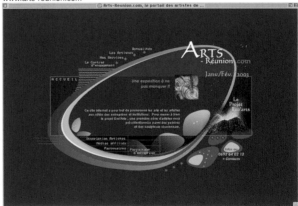

www.arsfutura.ch

arsFutura
G A L E R I E

BLEICHERWEG 45 CH - 8002 ZÜRICH

CH C

www.annthinghuus.com

annthinghuus.com
abstract expressionism

portfolio | profile | contact | news & events

Upcoming Events

Diversity
Art Works Gallery (www.artworksbc.com)
March 28-29
225 Smithe Street
Vancouver, BC, V6B 4X7
Partial proceeds go to 'A Step Ahead' Foundation

Halde Galerie
CoLor
March 28, 2003
www.haldegalerie.ch
Haldenstrasse 24
8967 Widen
Switzerland

Abstract Expressionism

A term first used in connection with <u>Kandinsky</u> in 1919, but more commonly associated with post-war American art. Robert Coates, an American critic, coined it in 1946, referring to <u>Gorky</u>, <u>Pollock</u> and <u>de Kooning</u>. By 1951, the term was used to refer to all types of non-geometric abstraction in the Museum of Modern Art exhibition 'Abstract Painting and Sculpture in America'.

There are two distinct groups with in the movement; Colour Field with artists like <u>Rothko</u>, <u>Newman</u> and <u>Still</u> who worked with simple, unified blocks of colour. And then there are gestural painters like Pollock, de Kooning and <u>Hofman</u> who made use of surrealist techniques of automatic art. Not all the artists associated with the term produced either purely abstract, or purely expressionist work

Ann Thinghuus's abstracts result from the building and exposing layers of color and hues. Moving around her paintings, the repositioning of light reveals entirely new perspectives. Tension and balance through the blending of colours and hues evokes deep emotional reactions from the observer. The creator and viewer meet on the canvas to collaboratively experience individual thoughts and perceptions.

GA P

www.avocade.com

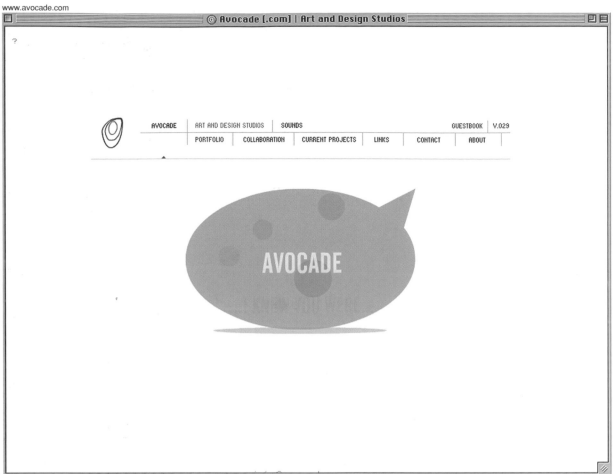

@ Avocade [.com] | Art and Design Studios

?

AVOCADE   ART AND DESIGN STUDIOS   SOUNDS   GUESTBOOK   V.029

PORTFOLIO   COLLABORATION   CURRENT PROJECTS   LINKS   CONTACT   ABOUT

AVOCADE

USA F P

www.artsa.co.za

ArtSa Gallery

ART SA Home | African | Contemporary | Wildlife | About us | Order / Contact Us

ART SA GALLERY

ORIGINAL FINE ART FROM SOUTH AFRICA

To view, click gallery below

AFRICAN
CONTEMPORARY
WILDLIFE

Best viewed - 800 x 600

Copyright ART SA / artist © All rights reserved

ZA C

www.gladstonegallery.com

Barbara Gladstone Gallery

Exhibitions   Artists   Gallery   Publications

BARBARA GLADSTONE GALLERY

515 West 24th Street
New York, New York 10011
Telephone 212 206 9300
Fax 212 206 9301

USA F C

www.bmathesgallery.com

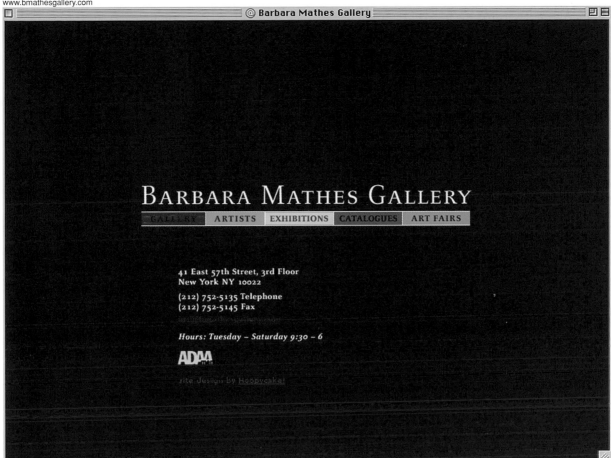

www.bauhaus.de

www.teien-art-museum.nc.jp

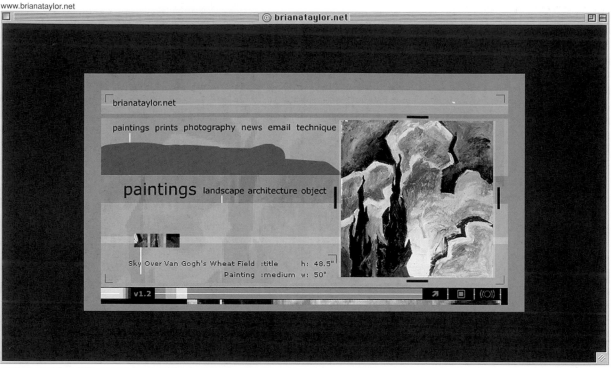

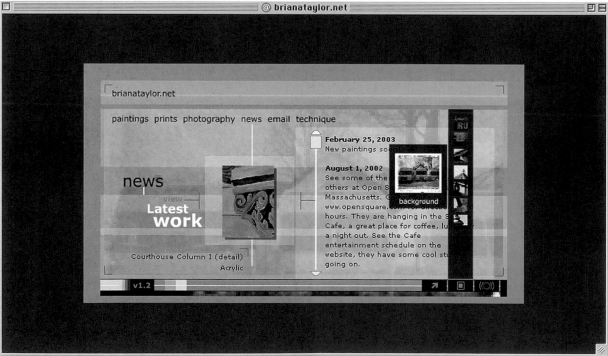

http://www.bigtorino.net/english/index.htm

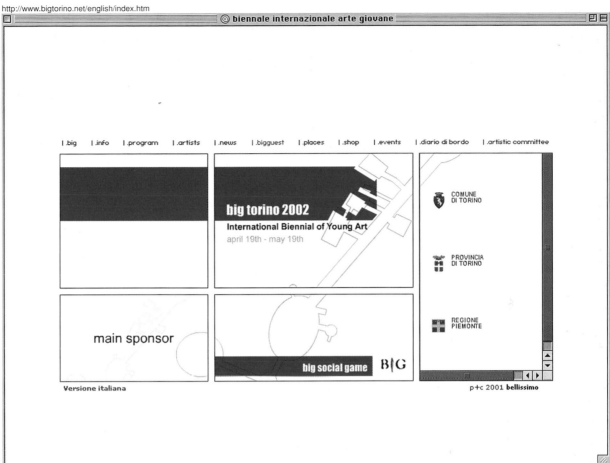

l .big   l .info   l .program   l .artists   l .news   l .bigguest   l .places   l .shop   l .events   l .diario di bordo   l .artistic committee

big torino 2002
International Biennial of Young Art
april 19th - may 19th

COMUNE
DI TORINO

PROVINCIA
DI TORINO

REGIONE
PIEMONTE

main sponsor

big social game   B|G

Versione italiana

p+c 2001 **bellissimo**

http://www.cnac-gp.fr/Pompidou/Home.nsf/docs/fhome

Centre
Pompidou

En raison d'un mouvement de

Expositions   Événements

Bpi   Documentation   Éditions

Ircam

english
information
& newsletter   laissez passer   what's your view?   UNE TOUR EIFFEL HAUTE EN COULEURS   WEBCAM

informations   agenda   le laissez-passer   rechercher   s'inscrire   contacter   www   professionnels

www.caam.net

CAAM.net

CENTRO ATLANTICO DE ARTE MODERNO

Español   English

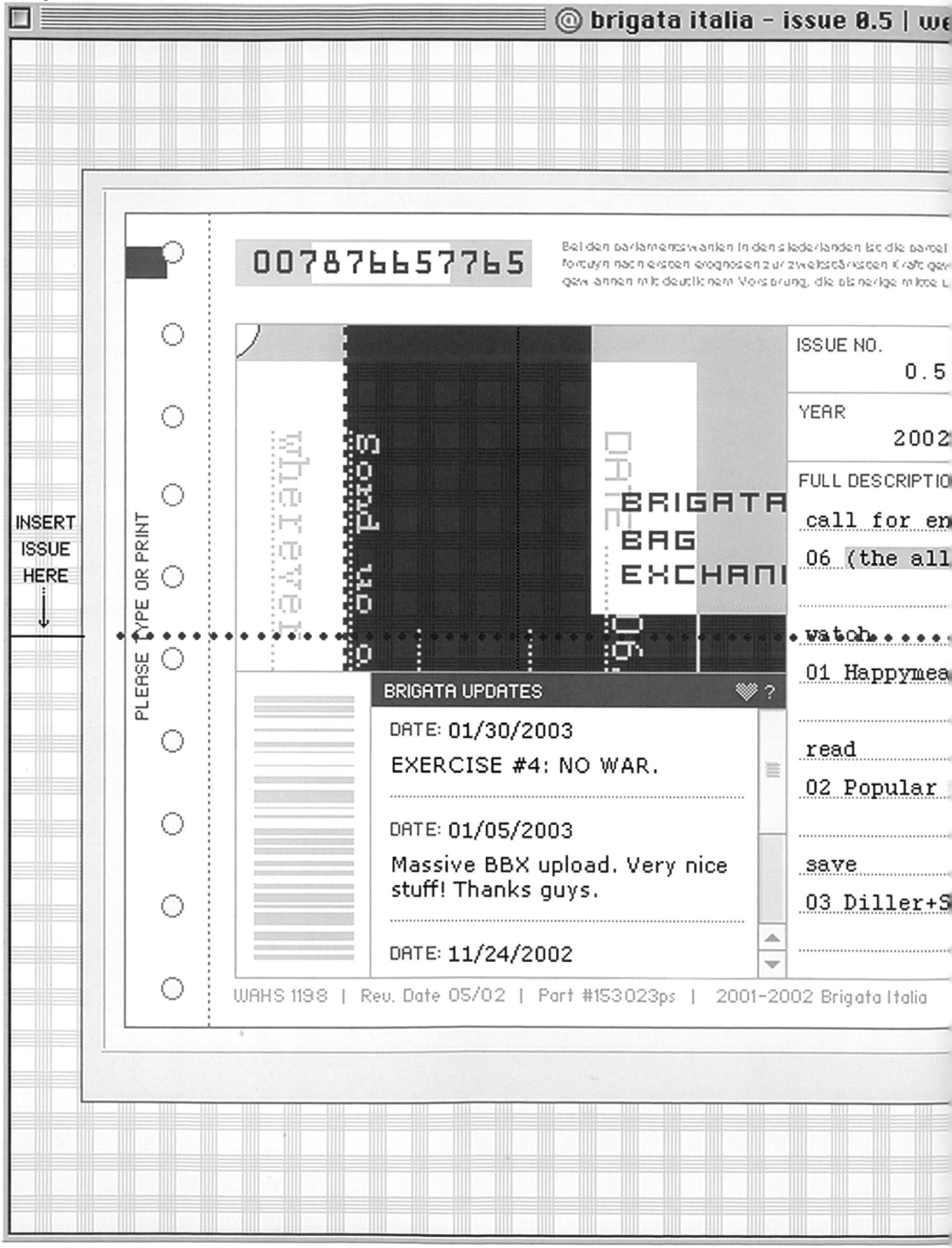

00787665765

Bei den parlamentswahlen in den niederlanden ist die partei
forzuyn nach ersten prognosen zur zweitstärksten Kraft gew
gew annen mit deutlichem Vorsprung, die als nerige in tote u

ISSUE NO.

0.5

YEAR

2002

FULL DESCRIPTIO

call for en

06 (the all

watch

01 Happymea

BRIGATA
BAG
EXCHANI

INSERT
ISSUE
HERE
↓

PLEASE TYPE OR PRINT

BRIGATA UPDATES ♥ ?

DATE: 01/30/2003

EXERCISE #4: NO WAR.

DATE: 01/05/2003

Massive BBX upload. Very nice
stuff! Thanks guys.

DATE: 11/24/2002

read

02 Popular

save

03 Diller+S

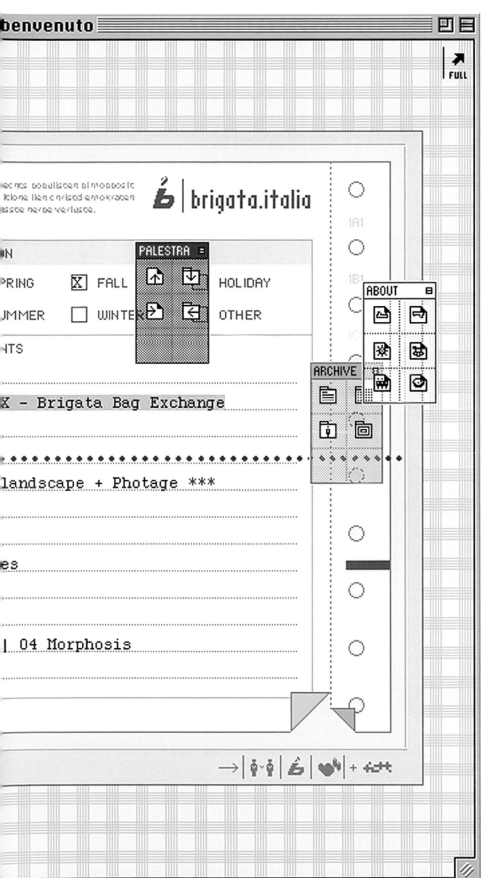

clandestina
ARTISTAS EN CONFLICTO

COLORS   TRIPS

NEWSLETTER · LINKS · INFO · CONTACTO

03
magicplaces

Una mirada desde la alcantarilla
puede ser una visión del mundo
la rebelión consiste en mirar una rosa
hasta pulverizarse los ojos

Alejandra Pizarnik

TRIPS   11

COLORS   11

CD COVERS

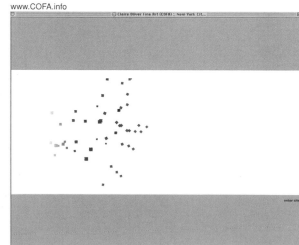

POWERED BY *la vertical*
:: studio

WHAT'S NEW

Alegria celebrates its 3,000th performance!
We invite you to discover the virtual universe of the
show. Enter the Club to read more from our artists on
tour.

ZUMANITY · Discover another
side of Cirque du Soleil!

Cirque du Soleil is innovating once again with a new
production: *ZUMANITY*. If you are 18 or over, we invite
you to experience the creative climax of sensuality,
humanity and art.

JOIN
CIRQUE
CLUB

EXPLORE SPECTACULAR

TRAILERS

Currently traveling through Europe: *Saltimbanco!*

Watch a clip!

SHOWS TICKETS MULTIMEDIA CIRQUE CLUB BOUTIQUE JOIN CIRQUE THE COMPANY PRESS ROOM   Français

Home   Credits Contact Us FAQ Profile

enter site

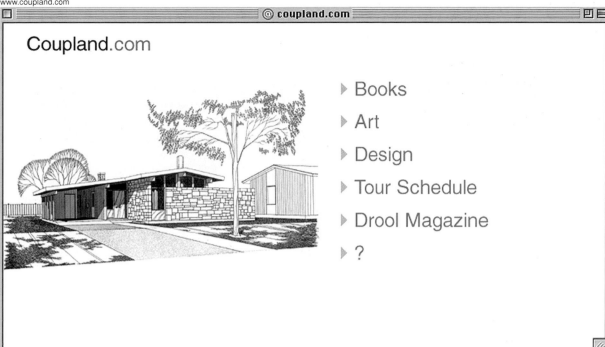

CLINE FINE ART
SANTA FE · SCOTTSDALE

Santa Fe
135 West Palace Avenue
Santa Fe, NM 87501
Tel 505-982-5328
Fax 505-982-4762
info@clinefineart.com

Scottsdale
4200 North Marshall Way
Scottsdale, AZ 85251
Tel 480-941-1811
Fax 480-941-1812
info@clinefineart.com

> *Enter*

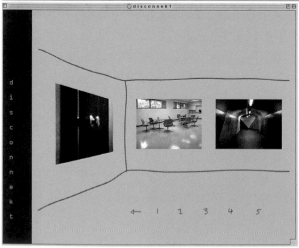

DE

www.districtsix.co.za

www.e-flux.com

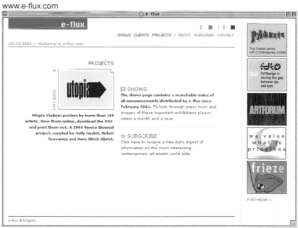

www.eegallery.com

☰ ELEANOR ETTINGER GALLERY

HOME | EXHIBITION | ARTISTS | SEARCH | ABOUT | SITE MAP | CONTACT | PRIVATE

WELCOME TO THE GALLERY

CURRENT   UPCOMING   PREVIOUS   ARTISTS

ESTABLISHED 1975

119 SPRING STREET, GROUND FL, NEW YORK NY 10012 TEL: (212) 925-7474 FAX: (212) 925-7734

USA F C

---

www.foe156.de

eins

FOE 156

Kunst und Architektur im Ausstellungsforum

[Ausstellungen]   [Rückblick]   [Künstler]   [Kataloge]   [Kontakt]   [Informationen]

DE I

---

http://www.noiselabmedia.com/espaciotres/

espaciotres

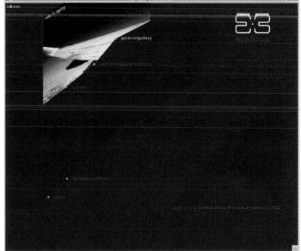

MY F C

voltz.jp   devilock.com
lazymf.com   swishnyc.com
djtommy.com   revolholic.com

interview on evilmonito.com (summer
interview on figures.com (jan. 02)

site design: dhky.com

personal work _

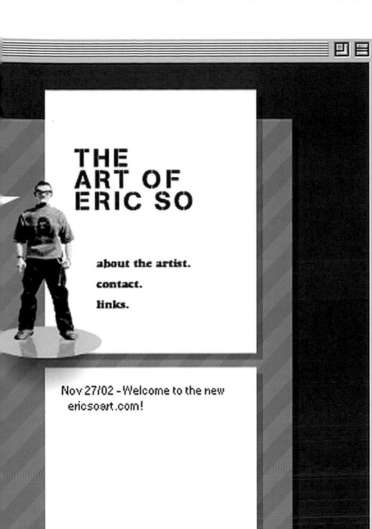

THE ART OF ERIC SO

about the artist.

contact.

links.

Nov 27/02 – Welcome to the new ericsoart.com!

nese "www.ericsoart.jp"

@ Flying Puppet

Flying Puppet

français

english

18-05-2003

optimized for a 1024x768 resolution and true color 32 bits

requires the Flash and Shockwave plug-ins

nicolas clauss © 2001-2003

www.daiichi-museum.co.jp

www.fkv.de

www.petzel.com

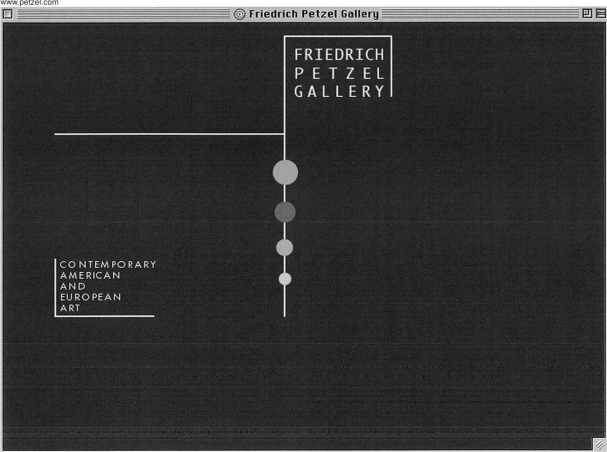

FRIEDRICH
PETZEL
GALLERY

CONTEMPORARY
AMERICAN
AND
EUROPEAN
ART

www.frithstreetgallery.com

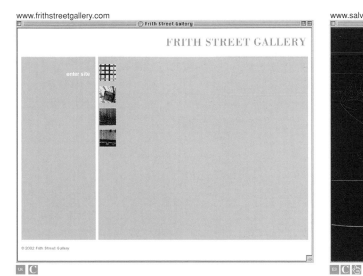

FRITH STREET GALLERY

enter site

© 2002 Frith Street Gallery

www.salvador-dali.org

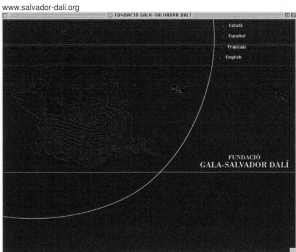

Català
Español
Français
English

FUNDACIÓ
GALA-SALVADOR DALÍ

@ Fundació Miró

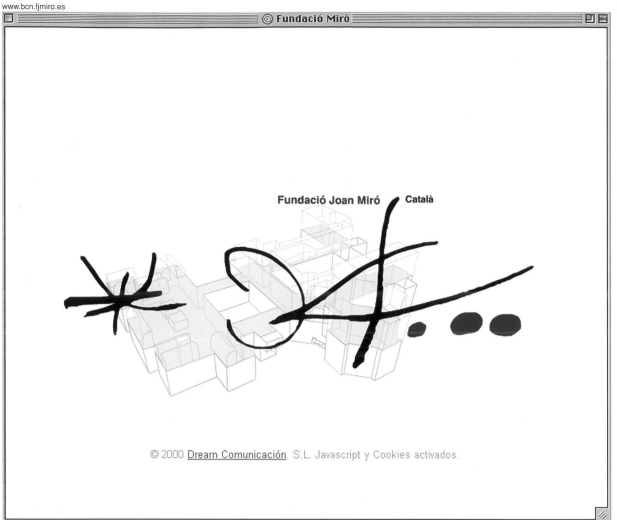

Fundació Joan Miró   Català

© 2000 Dream Comunicación. S.L. Javascript y Cookies activados.

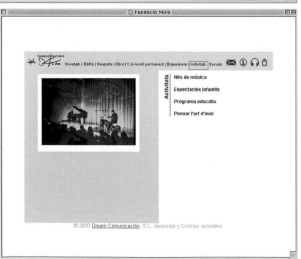

www.fbarrie.org

Fundación
Pedro Barrié de la Maza

Español
Galego
English

ES F I

www.future-factory.org

UK F C

www.gagosian.com

USA F C

@ Galerie Max Hetzler - Berlin

Contact | Publications | Artists | Exhibitions

Richard Phillips

May 3 – May 31, 2003   Holzmarktstrasse 15–18

Werner Büttner
Paintings and Drawings from the Eighties

May 4 – May 31, 2003   Zimmerstrasse 90/91

View exhibition | Gallery calendar

Galerie Max Hetzler

**Holzmarktstrasse 15–18 S-Bahnbogen 48 D-10179 Berlin-Mitte   Phone (+49 30) 24 04 56 30   Fax 24 04 56 32
Zimmerstrasse 90/91 D-10117 Berlin-Mitte Phone (+49 30) 229 24 37   Fax 229 24 17**

Site management by artindata | Design by Hans Werner Holzwarth

DE C

---

www.galerie-nagel.de

@ Galerie Christian Nagel

CN

Galerie Christian Nagel

DE F K C

---

www.gallery49.com

@ GALLERY 49 | CONTEMPORARY FINE ART

GALLERY@49
notartcontemporary

artists | exhibitions | about | contact | mailing list

DAVID TOBEY
MAY 10 – JUNE 7, 2003

The Structure of Energy

opening reception:
SATURDAY | MAY 10, 2003 | 4 - 7PM

solo contemporary guitar performance by Oren Fader

view work | press release

home | artists | exhibitions | about | contact | mailing list
©2003. Gallery@49. Copyright information and credits. Visual material cannot be used without permission. Design: gui | studio

USA C

www.gasworks.org.uk

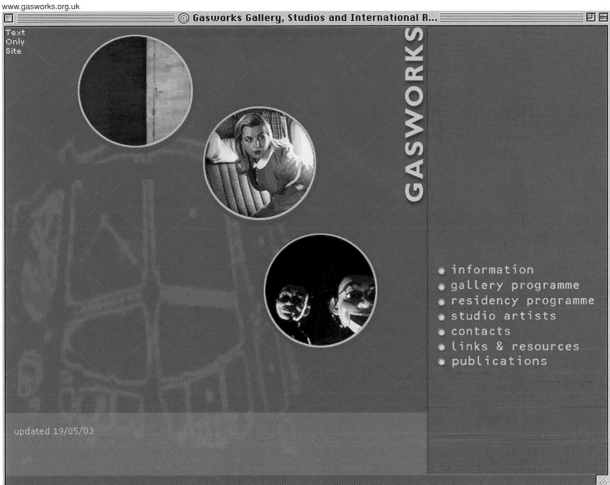

Text
Only
Site

GASWORKS

- information
- gallery programme
- residency programme
- studio artists
- contacts
- links & resources
- publications

updated 19/05/03

www.lehmannmaupin.com

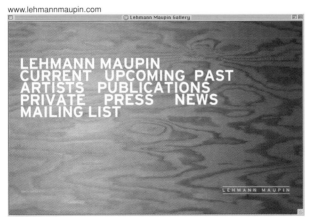

LEHMANN MAUPIN
CURRENT UPCOMING PAST
ARTISTS PUBLICATIONS
PRIVATE PRESS NEWS
MAILING LIST

LEHMANN MAUPIN

www.goodman-gallery.com

GOODMAN
GALLERY

@ Graphische Sammlung der ETH Zürich – Lange Na...

ETH
Eidgenössische Technische Hochschule Zürich
Swiss Federal Institute of Technology Zurich

english

GRAPHISCHE SAMMLUNG

sammlung   forschung   publikationen   information   im ausstellungsraum

Kunst am
Montagmittag
Thematische Führungen
jeweils montags von
12.30 bis 13 Uhr

Aktuelle Ausstellung:
Marc-Antoine Fehr - Journal
de Pressy
Ein Zyklus von 366
Zeichnungen

Das *Journal de Pressy* spiegelt
Fehrs ganze künstlerische
Tätigkeit: Porträts,
Interieurs, Landschaften und
seine Arbeit am Bild *Die
Grosse Mühle*.

Nächste Führung
**Ein Bildertagebuch von Marc-Antoine Fehr:
Das "Journal de Pressy"**
Montag, 26. Mai, 12.30 Uhr

7. Mai – 11. Juli 2003

● newsmail abonnieren

impressum   aktualisiert 19.5.03_ab

www.diacenter.org

Dia Art Foundation

Dia: Beacon Chelsea Sites Affiliations Artists' Web Projects Books Information

Dia:

Dia Art Foundation was founded in 1974. A nonprofit institution, Dia plays a vital role among visual
arts organizations nationally and internationally by initiating, supporting, presenting, and preserving
art projects, and by serving as a locus for interdisciplinary art and criticism. In addition to
presenting exhibitions and public programming at Dia:Chelsea, (formerly Dia Center for the Arts)
Dia maintains long-term, site-specific projects in the western United States, in New York City, and on
Long Island. On May 18, 2003, Dia will open Dia:Beacon, a new museum in Beacon, New York, to
house its renowned collection of art from the 1960s to the present. For more information about
Dia's history, click here.

Dia's administrative offices are located at:

535 West 22nd Street
New York, NY 10011
T: 212.989.5566
F: 212.989.4055

© 1995-2003 Dia Art Foundation

USA I

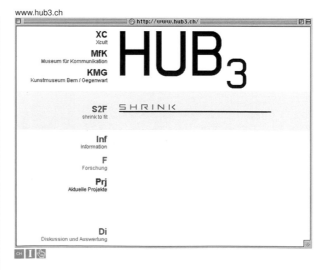

www.hub3.ch

© http://www.hub3.ch/

XC
Xcult

MfK
Museum für Kommunikation

KMG
Kunstmuseum Bern / Gegenwart

HUB₃

S2F
shrink to fit

SHRINK

Inf
Information

F
Forschung

Prj
Aktuelle Projekte

Di
Diskussion und Auswertung

CH I

www.gegenwart.com

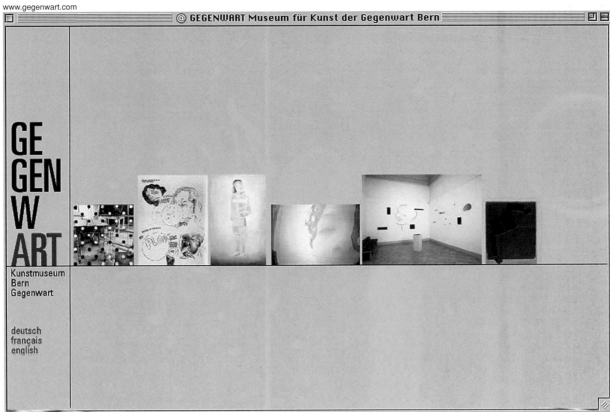

www.artb.co.za

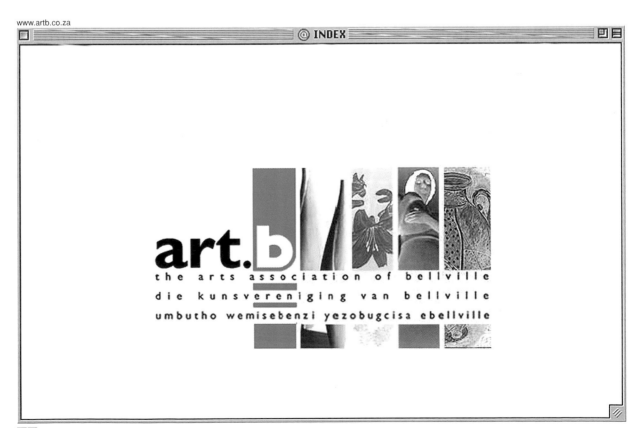

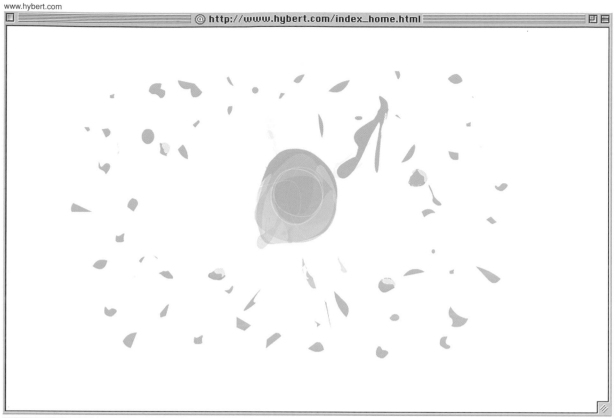

http://www.hybert.com/   FR SW I

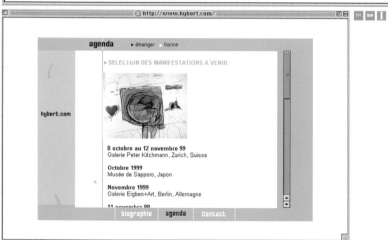

http://www.hybert.com/

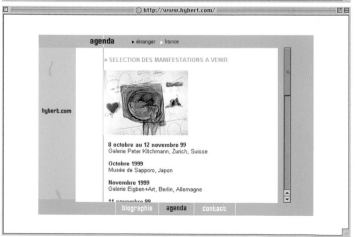

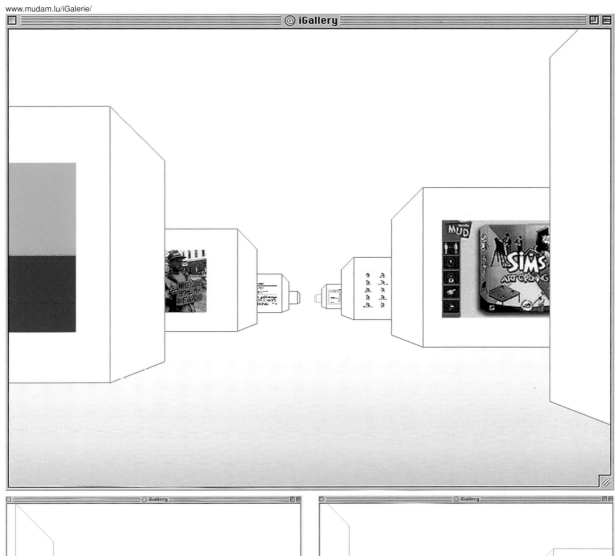

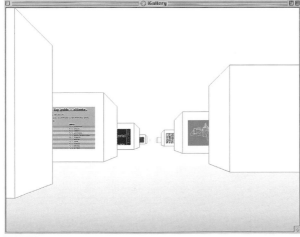

art

INGEN SKAM Å SNU

MIKKEL McALINDEN
PHOTO GALLERY

MIKKEL McALINDEN
PHOTO GALLERY

FIRST F

GROUND

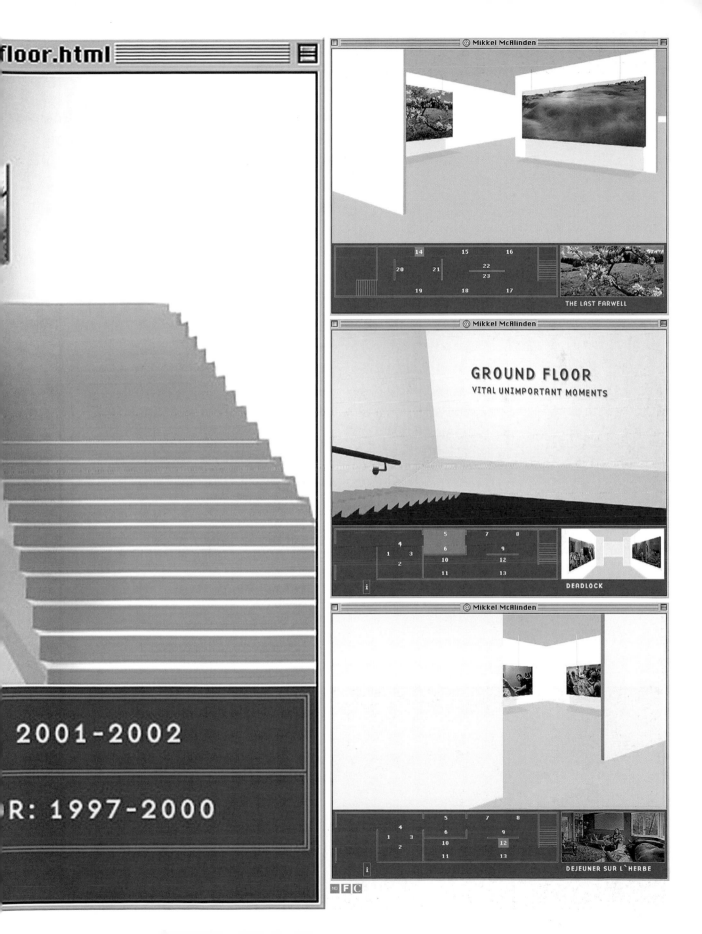

@ Ingvar Cronhammar

18389 besøgende

Forsiden   Biografi   Værker   CV   Kontakt

Aktuelt

"Blodrummet" - permanent installation
i lokale på Sønderjyllands Kunstmuseum i Tønder
Maj 2002 - gave fra Ny Carlsbergfondet.

Byrumsinstallation, "Redfall", Randers
Forventet indvielse maj/juni 2002

Byrumsinstallation, "Eye of the Shadow", Struer
Nybearbejdning, forår 2002

Separat udstilling, "Det Ny Kastet", Thisted
Forår 2003

Udstillingen "Sofienholm"
Forår 2003, i samarbejde med Thomas Bang og Poul
Ingemann

Boligbyggeri i Gjellerup
i samarbejde med arkitektfirmaet Søren Jensen,
Herning
Forventet opførelse 2003

Separat udstilling, Gallerie Nils Stærk
Efterår 2003

www.Gallerie.net

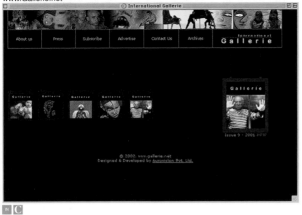

www.jamescohan.com

www.artsouth.co.za

www.kiddersmithgallery.com

www.kkl-luzern.ch

www.kunsttermine.de

MENU

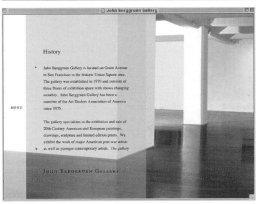

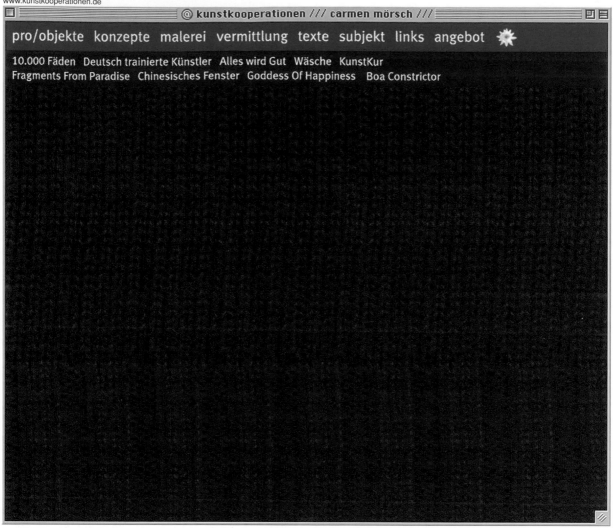

@ kunstkooperationen /// carmen mörsch ///

pro/objekte konzepte malerei vermittlung texte subjekt links angebot ✳

10.000 Fäden Deutsch trainierte Künstler Alles wird Gut Wäsche KunstKur
Fragments From Paradise Chinesisches Fenster Goddess Of Happiness Boa Constrictor

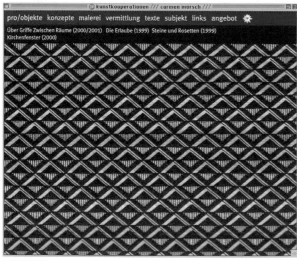

@ kunstkooperationen /// carmen mörsch ///

pro/objekte konzepte malerei vermittlung texte subjekt links angebot ✳

Über Griffe Zwischen Räume (2000/2001) Die Erlaube (1999) Steine und Rosetten (1999)
Kirchenfenster (2000)

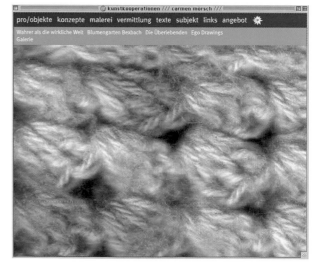

@ kunstkooperationen /// carmen mörsch ///

pro/objekte konzepte malerei vermittlung texte subjekt links angebot ✳

Wahrer als die wirkliche Welt Blumengarten Bexbach Die Überlebenden Ego Drawings
Galerie

www.kunstsammlung.de

www.luhringaugustine.com

www.mariangoodman.com

www.marcjancou.com

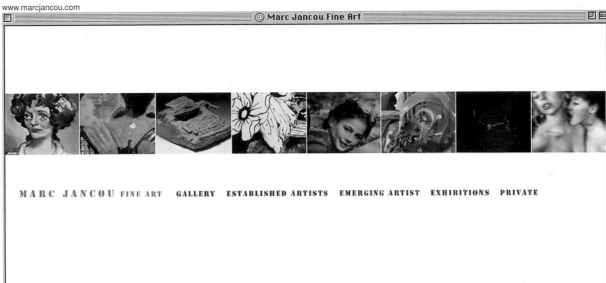

MARC JANCOU FINE ART   GALLERY   ESTABLISHED ARTISTS   EMERGING ARTIST   EXHIBITIONS   PRIVATE

Site by exhibit-E™

www.madame-tussauds.com

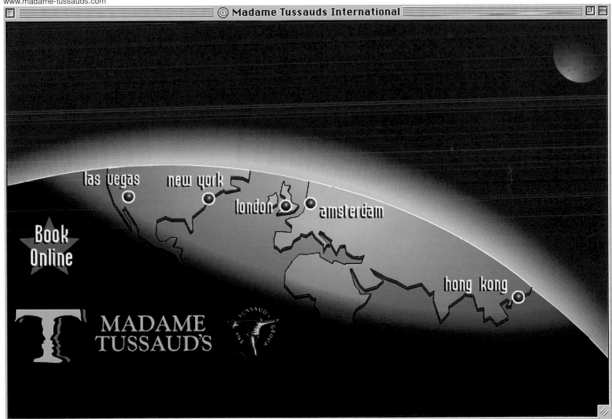

www.malba.org.ar

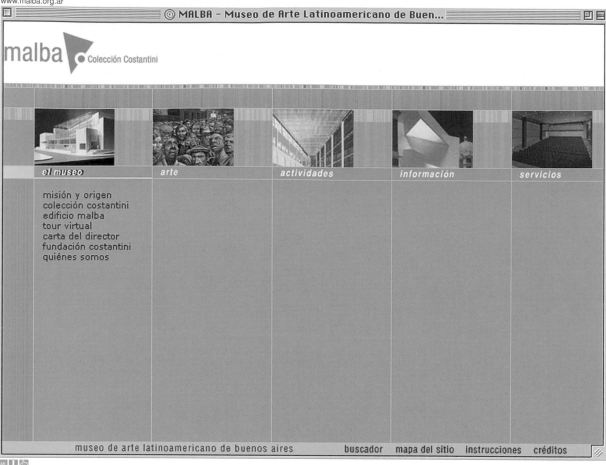

@ MALBA – Museo de Arte Latinoamericano de Buen...

malba Colección Costantini

el museo   arte   actividades   información   servicios

misión y origen
colección costantini
edificio malba
tour virtual
carta del director
fundación costantini
quiénes somos

museo de arte latinoamericano de buenos aires   buscador   mapa del sitio   instrucciones   créditos

www.mca.com.au

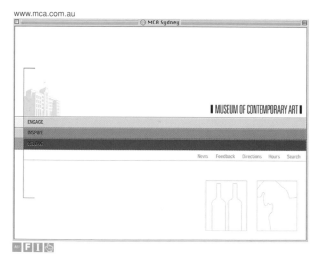

MCA Sydney

MUSEUM OF CONTEMPORARY ART

ENGAGE
INSPIRE
BELONG

News   Feedback   Directions   Hours   Search

www.michaelrosenfeldart.com

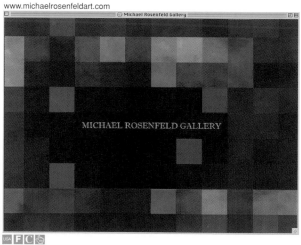

Michael Rosenfeld Gallery

MICHAEL ROSENFELD GALLERY

www.minettabrook.org

AND THE WIND AND THE RAIN

Please join us for the opening of Watershed: The Hudson Valley Art Project
Click here for more information.

| MINETTA BROOK | ARTISTS | PROJECTS | PUBLICATIONS |

MINETTA BROOK

Minetta Brook   105 Hudson Street No 411   New York NY 10013

Telephone +1 212 431 7165   Fax +1 212 431 1504   Email info@minettabrook.org

subscribe mailinglist

Erisma

Impressum

AKTUELL

54 CH-8004 Zürich 01 241 77 12

www.mnw.art.pl

@ MUZEUM NARODOWE W WARSZAWIE

MUZEUM NARODOWE W WARSZAWIE

POLSKI   ENGLISH

---

www.ruthprowse.co.za

@ Ruth Prowse School of Art

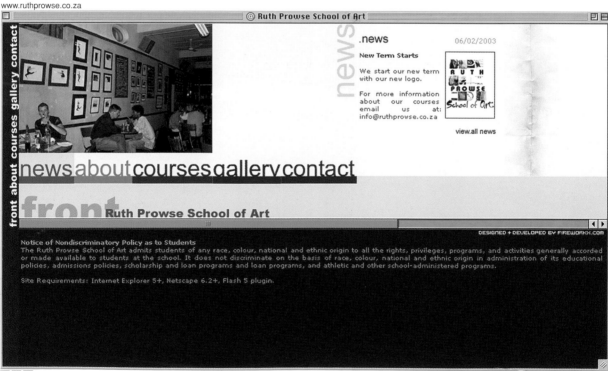

news about courses gallery contact

front Ruth Prowse School of Art

.news   06/02/2003

New Term Starts

We start our new term with our new logo.

For more information about our courses email us at: info@ruthprowse.co.za

view.all news

DESIGNED + DEVELOPED BY FIREWORKX.COM

Notice of Nondiscriminatory Policy as to Students
The Ruth Prowse School of Art admits students of any race, colour, national and ethnic origin to all the rights, privileges, programs, and activities generally accorded or made available to students at the school. It does not discriminate on the basis of race, colour, national and ethnic origin in administration of its educational policies, admissions policies, scholarship and loan programs and loan programs, and athletic and other school-administered programs.

Site Requirements: Internet Explorer 5+, Netscape 6.2+, Flash 5 plugin.

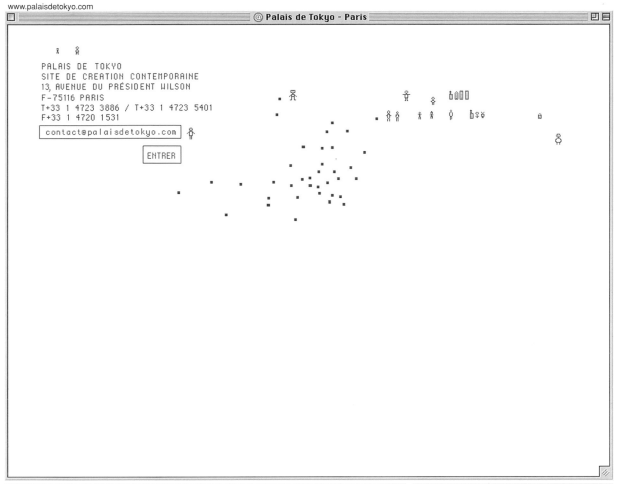

PALAIS DE TOKYO
SITE DE CRÉATION CONTEMPORAINE
13, AVENUE DU PRÉSIDENT WILSON
F-75116 PARIS
T+33 1 4723 3886 / T+33 1 4723 5401
F+33 1 4720 1531

contact@palaisdetokyo.com

ENTRER

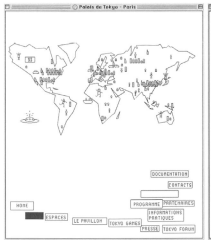

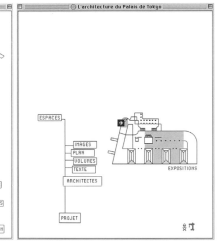

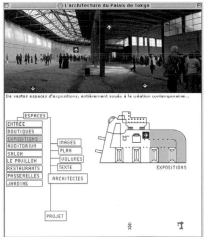

De vastes espaces d'expositions, entièrement voués à la création contemporaine...

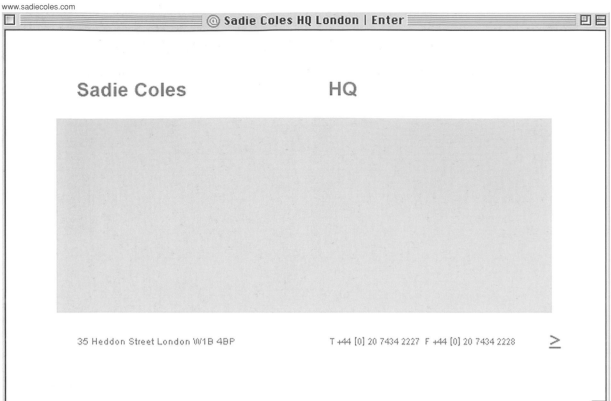

Sadie Coles HQ London | Enter

Sadie Coles HQ

35 Heddon Street London W1B 4BP   T +44 [0] 20 7434 2227 F +44 [0] 20 7434 2228   ≥

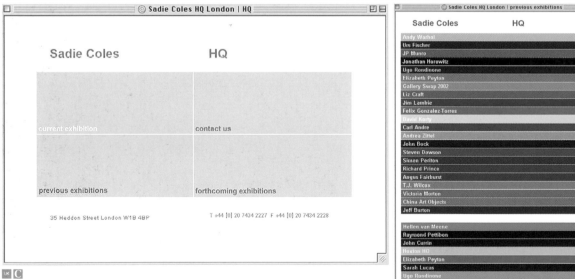

Sadie Coles HQ London | HQ

Sadie Coles HQ

current exhibition

contact us

previous exhibitions

forthcoming exhibitions

35 Heddon Street London W1B 4BP   T +44 [0] 20 7434 2227 F +44 [0] 20 7434 2228

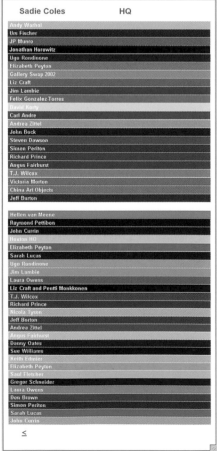

Sadie Coles HQ London | previous exhibitions

Sadie Coles HQ

Andy Warhol
Urs Fischer
JP Munro
Jonathan Horowitz
Ugo Rondinone
Elizabeth Peyton
Gallery Swap 2002
Liz Craft
Jim Lambie
Felix Gonzalez-Torres
David Korty
Carl Andre
Andrea Zittel
John Bock
Steven Dowson
Simon Periton
Richard Prince
Angus Fairhurst
T.J. Wilcox
Victoria Morton
China Art Objects
Jeff Burton

Hellen van Meene
Raymond Pettibon
John Currin
Hoxton HQ
Elizabeth Peyton
Sarah Lucas
Ugo Rondinone
Jim Lambie
Laura Owens
Liz Craft and Pentti Monkkonen
T.J. Wilcox
Richard Prince
Nicola Tyson
Jeff Burton
Andrea Zittel
Angus Fairhurst
Danny Oates
Sue Williams
Keith Edmier
Elizabeth Peyton
Saul Fletcher
Gregor Schneider
Laura Owens
Don Brown
Simon Periton
Sarah Lucas
John Currin

≤

www.swissinstitute.net

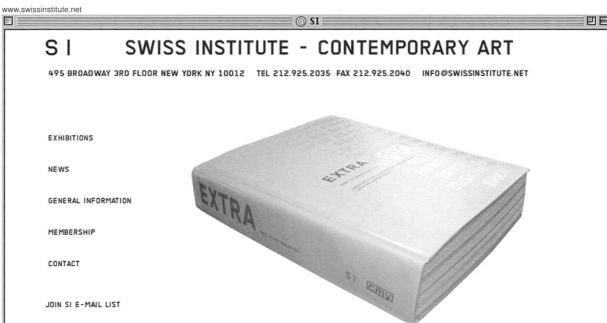

www.secession.at

www.simonrobinsonsculptor.com

www.designindaba.com

www.pulitzerarts.org

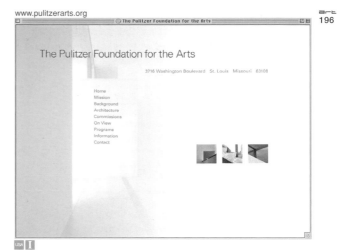

www.royalacademy.org.uk

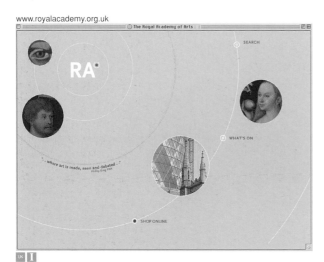

www.vanessabeecroft.com

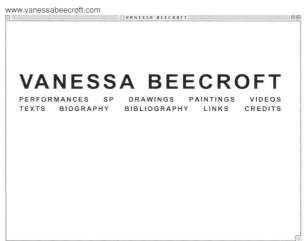

www.likeyou.com

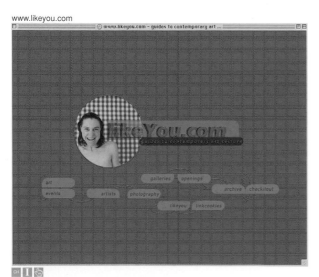

www.art.pref.tochigi.jp

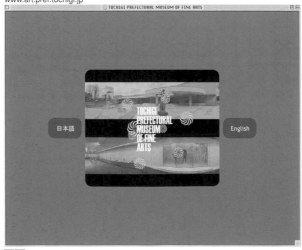

www.wildenstein.com

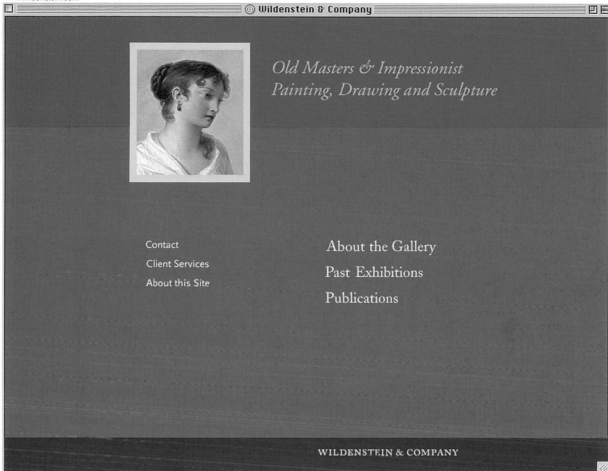

www.bell-roberts.com

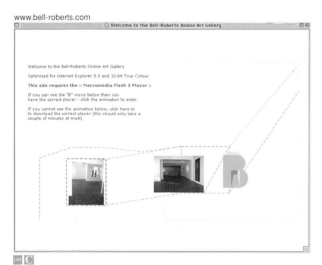

www.whitecube.com

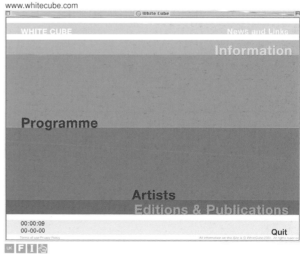

www.carliergebauer.com

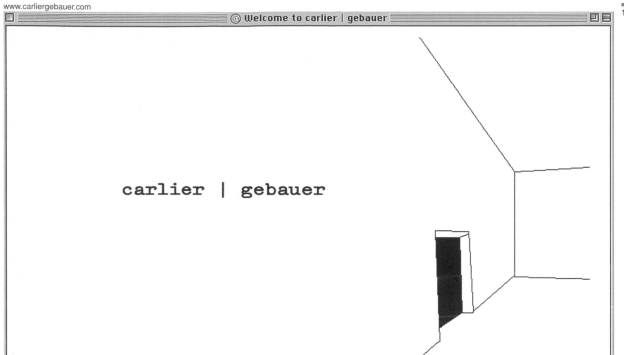

@ Welcome to carlier | gebauer

carlier | gebauer

DE P

www.warhol.org

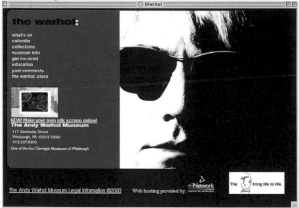

USA I

www.vmcaa.nl

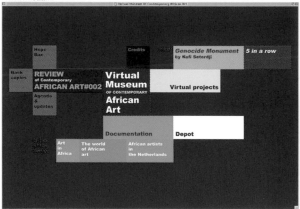

NL I

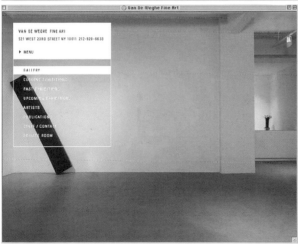

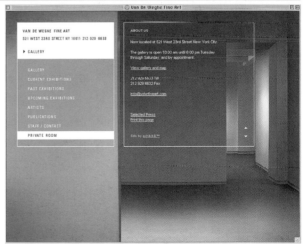

www.rocketpoweredmice.com

www.sunsector.com

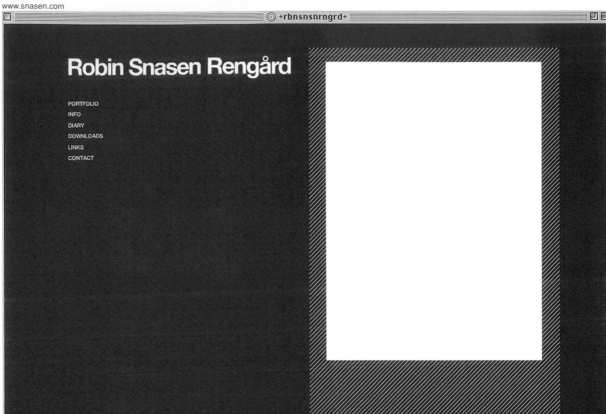

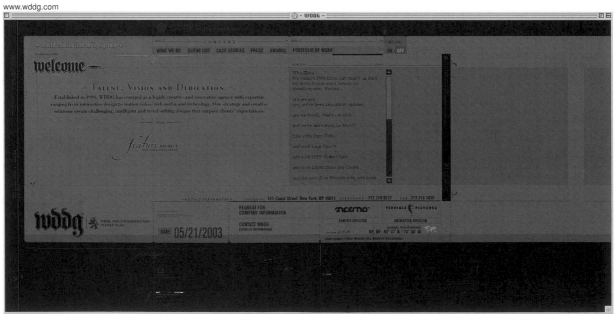

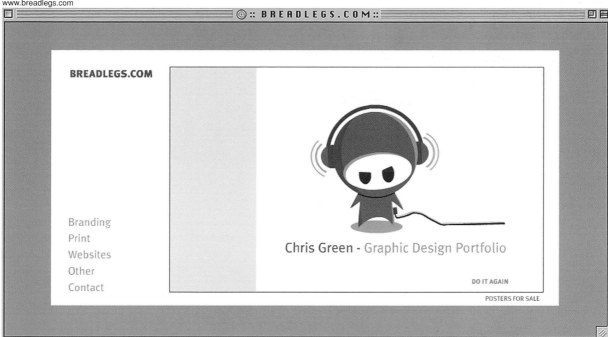

www.saman.rahmanian.at

welcome to **arkndesign**.com

v2.0 : require: flash 5 plugin + quicktime 5 + ie 5 + 800x600 rez >

@ : : : **arkndesign** : : :

home | cover | showroom

lastest news | all news

28/02/03 > 18:50
71Lab has been updated !
(thanks Stephanie !) >>

28/02/03 > 17:50
haaa haaa ~
make pixels not war !
(thanks Michael !) >>

17/02/03 > 17:40
this coming Saturday is
Designer's Saturday
(in hongkong island) >>

17/02/03 > 17:35
db-db version 4 !!! >>

28/01/03 > 10:05

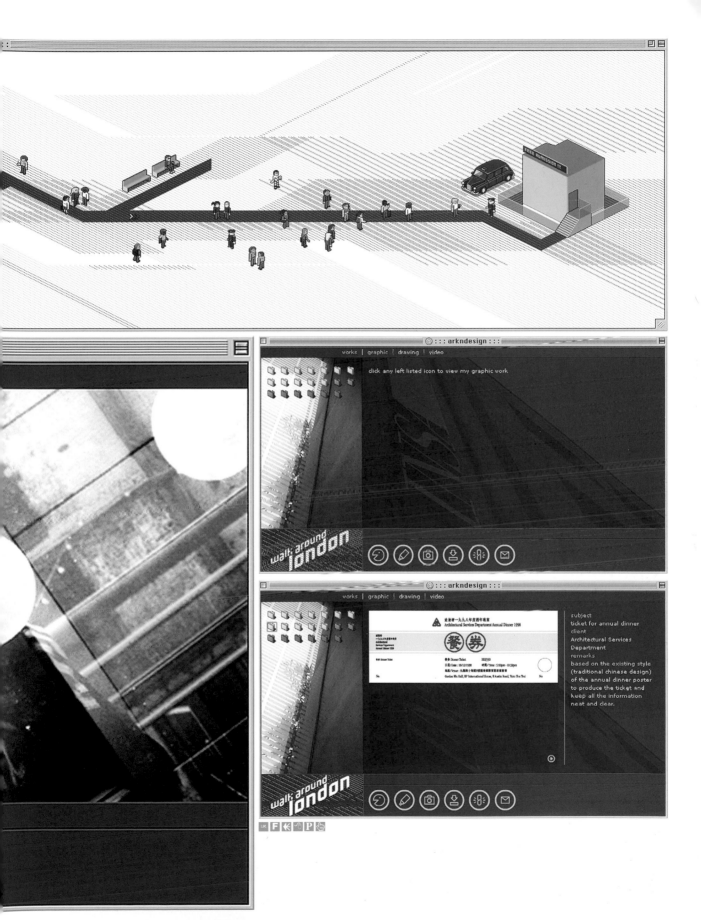

works | graphic | drawing | video

click any left listed icon to view my graphic work

walk around london

works | graphic | drawing | video

subject
ticket for annual dinner
client
Architectural Services
Department
remarks
based on the existing style
(traditional chinese design)
of the annual dinner poster
to produce the ticket and
keep all the information
neat and clear.

walk around london

:: elev8|design ::

elev8|design

MAIN   RESUME   PORTFOLIO   CONTACT

My name is Geoff Small, and Elev8 Design is my online portfolio.

I am experienced in both print and online media, having designed websites, Flash animations, corporate identities, marketing materials, brochures, business cards, and pretty much anything else you can make out of pixels and/or paper.

If you would like to see samples of my work, please feel free to check out the Portfolio section. You'll find print and interactive work from both employers and freelance clients. In addition you can browse through photographs taken on my many adventures.

Whether you are a large corporation or an independent business person, Elev8 Design can create a design solution tailored to meet your needs.

News

10/28/02
Recently completed a website for Motivational Speaker and Author, Scott Stawski. You can check it out here.

09/30/02
Currently looking for work in Southern Ontario, please let me know if you have any opportunities.

09/06/02
SmartForce, my employer has just merged with another company, Skillsoft.

more news

CA F C

www.unburro.com

www.velocitystudio.com

www.aptagraphics.com

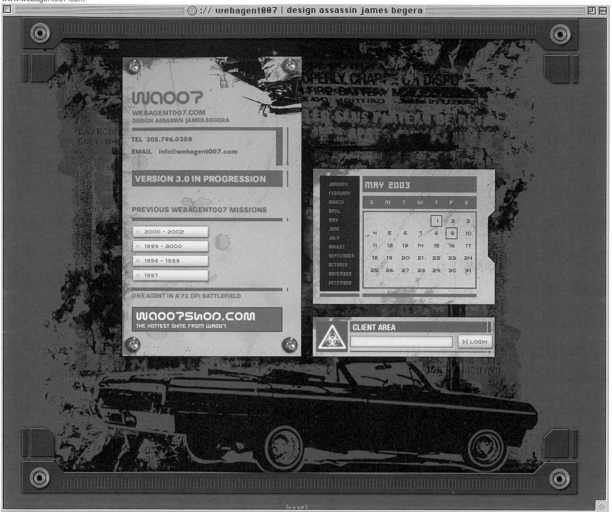

www.ascension1.com

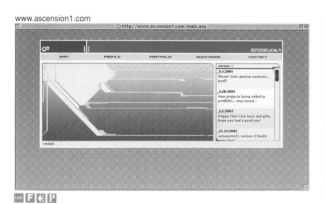

www.strukt.at

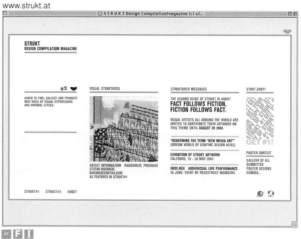

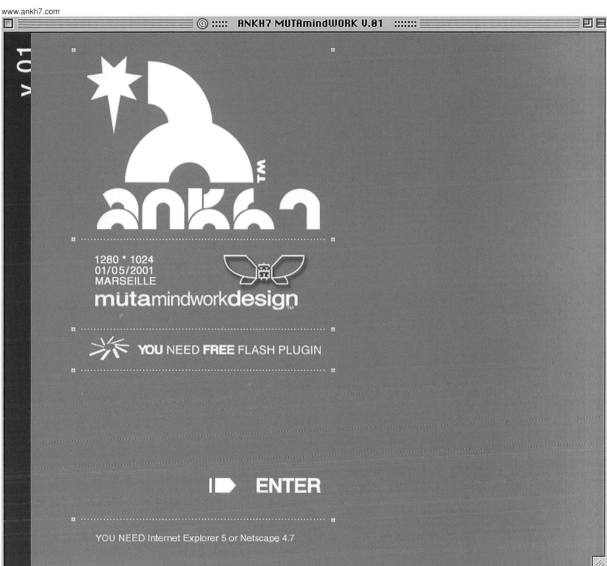

v.01

1280 * 1024
01/05/2001
MARSEILLE

mūtamindworkdesign™

YOU NEED FREE FLASH PLUGIN

▷ ENTER

YOU NEED Internet Explorer 5 or Netscape 4.7

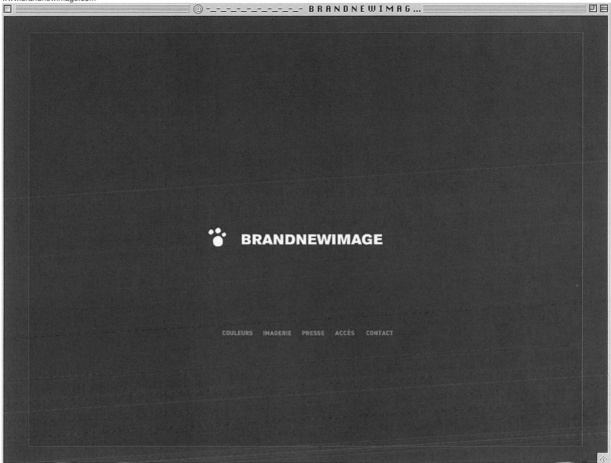

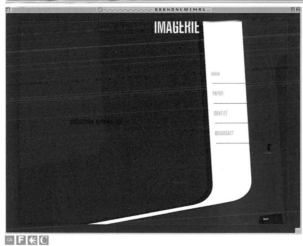

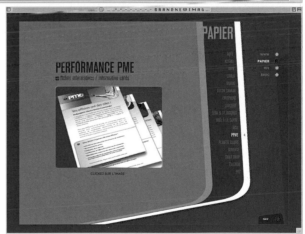

.:: IAAH ::.

www.210879.com

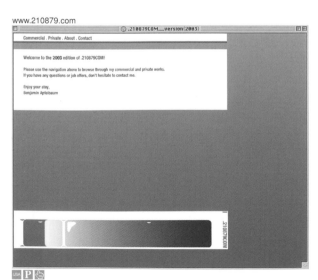

@ .210879COM__version(2003)

Commercial . Private . About . Contact

Welcome to the 2003 edition of .210879COM!

Please use the navigation above to browse through my commercial and private works.
If you have any questions or job offers, don't hesitate to contact me.

Enjoy your stay,
Benjamin Apfelbaum

www.120seconds.com

120seconds.com - Bite-sized Entertainment

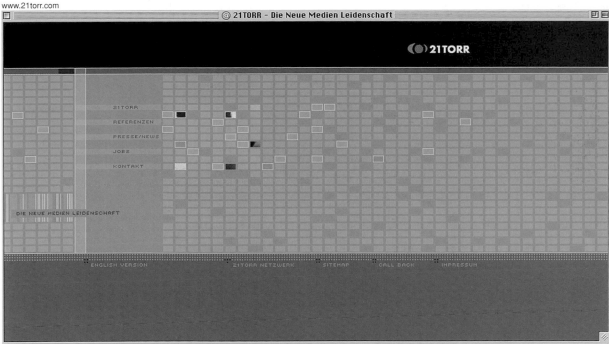

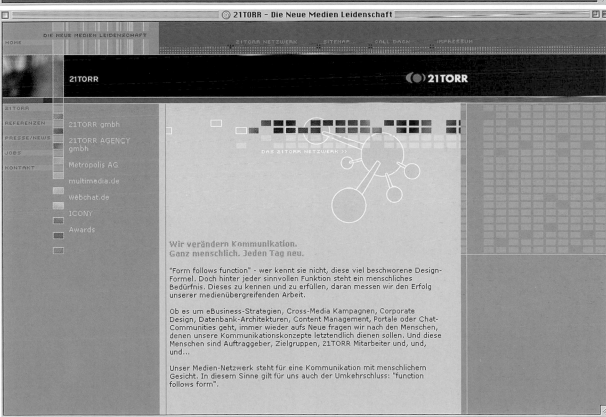

**Wir verändern Kommunikation.
Ganz menschlich. Jeden Tag neu.**

"Form follows function" - wer kennt sie nicht, diese viel beschworene Design-Formel. Doch hinter jeder sinnvollen Funktion steht ein menschliches Bedürfnis. Dieses zu kennen und zu erfüllen, daran messen wir den Erfolg unserer medienübergreifenden Arbeit.

Ob es um eBusiness-Strategien, Cross-Media Kampagnen, Corporate Design, Datenbank-Architekturen, Content Management, Portale oder Chat-Communities geht, immer wieder aufs Neue fragen wir nach den Menschen, denen unsere Kommunikationskonzepte letztendlich dienen sollen. Und diese Menschen sind Auftraggeber, Zielgruppen, 21TORR Mitarbeiter und, und, und...

Unser Medien-Netzwerk steht für eine Kommunikation mit menschlichem Gesicht. In diesem Sinne gilt für uns auch der Umkehrschluss: "function follows form".

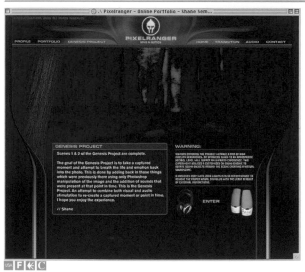

www.28design.co.uk

@ 28 design | +44 20 7404 4828

discipline

28

design, planning, strategy and
consultancy, across all media

28

phone : +44 20 7404 4828
email : 28@28design.com
how to find us
client login

database fed screen design - find out more ●

UK F C

www.04.jp.org

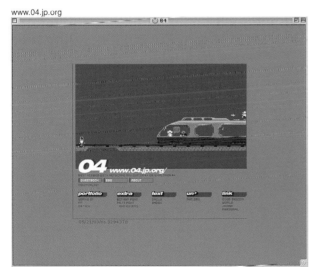

www.2doublezero1.com

www.310k.nl

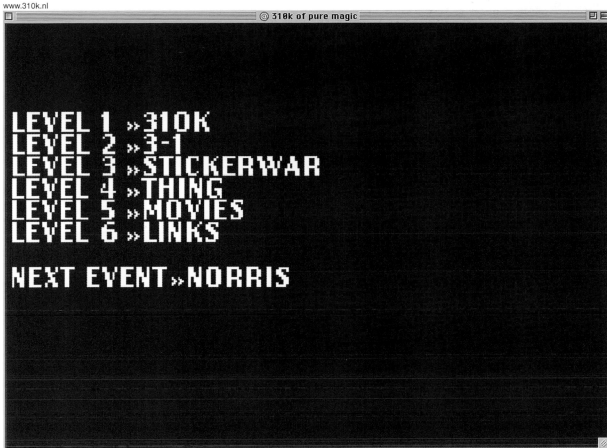

LEVEL 1 »310K
LEVEL 2 »3-1
LEVEL 3 »STICKERWAR
LEVEL 4 »THING
LEVEL 5 »MOVIES
LEVEL 6 »LINKS

NEXT EVENT»NORRIS

www.3w4u.de

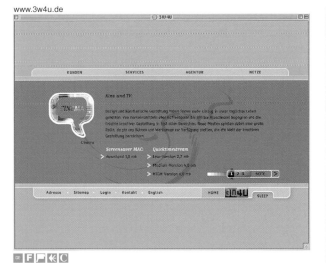

www.4vs5.com

Four versus Five™
Coffee-stained sketchbooks, and sleep-deprived design.

Featured Projects_
Just wrapped up the identity for (1) **Dovetail Workshop**, finished a few more logo and deck concepts for (2) **ABC Skateboards**, and take a glimpse at the conceptual (3) **Pickup Line book.** Plans are in the works for printed copies available this summer.

Now Working On_
A website for a software company, 2 identity projects, and the relaunch of **Campfire Collective™**.

3 Cups of Coffee_
Check out the **Profile** section and fill up on more information than you'll know what to do with.

Subscribe_
Submit your e-mail to keep up with what's happening at 4vs5.

[Your e-mail] [Submit]

@ Copyright 2003 4vs5™. Hosting paid for the old-fashioned way.

Latest News_
(May 17, 2003)
New work coming soon! Keep an eye out for a new identity project for **Nando Costa** over at **Nalof™**, 4vs5 Tshirts (finally!), unreleased work from an old sketchbook.

Older News_
(May 3, 2003)
Whew, the long-awaited 4vs5 CD Sampler is soon on its way. Sorry for the long wait (for those who've requested a copy long ago) but there is tons of new work that has been added at the last minute. Keep your eyes peeled...

Really Old News_
(April Fools Day)
Okay, for those who've been waiting and those who haven't...the 1st Edition 4vs5 Newsletter is soon on its way...

Site Last Updated_
On the mostly-sunny morning of May 17th, 2003

@ 5inch.com: blank CDR and cases

5inch®

CUSTOM DESIGNED BLANK CDR'S AND CASES

PRINTED CDR BLANK CDR DVD CASES SETS STORAGE WEARABLES HARDWARE

VIEW CART
HAS 0 ITEMS

Welcome to 5inch.com. We offer pre-designed silkscreened blank cdr's to suit all your data, as well as equally unique cd cases. DVD-Rs, unprinted 5" and 3" cdrs, and cdr-ws can be found in the Blank CDR section. Look in Storage and Wearables for one of a kind accessories.

SEE US IN CHICAGO AT CB2, PAPERSOURCE, ORANGESKIN, & ELEMENTS, OK STORE IN LA, ULTRAHOUSE IN SANTA MONICA, URBAN OUTFITTERS NATIONWIDE, MOJOE IN BRIGHTON UK and HOW&WHY IN MALAYSIA.

issue 12/02

5INCH GIFT CERTIFICATES ARE NOW AVAILABLE

25 DOLLARS
GIFT CERTIFICATE

> WEARABLES <

> STORAGE <

> SETS OF CDR'S AND CASES <

> PRE-DESIGNED SILKSCREENED CDR'S <

> CDR SET BUNDELS <

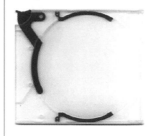
> CDR AND DVD CASES <

>> YOUR CUSTOM DESIGN
LEARN MORE ABOUT GETTING YOUR OWN CDR

>> CDR SAMPLER PACK
PICK ANY 10 CDR'S OF YOUR CHOICE FOR $15

>> SETS SAMPLER PACK
PICK ANY 10 SETS OF YOUR CHOICE FOR $30

>> THE FULL COLLECTION
INCLUDES ALL 53 SILKSCREENED CDR'S

>> THIS WEEKS SPECIAL
DISCOUNTED LIMITED TIME OFFERS

ALL DESIGNS ℗+© 2003 5INCH. 5INCH IS A SERVICE MARK OF T-26 AND SEGURA INC. T.26

GIFT CERTIFICATES | MAILING LIST | TELL A FRIEND | FAQ/HELP | LINKS | CUSTOM DESIGNS | POLICIES/LEGAL | CONTACT US

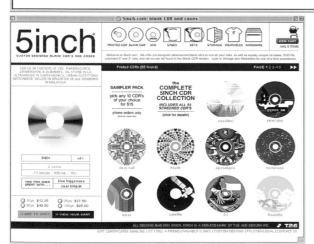

USA C

www.charlgrabe.co.za

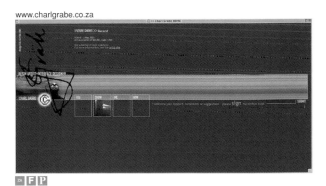

www.plusism.com

www.cubadust.com

www.designmuseum.org

http://users.yesmate.com/d2k

www.regleszero.com

www.inkgraphix.com

http://angeloplessas.com

a representation of my past clients / companies where I created / developed design strategies.

1 2 3 4 5   design

http://julien.moulin.free.fr

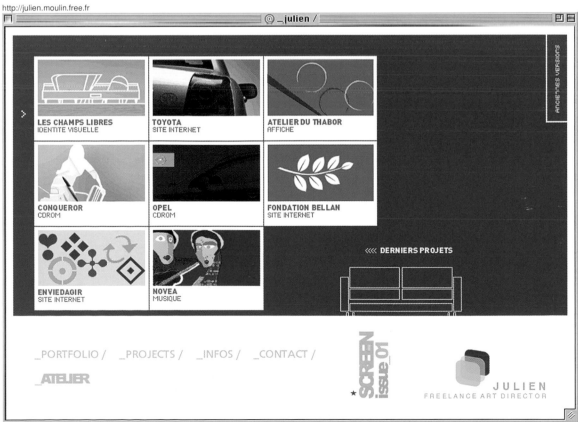

@ aaron braun

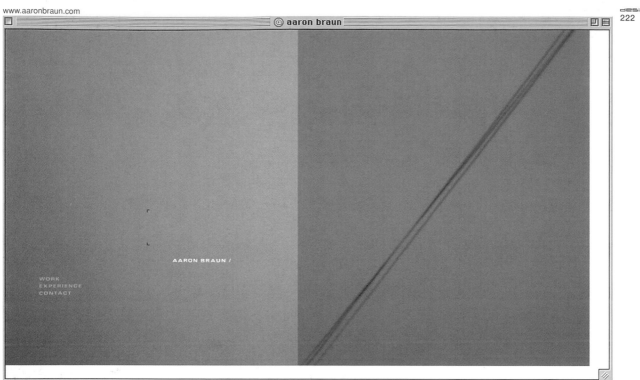

AARON BRAUN /

WORK
EXPERIENCE
CONTACT

@ aaron braun

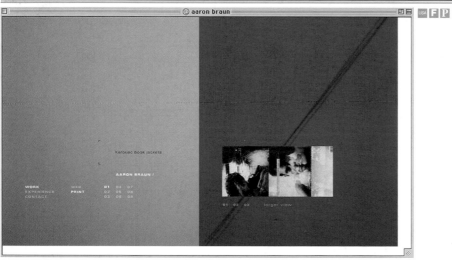

Kerouac book jackets

AARON BRAUN /

WORK	WEB	01	04	07
EXPERIENCE	PRINT	02	05	08
CONTACT		03	06	09

01 02 03   larger view

@ aaron braun

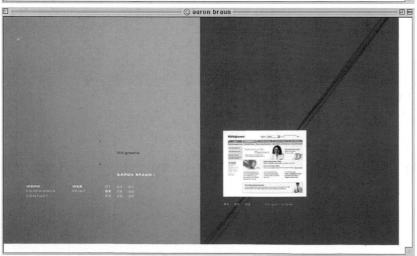

Walgreens

AARON BRAUN /

WORK	WEB	01	04	07
EXPERIENCE	PRINT	02	05	08
CONTACT		03	06	09

01 02 03   larger view

www.addis.com

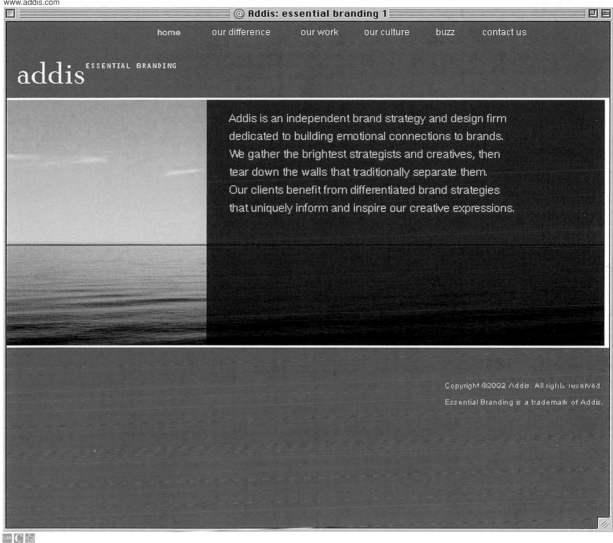

www.aestheticapparatus.com

www.amo.pl

www.amokone.com

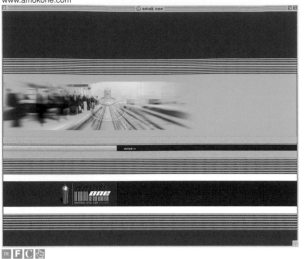

www.andreaskallbom.com

DE F C

SE F P

www.arabictypography.com

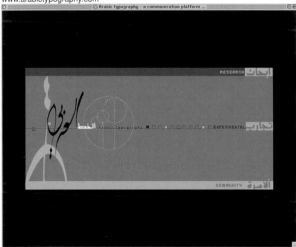

www.artxact.com

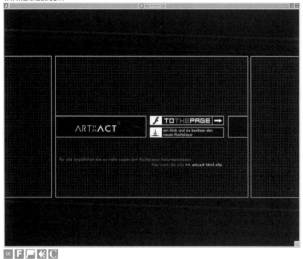

NL F I

DE F C

www.asmallpercent.com

www.asterikstudio.com

USA P

USA F C

www.astrostudios.com

http://atysdesign.com

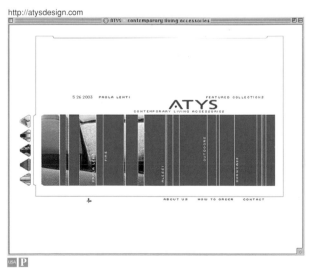

www.australiapresents.com

http://avocadolite.com

www.babysteps.tv

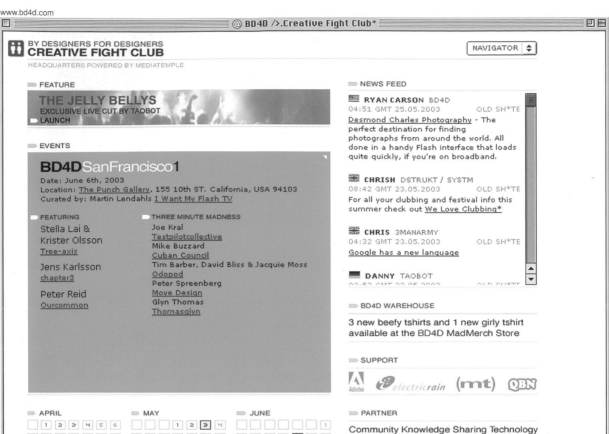

BY DESIGNERS FOR DESIGNERS
CREATIVE FIGHT CLUB

HEADQUARTERS POWERED BY MEDIATEMPLE

NAVIGATOR

FEATURE

THE JELLY BELLYS
EXCLUSIVE LIVE CUT BY TAOBOT
LAUNCH

EVENTS

BD4D SanFrancisco1

Date: June 6th, 2003
Location: The Punch Gallery, 155 10th ST, California, USA 94103
Curated by: Martin Lendahls I Want My Flash TV

FEATURING

Stella Lai &
Krister Olsson
Tree-axis

Jens Karlsson
chapter3

Peter Reid
Ourcommon

THREE MINUTE MADNESS

Joe Kral
Testpilotcollective
Mike Buzzard
Cuban Council
Tim Barber, David Bliss & Jacquie Moss
Odopod
Peter Spreenberg
Move Design
Glyn Thomas
Thomasglyn

NEWS FEED

RYAN CARSON BD4D
04:51 GMT 25.05.2003   OLD SH*TE
Desmond Charles Photography - The
perfect destination for finding
photographs from around the world. All
done in a handy Flash interface that loads
quite quickly, if you're on broadband.

CHRISH DSTRUKT / SYSTM
08:42 GMT 23.05.2003   OLD SH*TE
For all your clubbing and festival info this
summer check out We Love Clubbing*

CHRIS 3MANARMY
04:32 GMT 23.05.2003   OLD SH*TE
Google has a new language

DANNY TAOBOT
02:52 GMT 22.05.2003   OLD SH*TE

BD4D WAREHOUSE

3 new beefy tshirts and 1 new girly tshirt
available at the BD4D MadMerch Store

SUPPORT

Adobe   electricrain   (mt)   QBN

PARTNER

Community Knowledge Sharing Technology
Inspiration Ideas Networking Passion Fun
Voices That Matter
BD4D + New Riders

New
Riders

APRIL

1	2	3	4	5	6
7	8	9	10	11	12	13
14	15	16	17	18	19	20
21	22	23	24	25	26	27
28	29	30	31		

MAY

		1	2	3	4
5	6	7	8	9	10	11
12	13	14	15	16	17	18
19	20	21	22	23	24	25
26	27	28	29	30	31

JUNE

					1
2	3	4	5	6	7	8
9	10	11	12	13	14	15
16	17	18	19	20	21	22
23	24	25	26	27	28	29
30					

USA

Beautiful Information

Beautiful Information

Work   Play   Kontakt
              1 2 3 4 5 6 7 8 9 10 11 12

BGDI : Strategic Brand Solutions

BGDI
STRATEGIC BRAND SOLUTIONS

Company   Services   Solutions   News & Press   Clients   Contact Us

accelerating brands™

Build your
web
presence

Brand Guidance + Design

FEATURE ARTICLE

R.O.I and Some Observations
on the Darwinian Market Place

Identity, Image and Brand -
What Creates Value?

BGDI Creates Online
Buffer's Identity

MORE ABOUT...

BGDI Revenue Focused Programs

CNET News Video: BGDI Brands On-line
Companies

BGDI Names Web Start-up diCarta

BGDI Redesigned Business Portal
Solutions Company Verity

BRANDING   MARKETING   DESIGN   WEB

Job Opportunities

Client Access

USA

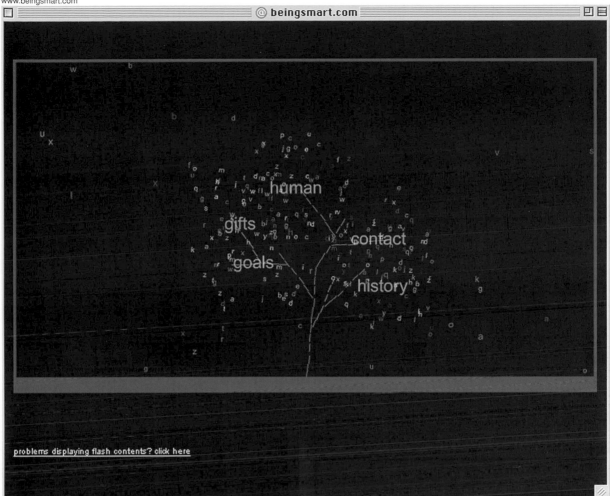

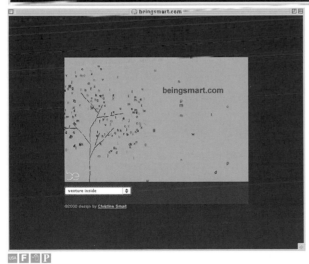

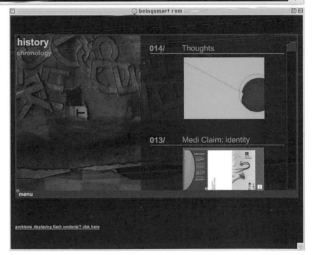

BIG CODE

GOOD DESIGN PUTS TECHNOLOGY TO WORK.

ENTER SITE

News

March 14, 2003
Here are a couple photography sites. Tim
Carpenter's Untitled And Unsung has some
great, subtle, quiet photography. And here
are some photos from Nat's trip to Japan.

February 1, 2003
Ongoing project Boom By Atom has been
launched. Watch the animated story every
month. Break the codes and win spy gear.
See the posters and Max Racks postcards
throughout New York City.

October 14, 2002
Thanks UAI Lab.

October 1, 2002
We've been busy these past few months. So
busy in fact we neglected updating this news
section. Here are some new projects:

HELLTHY entertainment is our
entertainment outlet. A new site. A new
magazine. New artists. Make sure you listen
to the radio. We also created a compilation
CD with MOJA DESIGN promoting their new
BOOM by Atom line of eyewear.

And speaking of MOJA DESIGN: take a look
at their new Big Code site: MOJA DESIGN.
Created with Rubenstein Technology Group.

Take a look at the portfolios our partners in
crime: the Sound of Snow.

Thanks to Net Inspiration and Visual
Orgasm for the support.

March 27, 2002
See the New York City 9.11.01 show
at the New York Historical Society
Museum. which is now showing. The project
documents people's feelings about the
events of Sept 11th through photographs
and words. Big Code created an interactive
kiosk that reveals the interviews conducted
by the New York City 9.11.01 project.

March 22, 2002
Check out the new musical addition to the
young Hellthy Entertainment family: The
Biscuit Boys. Site by Big Code.

March 15, 2002
Thanks for the support
NewsToday
ThreeOh
StyleBoost
HalfProject
Xpaider
StereoTypography
The Design Girl
Linkdup
No Limit Media
ChaoticRoots
RedCricket
9Zaku
HuriKuri
Yevknee
Visual Orgasm
Plastikon
Were-Here
Sticking Out Tongues
DigitalCulture
BMSON
MI3dot.org
Poows
Fimoculous
DeadBrains
I Love Everything
ArtEye
UltraShock
Digital Ultras
Design Box Set
Urbanoia
Flash-Up

March 11, 2002
Big Code has created a design-inspiration-
and-time-wasting tool we call the Content
Tower. We bring you great web sites every
time you open your browser. Experience
pretty sites, get enlightened with knowledge
like "How to hot wire a car," and much more.
Refresh often!

February 6, 2002
Big Code is creating an interactive kiosk for
the New York City 9.11.01 show at the New
York Historical Society. The project
documents people's feelings about the
events of Sept 11th through photographs
and words. Please come visit this project
this March at
the Historical Society Museum.

February 1, 2002
Welcome to the new site. Meet MegaPhil,
SARU-69 and the whole Big Code family. We
are still adding things here and there so
come back often. And enjoy.

Contact Us

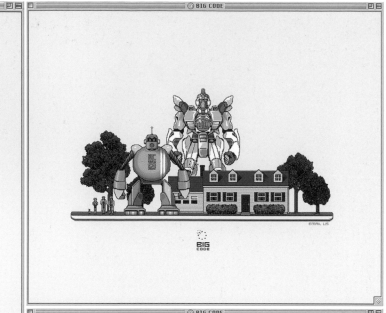

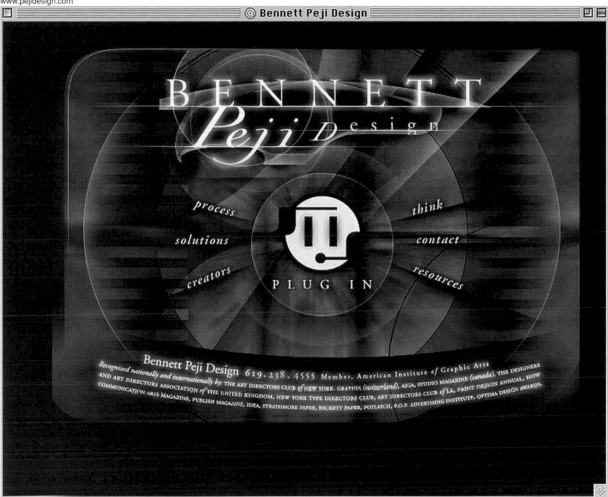

www.bludot.com

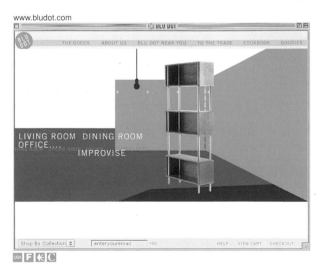

www.adenek.com

K portfolio v003.0"
ved

_Resume   _Contact

_Print   _Multimedia

Prvni Multimedialni   Volkswagen
Porsche   Tupe Strojarne
Citroen   Blank
Orange   MediaCom
Sony Mobile   Scomad
Inertia   CMS S

_Contact

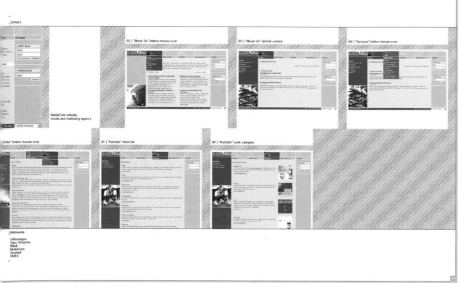

_Multimedia

Volkswagen
Tupe Strojarne
Blank
MediaCom
Scomad
CMS S

WLF OLÁ! LOCO LOB WONDER PIANO! BUY THE WAY

Brand Portal

TUTTO QUADRA.

created by olà!

www.brandequity.com

BrandEquity™

Creating Great Brands for Over Forty Years.....

www.bsur.com

bs ur.

01 | 00
ISSUE No 03
launch date 04 sep 01
published by bsur

flash 5/dhtml version*
* netscape 6 and internet explorer do not fully support the flash 5 plugin,
please visit our site with netscape 4

or visit the dhtml version

bsur sample

or visit

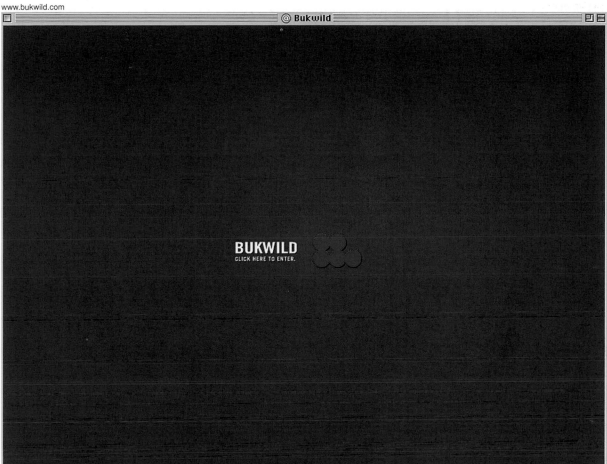

BUKWILD
CLICK HERE TO ENTER.

9.13.03 We have been selected to develop the online identity for award-winning sound designer, Bongo Post, whose client list includes; NBC, Disney, Warner Bros. and so on. We look forward to an innovative site.

5.7.03 We added the new "rap" theme today. Let us know what you think. We also added an awards section, and updated the portfolio with a ton of new-ish work. Oh, and we also made the sites in the portfolio linkable...finally. Enjoy.

5.6.03 Bukwild has been chosen to re-develop record company Geles Record's website. This is going to be a ground breaking label site, check for it in the next couple months.

5.6.03 We will be developing new sites for hip hop artists DJ Maq, and Verbs. Look for them in the next several weeks.

5.5.03 Great news! Bukwild was just awarded the respected FWA award for the Reliant K site. You can check it out here. Thanks FWA.

RECENT ▓ NEWS

HOME STUDIO PORTFOLIO

NEWS THEME

BUKWILD
DESIGN. DEVELOPMENT.

HOME STUDIO PORTFOLIO

WEB INTERACTIVE PRINT IDENTITY

BUKWILD
DESIGN. DEVELOPMENT.

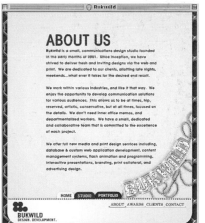

ABOUT US

Bukwild is a small, communications design studio founded in the early months of 2001. Since inception, we have strived to deliver fresh and inviting designs via the web and print. We are dedicated to our clients, allotting late nights, weekends...what ever it takes for the desired end result.

We work within various industries, and like it that way. We enjoy the opportunity to develop communication solutions for various audiences. This allows us to be at times, hip, reserved, artistic, conservative, but at all times, focused on the details. We don't need inner office memos, and departmentalized workers. We have a small, dedicated and collaborative team that is committed to the excellence of each project.

We offer full new media and print design services including, database & custom web application development, content management systems, flash animation and programming, interactive presentations, branding, print collateral, and advertising design.

HOME STUDIO PORTFOLIO

ABOUT AWARDS CLIENTS CONTACT

BUKWILD
DESIGN. DEVELOPMENT.

www.cdesigngrafico.com.br

BR F C

www.craigkroeger.com

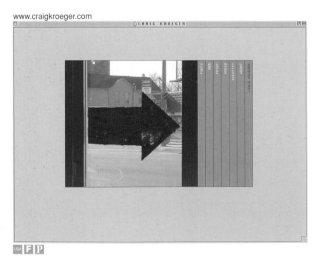

USA F P

www.trashlab.net/chris

SE P

@ sense-net

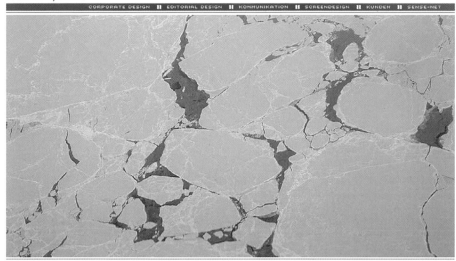

SENSE/NET

CORPORATE DESIGN ▌ EDITORIAL DESIGN ▌ KOMMUNIKATION ▌ SCREENDESIGN ▌ KUNDEN ▌ SENSE-NET

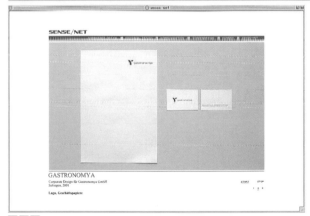

GASTRONOMYA
Corporate Design für Gastronomya GmbH
Solingen, 2001

Logo, Geschäftspapiere

START   STOP
1 2 3

CM4all
Postkarten, Folder, Anzeigen, Plakate,
Beschriftung Messestand

Verschiedene Formate

START   STOP
1 2 3 4 5 6 7 8

@ 8EDGE.COM

SKIP INTRODUCTION

USA F P

www.crockerinc.com

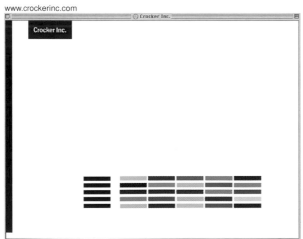

Crocker Inc.

USA F C

www.d2m-inc.com

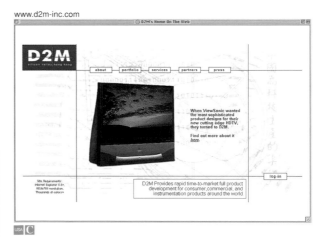

D2M
silicon valley, hong kong

about   portfolio   services   partners   press

When ViewSonic wanted
the most sophisticated
product designs for their
new cutting edge HDTV,
they turned to D2M.

Find out more about it
here.

log-in

Site Requirements:
Internet Explorer 5.5+,
1024x768 resolution,
Thousands of colors+

D2M Provides rapid time-to-market full product
development for consumer, commercial, and
instrumentation products around the world

USA C

© DESIGN MADE IN GERMANY

Design made in Germany

News

Forum

Links

Köpfe

Webcams

Impressum

Mediadaten

Personalisierung

Vorname Nachname

••••••••

>

Registrieren

Werbung

Aktuelles

Every Day Life

Webseiten

R9005 Designportal

Spotleid

Photocase

Designbooks

Bigsexyland

Public Relation Services

DSPR

Hosting Services

Notraffic Webserver

Zeitschriftenabonnements

Der Spiegel

Börse Online

Capital

FOCUS

Focus Money

Manager

Stern

Wirtschaftswoche

Chip

Art

Die Welt

Welt am Sonntag

Financial Times Deutschland

Die Zeit

Finanzen

Kreditkarte Students

Kreditkarte Classic

Kreditkarte Business

Kreditkarte Gold

Newsmagazin

Aktuelle Magazinartikel:

MX-Magazin: Interview mit Stefan D'Amore (Verleger)

Redesign clan.drei: Interview mit Kai Brunning (Geschäftsführer/CD)

Cebit 2003: Bericht/Kommentar von Torsten Bergler

Strukt #1: Buchreview von Torsten Bergler

R9005 Designportal: Interview mit Joanna Nottebrock (Verantwortlich)

Persönliches
Tanja Kimme (1)

Tanja Kimme, eigentlich aus Deutschland - lebt aber im Moment in Sydney, ist eingeladen worden Ende des jahrens in Berlin Ihre Arbeiten auszustellen. Zur finanzierung verkauft sie CDs mit 20 von ihren Fotos fuer 15$. Die Fotos sind Royality Free!

http://www.australianinfront.com.au/tanjakimme

Surftipps
planetjump (4)

mal wieder was neues aus deutschland...

http://www.planetjump.de

Surftipps
Schöne Fotos ... (1)

findet man man im Portfolio des Fotografen Jörn Lies ... besonders interessant die Zoo/Tierpark-Fotos ...

check !

http://www.timescapes.de

Surftipps
3D Games... (1)

Das ist jetzt schon ziemlich krass... man kennt es zwar von den Osbournes, ich find das trotzdem end faszinierend.

http://www.shipoffools.com/theark/enter.php

Surftipps
Todd Hido (8)

atmosphäre.pur

http://www.toddhido.com

Surftipps
Loretta Lux (5)

aussagekräftige people photos

http://www.lorettalux.de

Surftipps
Desmond Charles (2)

Super. Und vor allem unheimlich viel. Gefiel mir.

Newstodaylink

http://www.desmondcharles.com/main.html

Surftipps
code4me (13)

nun doch noch online nach langer zeit...

http://www.code4me.net

Surftipps
BERLIN GOLD (0)

beim surfen entdeckt und vorher nicht gekannt, ein berliner büro mit sehenswerten arbeiten.

http://www.berlin-gold.de

Surftipps
Sueddeutsche.de (4)

Sueddeutsche.de Redesign

http://www.sueddeutsche.de

Ältere News

News suchen

Stichwort

>

Newsletter

Email

⦿ eintragen ◯ austragen

>

DESIGNFORFREEDOM™
BUILT
DESIGN
VERSION_00.2.1
START

This is a silent launch of the Freedom Project. We decided to finish the running of the project with our own submission. This was something we took very serious, being the ones who have asked so many to share their idea of "freedom" with us artistically. Over the last year we have conceptualised a book to be made in limited quantity, hand produced and given to friends. This book has finally become a reality to us. This wouldn't have been possible without the contributions of many friends. Thank you to all who have helped and supported us, we are very grateful.

DFF

We would like to thank everyone who made our first BD4D a great success. We had a great night with 756 of our closest friends. If you were not able to make it you can see what you missed here. Big up to Olivier at SUBSTITUD for putting together this great mini-site.

DFF POSTER We are very happy to see the poster we organized for the computerlove design contest available to the public. Have a look at the great job computerlove did with the posters.

Kozy n Dan have just launched Lucky Disc! Some super hot CDR's available there. And you should check out their store while you are at it.

FREEDOM PROJECT_

Give a group of designers one goal. To create art that expresses FREEDOM to them. Whatever they want, as long as it can be displayed on the screen.

SCHEDULED ARTISTS_

DESIGNFORFREEDOM

PRESENTATION_LOCATION
DISPLAY

+DFF:
+
We express our freedom by creating this book with and for our friends. Not letting challenges stop us from doing what we want.

We are grateful for our freedoms.
Freedom to communicate.
Freedom to express.
Freedom to inspire.
Freedom to create.
Freedom to love.

Freedom is individual.

POINT.

POINT

VIEW BOOK

VIEW MOVIE (LO-RES)
VIEW MOVIE (HI-RES)

_LOCATION: _USA.ATLANTA
_TIME: Mon May 26 07:39:23 GMT+0200 2003
_33° 39' N _84° 26' W

DEMONSTRATION
EXPRESS.FREEDOM

ARCHIVE.

ON DISPLAY_

On Feb21st DFF hosted BD4D Atlanta.
We would like to share the experience with all of you.

CREATE.BEAUTIFUL.THINGS

VIEW_PROJECT
EXTERNAL

SCOUTT_

DFF™ is proud to present SCOUTT.
In an attempt to document what happens around us and in our lives, we have created this online presentation. Future release will be available as content is created.

SCOUTT is a production of the DFF™ minds.

VIEW_PROJECT
LOCAL

ARCHIVE.

CALENDAR PROJECT_

To promote web artists who create beautiful things.
We will feature the work of one artist everyday for a year.
Help us to strengthen the global design community.

VIEW_PROJECT
EXTERNAL

TODAYS FEATURED ARTIST_

DISPLAY PREVIEW_

MISSION.STATEMENT
_

Design for Freedom seeks to impact the future by exploring art and design as vehicles for communicating passion, creativity, viewpoint, perspective, need, awareness, involvement, contribution and community. We will provide a platform for artists to present their creations. We are passionate about what we do, and hope to help others, and ourselves feed that passion. We strive for total creative freedom.

design_develop_create

CONTACT.

THE FREEDOM PROJECT™ 2002

DEVELOPED FOR LOVE

HOSTING

Acta Divina

PEER 1 NETWORK

DESIGN.FOR.FREEDOM IS SPONSORED BY:

© Designgraphik™

Users currently on = **0**

Designgraphik™   Proud Division of WeWorkForThem™   Super Nice Hosting by **MediaTemple**™

Subject   **<<Artwork**

Review   Information

About   Designgraphik™:
Latest News
Achievements   First off we would like that thank those of you who have been
Join Our Newsletter   following Designgraphik since 1998. Without the support and constant
Contact Us   support weather it be positive or negative, we could have not made it
          here without it.
Buy Our Products
          Designgraphik is an online sketch book that I (Michael Young) started
          in 1998. I started this site as a way to express my ideas, techniques,
          concepts, and styles in which I was not able to execute to my fullest
          in my everyday commercial employment. Since 1998 I have created
          six versions, this current version being number six in the lineup. Four
          of the past six versions always consisted of a large group of work
          that was released as one entire version, similar to how a musician
          might release a compact disc with 12 tracks to complete the release.
          In version five I changed my outlook on this, and enjoyed the fact the
          web gave me the chance to update whenever I liked. I then developed
          an interface that would allow for updating the site with new works
          whenever I pleased. I could update my interface 20 times a week with
          new work, or I could just never update it. This interface was great for
          me personally, but to the viewers it was unsuccessful. This was
          because visually it was too abstract for the majority of Designgraphik
          visitors to even know it had been updated.

          After all these lessons, nightmares, and advancements it has led me
          to this current sixth version, titled DGVI. With this current version I
          hope to always find ways to improve not only my artwork, but also
          the way in which the site provides information about the artwork.
          Over time you might notice features added, deleted, or improved to
          help better present the work. I did not create this interface to be what
          lured people to Designgraphik like I did in past versions. Yet I created it
          to be what helped viewers easily navigate all the artwork and its
          information in a straight forward manner.

          The artwork posted in this sixth version will be created not only be me
          Michael Young. I will be posting a huge amount of published and
          unpublished work that has been created by WeWorkForThem™.
          WeWorkForThem™ is the art and design agency that Michael Cina
          and I created in 2001. The information posted for each work will
          express if the work was a joint effort, or if it was an execution of my
          own. Ever since the year 2001, 99% of my work has been a full
          collaborative effort with Michael Cina under the WeWorkForThem™
          name. Since this has happened, you will hardly ever find me taking full
          credit for most the work that is published on Designgraphik.

          I will continue to post work in version six as time permits me too. The
          work on Designgraphik is not a commercial portfolio, but yet more of a
          personal diary, sketchbook, gallery, and collection of published and
          unpublished works I have chosen to present.

          If you are interested in wanting to view any of the old versions of
          Designgraphik or Submethod, you can buy them as apart of the **One**
          book+cdrom. You can preview and purchase this item at:
          YouWorkForThem

          To view our commercial portfolio,
          visit the main division **WeWorkForThem**™.

          If you are interested in buying any art and products that we make,
          you can buy them from our secure online store **YouWorkForThem**.

          (mt)   Super Nice Hosting by **MediaTemple**™

Everyday

DU

DesignUnion

1561 S. Barrington Ave.
Suite 104
Los Angeles, CA 90025

info@designunion.net

Enter

Flash 5 Plug-in Required

USA F C

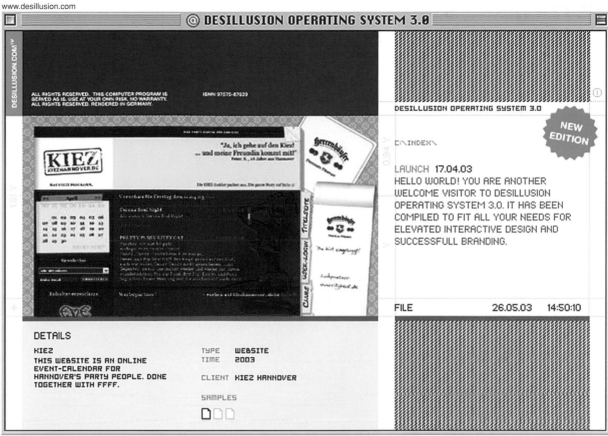

DESILLUSION OPERATING SYSTEM 3.0

C:\INDEX\

LAUNCH 17.04.03
HELLO WORLD! YOU ARE ANOTHER
WELCOME VISITOR TO DESILLUSION
OPERATING SYSTEM 3.0. IT HAS BEEN
COMPILED TO FIT ALL YOUR NEEDS FOR
ELEVATED INTERACTIVE DESIGN AND
SUCCESSFULL BRANDING.

FILE   26.05.03   14:50:10

DETAILS

KIEZ
THIS WEBSITE IS AN ONLINE
EVENT-CALENDAR FOR
HANNOVER'S PARTY PEOPLE. DONE
TOGETHER WITH FFFF.

TYPE   WEBSITE
TIME   2003

CLIENT KIEZ HANNOVER

SAMPLES

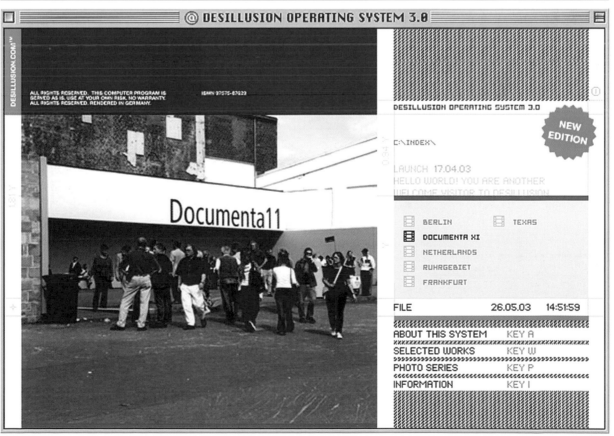

DESILLUSION OPERATING SYSTEM 3.0

C:\INDEX\

LAUNCH 17.04.03
HELLO WORLD! YOU ARE ANOTHER
WELCOME VISITOR TO DESILLUSION

BERLIN   TEXAS
DOCUMENTA XI
NETHERLANDS
RUHRGEBIET
FRANKFURT

FILE   26.05.03   14:51:59

ABOUT THIS SYSTEM   KEY A
SELECTED WORKS   KEY W
PHOTO SERIES   KEY P
INFORMATION   KEY I

AU
SYDNEY/APRIL
MELBOURNE

THANKS AUSTRALIA / BE BACK SOON   CONTACT

100X100 PROJECT >   OLD SHITE >

www.dieselprint.com

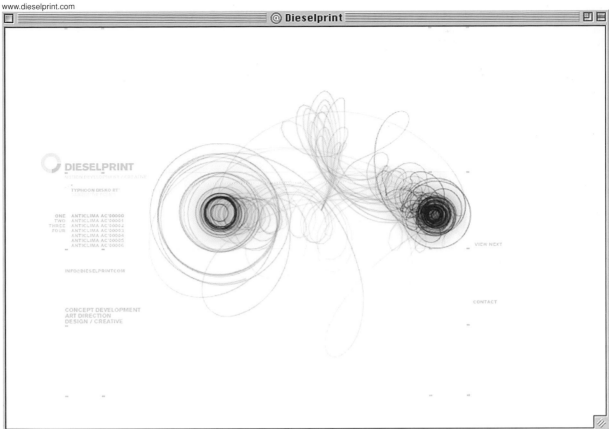

www.dinnickandhowells.com

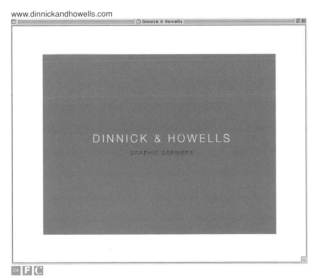

http://ycrop.com/

all works copyright © 1997–2003 dhky   + contact

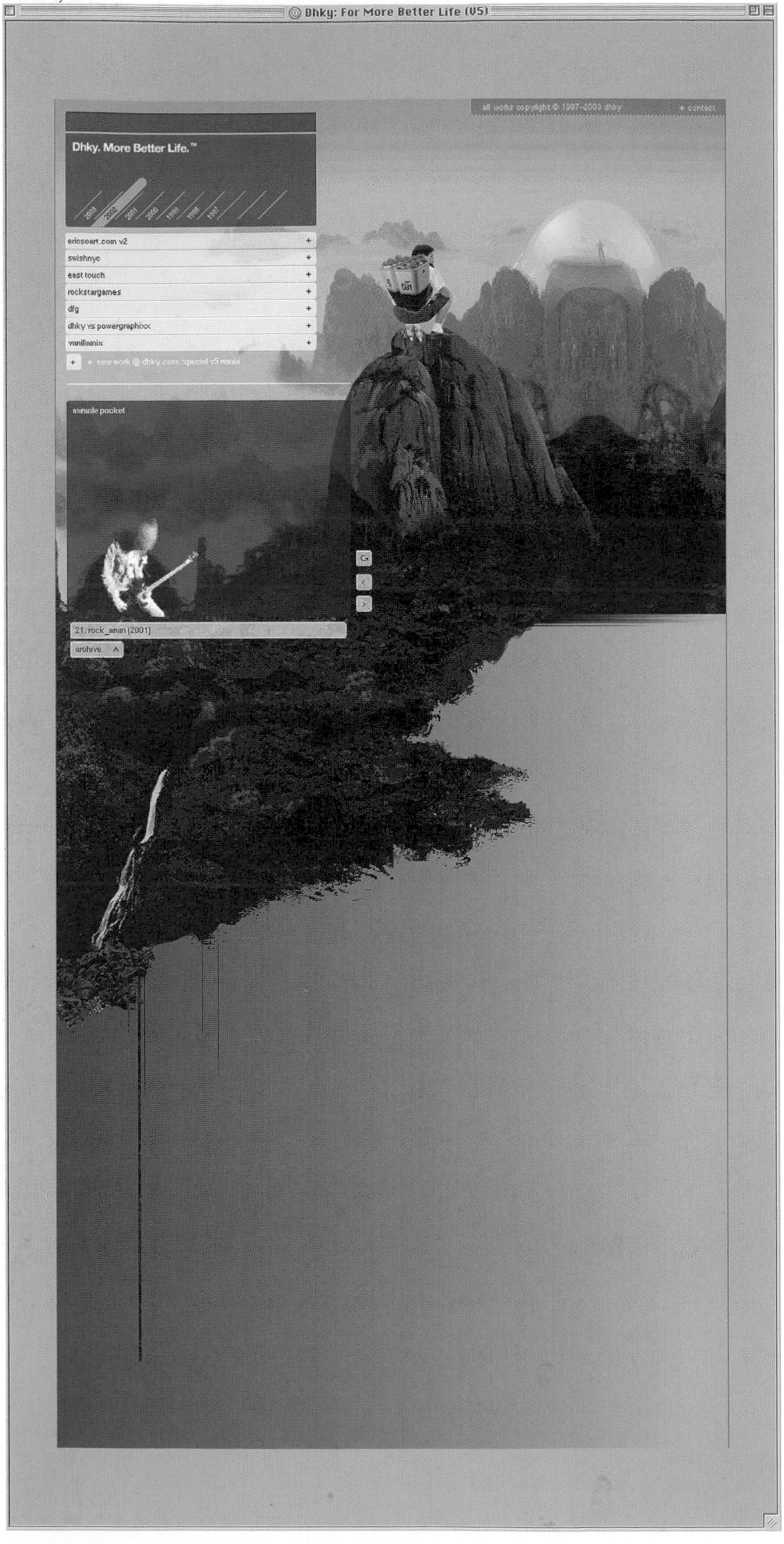

Dhky. More Better Life.™

ericsoert.com v2   +
swishnyc   +
east touch   +
rockstargames   +
dfg   +
dhky vs powergraphixx   +
vanillamix   +

+   » new work @ dhky.com. special v5 remix

mimale pocket

21. rock_arian (2001)

archive   ^

www.singlecell.org

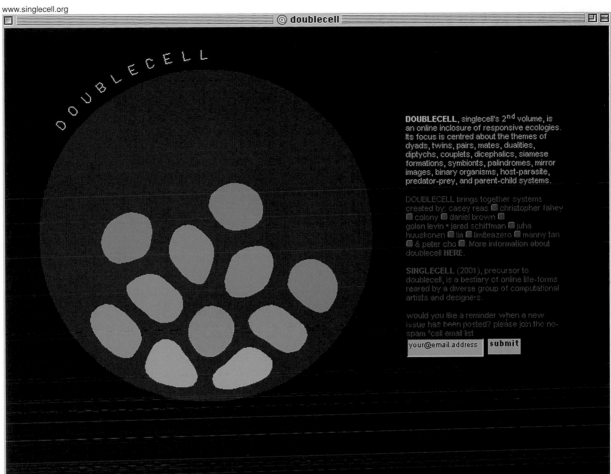

DOUBLECELL, singlecell's 2nd volume, is an online inclosure of responsive ecologies. Its focus is centred about the themes of dyads, twins, pairs, mates, dualities, diptychs, couplets, dicephalics, siamese formations, symbionts, palindromes, mirror images, binary organisms, host-parasite, predator-prey, and parent-child systems.

DOUBLECELL brings together systems created by: casey reas ■ christopher fahey ■ colony ■ daniel brown ■ golan levin * jared schiffman ■ juha huuskonen ■ lia ■ limiteazero ■ manny tan ■ & peter cho ■. More information about doublecell HERE.

SINGLECELL (2001), precursor to doublecell, is a bestiary of online life-forms reared by a diverse group of computational artists and designers.

would you like a reminder when a new issue has been posted? please join the no-spam *cell email list

your@email.address   submit

www.abnormalbehaviorchild.com

www.dumper.no

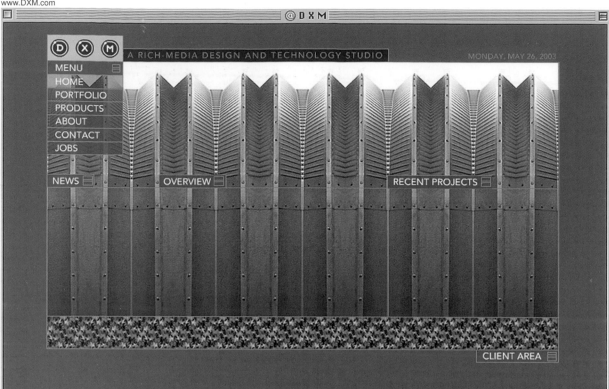

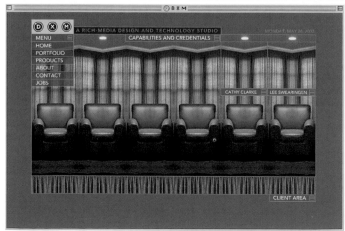

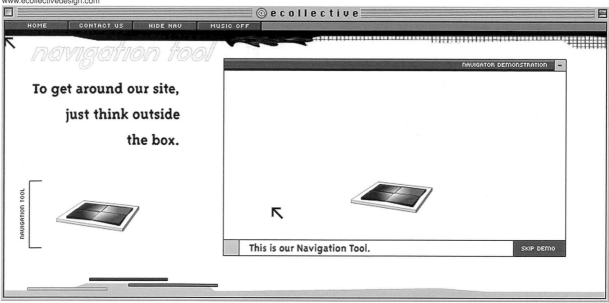

To get around our site,
just think outside
the box.

This is our Navigation Tool.

SKIP DEMO

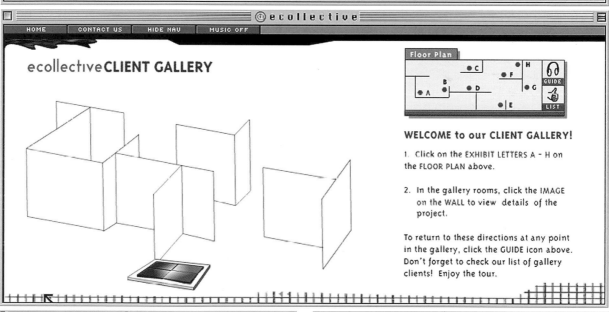

ecollective**CLIENT GALLERY**

Floor Plan

WELCOME to our CLIENT GALLERY!

1. Click on the EXHIBIT LETTERS A – H on the FLOOR PLAN above.

2. In the gallery rooms, click the IMAGE on the WALL to view details of the project.

To return to these directions at any point in the gallery, click the GUIDE icon above. Don't forget to check our list of gallery clients! Enjoy the tour.

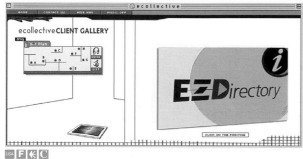

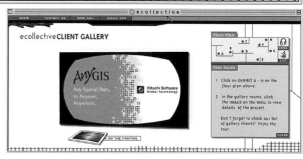

www.8plus9.com

USA F K C

www.emptydrome.com

CR F K C

www.evolutiontwo.com

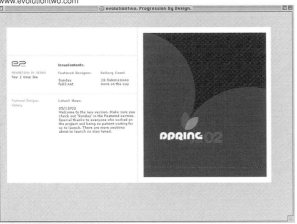

USA F F K I

www.evskion.de

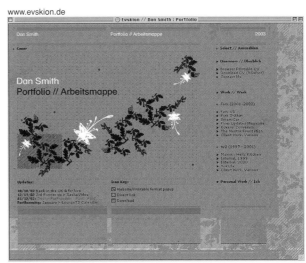

UK F P

www.exile.com.au

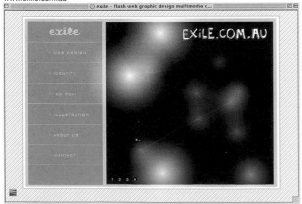

AU F C

www.enterexit.co.uk

UK F K C

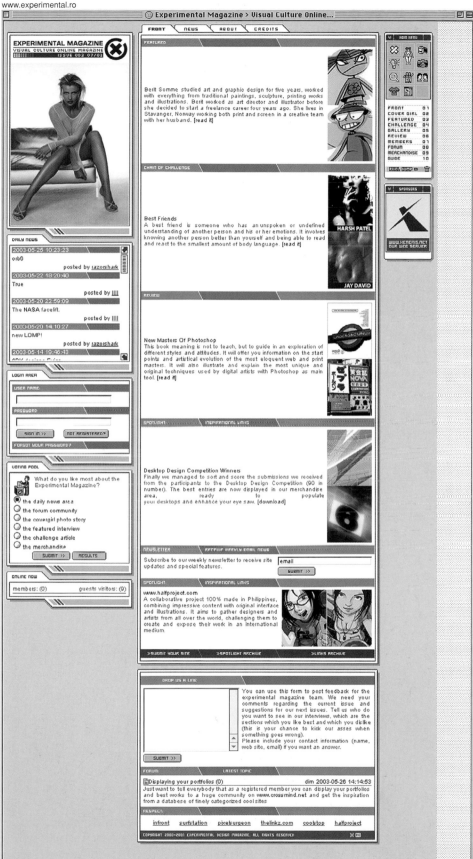

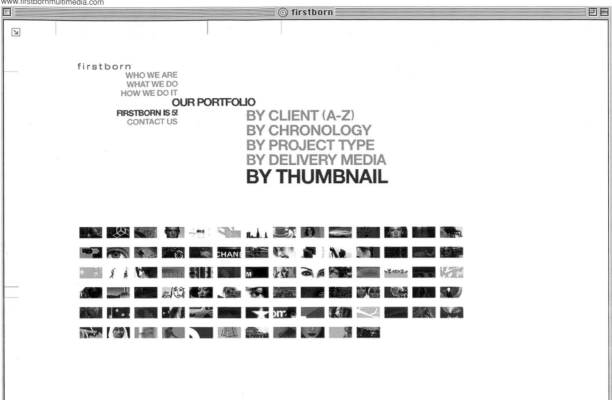

@ firstborn

firstborn

WHO WE ARE
WHAT WE DO
HOW WE DO IT

OUR PORTFOLIO

FIRSTBORN IS 5!
CONTACT US

BY CLIENT (A-Z)
BY CHRONOLOGY
BY PROJECT TYPE
BY DELIVERY MEDIA
BY THUMBNAIL

www.clusta.com

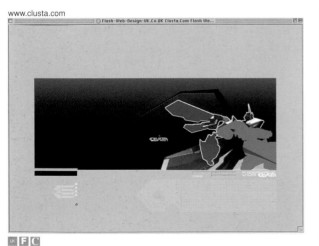

www.frontmedia.co.uk

" Initial consultation gave us the confidence to choose
them as a long-term partner. Frontmedia have been
a model supplier. They were very willing, nothing was
impossible, technically excellent and quickly
understood our business and systems requirements. "

Ketan Patel, Business Analyst, Aveva Group PLC.

are you looking for **anything in particular**?

web design
print
client list
ideas
us

frontmedia

T : +44 (0)1245 266684   E : info@frontmedia.co.uk

http://gridplane.com

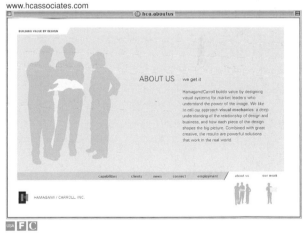

www.hcassociates.com

@ harald peter ström

| ARTON.NU | GRAND RECORDINGS | WEBBOKEN2000 | ABOUT, CONTACT
| BURNFIELD | PLUXEMBURG | | EXPLANATIONS &
| HEJ EUROPA | PLUXUS | | BRAG
| FLUORTANTEN | ROLE MODEL | OTHER PROJECTS |
| FRANKOSAUR.COM | SPEEDWAY | MISC THINGS | HOME

PREV

NEXT

WELCOME!

This is some selected work from me, peter ström – enjoy. And contact me for freelance work – i'll do anything for ca$h.

LATEST NEWS

2003.04.17
Major update!
Frankosaur – Finally online! A project i started almost a year ago is finally (more or less at least...) finished and put online.

Misc Things – A new section with a lot of different stuff. From "real" projects and illustrations to sketches and such.

Other projects – Updated with a preview of the work i did for the new Djuice-site, aswell as a flyer illustration I did for LSU.

Pluxemburg – Updated with an ad in Sex Magazine (click to number 4) and the old business cards we made 2 years ago.

Burnfield – A spread for a hong kong magazine on the theme animals, together with Martin.

+ I have also added some things to this page, such as links! Look to the right »

SHORTCUTS

NEWSLETTER

Sign up to recieve great news from me!

my@emailadress   OK!

LINKS

Friends etc	Music	Looks good
Baby	APC	Meomi
Karin	Beans	Syruphelsinki
Mattias	Kompakt Rec.	Indian covers
Stefan	Gigolo Rec.	
Ben	K7! Rec.	**Important**
Benninge	Swayzak	M Moore
Daniel	Legowelt	Antiwar.com
Oskar	Puppetmstz	Amnesty
Farsan	Kitty-yo	
Jmy	Martini Brös	
Miika	Bpitchcntrl	
Samuel	Superpitcher	
Ola	Forte Rec.	
Sporty	Pluxemburg	

@ harald peter ström

SE F P

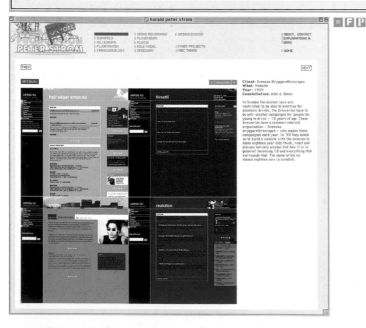

NEW

mic
SING IN THE SHOoOOOoOWER

CREATION EDITION

SHOW ROOM 17 RUE LAMBERT — 75018 PARIS

ENTER

BEST WITH INTERNET EXPLORER

ATYPYK

ATYPYK::GREETINGS

FR F C

GREETINGS !

CHOOSE : GRADUATION, MOTHER'S DAY, FATHER'S DAY, CHRISTMAS, NEW YEAR, VALENTINE'S DAY, BIRTHDAY, NEW BORN, WEDDING, RETIREMENT.
AND SEND.

SIZE : DIAM. 18 CM (POST CARD)
NEXT

Products...

CREATION EDITION

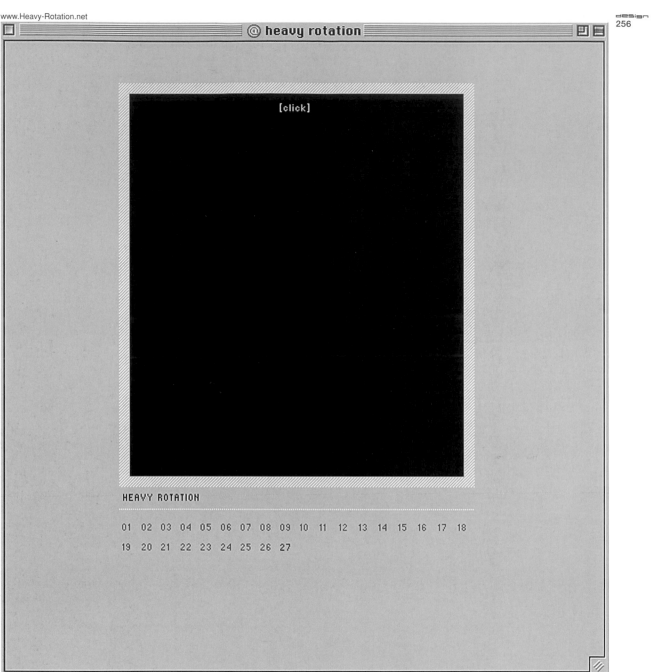

@ heavy rotation

[click]

HEAVY ROTATION

01 02 03 04 05 06 07 08 09 10 11 12 13 14 15 16 17 18
19 20 21 22 23 24 25 26 27

www.heine-lenz-zizka.com

http://www.kyamk.fi/~vi9gvisa/Index2.html

@ home1

Un petit air de loft new-yorkais. Telle est la première impression que l'on a en pénétrant d'espace, donnant à l'endroit une atmosphère à la fois chaleureuse

ESSENCEDESIGN
INFORMATION
INTERACTION
CORPORATE
_DESIGN

◄ ENTER BUT YOU NEED FLASH 5

◄ QUICK VIEW NO FLASH REQUIRED

◄ **OUT NOW**

NESCAFE
35MM ADVERT.

HOPITAL DE L'ENFANCE
ANNUAL REPORT 2001

SAPHIR WERK
INSTITUTIONAL IMAGERY

EUROWATT COMMERCE
NEW FLASH INTRO

F1   F2 F8   RR

◄ GRAND PONT 2B
CH-1003 LAUSANNE
SWITZERLAND
++ 41 21 343 24 13
INFO@ESSENCE.CH

@ +essencedesign--

SELF-EXPRESSION   F1   F2

CONDITION   ABOUT   ESSENCEGALLERY

350 M2

MIXED
MODE

01/1

CORPORATE
INFORMATION
INTERACTION
_DESIGN

-UG
GALLERY
SOFA
CONTACT

1

Sound off

LF-EXPRESSION

F1

F2

ABOUT

ESSENCEGALLERY

VMFP-3

AF931
VELOCITE ENGINE

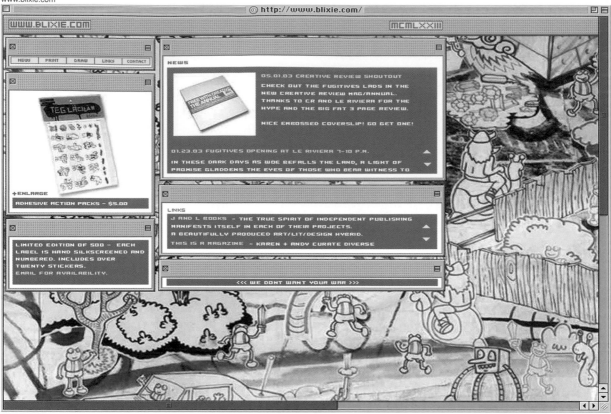

English   Français   Italiano   Deutsch   РУССКИЙ

Design by Web-Workstyle 2002

@ **http://www.smartdesignusa.com/flash.html**

smart is   smart does   smart now   get smart

SMART   DESIGN

www.inkbytedesign.com

inkbyte design inc. — graphic...

ABOUT US   OUR WORK   CONTACT US

we do design.

inkbyte design

We are a small print and web studio that specializes in creating excellent design solutions to help you succeed.

Take a look around. You'll see what we mean.

we listen

©2003 Inkbyte Design, Inc. All Rights Reserved

www.ideo.com

ideo.com

IDEO helps companies innovate.
We design products, services, environments, and interactions.

Enter IDEO

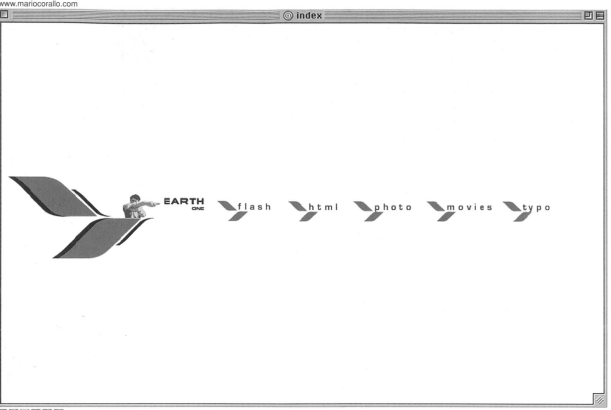

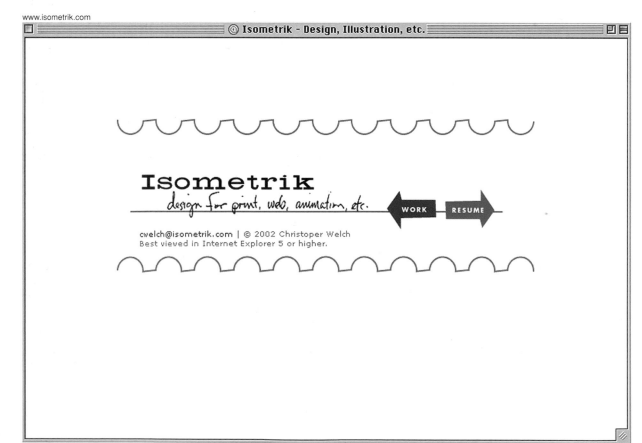

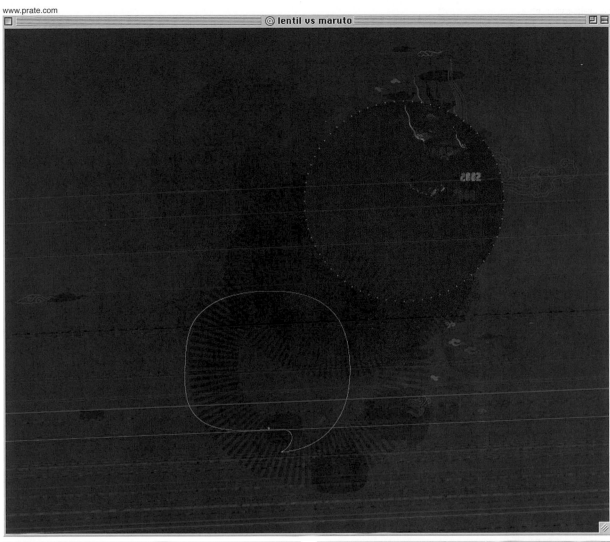

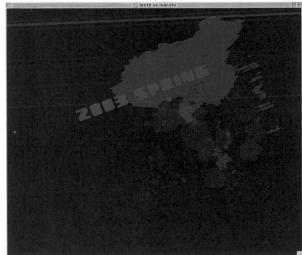

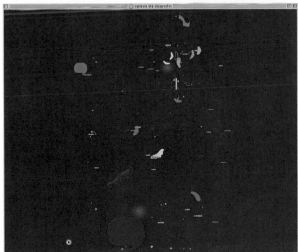

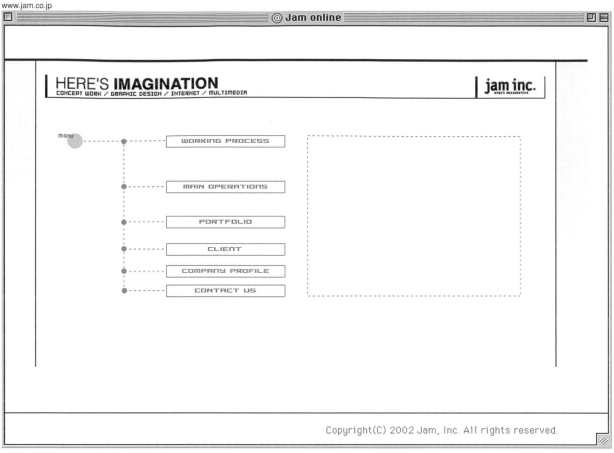

HERE'S **IMAGINATION**
CONCEPT WORK / GRAPHIC DESIGN / INTERNET / MULTIMEDIA

jam inc.

menu

- WORKING PROCESS
- MAIN OPERATIONS
- PORTFOLIO
- CLIENT
- COMPANY PROFILE
- CONTACT US

HERE'S **IMAGINATION**
CONCEPT WORK / GRAPHIC DESIGN / INTERNET / MULTIMEDIA

jam inc.

WORKING PROCESS | MAIN OPERATIONS | PORTFOLIO | CLIENT | COMPANY PROFILE | CONTACT US

Working Process

[design] – デザインとは考え方

私たちがご提案させて頂く商品は創造（考え方）。
そのツールが本当に最も効果的な手段であるか？
最終的な目的のためには他の方法は無いのか？

煩雑な情報化社会の中でシンプルで効果的な考え方。

一つのツールを制作するにあたり私たちはプロジェクトを立て、
利用シーンを創造し、様々なメディアとのコラボレーションを構築して、
最も効果的なツールのご提案をさせていただきます。

HERE'S **IMAGINATION**
CONCEPT WORK / GRAPHIC DESIGN / INTERNET / MULTIMEDIA

jam inc.

WORKING PROCESS | MAIN OPERATIONS | PORTFOLIO | CLIENT | COMPANY PROFILE | CONTACT US

Portfolio

キャンペーン企画・運営

ロゴマーク/C企画
1 | 2 | 3 | 4 | 5

キャラクター制作
会社案内
パンフレット・カタログ
パッケージ／包装デザイン
インターネット・マルチメディア関連
空間プロデュース
各種イベント
ノベルティ

CLIENT:
医療法人　治仁会
のぞみの丘ホスピタル

PROJECT:
建設ロゴ

DATE:
2002 –

のぞみの丘ホスピタル

@ **johncrumpton.com**

johncrumpton
works/profile/contact

www.kaliforniarepublik.com

@ KALIFORNIAREPUBLIK V.6.

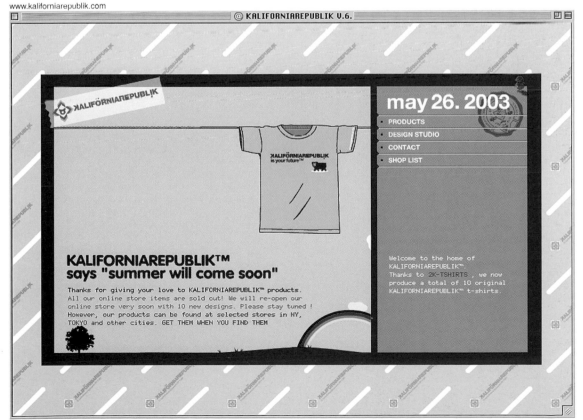

USA F K C

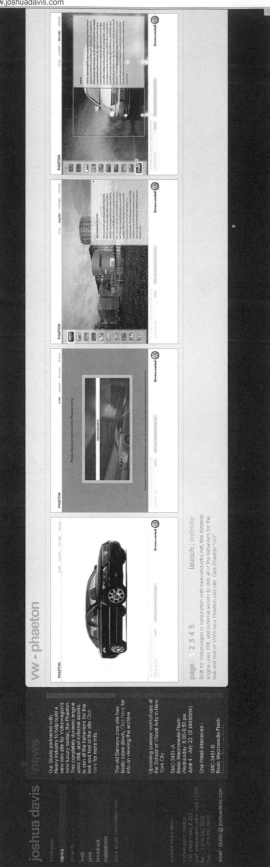

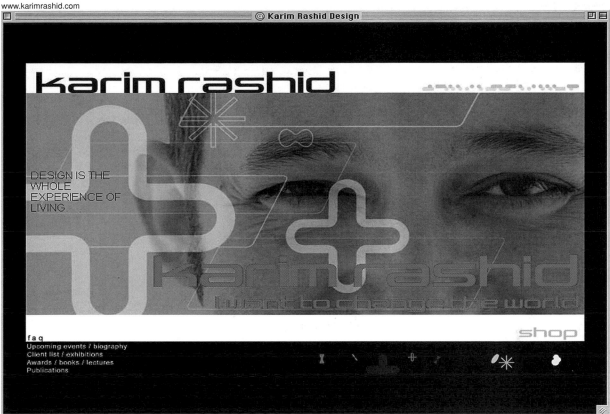

DESIGN IS THE
WHOLE
EXPERIENCE OF
LIVING.

f a q
Upcoming events / biography
Client list / exhibitions
Awards / books / lectures
Publications

shop

USA F C

www.knoll.com/a3i/

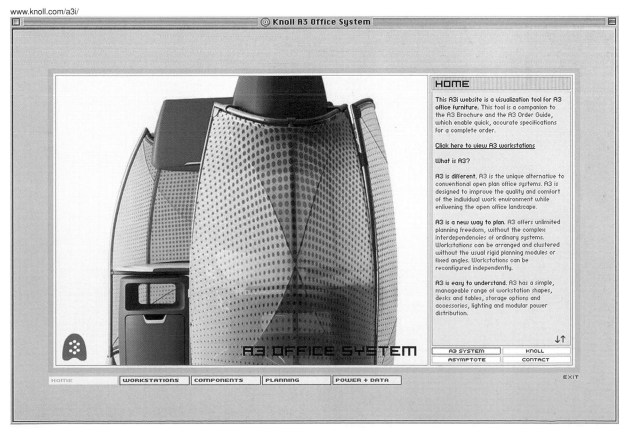

HOME

This A3i website is a visualization tool for A3 office furniture. This tool is a companion to the A3 Brochure and the A3 Order Guide, which enable quick, accurate specifications for a complete order.

Click here to view A3 workstations

What is A3?

A3 is different. A3 is the unique alternative to conventional open plan office systems. A3 is designed to improve the quality and comfort of the individual work environment while enlivening the open office landscape.

A3 is a new way to plan. A3 offers unlimited planning freedom, without the complex interdependencies of ordinary systems. Workstations can be arranged and clustered without the usual rigid planning modules or fixed angles. Workstations can be reconfigured independently.

A3 is easy to understand. A3 has a simple, manageable range of workstation shapes, desks and tables, storage options and accessories, lighting and modular power distribution.

| A3 SYSTEM | KNOLL |
| ASYMPTOTE | CONTACT |

| HOME | WORKSTATIONS | COMPONENTS | PLANNING | POWER + DATA | EXIT |

USA F C

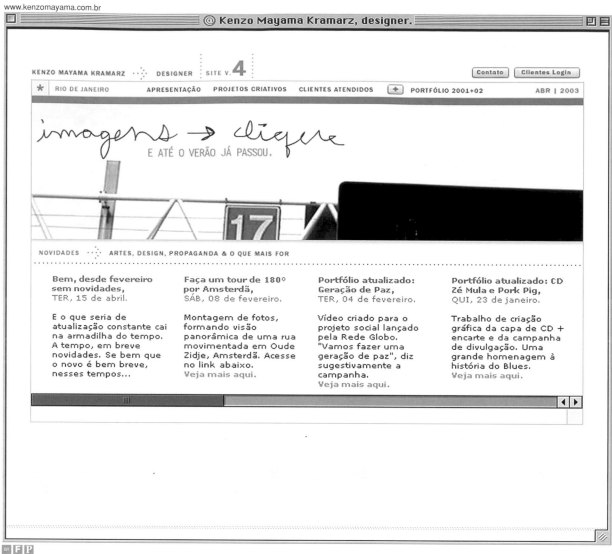

@ Kenzo Mayama Kramarz, designer.

KENZO MAYAMA KRAMARZ ···· DESIGNER SITE v. **4**

Contato | Clientes Login

* RIO DE JANEIRO APRESENTAÇÃO PROJETOS CRIATIVOS CLIENTES ATENDIDOS + PORTFÓLIO 2001+02 ABR | 2003

imagens → clique
E ATÉ O VERÃO JÁ PASSOU.

NOVIDADES ···· ARTES, DESIGN, PROPAGANDA & O QUE MAIS FOR

Bem, desde fevereiro sem novidades,
TER, 15 de abril.

E o que seria de atualização constante cai na armadilha do tempo. A tempo, em breve novidades. Se bem que o novo é bem breve, nesses tempos...

Faça um tour de 180° por Amsterdã,
SÁB, 08 de fevereiro.

Montagem de fotos, formando visão panorâmica de uma rua movimentada em Oude Zidje, Amsterdã. Acesse no link abaixo.
Veja mais aqui.

Portfólio atualizado: Geração de Paz,
TER, 04 de fevereiro.

Vídeo criado para o projeto social lançado pela Rede Globo. "Vamos fazer uma geração de paz", diz sugestivamente a campanha.
Veja mais aqui.

Portfólio atualizado: CD Zé Mula e Pork Pig,
QUI, 23 de janeiro.

Trabalho de criação gráfica da capa de CD + encarte e da campanha de divulgação. Uma grande homenagem à história do Blues.
Veja mais aqui.

www.kvad.com/v6/toc.html

http://lauckgroup.com/

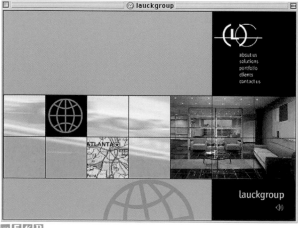

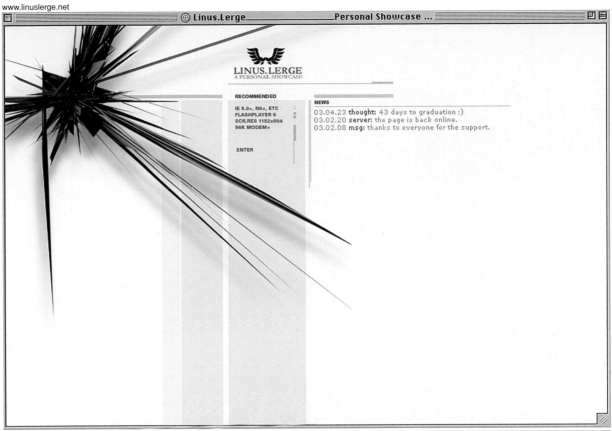

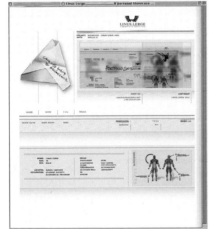

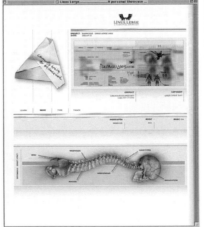

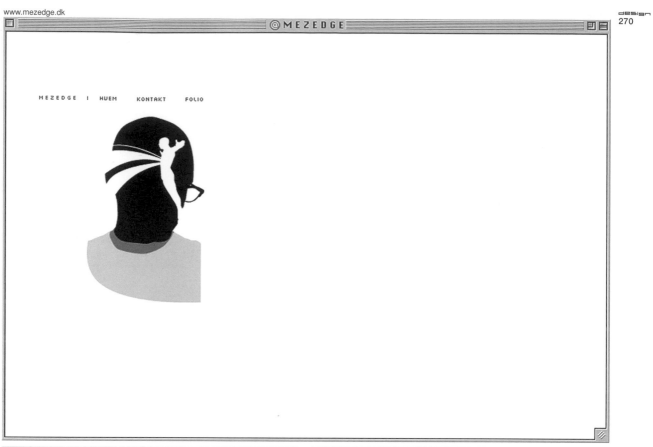

MEZEDGE | HUEM KONTAKT FOLIO

MEZEDGE | HUEM KONTAKT FOLIO!

< ▶ FODBOLDPROJEKT 2-2

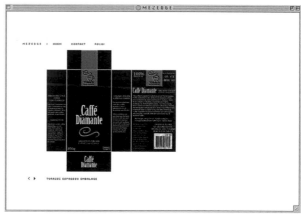

MEZEDGE | HUEM KONTAKT FOLIO!

< ▶ TORRISI ESPRESSO EMBALAGE

DK F P

Louis Nelson

©LOUIS NELSON ASSOCIATES   info@louisnelson.com   ▶ Skip Intro

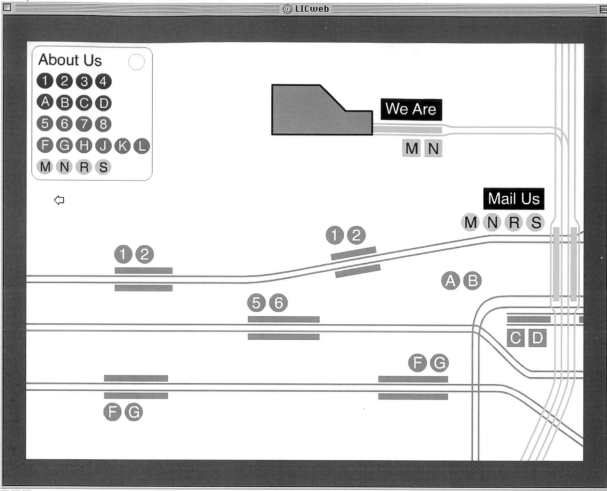

@ LICweb

About Us

① ② ③ ④
Ⓐ Ⓑ Ⓒ Ⓓ
⑤ ⑥ ⑦ ⑧
Ⓕ Ⓖ Ⓗ Ⓙ Ⓚ Ⓛ
Ⓜ Ⓝ Ⓡ Ⓢ

We Are
Ⓜ Ⓝ

Mail Us
Ⓜ Ⓝ Ⓡ Ⓢ

① ②

① ②

Ⓐ Ⓑ

⑤ ⑥

Ⓒ Ⓓ

Ⓕ Ⓖ

Ⓕ Ⓖ

UK F C

www.liquidpixels.co.uk

liquidpixels | speaks volumes :: e:inspired...

This domain name is now under offer!!
so my site will be moving to a new domain soon...

liquidpixels | speaks volumes

ENTER >>

site.requirements. v1.0

internet explorer 4.0+   netscape 4.0+
800 x 600 resolution+   macromedia flash 5.0+ (optional)

USA F C

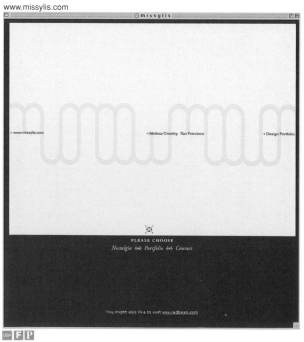

www.missylis.com

missylis

www.missylis.com   Melissa Crowley. San Francisco   Design Portfolio

PLEASE CHOOSE
Nostalgia ❧ Portfolio ❧ Contact

You might also like to visit www.redbean.com

USA F P

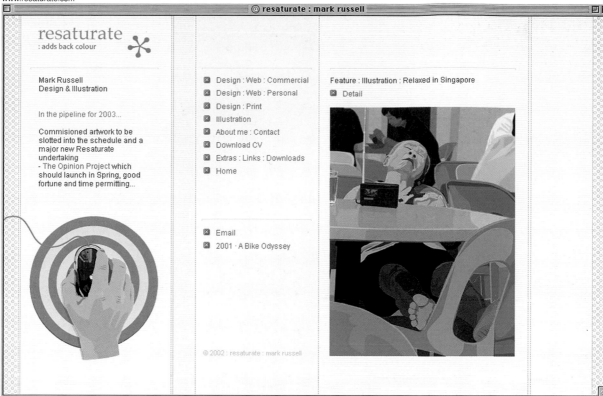

resaturate
: adds back colour

Mark Russell
Design & Illustration

In the pipeline for 2003...

Commisioned artwork to be
slotted into the schedule and a
major new Resaturate
undertaking
- The Opinion Project which
should launch in Spring, good
fortune and time permitting...

☒ Design : Web : Commercial
☒ Design : Web : Personal
☒ Design : Print
☒ Illustration
☒ About me : Contact
☒ Download CV
☒ Extras : Links : Downloads
☒ Home

☒ Email
☒ 2001 · A Bike Odyssey

Feature : Illustration : Relaxed in Singapore
☒ Detail

© 2002 : resaturate : mark russell

UK F P

www.serialcut.com

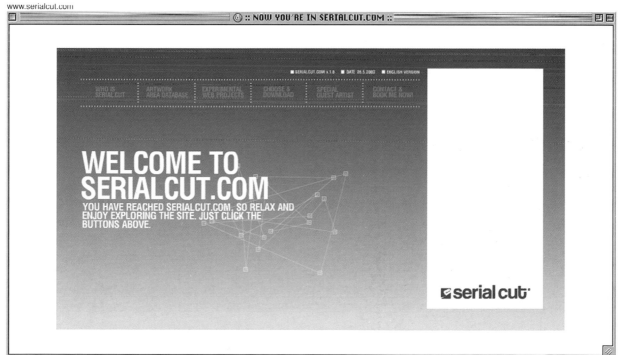

SERIALCUT.COM v.1.0 ▪ DATE 26.5.2003 ▪ ENGLISH VERSION

WHO IS
SERIAL CUT

ARTWORK
AREA DATABASE

EXPERIMENTAL
WEB PROJECTS

CHOOSE &
DOWNLOAD

SPECIAL
GUEST ARTIST

CONTACT &
BOOK ME NOW!

WELCOME TO
SERIALCUT.COM
YOU HAVE REACHED SERIALCUT.COM. SO RELAX AND
ENJOY EXPLORING THE SITE. JUST CLICK THE
BUTTONS ABOVE.

serial cut·

USA F P

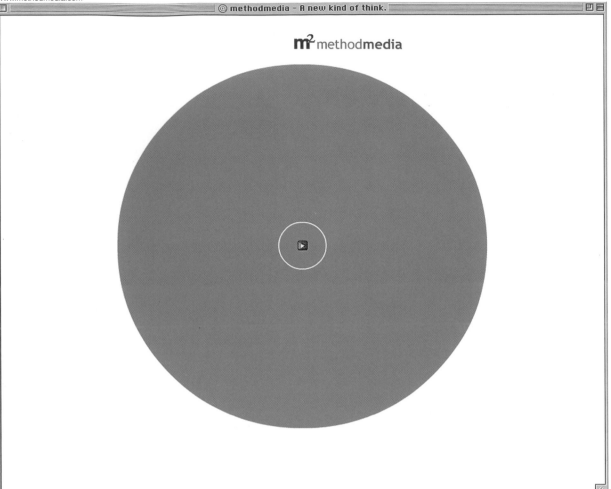

www.dmimagelabs.com

MX F C

www.motivdesign.com

USA F P

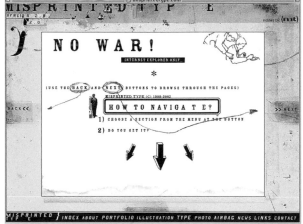

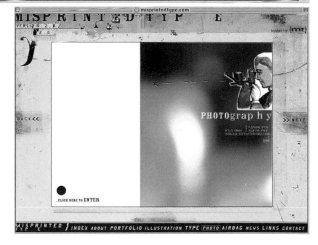

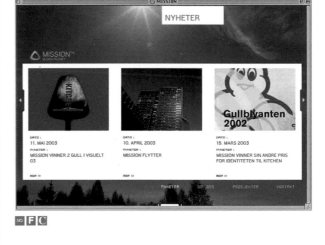

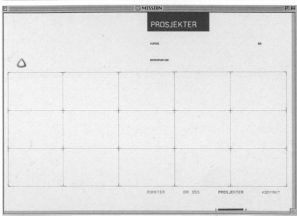

@ MOCCU.COM

HOME   COMPANY   PROJECTS   PRESS RELEASE   ENTERTAINMENT   CONTACT

BILLBOARD

FOR FURTHER INFORMATION PLEASE CLICK HERE ▶

NEWSBOARD

Feb 18, 2003 Scenery made by Moccu leads up to the Echo Awards read more

Feb 17, 2003 Moccu maintains its position in the "Horizont" ranking read more

Feb 07, 2003 Re-launch of moccu.com read more

Nov 12, 2002 DaimlerChrysler Bank with new Leasing Interface by Moccu read more

@ MOCCU.COM

HOME   COMPANY   PROJECTS   PRESS RELEASE   ENTERTAINMENT   CONTACT

ADVERTISING GAME "VITALFORCE"

CMA - Online
Game "VitalForce"

DC Bank -
Leasing
Applikation

Neue Sentimental
Film - Website

CMA - CENTRALE MARKETING-GESELLSCHAFT DER
DEUTSCHEN AGRARWIRTSCHAFT

Development of didactic as well as playful themes, to
increase the popularity of German agricultural products in
the young target group.

A game plus matching content were integrated in the
existing "Young 'n' Fun" area. One main aim was to raise
awareness for the issue of a conscious and balanced diet.
As skater "Indy" or "Xenia", the player gets to know the
products and their positive effects in a playful way.

SUCCESS: Putting new life into the community, and
increasing the website traffic with the help of
banner games and advertising.

ONLINE: www.cma.de/vitalforce

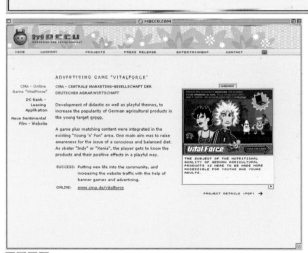

THE SUBJECT OF THE NUTRITIONAL
QUALITY OF GERMAN AGRICULTURAL
PRODUCTS IS HERE TO BE MADE MORE
ACCESSIBLE FOR YOUTHS AND YOUNG
ADULTS.

PROJECT DETAILS (PDF) →

@ MOCCU.COM

HOME   COMPANY   PROJECTS   PRESS RELEASE   ENTERTAINMENT   CONTACT

ANIMATED ECARDS

2003
2002
2001
2000

CMA - CENTRALE MARKETING-GESELLSCHAFT DER
DEUTSCHEN AGRARWIRTSCHAFT

As an extension of the CMA-Website youth area, Moccu
developed 13 animated e-cards with the appealing
VitalForce characters.
The issues love, party, greetings and cooking invite to
laugh, dance, sing and celebrate. Thus, there is
something for everyone and every occasion, to make the
community happy.

SUCCESS: The marketing instrument offers a multiplying
effect: after receiving an appealing e-card,
people send out e-cards themselves,
encourage other Internet users, etc.

ONLINE: http://www.cma.de/young_76506.php

← BACK

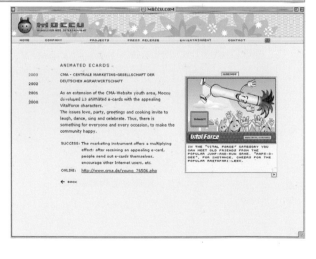

IN THE "VITAL FORCE" CATEGORY YOU
CAN MEET OLD FRIENDS FROM THE
POPULAR JUMP-AND-RUN GAME, "RAPS-O-
DEE", FOR INSTANCE. CHEERS FOR THE
POPULAR RASTAFARI-LEEK.

DE F C

www.murphydesign.com

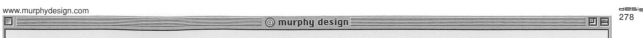

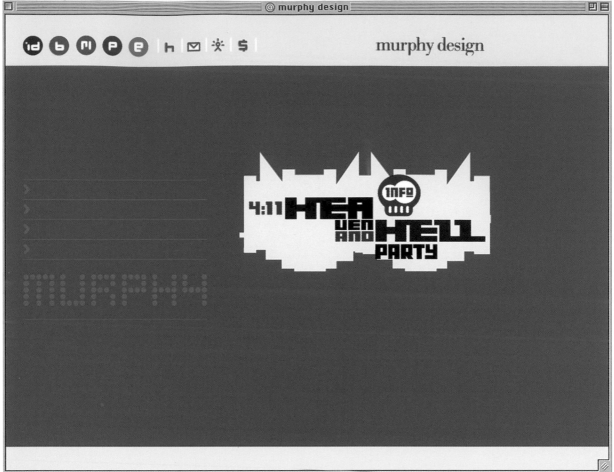

www.notsosimpleton.com

Nonstop®

Nonstop @ Work

Nonstop@Work 2003
Graphic Design, Styling and Sick Shit

Last update - 23.04.2003

Graphic Design
Illustration
Styling
Photography
Contact & Info

THIS IS MY WORK

Nonstop Newsletter

Enter your email address to receive
information about updates on this site.

| who@where.what? | go! |

**ROMEO
IS BLEEDING...**

Nonstop @ News For You ~ 24th April 2003

Here we go again. The first proper update since January.
Few new illustration works here and few pieces of graphic design at here.

This site is a portfolio of freelance graphic designer, stylist and consultant
Miika Saksi. Have been working among graphical and style matters since the
winter of 1995. Actually, right now trying to find a part time job or something.

Big thank to Jani@Notwest, who helped me out with code.

Any questions, just hit me with an e-mail.

Alright, Romeo is still bleeding.

Nonstop / Miika Saksi - Tel. +358-50-545 7774 - nonstop@non-stops.com - www.non-stops.com

---

www.superswede.com

Portfolio of Joakim Jansson

www.pontagram.com

Pentagram

© NowGoCreate: Artist Resource & Community

 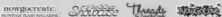

nowgocreate. MONTHLY FLASH MAGAZINE | Showcase | Threads by NowGoCreate | NowGoLove

MAGAZINE | CURRENT ISSUE | ARCHIVES | MEMBERS | SIGNUP | INFORMATION | DIRECTORY | THREADS

WELCOME TO NOWGOCREATE
YOU ARE CURRENTLY NOT LOGGED IN
LOGIN
>>
FORGOT PASSWORD?

If this is your first time at NowGoCreate or want to learn more
Click Here for Details
or
Sign Up Now

THREADS

CREATE A NEW CHAT | START A BATTLE

FORMAT	TITLE	AUTHOR	REPLIES	LAST REPLY	LAST POSTER
CHAT	join the admin gang	FM	31	10:05PM Apr 05	Reconfine
CHAT	DID YOU GUYS NOT READ MY ENTRY DESCRIPTION??? Morons!	Trevor	3	4:18PM Apr 05	Says who
CHAT	NGC SURVIVOR		23	12:51AM Feb 28	N/A
CHAT	Apology --> (from "corrupt administration)	Dephekt	0	5:21PM Feb 26	N/A
CHAT	SNOW!!!	Complete2	1	4:17PM Feb 25	Justin

NEWS

TIMEZONES | SEARCH

Warning: Wrong parameter count for mysql_result() in /home/nowgocreate/www/www.nowgocreate.com/2/db_news.php on line 95

Free research for artists
SEND MESSAGE | VIEW PROFILE
Posted by PeterS

Warning: Wrong parameter count for mysql_result() in **/home/**nowgocreate/www/www.nowgocreate.com/2/db_news.php on line 95

NoRedStars presents the **Permanent Contest Section**
Always there will be an open contest to let you play! We want to hear+see from every part of the world! First Act: NRS Wallpaper Contest ENJOY!
SEND MESSAGE | VIEW PROFILE
Posted by Babanetcom

Warning: Wrong parameter count for mysql_result() in **/home/**nowgocreate/www/www.nowgocreate.com/2/db_news.php on line 95

Oh dear god, what has happened here?

whos ill?
SEND MESSAGE | VIEW PROFILE
Posted by David

Warning: Wrong parameter count for mysql_result() in **/home/**nowgocreate/www/www.nowgocreate.com/2/db_news.php on line 95

man, i fucking rule.
SEND MESSAGE | VIEW PROFILE
Posted by Damon

Warning: Wrong parameter count for mysql_result() in **/home/**nowgocreate/www/www.nowgocreate.com/2/db_news.php on line 95

ill tell you who killed you if you give my powers back
SEND MESSAGE | VIEW PROFILE
Posted by Jesse

Warning: Wrong parameter count for mysql_result() in **/home/**nowgocreate/www/www.nowgocreate.com/2/db_news.php on line 95

to whoever killed me this morning:
like jesus, im back. ha
SEND MESSAGE | VIEW PROFILE
Posted by FM

Warning: Wrong parameter count for mysql_result() in **/home/**nowgocreate/www/www.nowgocreate.com/2/db_news.php on line 95

damon i love you...
your silly blue and red thing made my sister think she was going into epileptic shock....
and it made my white shirt look like it changed colors when i stood in front of the screen.
SEND MESSAGE | VIEW PROFILE
Posted by Marcy

Warning: Wrong parameter count for mysql_result() in **/home/**nowgocreate/www/www.nowgocreate.com/2/db_news.php on line 95

He didn't :)
SEND MESSAGE | VIEW PROFILE
Posted by Richardm

Warning: Wrong parameter count for mysql_result() in **/home/**nowgocreate/www/www.nowgocreate.com/2/db_news.php on line 95

SHOWCASE

FILE TYPE	TITLE	AUTHOR	RATING	NOTES
JPG	...	Euphoria3	2	2
JPG	Shoe	Euphoria3	4	2
JPG	You tell me	Euphoria3	N/A	
JPG	shady lives	Reborn	N/A	
JPG	more trucks for kids	Reborn	4	2
JPG	flower for her	Paradox	3	1
JPG	Justin new version	RaW	3	1
JPG	goddess of the highway	Ghostco	5	6
JPG	Luuurrrvee e MMEEhhh !	Justin	2	1
JPG	coming up for air	GenOx	3	1
JPG	Da Feces	Bull ISH	3.5	6
JPG	Brother and sister.	Justin	4.5	2
JPG	Uni-eye.	Justin	3	2
JPG	My Brother, Retardous	Justin	5	1
JPG	damon likes hot dogs	Reborn	3.67	3
JPG	i still want your soul!!	Trevor	2.5	4
JPG	i want your soul!!!	Trevor	1.4	5
JPG	shhhhhhhhhhh	Tyler	3.4	5
JPG	let it go	Sk8er08	3.75	4
JPG	second front	Sentient	3.67	3
JPG	they\'re watching	Sk8er08	3.6	5
JPG	saudade	RaW	4.75	4

PREVIOUS PAGE | NEXT PAGE

Warning: Supplied argument is not a valid MySQL result resource in /home/nowgocreate/www/www.nowgocreate.com/2/whosonline.php on line 6
No members online
Warning: Supplied argument is not a valid MySQL result resource in /home/nowgocreate/www/www.nowgocreate.com/2/whosonline.php on line 8

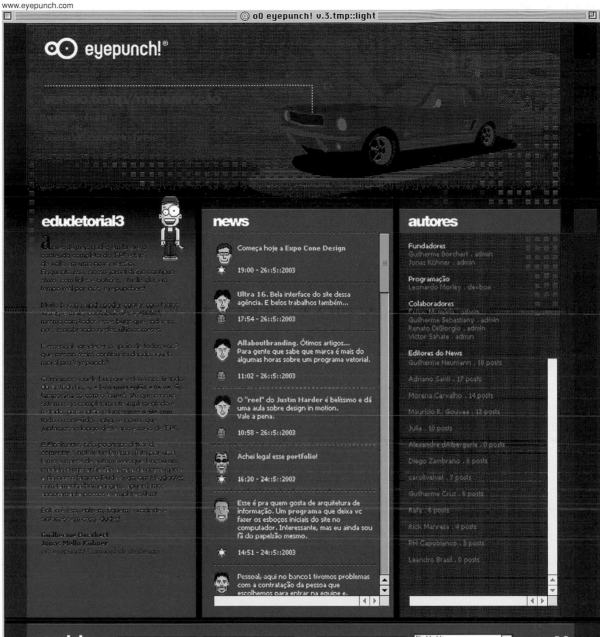

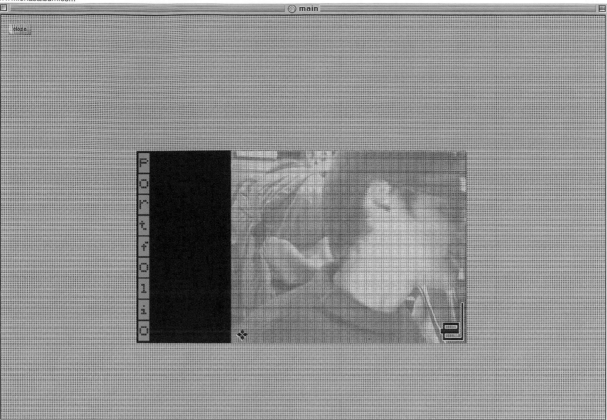

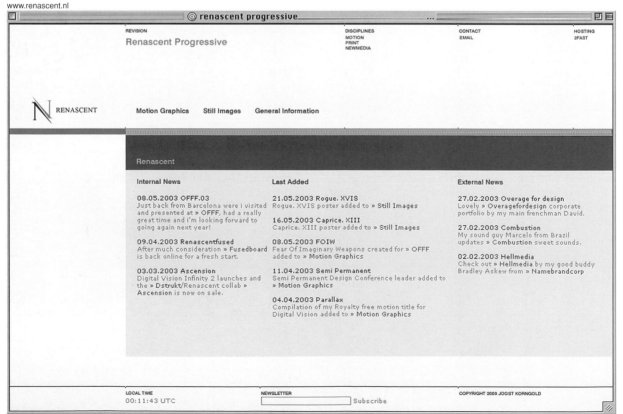

TXT 01/PR

TXT 02/INNT

MRK.

TXT 03/2003PORT

PR INNT — 2003PORT

KRISTOFERFOLIO

TXT 04/KRISTOFER   TXT 05/VOID

PR

1 BEATNYK	1 GUCCI	1 RINGSIDE
2 FLASHMAN	2 BUNKER	2 DONNA KARAN
3 VON DUTCH	3 PRINNT	3 BPR
4 MICHAEL MULLER	4 GETLA	4 PARU
5 BCA	5 NEWSTOONS	5 THE VICTOR
6 GIANT	6 COCA COLA	6 SOUNDLORD
7 REST HOTEL	7 QUORPORATION	

MAIN MENU
TOGGLE MENU

muller®

MICHAEL MULLERS EXTENSIVE PORTFOLIO OF PHOTOS DESERVED A MARK THAT WOULD REFLECT HIS ELITE CLIENTELE. WITH ASSISTANCE FROM _____, WE FOCUSED ON THE M IN MULLER WITHIN THE FORM OF A CROWN. IT WAS REQUIRED THAT THE LOGOMARK BE ABLE TO DISPLAY WITHOUT THE WORDMARK AND PRODUCE STICKERS ALLOWING FOR QUICK AND UNOBTRUSIVE BRANDING ON THE PHOTOS THEMSELVES WHEN REQUIRED.

CONTINUE

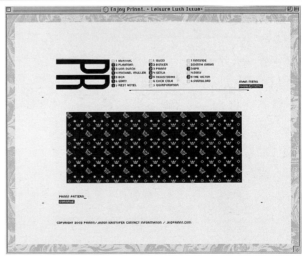

PR

1 PLAYMAL	1 GUCCI	1 RINGSIDE
2 FLASHMAN	2 BUNKER	2 DONNA KARAN
3 VON DUTCH	3 PRINNT	3 BPR
4 MICHAEL MULLER	4 GETLA	4 PARU
5 BCA	5 NEWSTOONS	5 THE VICTOR
6 GIANT	6 COCA COLA	6 SOUNDLORD
7 REST HOTEL	7 QUORPORATION	

MAIN MENU
TOGGLE MENU

PRINNT PATTERN
CONTINUE

say
hello

Quikanddirty

VOL.07.AUGUST.2002

NEW!!

issue #01
Aug 2002

issue #02
Feb 2003

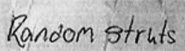

@ random

"Struts" is the swedish word for Ostrich.
Press F5 to reload and see a new Struts appear...

Click on the struts to see my portfolio

Have fun/ Mattias

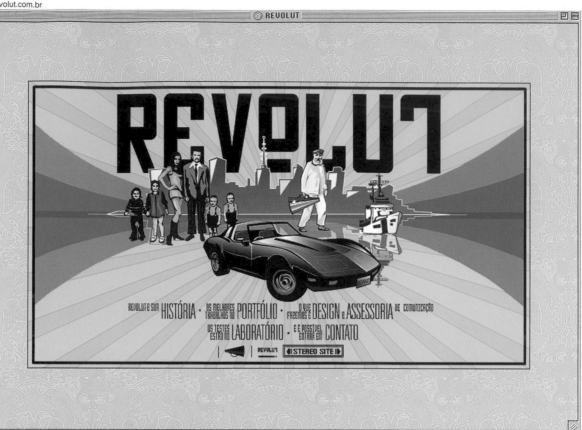

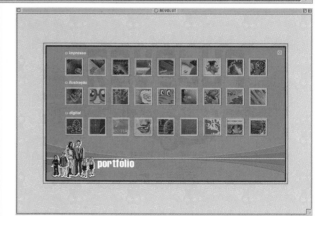

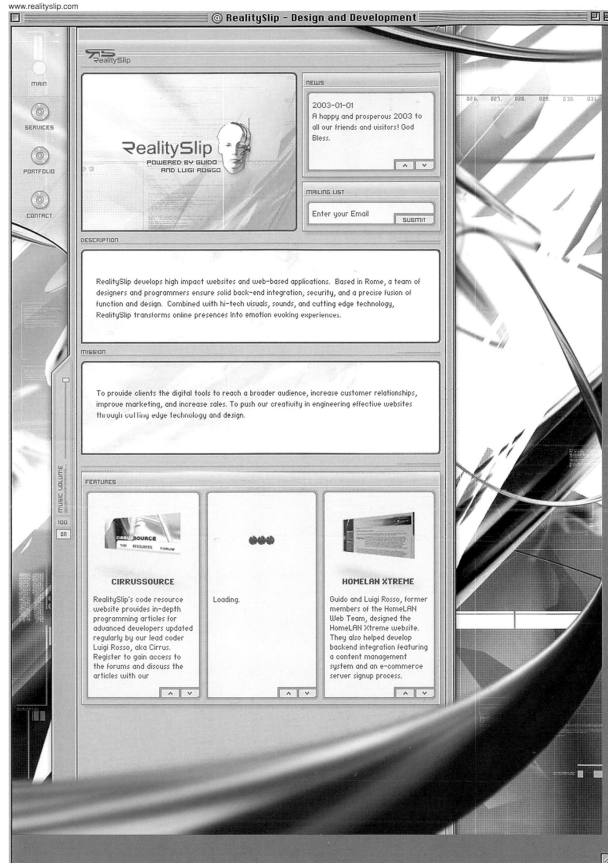

RealitySlip
POWERED BY GUIDO
AND LUIGI ROSSO

NEWS

2003-01-01
A happy and prosperous 2003 to all our friends and visitors! God Bless.

MAILING LIST

Enter your Email   SUBMIT

MAIN
SERVICES
PORTFOLIO
CONTACT

MUSIC VOLUME
100
ON

DESCRIPTION

RealitySlip develops high impact websites and web-based applications. Based in Rome, a team of designers and programmers ensure solid back-end integration, security, and a precise fusion of function and design. Combined with hi-tech visuals, sounds, and cutting edge technology, RealitySlip transforms online presences into emotion evoking experiences.

MISSION

To provide clients the digital tools to reach a broader audience, increase customer relationships, improve marketing, and increase sales. To push our creativity in engineering effective websites through cutting edge technology and design.

FEATURES

CIRRUSSOURCE

RealitySlip's code resource website provides in-depth programming articles for advanced developers updated regularly by our lead coder Luigi Rosso, aka Cirrus. Register to gain access to the forums and discuss the articles with our

Loading.

HOMELAN XTREME

Guido and Luigi Rosso, former members of the HomeLAN Web Team, designed the HomeLAN Xtreme website. They also helped develop backend integration featuring a content management system and an e-commerce server signup process.

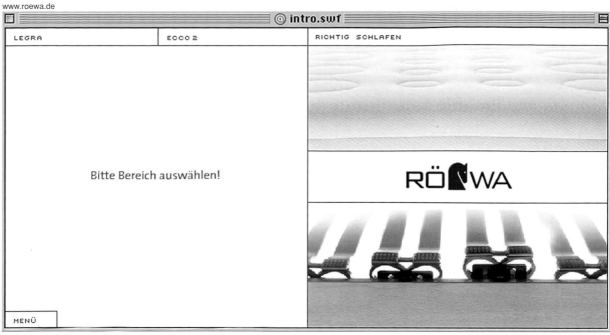

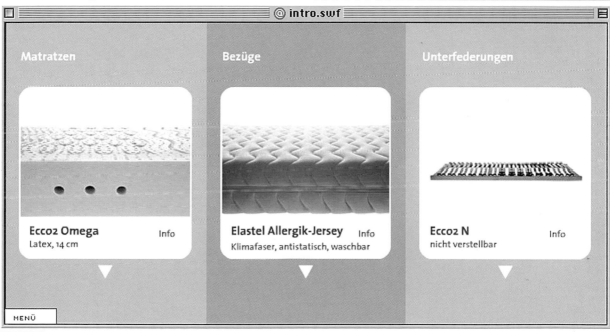

@ sadee

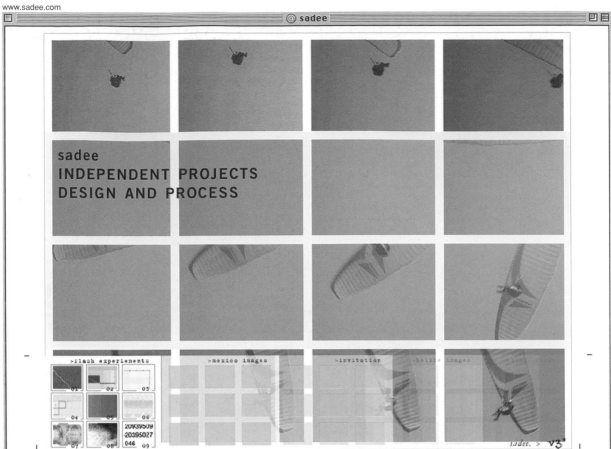

sadee
INDEPENDENT PROJECTS
DESIGN AND PROCESS

>flash experiments   >mexico images   >invitation   >helice images

01 02 03
04 05 06
07 08 09
20939509
20395027
046

sadee. > v3²

contact

USA F P

@ Sedus Homepage

sedus   ■ Deutsch   English   Français   Nederlands   Italiano   Español

Produkte
Design
Ergonomie
Unternehmen
Infoservice
Sitemap
Impressum

a-matter
Gesika
Partnernet

Einrichtungen für den Lebensraum Büro.
Life inspires.

DE F C

"SFAUSTINA design"

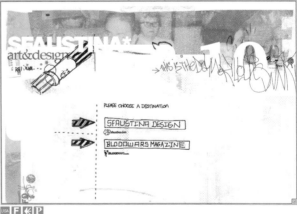

SFAUSTINA*
art&design

PLEASE CHOOSE A DESTINATION

SFAUSTINA DESIGN

BLOODWARS MAGAZINE

USA F K P

@ Site

01   **TOSHIBA** PORTEGE 2800

:.Art Direction:.

Very good knowledge of visual
communication, user experience
and design basics. Expertise in
creating styles guides.

:.Production:.

Full knowledge of the production
processes for the following media:
- interactive applications.
- Print design.

:.Typography:.

Expertise in the rules of
typography and creating fonts
optimized for the screen.

Sam Dallyn:.

the work shown is this folio
is only a small portion of
my work.

contact

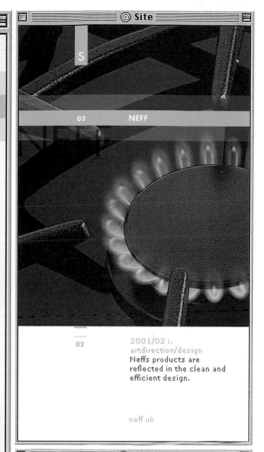

@ Site

02   NEFF

02   2001/02 :.
      artdirection/design
      Neffs products are
      reflected in the clean and
      efficient design.

      neff uk

@ Site

05   **B / S / H** APPLIANCE CARE

05   2002 :.
      artdirection/design
      This site is designed to be
      very functional giving
      Bosch, Siemens, Neff and
      Gaggenau users after
      sales help.

      B/S/H

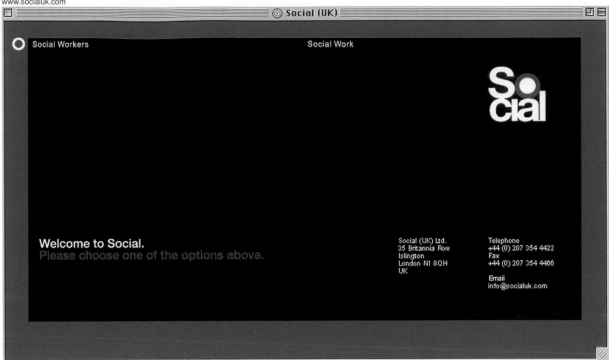

www.unit8.net

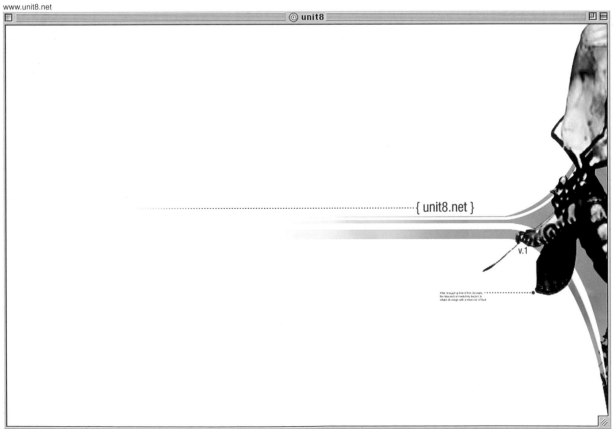

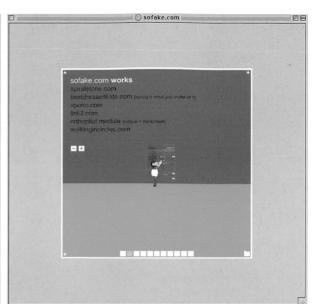

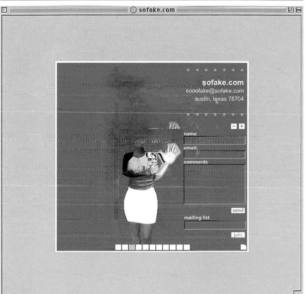

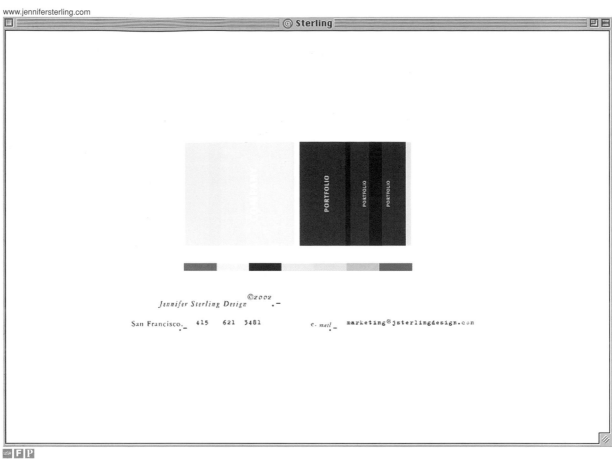

@ Sterling

PORTFOLIO PORTFOLIO PORTFOLIO

Jennifer Sterling Design ©2002 .-

San Francisco._ 415 621 3481   e. mail_ marketing@jsterlingdesign.com

USA F P

@ Super Natural Design

THIS SITE REQUIRES THE FLASH PLUG-IN
ENTER >>>

super natural design

SND

©2002 SUPER NATURAL DESIGN

CONTACT: INFO@SUPERNATURALDESIGN.COM

TEL 415-641-8088
FAX 415-641-8088

MORE OF OUR WORK CAN BE VIEWED AT ALTPICK.COM

USA F C

@ SUGATI

AUTHENTIC NYC DESIGNER
ONLY $19.95 CALL NOW!
OUR OPERATORS ARE STANDING BY.

USA P

▌ ON THE MOVE
I have decided to leave Paregos and Sweden and move to Kuala Lumpur. I will be leaving in early October.

▌ LOCATION CHANGE
I'm going to be on vacation in Kuala Lumpur, Malaysia, from the 1st of august until sometime in early september.

▌ SUBDISC V2
Finally! It's online, the new version of subdisc, never thought I would be able to get it done but here it is. Let me know what you think.

▌ NEW RELEASE
Just finished a project that has been going on for a long time, Vodafone and Ferrari F1 banners, check 'em out in the exhibition.

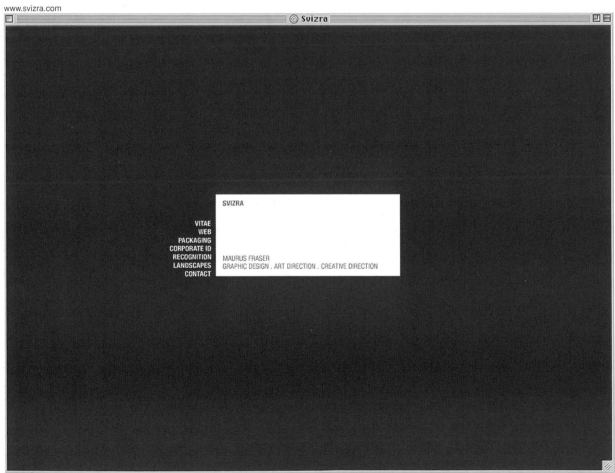

www.onetwothreefour.net

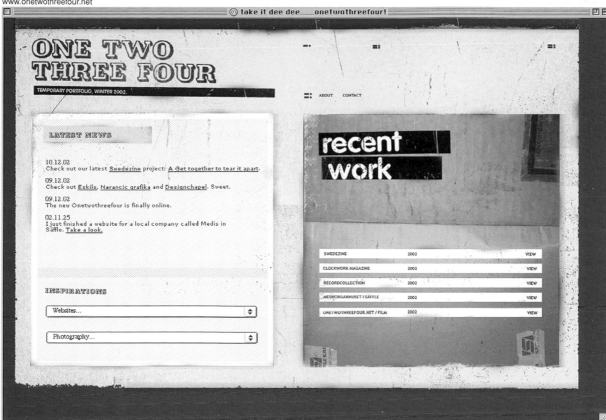

www.tmarksdesign.com

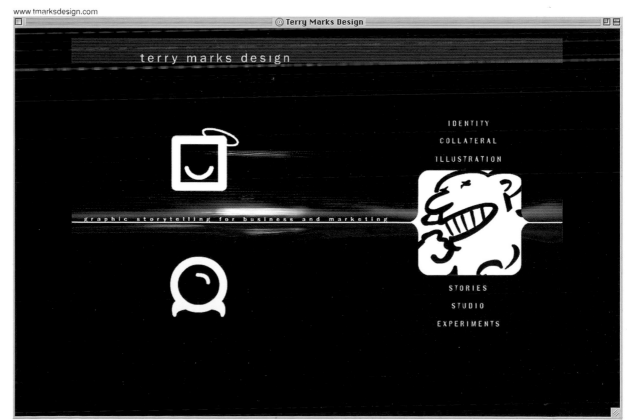

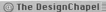

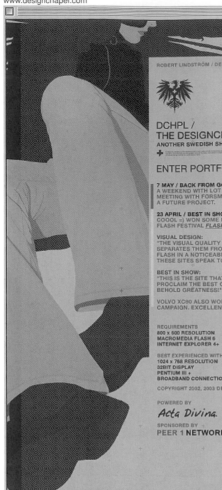

ROBERT LINDSTRÖM / DESIGNCHAPEL.COM

DCHPL /
THE DESIGNCHAPEL
ANOTHER SWEDISH SHOWCASE

ENTER PORTFOLIO

7 MAY / BACK FROM GOTHENBURG
A WEEKEND WITH LOT OF PARTY AND A
MEETING WITH FORSMAN & BODENFORS ABOUT
A FUTURE PROJECT.

23 APRIL / BEST IN SHOW / CANADA
COOOL =) WON SOME PRICES AT CANADA'S
FLASH FESTIVAL *FLASH IN THE CAN.*

VISUAL DESIGN:
"THE VISUAL QUALITY OF THESE SITES IS WHAT
SEPARATES THEM FROM THE REST. UTILIZING
FLASH IN A NOTICEABLE, MEANINGFUL WAY,
THESE SITES SPEAK TO THE EYE ABOVE ALL."

BEST IN SHOW:
"THIS IS THE SITE THAT THE JUDGES PROUDLY
PROCLAIM THE BEST OF THE FESTIVAL.
BEHOLD GREATNESS!"

VOLVO XC90 ALSO WON FOR BEST INTEGRATED
CAMPAIGN. EXCELLENT! =)

REQUIREMENTS
800 x 600 RESOLUTION
MACROMEDIA FLASH 6
INTERNET EXPLORER 4+

BEST EXPERIENCED WITH
1024 x 768 RESOLUTION
32BIT DISPLAY
PENTIUM III +
BROADBAND CONNECTION

COPYRIGHT 2002, 2003 DESIGNCHAPEL

POWERED BY
Acta Divina.

SPONSORED BY
PEER 1 NETWORK

SE F K P

the5k.org : home page

T·H·E **5k**
AN AWARD FOR EXCELLENCE
IN WEB DESIGN AND
PRODUCTION

Login | Register

Important Announcement!
5k Authorities to turn the 5k over to "The People"

This is something that we should have done a long time ago. But hey, at least we are doing it now.

Since we have never had sufficient time to devote to the 5k, it has been existing for a long time with too much potential. And potential is a bad thing which should be eliminated, through the actualization of all the good possibilities.

For more information, browse the **5k yahoo group**.

And, if you are interested in the latest reason we don't have enough time to 5k-ate, then have a look at the greatest game the web will ever see: **The Game Neverending!**

* * *

And now back your regular programming ...

For Your Pleasure: The 2002 Anything Goes Winners

The Winners

(Not that the public ratings and the complete list of entries weren't capable of pleasuring you as well.)

See also: **THE EDITOR'S PICKS**

* * *

Yes, yes, the competition stopped taking new entries on June 6th, and the 366 entries in the 2002 5k "Anything Goes" competition are now public (there were about 500 entries in all, but we have removed the duplicates, broken links and over-the-limit entries).

>>> **THE 2002 5K "ANYTHING GOES" ENTRIES!** <<<

Please take the time to rate the entries: collaborative filtering is what [it]'s all about. And ask questions (each entry has a discussion thread attached to it). And, if you particularly like something, let the creator know! They love to hear it.

* * *

The 5k recognizes the roles that constraints play in creativity and discipline in craftsmanship. Please make beautiful things!

The 2002 "Anything Goes" Winners!

All the Entries

Editor's Picks

2002 Call for Entries

2002 FAQ

2002 Judges

Tuesday, February 11

:: Interlude: while we are in statis (which shouldn't be too much longer), may we suggest that you check out Andy King's new book **Speed Up Your Site: Web Site Optimization** (and the accompanying **site**). Sure to please the 5k-inclined.

Saturday, September 28

:: People ask: "Hey! You dolts! When is the next 5k going to run!?" Well, here is a thing: you tell us! After 2-1/2 years of intense soul searching, extreme meditation and other related hippy things, we have decided to do what we should have done 2-1/4 years ago: make the 5k a real .org! Details will be provided very shortly and an email announcement will be sent to all site members.

If you want to provide your services (coding, design, organization, translation, moderation, etc.) or resources (servers, bandwidth, etc.) then what you need to do is join **the 5k yahoo group** where, hopefully, a new 5k order will spontaneously emerge. We hope that some good arrangement will spontaneously arise, but the 5k Authorities will select what they consider the best proposal if there are competing but incompatible ideas.

Wednesday, August 7

:: The winners have been announced. (Look over that a way <--).

:: By about 8:42pm Pacific Time (GMT-8) the winners will be announced.

Powered by Blogger XML

home | about | contact us

© 2000. All entries owned by the entrants. Steal anything else.

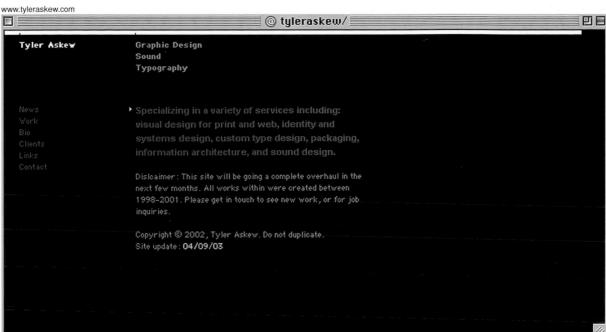

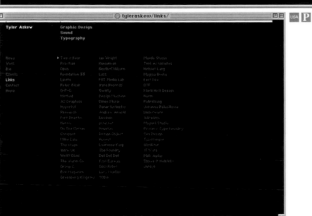

typisk .... WEBSITE

grafisk design.......

strandgade 100 a ...

1401 københavn k..

....

info@typisk.nu .....

....

....

kort fortalt ....

....

projekter............

skrifter.............

fotos ....

småting.............

....

links...............

....

....

....

....

....

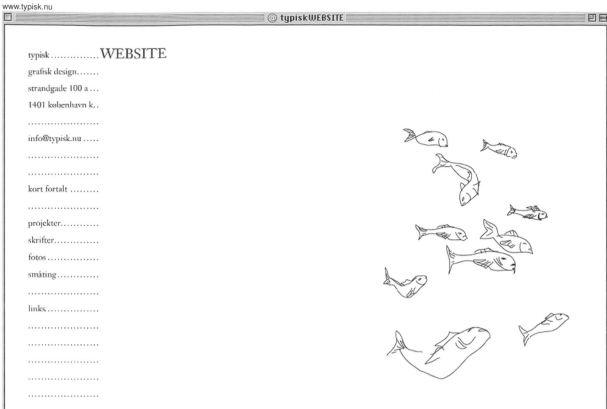

http://uoa7.free.fr/

uoa7

www.kastbuilt.com

KAST 1
A COLLECTION OF
IDEAS AND SELF-DISCOVERY

1. REPUBLICA
2. EVOLUTION
3. ASSASSIN

UPDATES COMING

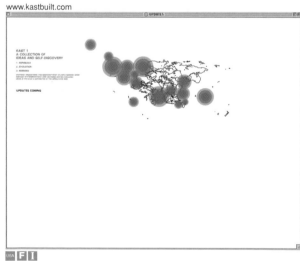

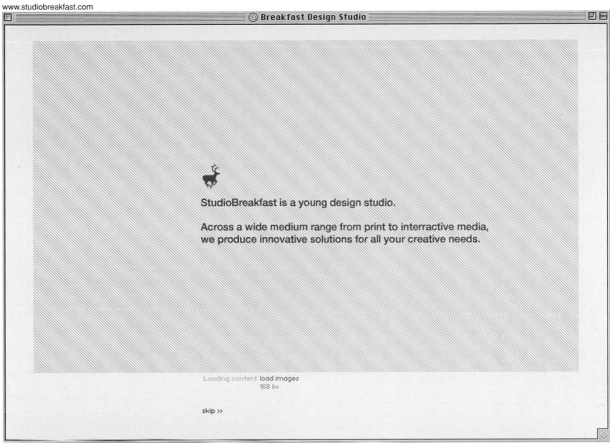

StudioBreakfast is a young design studio.

Across a wide medium range from print to interractive media,
we produce innovative solutions for all your creative needs.

Loading content **load images**
168 ko

skip »

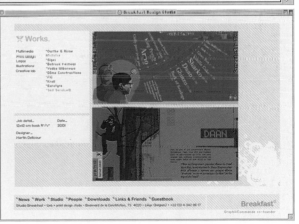

2002(C)(0)

DIGITAL.GRAPHICS

VISUAL STUDY

SOLOFLOW.V4 (FLASH)

DIGITAL.PHOTOGRAPHY

ASSORTED

ICELAND

TENERIFE

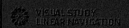

www.design-museum.de

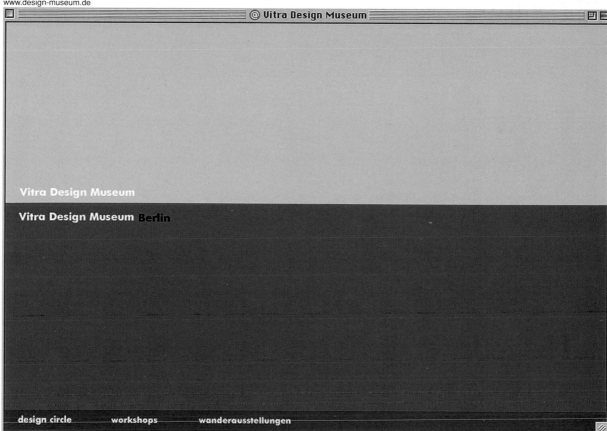

Vitra Design Museum

Vitra Design Museum

Vitra Design Museum Berlin

design circle   workshops   wanderausstellungen

DE C

www.volumeone.com/dev/22

USA F P

www.digerati.info

UK F

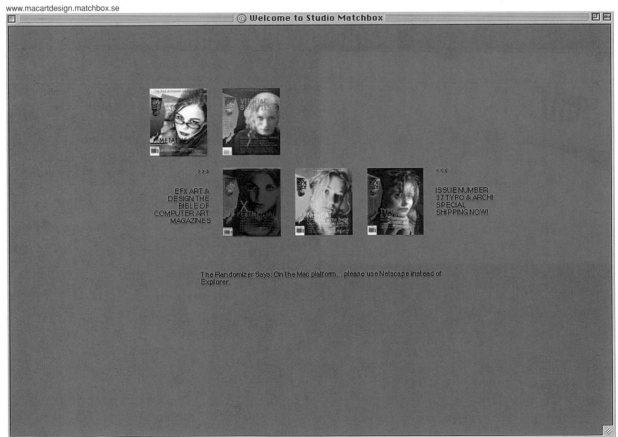

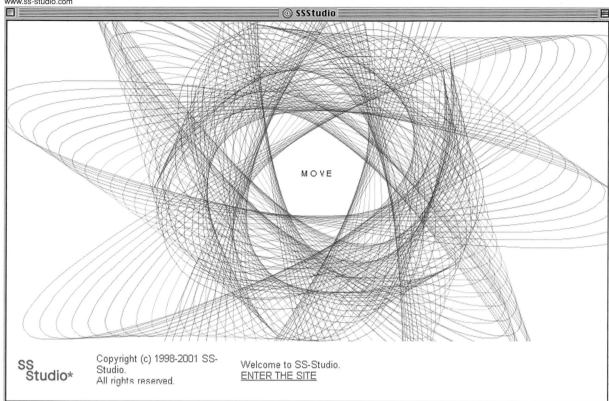

MOVE

SS Studio*

Copyright (c) 1998-2001 SS-Studio.
All rights reserved.

Welcome to SS-Studio.
ENTER THE SITE

FINAL HOME ART DIRECTION FOR ADVERTISING (US MARKET). CLIENT: ISSEY MIYAKE, USA
PHOTO: KELLY RYERSON PRODUCER: SASHA TULCHIN

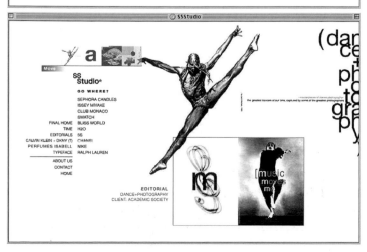

EDITORIAL
DANCE+PHOTOGRAPHY
CLIENT: ACADEMIC SOCIETY

Selection

WeWorkForThem™

Company   Timezones
> Profile   .Baltimore   .Minneapolis
> Achievements   .06.35.48   .05.35.48
> Recognitions
> Updates
> Subscribe
> Contact   .EST   .CST

Portfolio
> Typefaces
> Trademarks
> Print:1996-2001
> Print:2002
> Web
> Broadcast
> Systems
> **Buy Products**

USA F C

www.wrecked.nu

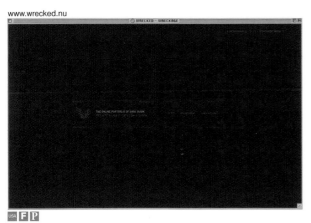

USA F P

www.x-entrik.com

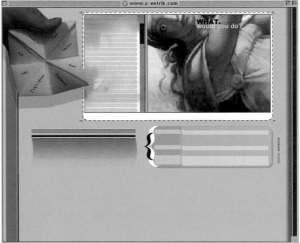

USA ◻ ◀ C

www.xrtions.net

www.xtrapop.com

www.xtremities.com

May 26, 2003

» Alright, I'm back home - but tired from driving 13 hours straight.. so not much in terms of posting for the time being. I was going to upload a bunch of pics from my last San Francisco trip, but the majority of pics that came back were of Nashville and jacked up. Either my Lomo is on it's way out, or I had a light leak that's hopefully been plugged (we'll find out on the next roll). But in the meantime, you can enjoy the shots to tide you over... Will post more about Austin later...

11:35 PM » [Comments (0)]

May 22, 2003

» I'm off to Austin, TX for a few days. So expect no updates in that time. Wireless networks will be sparse and Powerbook time will be even less. So, enjoy the rest of the Internet.

12:20 AM » [Comments (1)]

YEWKNEE.COM

ABOUT
CONSUMED
CONTACT
DWNLOAD
SUPPORT
WORDS

http://youworkforthem.com

@ YouWorkForThem

yWFt

Products
Art
Clothing
Multimedia
Print
Typefaces
Eps

About
Contact
Subscribe
Profile
Policies
Help

Your Cart Details
0 Items In Cart
View Item Details
Check Out
Your Account

Featured

Latest News

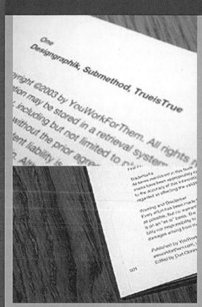

05.20.2003
Don't Make Me Over shirts by
Typevsm are for sale.

05.19.2003
Six new drawings by James
Paterson up in the Art Section.

04.28.2003
Neue Hardcovers:
Tom Hingston
Ryan McGinness
Geoff McFetridge
Groovevisions
Tomato

Neue EPS:
Camouflage Patterns
YouWorkForThem: E1

04.04.2003
We are very proud to announce that
One and Arba are finally here! We
hope you like them as much as we
do. Over a year was spent writing,
producing, editing and publishing this
book and CD. Our biggest project to
date. Enjoy!

One
One is a Book+CD-Rom containing
interactive versions of Designgraphik,
TrueisTrue, and Submethod from
1998-2002. These projects no longer
exist online and can only be viewed
via the CD-ROM. The book describes
the projects thoughts & processes.

Take a look!

Don't Make Me Over
Don't Make Me Over is a 2 color
screen print on a maroon shirt by
Typevsm. A great mixture of graff
and heavy metal for the heads that
know.

Take a Look!

USA C

www.ziba.com

z i b a

Capabilities
Portfolio
News
Awards
Careers
Contact

Experience
the **Fedex**
Brand

USA F C

---

www.factor27.com

factor**twentyseven**

Where have all the Poster shows gone?

company

About Us
Bios / People
Stratigic Partner
Influences / Links

services

Branding / Logo
Web / New Media
Print / Packaging
Photography / QTVR

portfolio

Branding
New Media
Print
Poster
Photography

USA F C

---

www.refinariadesign.com.br

@ Refinaria Design

ENTRE

AMBIENTE
REFINADO

BR C

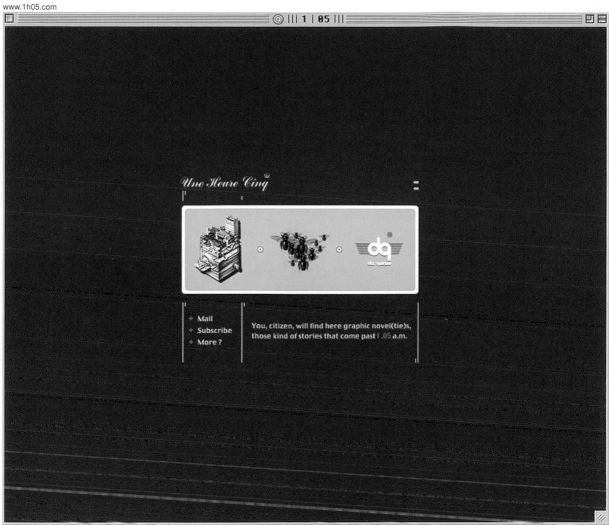

FR F K C

ARTISTSUPERLOOPER
VERSIONTHREEPOINTZERO
RELEASEDINJUNE2002
SECTIONCOVEROTHERSECTIONSAR
FONTSVISUALSLINKSDESKTOPSCO
USEDFONTSUPERSCOOP
PLEASE**ENTER**

play

design by: www.vectorize.de

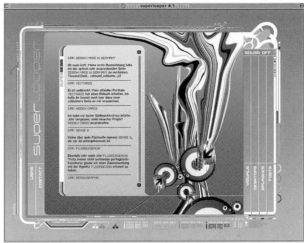

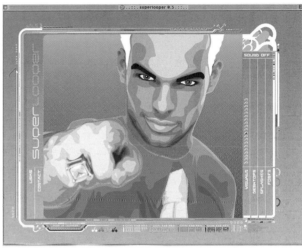

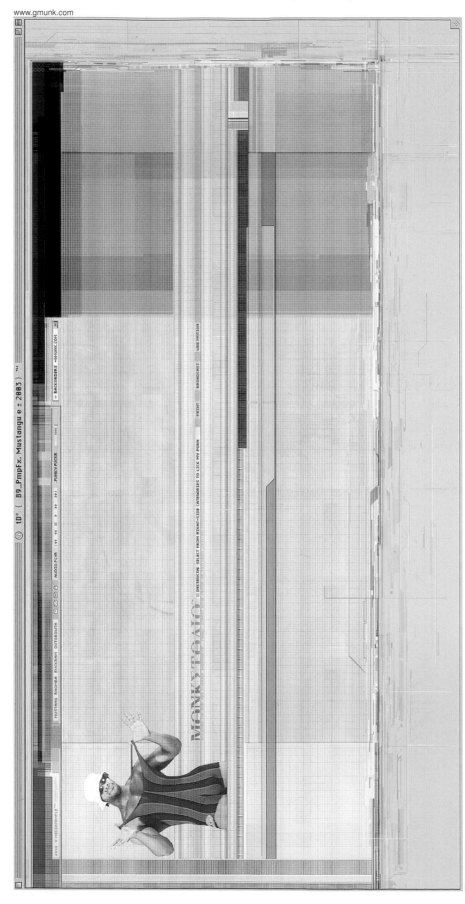

@ • core •

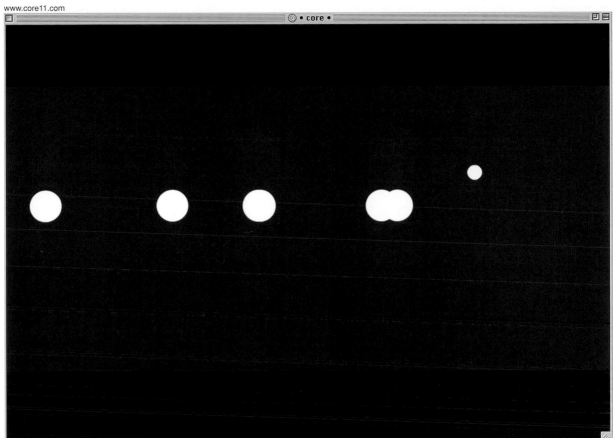

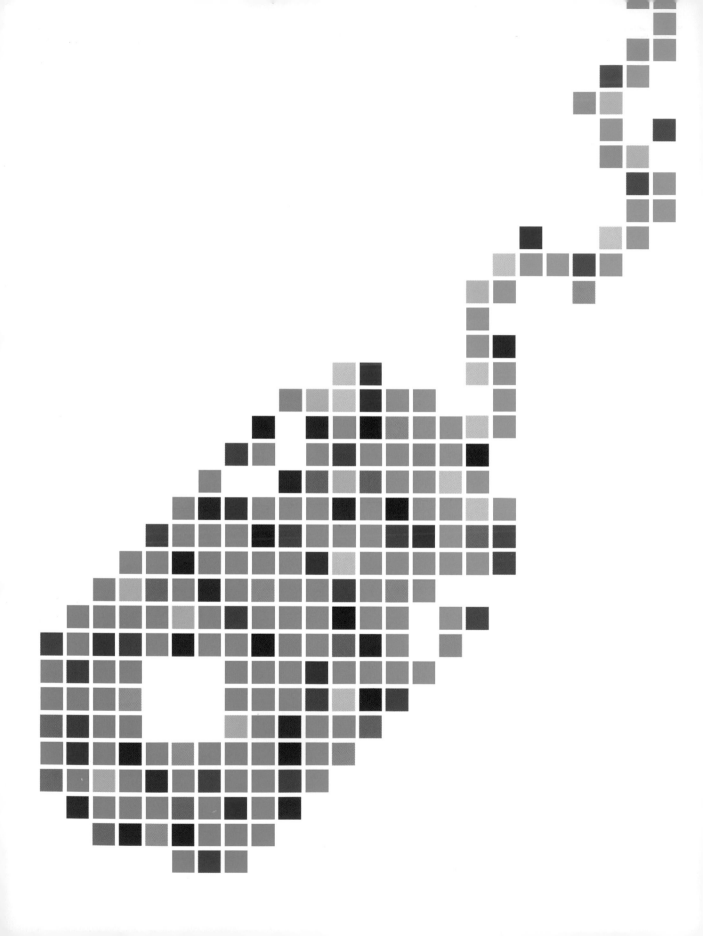

www.sixstation.com

UNLIMITED_VECTOR series
1_advanced wing   2_advanced wheel
view detail   view detail

New Package
+ Postcard

more to come...

cover page   contact
sphere   benny@sixstation.com
main visual
vector . visual . art   guestbook

2002 advancedwing

vectorvisualart
sixstation

Date. 2002-10-16 00.00
sixstation online tee shop is now open
come in and look for your favourite

copyright by sixstation all right reserved
made in Hong Kong

hkda design 2002 show - bronze award   web host : tigahost

HK F C

www.lavertical.com

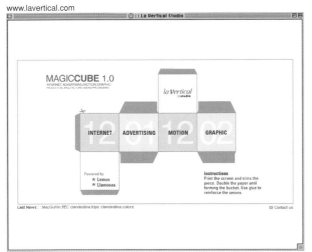

MAGIC CUBE 1.0
INTERNET ADVERTISING MOTION GRAPHIC
PRODUCTION ARCHITECTURE DESIGN PROGRAMMING

la Vertical
studio

12 01 12 02
INTERNET ADVERTISING MOTION GRAPHIC

Powered by
★ Lemos
★ Llamosas

Instructions
Print the screen and trims the
piece. Double the paper until
forming the bucket. Use glue to
reinforce the unions.

Last News : : MacGuffin.REC clandestina.trips clandestina.colors   Contact us

AR C

www.tomato.co.uk

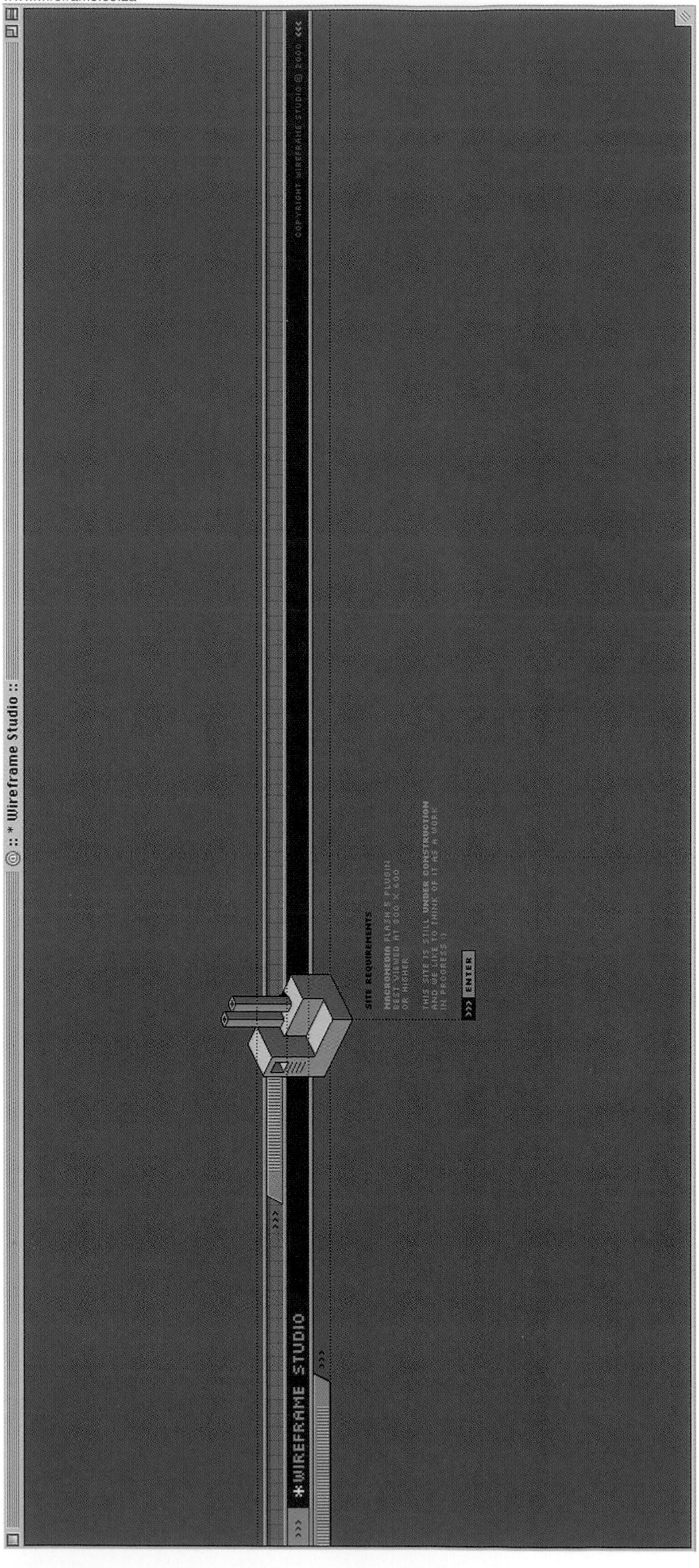

@ :: * Wireframe Studio ::

COPYRIGHT WIREFRAME STUDIO @ 2000 <<<

* WIREFRAME STUDIO

SITE REQUIREMENTS

MACROMEDIA FLASH 5 PLUGIN
BEST VIEWED AT 800 X 600
OR HIGHER.

THIS SITE IS STILL UNDER CONSTRUCTION
AND WE LIVE TO THINK OF IT AS A WORK
IN PROGRESS :)

>>> ENTER

www.envirium.com

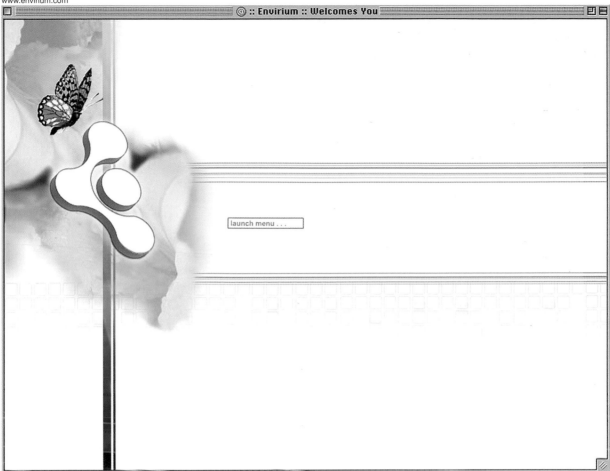

www.letsvamos.com

www.leogeo.com

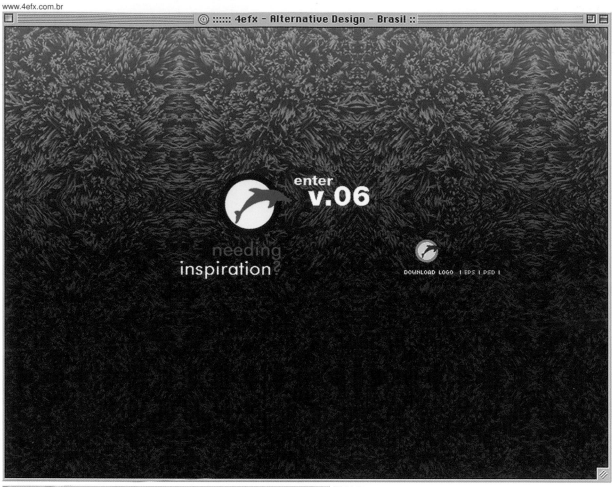

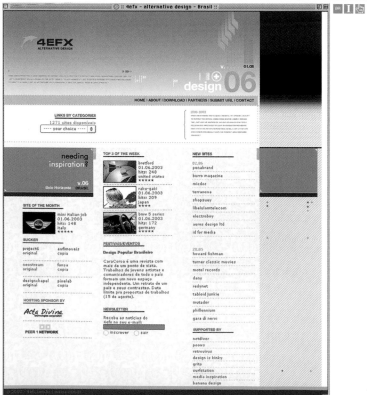

www.afterlab.com

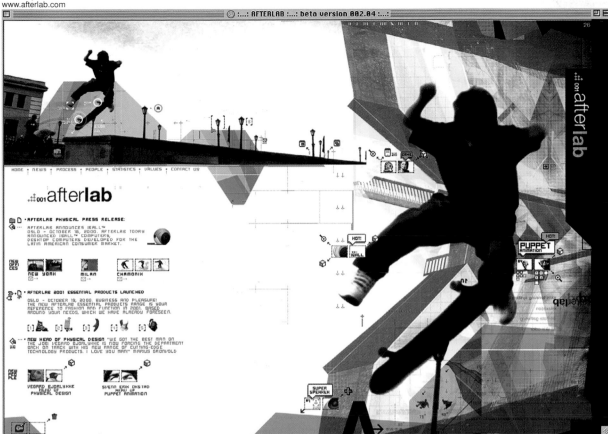

www.vianet.it/avatar

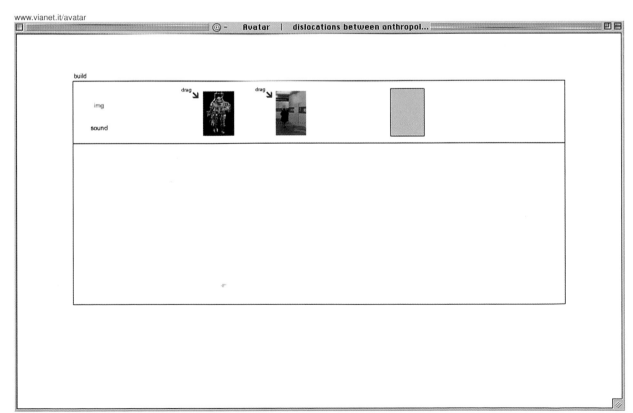

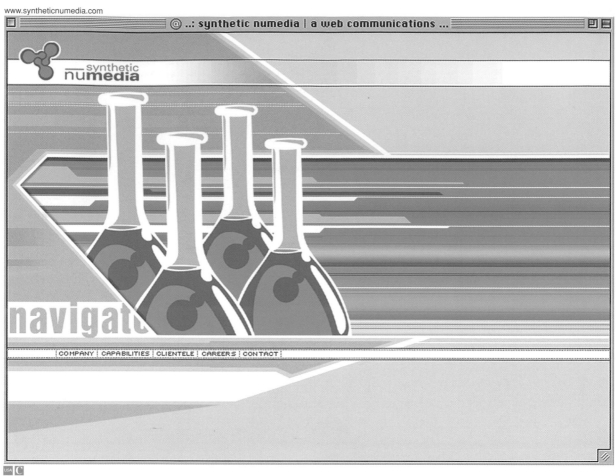

@ ..: synthetic numedia | a web communications ...

synthetic
nu**media**

navigate

COMPANY | CAPABILITIES | CLIENTELE | CAREERS | CONTACT

USA C

www.mileventos.com.br/jp/

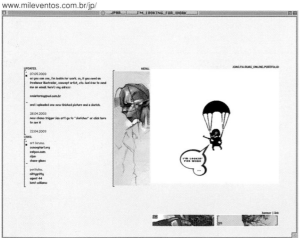

JPBR | I'M LOOKING FOR WORK

BR F P

www.graphicthinks.com

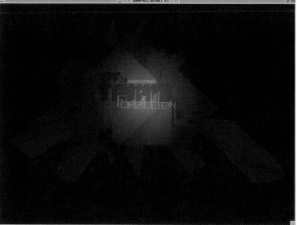

GRAPHICTHINKS 03

FR F C

www.pixelmuseum.com

PixelMuseum, a virtual museum with over 100 international top artists in
different sections as
"Photography", "Digital Art" and "Pixel Art".
Walk through more than 30 rooms!

Copyrights 2002-2003 by PixelMuseum.com

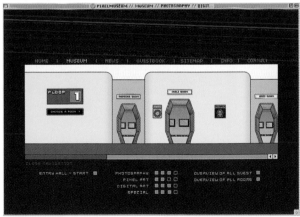

@ ////ELECTRONIC*ORPHANAGE\\\\

ELECTRONIC ORPHANAGE

ORPHANAGE ACTIVITIES

July 2003 exhibition by Angelo Plessas

May 16, 2003 Mai Ueda "Retrospective"

April 8, 2003 "About Yi " by Yi Zhou

NEEN.org

ELECTRONIC PROJECTS

Final version - whitneybiennial.com

Archive of the Electronic Orphanage

PRESS BOX

Articles

Electronic Orphanage press releases
Press photos and illustrations

Electronic Orphanage

View some orphans

Electronic Orphanage
975 Chung King Road
Los Angeles, CA 90012
directions

917.279.8372
212.228.7525
eo@electronicorphanage.com

Electronic Orphanage hours
random and by appointment

home

music by   gnac
play   stop

------angelo plessas------

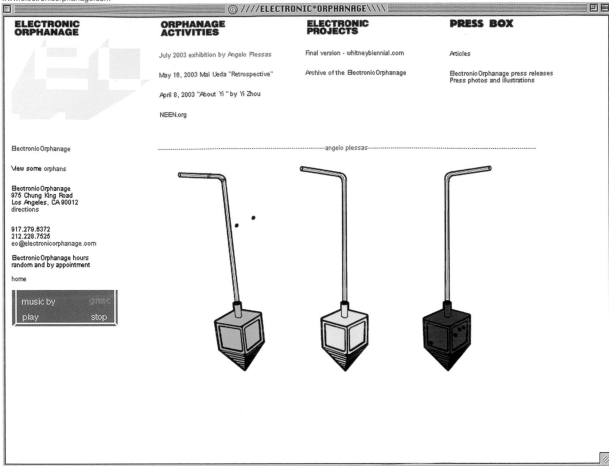

---

www.mdevelopment.com

@ //mdev//

http://arteye.com/

[ARTEYE 2002]

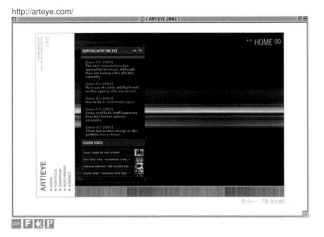

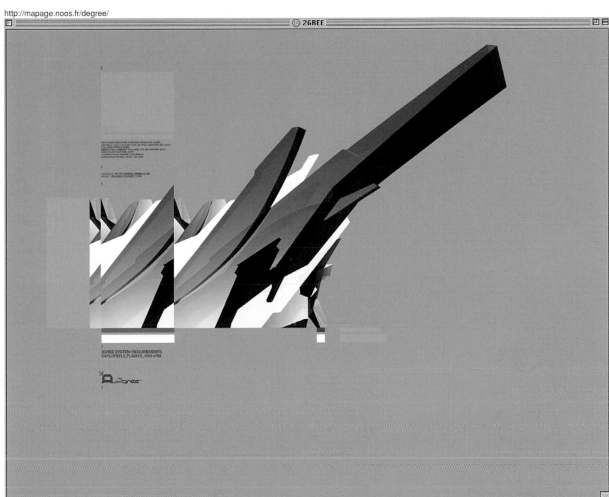

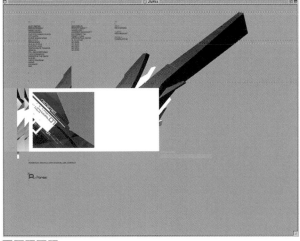

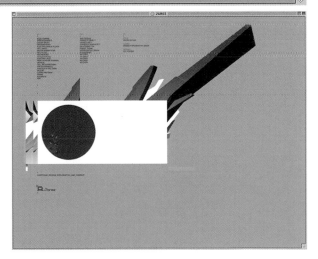

65media

/ enter

666 N. Robertson Blvd.
West Hollywood, CA 90069
310.855.0065
info@65media.com
www.65media.com

Download Flash 5 plugin
2002

65Media LosAngeles_06/03/03_06:45:41

Our Favorites
Company
Jobs
Awards
Contact

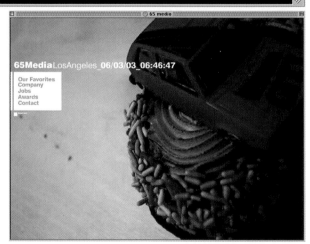

65Media LosAngeles_06/03/03_06:46:47

Our Favorites
Company
Jobs
Awards
Contact

@ [MTG Modern Games]

MODERN GAMES

"in labore pulchritudo"

ABOUT MODERN GAMES | **PROJECTS** | **DOWNLOADS**

NEWS

MAP

MTG Modern Games AB develops tailormade games and simulations.
Games are a storytelling device with enormous emotional and intellectual impact.

Our philosophy is to work with small, tight teams consisting of superior craftsmen with exceptional talent. Short, intense production cycles in close collaboration with clients has ensured major success.

Over the last 2 years, our team has been awarded with serveral international awards, most notably the French Cyber Lion Award and the American CLIO Award.

Check out our download section for more specific info!

MTG Modern Games AB
Engelbrektsgatan 20
S-211 33 Malmö, Sweden
Phone: +46 40 10 77 62
E-mail: info@moderngames.se

LILLA TORG

GUSTAV ADOLFS TORG

© COPYRIGHT MTG MODERN GAMES AB, 2002 & 2001

Superstars at MG (2003-01-15)
Three new employees have been added to our excellent staff. Daniel Olsén, 3D graphics, Evelina Persson, 3D graphics and Henrik Davidsson, Lead Programmer.

Expect them to rule!

Secret Project Success #1 (2003-01-07)
Our first milestone on the Secret Project was delivered in December. Mucho excited publisher and talk about moving production dates forward since the progress has been faster than they anticipated.

BMW Game breaks 25000 limit (2002-11-26)
MORE>

Democracy Game project (2002-11-15)
MORE>

Secret Contract (2002-10-15)
MORE>

Nominations (2002-10-02)
MORE>

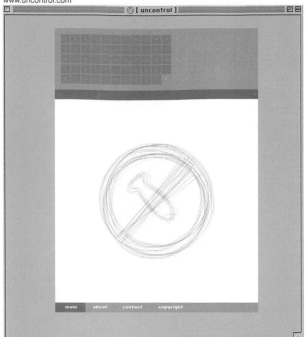

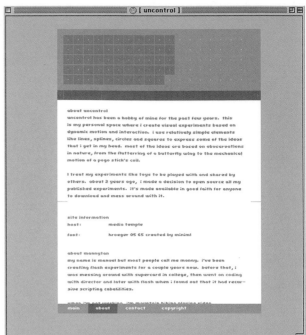

about uncontrol
uncontrol has been a hobby of mine for the past few years. this is my personal space where i create visual experiments based on dynamic motion and interaction. i use relatively simple elements like lines, splines, circles and squares to express some of the ideas that i get in my head. most of the ideas are based on observations in nature, from the fluttering of a butterfly wing to the mechanical motion of a pogo stick's coil.

i treat my experiments like toys to be played with and shared by others. about 2 years ago, i made a decision to open source all my published experiments. it's made available in good faith for anyone to download and mess around with it.

site information
host: media temple

font: kroeger 05 65 created by miniml

about mannytan
my name is manuel but most people call me manny. i've been creating flash experiments for a couple years now. before that, i was messing around with supercard in college, then went on coding with director and later with flash when i found out that it had recursive scripting capabilities.

when i'm not working, i'm mountain biking playing video

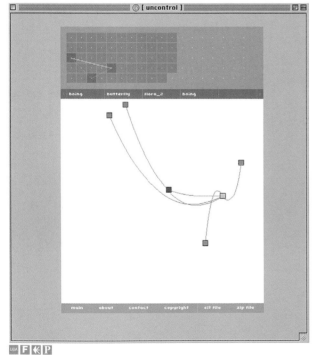

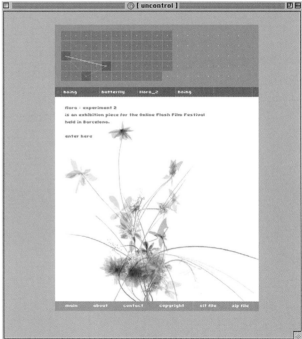

flora : experiment 2
is an exhibition piece for the Online Flash Film Festival held in Barcelona.

enter here

http://www.yestoall.com/flashAPI/index.html

@ [flashAPI]

#include "../lib/[flashAPI].as"
[03.02.03]

▶ español
english

www.missionmedia.net

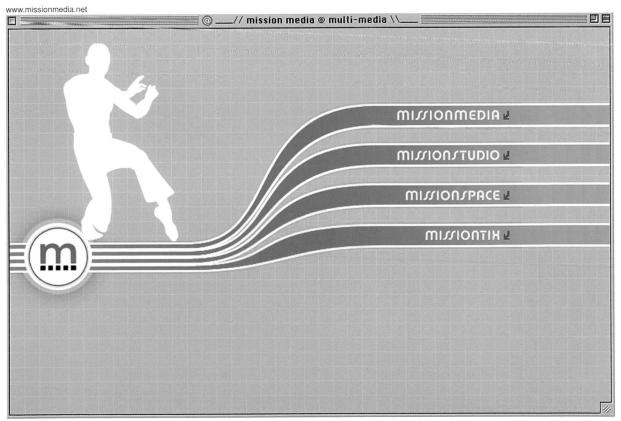

www.stuntkid.com

www.visualdata.org

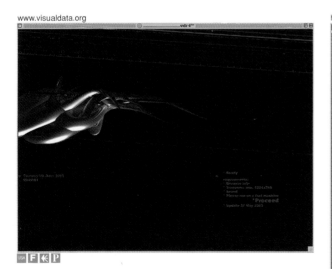

http://stu.aii.edu/~ky301/tempindex.htm

Absolut Kenneth Forty Seven®
Los Angeles - Orange County, USA
California and Nevada, PB. 1997 - 2002.
Imported from Taipei, Taiwan R.O.C. 1996
Hosted at the Art Institute of California - OC

Division of Faceblur Federation™
© Copyright 2002 - 2003
All Rights Reserved.

Printed in Taiwan
May 28, 2002

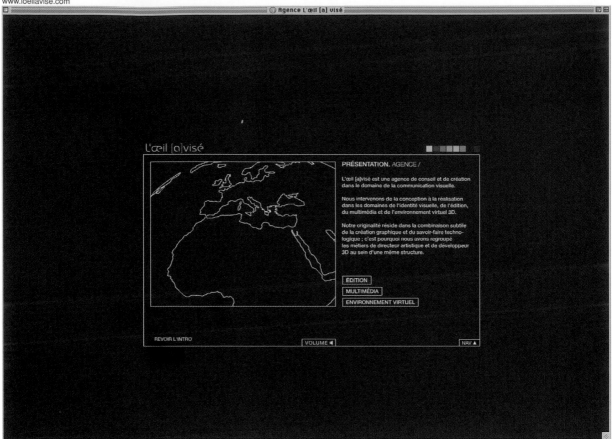

FR F C

www.amstudio.lt

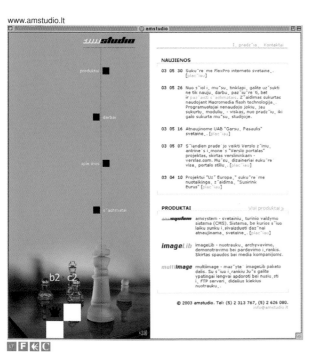

LT F C

www.astrotrain.com

USA F P

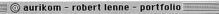

AURIKOM.COM
showcase ♥ playground

Welcome

Hello! I'm Robert Lenne,
a friendly designstudent
from Sweden. I'm looking
for a nice firm to do my
internship at this fall so
if you like what you see,
don't bee shy...

01 Showcase

02 Hyperisland

03 Pixelfonts

COMING
SOON!

ABCDEFGHIJKLM
abcdefghijklmr
1234567890

ABCDEFGHIJKLM
abcdefghijklmn
1234567890

04 About me

Contact

love@aurikom.com

+46 [0]70 356 09 65
UIN 19143193

---

04 About me

Creativity, Dedication, Details. These are things
that are important to me.

I am currently living a happy life in the small town
Karlskrona in Sweden, where I am studying at Hyper
Island - School of New Media Design.

In my work I pay strong attention to details and I
believe in doing everything I can to take a visual
concept to its purest form. True to the Scandinavian
tradition simplicity is also very important to me.

My strengths include a strong sense of responsibility
and an unwillingness for leaving work half-done. I
am also always very aware of how my project group
is working and I think I have a good understanding of
how a creative process works in a group.

I am also blessed with an extensive technical
knowledge. I am an experienced user of most
programming languages and gathering applications
related to the web (Se my CV for details), which
helps me a lot in my design work, when working
with concepts, and communicating with
technologists.

Now I am looking for a friendly company to do my
internship at for a period of three and a half or
seven months, starting August. If you believe that I
might fit in at your company, drop me a line (no
strings attached), and I will contact you.

• thoughts about me
• download cv
• contact me

back

---

04 HI application

ENLARGE

01 Lounge logotype
02 Helpbox
03 Pong logotype
04 HI application
05 Konvartposten
06 farmiddceit.com
07 Tank Trouble
08 Bomberboy

When applying to the Design & Technology course at
Hyper Island an important part of the application
process is the handing in of a piece of work.

I found the task very interesting and it didn't take
me long to come up with a concept. I wanted a
really interactive and almost game-like feel. I
made a shockwave movie that allowed the user to
control a small guy, representing myself, walking
around in my dream house. The user can click on
objects in the house, whereupon a small speech
bubble appears above the guy, explaining why I'm
fond of that object.

The solution required me to make a lot of
research on 2d game programming. I studied,
among others, The Sims and Diablo. The research
resulted in an isometric tile based engine.

When making the graphics I studied a lot of old
video games for ideas how to make isometric
graphic and sprite animation.

I'm very happy with result. But if I had applied
today I would probably have worked a lot harder
on creating a strong overall concept and not
focusing so much on technicalities.

• try it (pop-up)

back

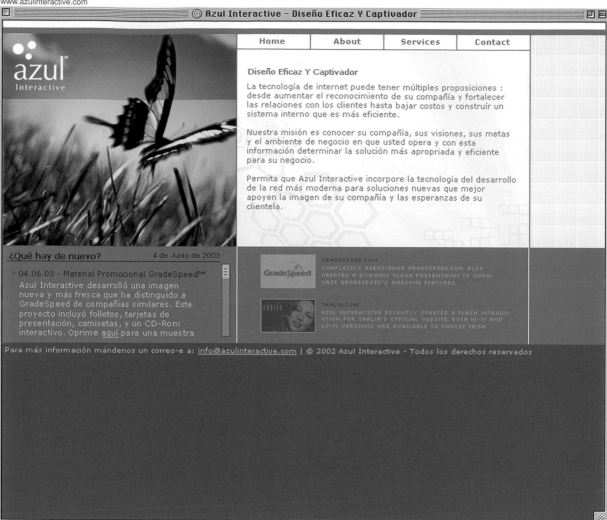

www.blue-lab.com

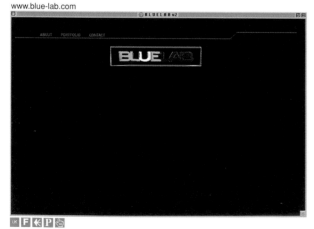

www.bionicdots.com

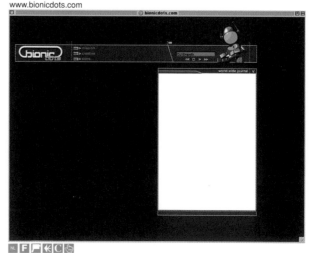

@ Barou point net (du tout)

FR F I

@ BlueMorpho

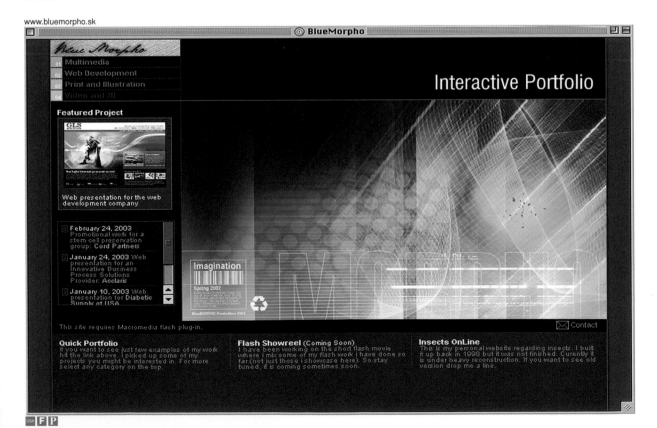

USA F P

http://jlapotre.free.fr/bpoem/

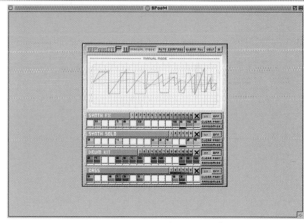

FR F ‹ P

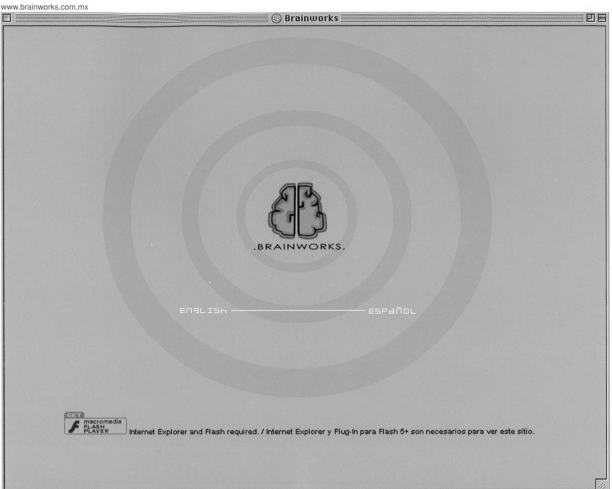

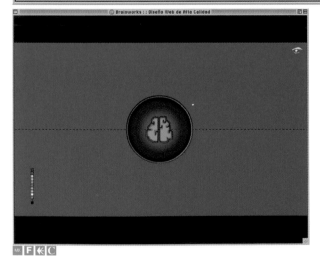

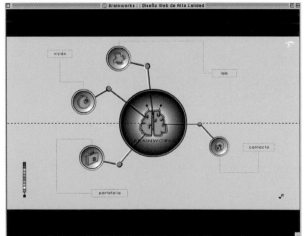

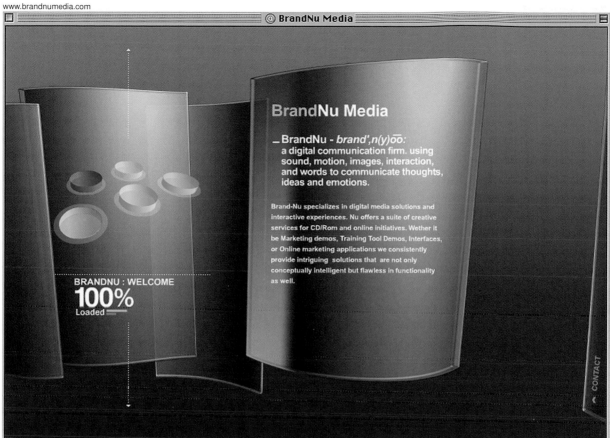

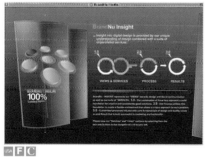

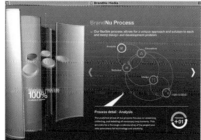

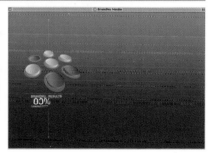

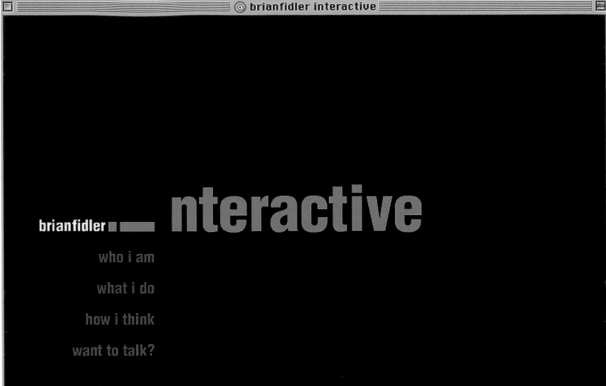

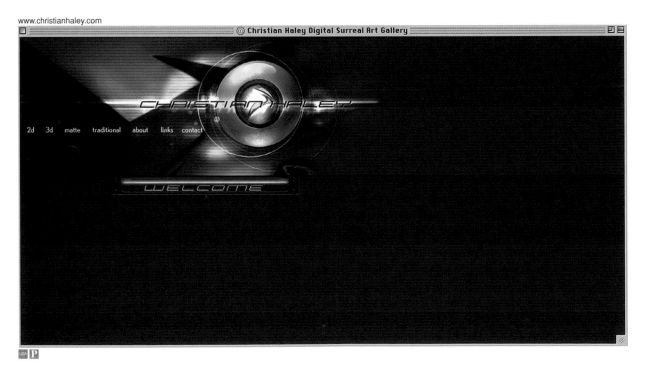

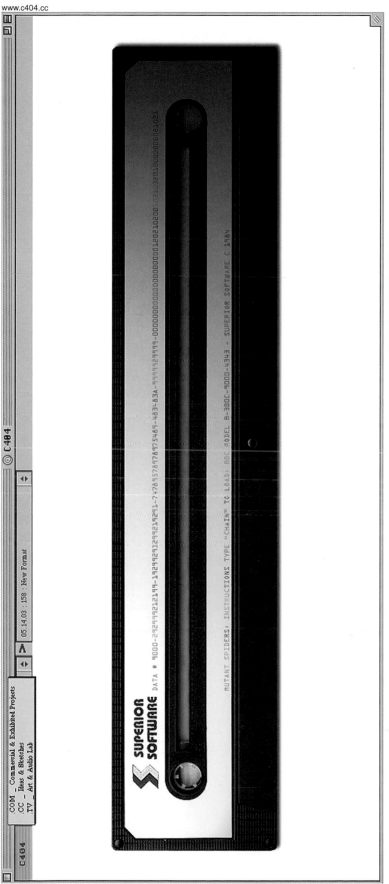

@ C404

05.14.03 : 158 : New Format

COM _ Commercial & Exhibited Projects
.CC _ Ideas & Sketches
.TV _ Art & Audio Lab

C404

www.d-realm.net

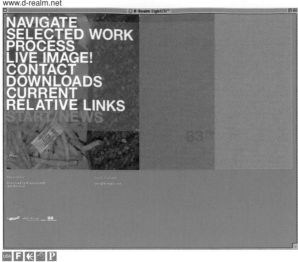

NAVIGATE
SELECTED WORK
PROCESS
LIVE IMAGE!
CONTACT
DOWNLOADS
CURRENT
RELATIVE LINKS
START NEWS

www.danielbrowns.com

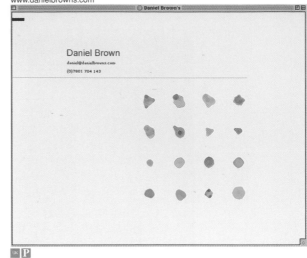

Daniel Brown
daniel@danielbrowns.com
(0)7801 704 143

www.e3direktiv.com

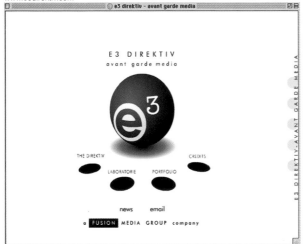

E 3 DIREKTIV
avant garde media

e³

THE DIREKTIV   CREDITS

LABORATORIE   PORTFOLIO

news   email

a FUSION MEDIA GROUP company

E 3 DIREKTIV - AVANT GARDE MEDIA

www.diesel.com/friendshipgallery

Friendship Gallery

Freedom Desire Temptation Pleasure
Delight Romance Fantasy Innocence
Temptation 2 Dreams Fun Memories
Passion Adventure Satisfaction Fun 2
Adventure 2

www.newmedia-works.com/arts

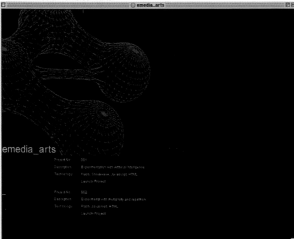

emedia_arts

www.empee3.net

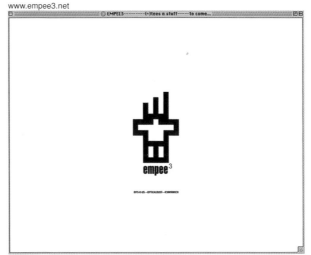

empee³

chewing gum for the eyes is part of the wheelhouse creative group

www.crashshop.com

ABOUT US   SELECTED WORK   NEWS   CONTACT US   STORE

ABOUT US: INTRO

INTRO   TEAM   CAPABILITIES   CLIENT LIST

You should hire us to build you a kick-ass website.

1.) Because we have experience managing some of the largest websites in the world, and examples of our work are displayed in museums like the San Francisco Museum of Modern Art.

2.) Because we're not a bloated Megacorp. We're a small, hand-picked team of experienced professionals. We can offer you less hassle and lower overhead than our larger competitors without sacrificing world-class quality.

3.) Because we love doing this. We're willing to put in the effort and the imagination required to make every project something truly beautiful.

Drop us a line.

JOBS AT CRASHSHOP

CrashShop is seeking a passionate, talented salesperson to promote the stuff we do! With several product launches coming soon, we are looking to grow.

If you are this person, please send a resume and cover letter to contact@crashshop.com.

CRASHSHOP

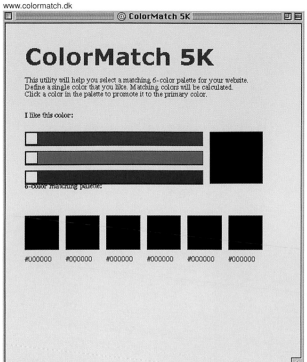

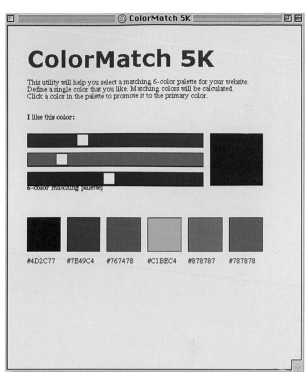

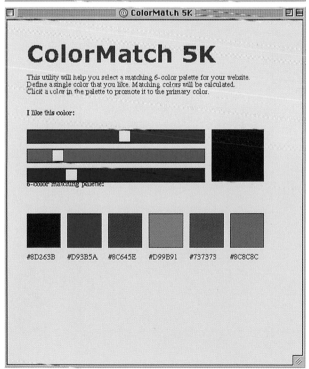

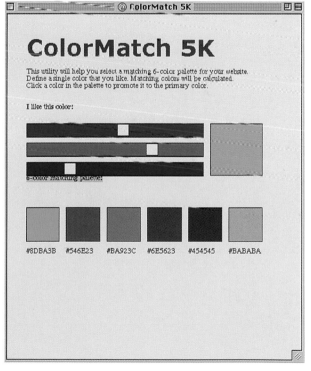

www.dchiang.com

www.sjufyra.se/honrik/

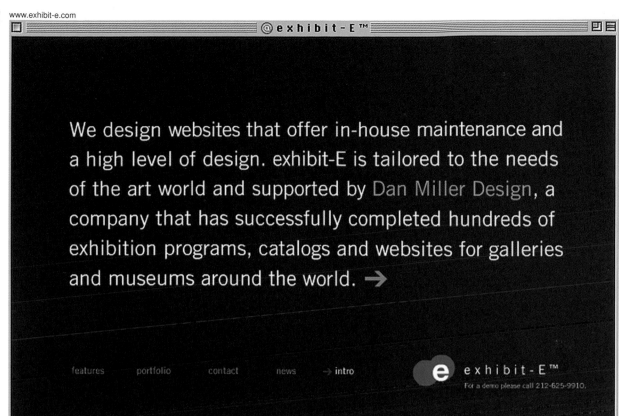

We design websites that offer in-house maintenance and a high level of design. exhibit-E is tailored to the needs of the art world and supported by Dan Miller Design, a company that has successfully completed hundreds of exhibition programs, catalogs and websites for galleries and museums around the world. →

features   portfolio   contact   news   → intro

exhibit-E™
For a demo please call 212-625-9910.

www.entropyswitch.com

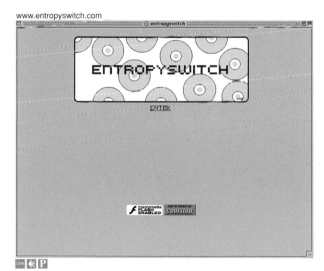

www.epeiron.com

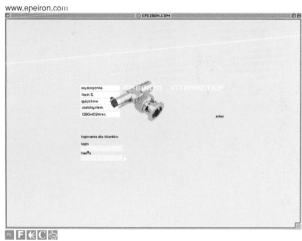

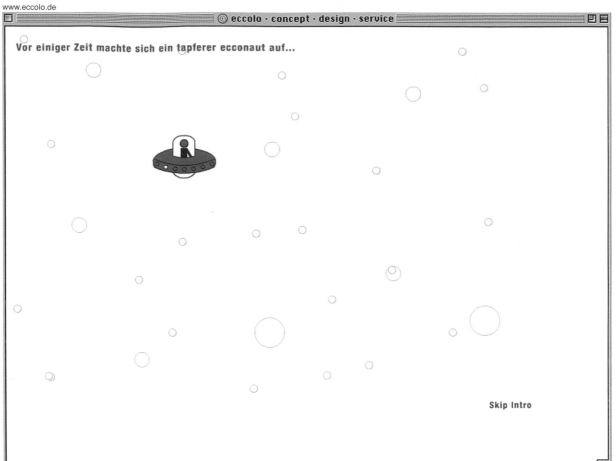

Vor einiger Zeit machte sich ein tapferer ecconaut auf...

Skip Intro

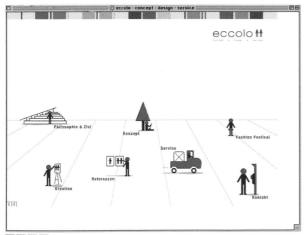

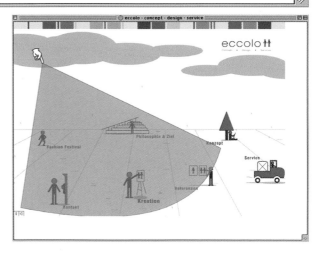

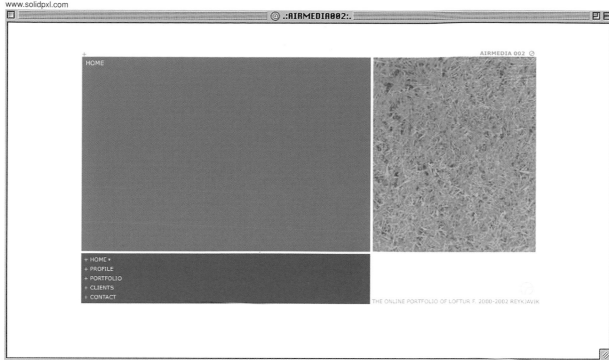

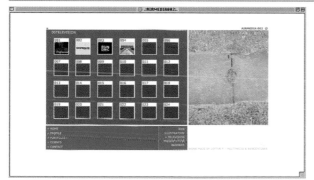

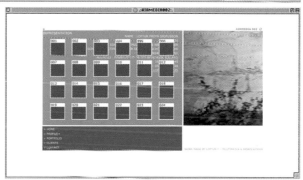

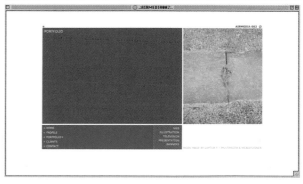

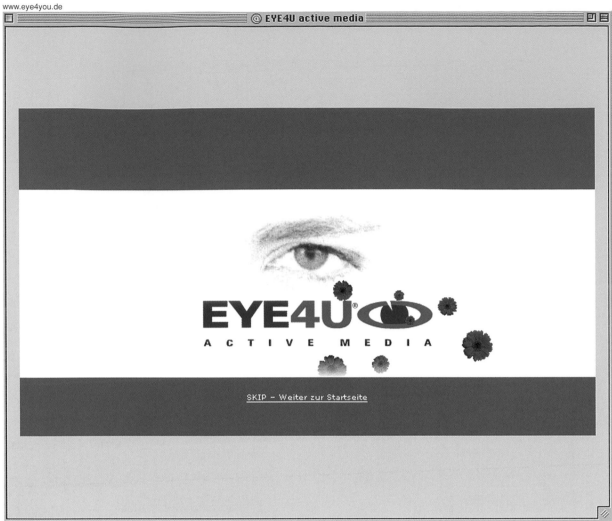

SKIP – Weiter zur Startseite

www.fix3r.com

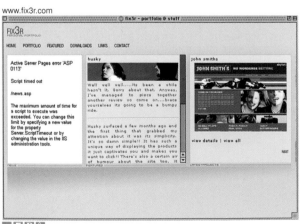

www.fixion.dk

www.fshuber.net

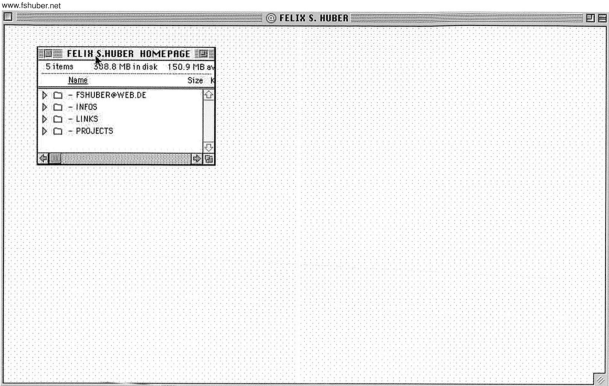

FELIX S.HUBER HOMEPAGE

5 items   388.8 MB in disk   150.9 MB av

Name   Size K

▷ ▢ – FSHUBER@WEB.DE
▷ ▢ – INFOS
▷ ▢ – LINKS
▷ ▢ – PROJECTS

DE P

www.grootlicht.com

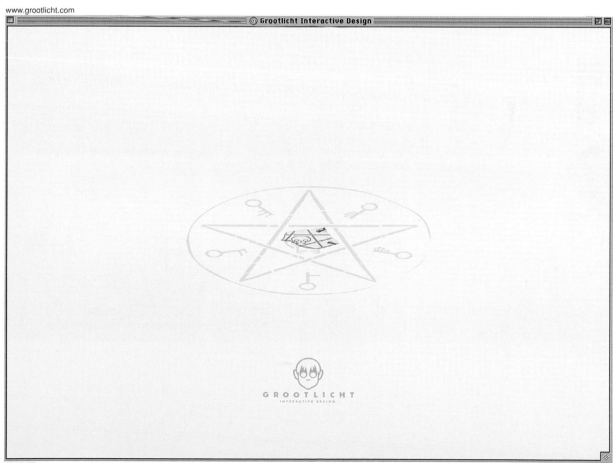

GROOTLICHT
INTERACTIVE DESIGN

NL F C

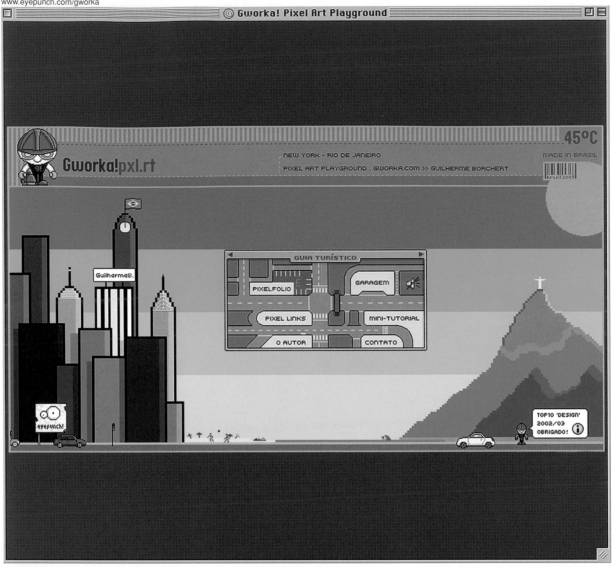

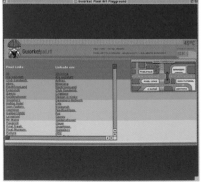

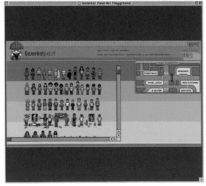

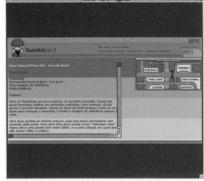

www.fontalicious.com

www.fontgraphic.com/zx26/

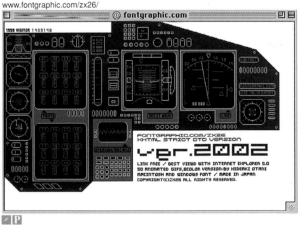

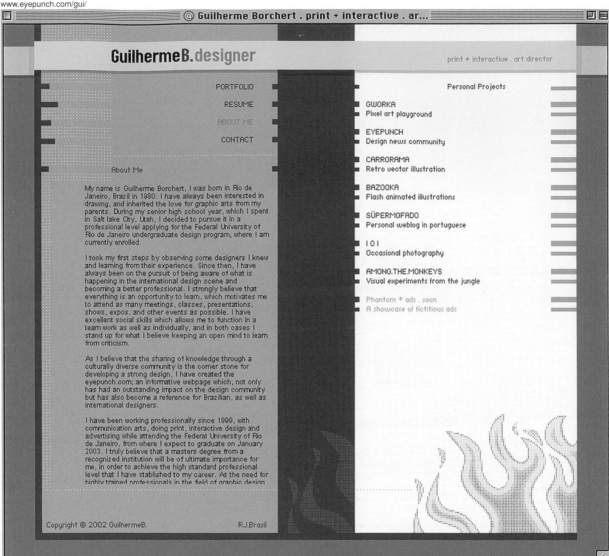

@ Guilherme Borchert . print + interactive . ar...

GuilhermeB.designer

print + interactive . art director

PORTFOLIO

RESUME

ABOUT ME

CONTACT

Personal Projects

GWORKA
Pixel art playground

EYEPUNCH
Design news community

CARRORAMA
Retro vector illustration

BAZOOKA
Flash animated illustrations

SÜPERMOFADO
Personal weblog in portuguese

I O I
Occasional photography

AMONG.THE.MONKEYS
Visual experiments from the jungle

Phantom * ads . soon
A showcase of fictitious ads

About Me

My name is Guilherme Borchert, I was born in Rio de Janeiro, Brazil in 1980. I have always been interested in drawing, and inherited the love for graphic arts from my parents. During my senior high school year, which I spent in Salt lake City, Utah, I decided to pursue it in a professional level applying for the Federal University of Rio de Janeiro undergraduate design program, where I am currently enrolled.

I took my first steps by observing some designers I knew and learning from their experience. Since then, I have always been on the pursuit of being aware of what is happening in the international design scene and becoming a better professional. I strongly believe that everything is an opportunity to learn, which motivates me to attend as many meetings, classes, presentations, shows, expos, and other events as possible. I have excellent social skills which allows me to function in a team work as well as individually, and in both cases I stand up for what I believe keeping an open mind to learn from criticism.

As I believe that the sharing of knowledge through a culturally diverse community is the corner stone for developing a strong design, I have created the eyepunch.com; an informative webpage which, not only has had an outstanding impact on the design community but has also become a reference for Brazilian, as well as international designers.

I have been working professionally since 1999, with communication arts, doing print, interactive design and advertising while attending the Federal University of Rio de Janeiro, from where I expect to graduate on January 2003. I truly believe that a masters degree from a recognized institution will be of ultimate importance for me, in order to achieve the high standard professional level that I have stablished to my career. As the need for highly trained professionals in the field of graphic design

BR F P

---

www.overage4design.com

http://www.overage4design.com/

● NOTHING HERE

● NOTHING HERE < Moving Back related

FR F P

---

www.stoav.be

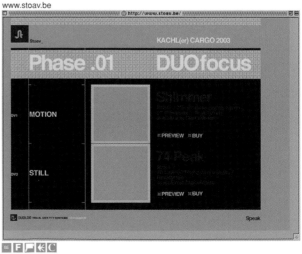

http://www.stoav.be/

Stoav

KACHL(er) CARGO 2003

Phase .01   DUOfocus

DV1   MOTION

DV2   STILL

PREVIEW BUY

PREVIEW BUY

Speak

BE F C

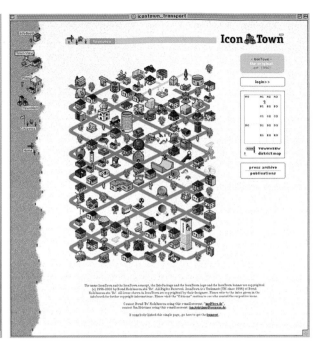

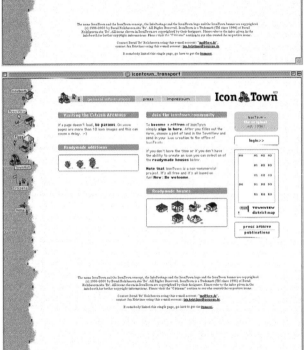

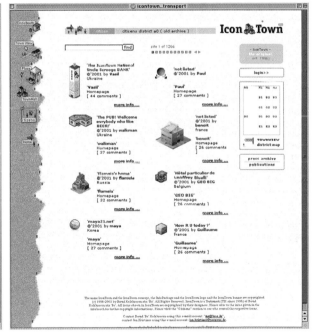

@ IDIOCASE™ – James Widegren

FEATURED PROJECT
2003/ Magasin Z Film

COPYRIGHT © 1999-2002
2003
2002
2001
2000
1999
WORK ▼
GENERAL ▼
INFO
CONTACT

01
Idiocase

Assembled identity, interactive, motion, photography and print projects 1999-2003 by art director James Widegren.

Available for assignments. Contact James

02 a
Recent Projects

📓 Magasin Z Film
📷 Karin K
🔲 Digital Vision

02 b
Current Projects

▣ Waytion

03 a
News

05.01.03 Co-Author: Photoshop Elements 2
05.01.03 In book: Metalheart 2
01.01.03 Interview: Pixel Conscious

03 b
Newsletter

your email address   Submit

IDIOCASE

AUDIO	BY ERRORENCOUNTERED	LEGEND ▼	ASSOCIATES		REQUIREMENTS	1024x768	HOSTING
STOP			CHAPTER3	SUPERSHAPES	INTERNET EXPLORER / NETSCAPE		ACTA DIVINA & PEER 1 NETWORK
			NGINCO	WAYTION	FLASH		
			ENDFORWARD	ENDEKKS	QUICKTIME		

SE F C

@ nomorespace welcomes you

nomorespace... ENTER HERE

REQUIREMENTS:
FLASH PLAYER 5
1024 X 768 RES. (OR BETTER)
A SENSE OF HUMOUR

attn: site opens in new full-screen window

USA F P

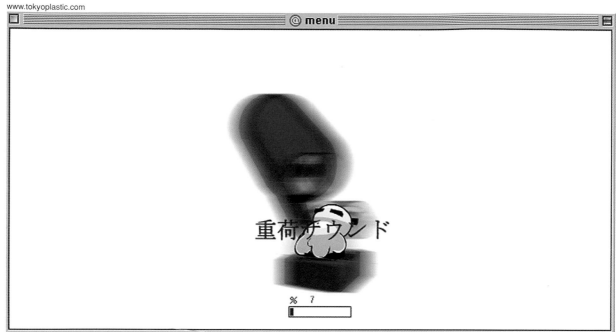

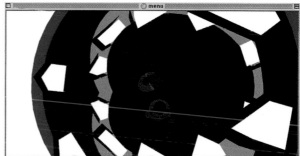

@ Insert Credit

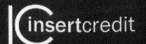

Welcome to insert credit
games studio, developer
of cutting edge browser
based games.

Q: How can a modern site
increase the time users stay
or more critically gain
repeat visits?

A: A beautifully crafted game,
of a carefully considered genre
with playability so good visitors
just have to come back.

If you would like to; purchase/
licence a game (all the games
shown on our site are available),
know more about how a great
game could help your site, or
just want to contact us, then
drop us an email to...

hello@insert-credit.com

LATEST **SUPERSOCCER**

SuperSoccer is our new football game, where
you take control of your team in friendlies,
the FA Cup, or the Premiership. Edit your
squad and formation (even individual players
tactics), Then test your skills against the best
of English football.

CLICK HERE TO PLAY

VAULT **MICRO JET RACERS**

Micro Jet Racers is a classic arcade racing
game. With 30 tracks in Normal, Arcade
and Tournament modes, and a custom
track builder... what are you waiting for?!

CLICK HERE TO PLAY

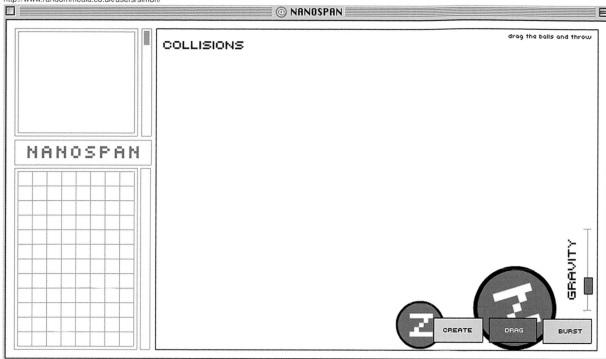

www.irrationalcontraption.net

www.olympusstudios.com

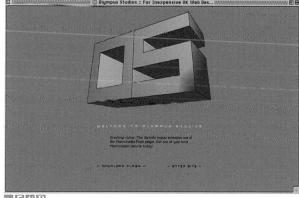

digital

@ Kaliber10000 { The Designers' Lu...

KALIBER10000 - THE GOOD VIBE PROVIDER v.6.25B
A.K.A. THE DESIGNERS' LUNCHBOX. LOCATED AT K10K.NET + .ORG. A CUBAN COUNCIL PRODUCTION

FRONT | ISSUES | NEWS | ★ SPECIALS | STORE

Kaliber Frontpage – A yummy grabbag o' design goodies

Issue 0125

No Issue
by K10k

ISSUE DESCRIPTION

We're not proud of ourselves, but due to an immense workload over our heads, the issues section is currently in a bit of disarray. We're very sorry.

We're dumb as squirrels. We hear voices and do what they command. We have broccoli in our socks.

ISSUE REQUIREMENTS

NONE	NONE	NONE	NONE

ISSUE RATINGS

⦙⦙⦙⦙⦙⦙⦙ HUMOR		⦙⦙⦙⦙⦙⦙ COMPLEXITY	
⦙⦙⦙⦙⦙⦙⦙ SMOOTHNESS		⦙⦙⦙⦙⦙⦙ INNOVATION	
⦙⦙⦙⦙⦙⦙⦙ AVERAGE		no. of ratings : 112	

Specials

★ KALIBER SPECIALS

PHOTOPACKS | ONDISPLAY | PXLPATTERNS

23 top images

CO.DESIGN TOUR 2002
PER-JESUS REPORTING FROM BOLOGNA, ITALY

★ KALIBER MATCHMAKER

RANDOM | LIST PROJECTS | WHAT IS THIS ?!!

SIGNOS en el CIE

'Signs in Heaven' – Onais ...

Desc : :: Onaisin.net :: the land of the magical p ...

Needed : We are back featuring "Signs in Heaven" an Icon ...

★ GLOBAL EVENT LOC...

LISTING | CALENDAR

Upcoming Events

**Jun 05
Jeff Minter Live**

One of the founding of the Bri ...

**Jun 05 – Jul 30
BoomBox : A Group**

BoomBox features Seattle's fre ...

★ GENERIC MEDUTAIN...

TRAILERPARK | MOO...

01	Cuckoo
02	Animated Ang...
03	Northfork

Store

NEW K10k TEES | ID #005
NIELSEN ESPECIAL

MOODSTATS APP | ID #002
Now also for OS X
MONITOR YOUR MOODS

HALF EMPTY #1
EMERGING ART...

Backissue 0001

Brazilian Anatomy
by nando costa

Wulffmorgenthaler's Daily

I want to trust her, but look at our kids! They're ...

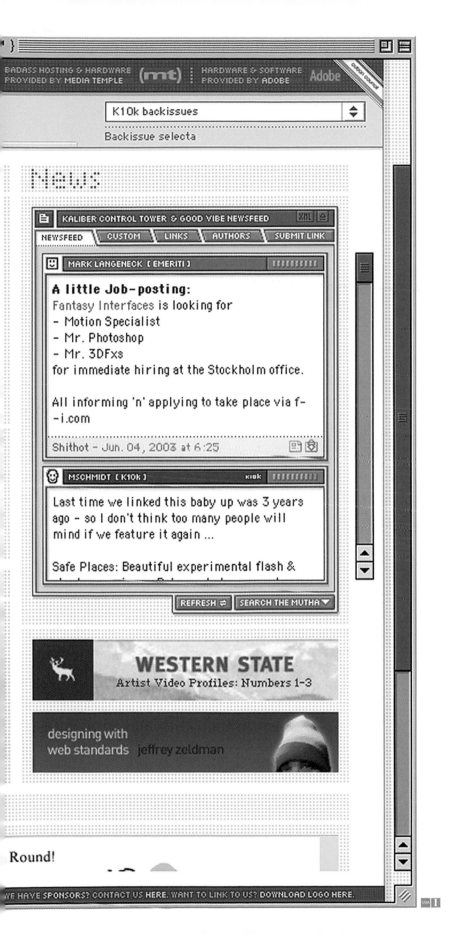

K10k backissues

Backissue selecta

News

KALIBER CONTROL TOWER & GOOD VIBE NEWSFEED   XML

NEWSFEED | CUSTOM | LINKS | AUTHORS | SUBMIT LINK

MARK LANGENECK [EMERITI]

A little Job-posting:
Fantasy Interfaces is looking for
- Motion Specialist
- Mr. Photoshop
- Mr. 3DFxs
for immediate hiring at the Stockholm office.

All informing 'n' applying to take place via f--i.com

Shithot - Jun. 04, 2003 at 6:25

MSCHMIDT [K10k]   KIOK

Last time we linked this baby up was 3 years ago - so I don't think too many people will mind if we feature it again ...

Safe Places: Beautiful experimental flash &

REFRESH ⇌ | SEARCH THE MUTHA ▼

WESTERN STATE
Artist Video Profiles: Numbers 1-3

designing with web standards jeffrey zeldman

Round!

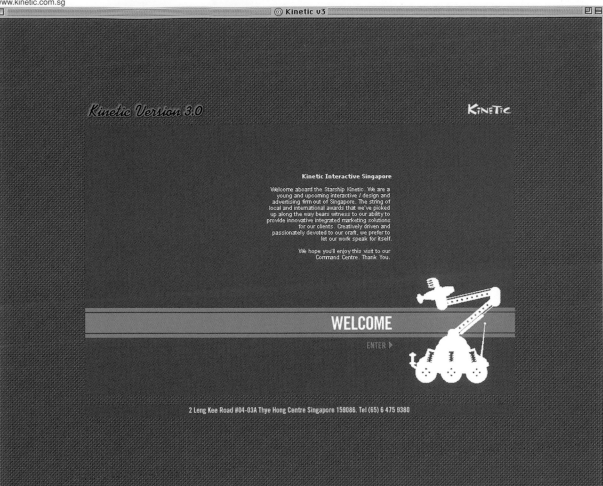

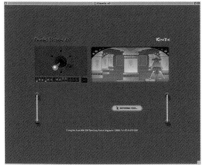

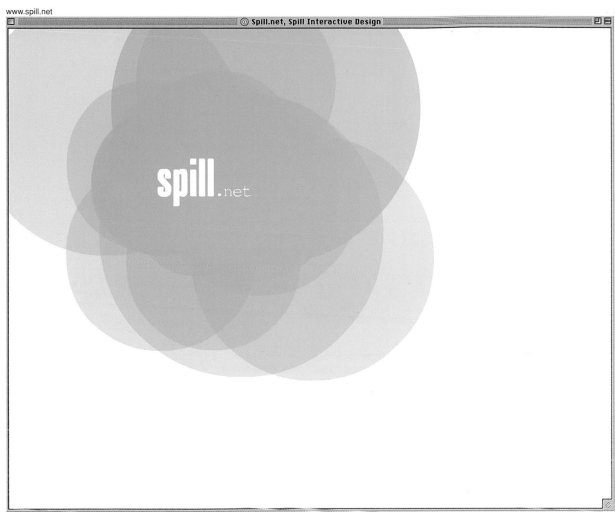

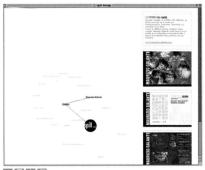

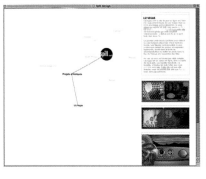

@ | miniml | v3 |

VERSION 3

Welcome to miniml.com!

To select a project, use the indexed list
to the left. You can sort content by
date (default), type, or name by clicking
on the corresponding word when you
rollover the miniml logo.

To download fonts, you must first
purchase an access pass. Click on the
access pass button for more details.

EMAIL

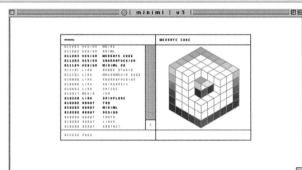

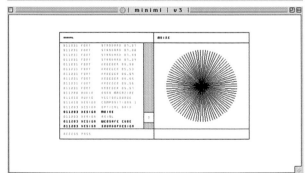

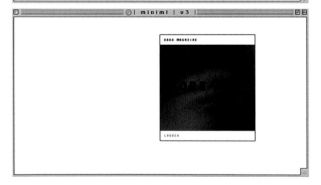

www.nooflat.nu

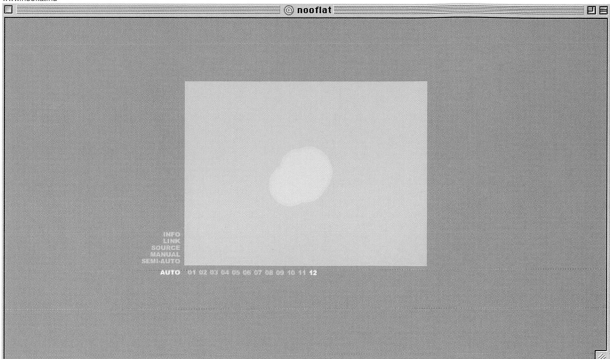

INFO
LINK
SOURCE
MANUAL
SEMI-AUTO
AUTO   01 02 03 04 05 06 07 08 09 10 11 12

www.noon.no

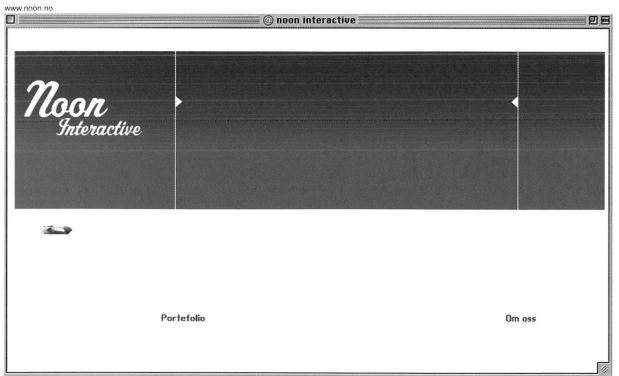

Portefolio   Om oss

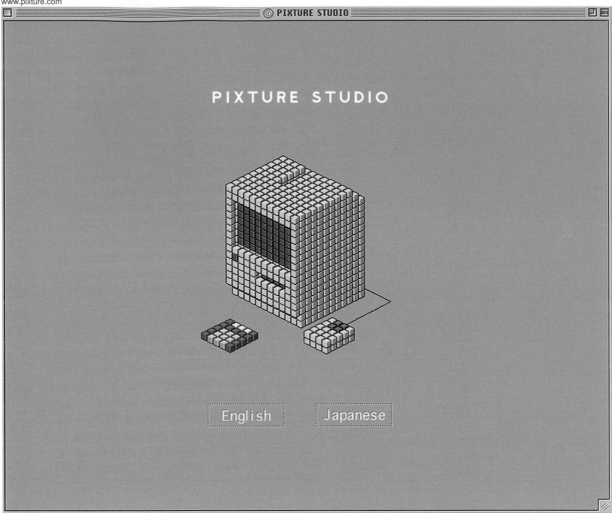

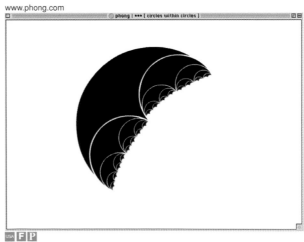

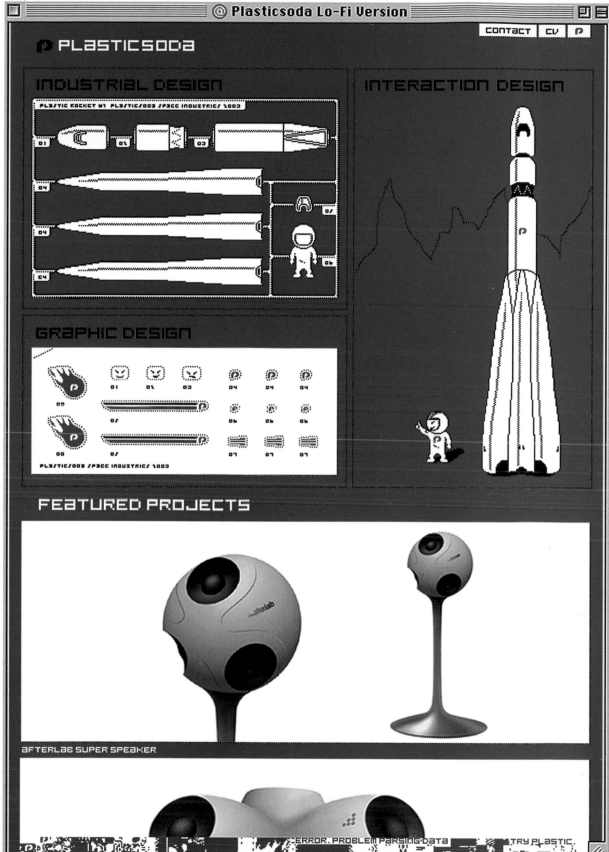

http://plotdev.com/

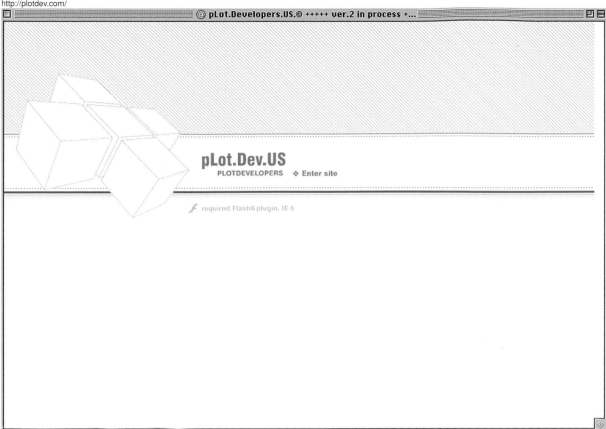

http://poligon.co.uk/

www.effects.it/ams/

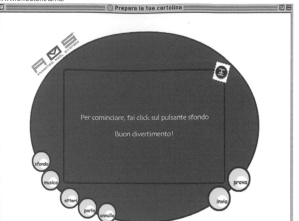

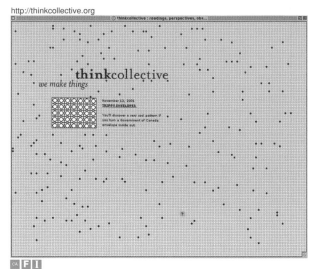

IT F C

CA F I

www.screenbow.de

www.screenpainting.com

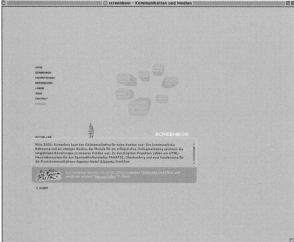

DE F C

AT F P

www.sweaterweather.org

www.soulsampler.com

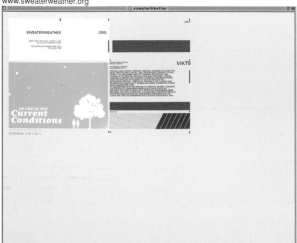

USA I

SE P

www.probe3.com

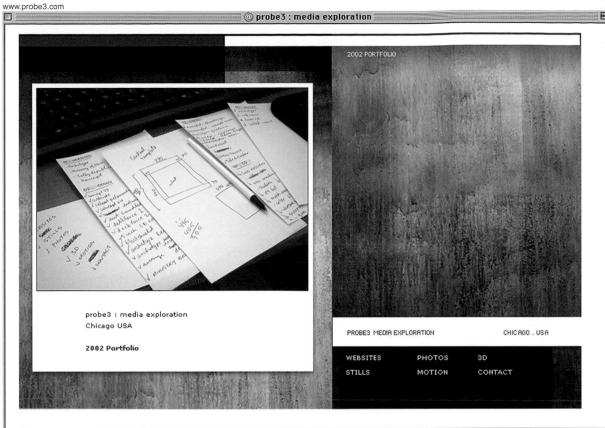

probe3 : media exploration
Chicago USA

2002 Portfolio

PROBE3 MEDIA EXPLORATION   CHICAGO . USA

WEBSITES   PHOTOS   3D

STILLS   MOTION   CONTACT

www.soppcollective.com

02.04.2003

We\'ve updated our work section so there are a few more pieces in the print, flyer and interactive section. We\'ve also created a link for the 'Ugress - Loungemeister' video in the moving image section so you can view or download it at: www.ugress.com under 'Videos/Fotos'.

06.03.2003

SCHATZ – POST TRASH
Here some pictures of our work at the exhibition at the Cruise Bar on Monday the 3rd of March.

news

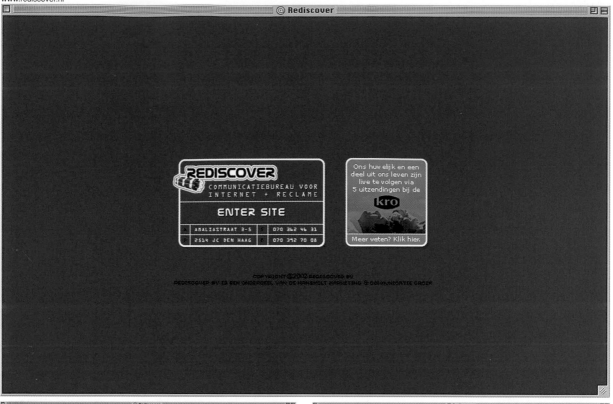

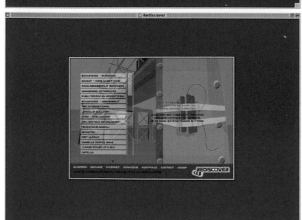

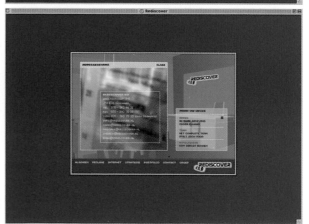

http://surface.yugop.com

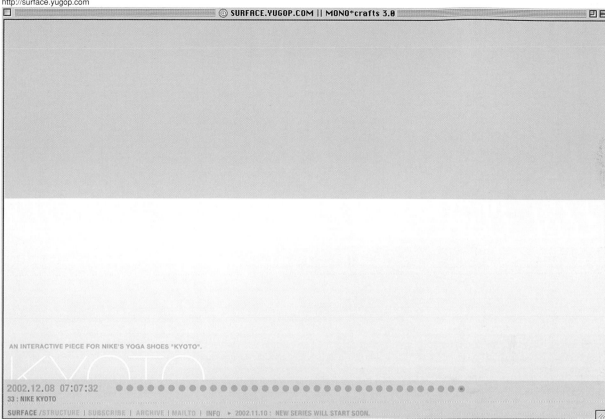

AN INTERACTIVE PIECE FOR NIKE'S YOGA SHOES "KYOTO".

KYOTO

2002.12.08 07:07:32 ●
33 : NIKE KYOTO

SURFACE /STRUCTURE | SUBSCRIBE | ARCHIVE | MAILTO | INFO ► 2002.11.10 : NEW SERIES WILL START SOON.

www.beonsite.com

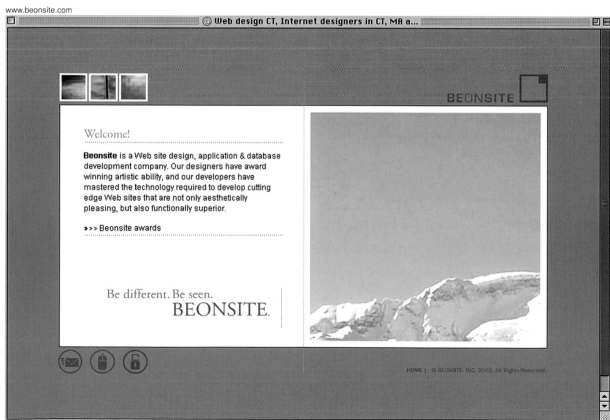

@ Web design CT, Internet designers in CT, MA a...

BEONSITE

Welcome!

Beonsite is a Web site design, application & database development company. Our designers have award winning artistic ability, and our developers have mastered the technology required to develop cutting edge Web sites that are not only aesthetically pleasing, but also functionally superior.

>>> Beonsite awards

Be different. Be seen.
BEONSITE.

HOME | © BEONSITE, INC. 2002. All Rights Reserved.

www.switchinteractive.com

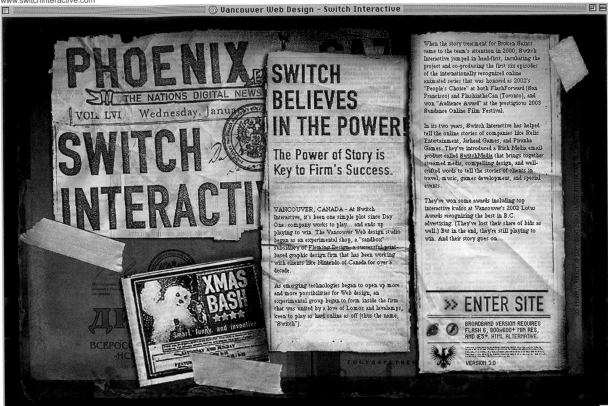

www.vectorpark.com

www.mmiweb.com

www.texturemedia.com

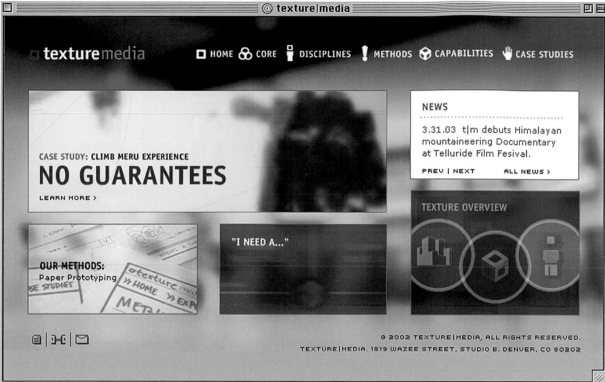

www.kluever.info

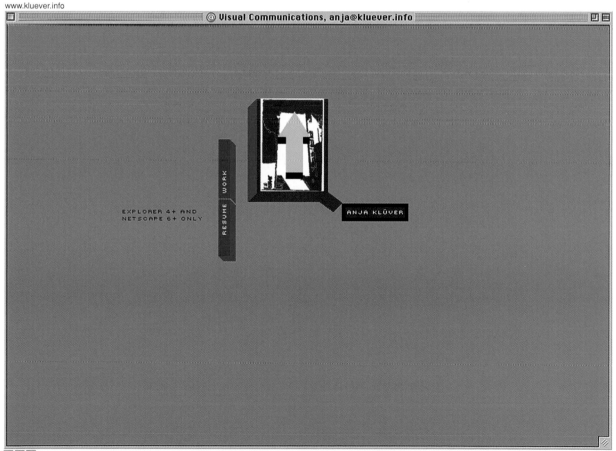

http://www.andressaurina.com/index2.htm

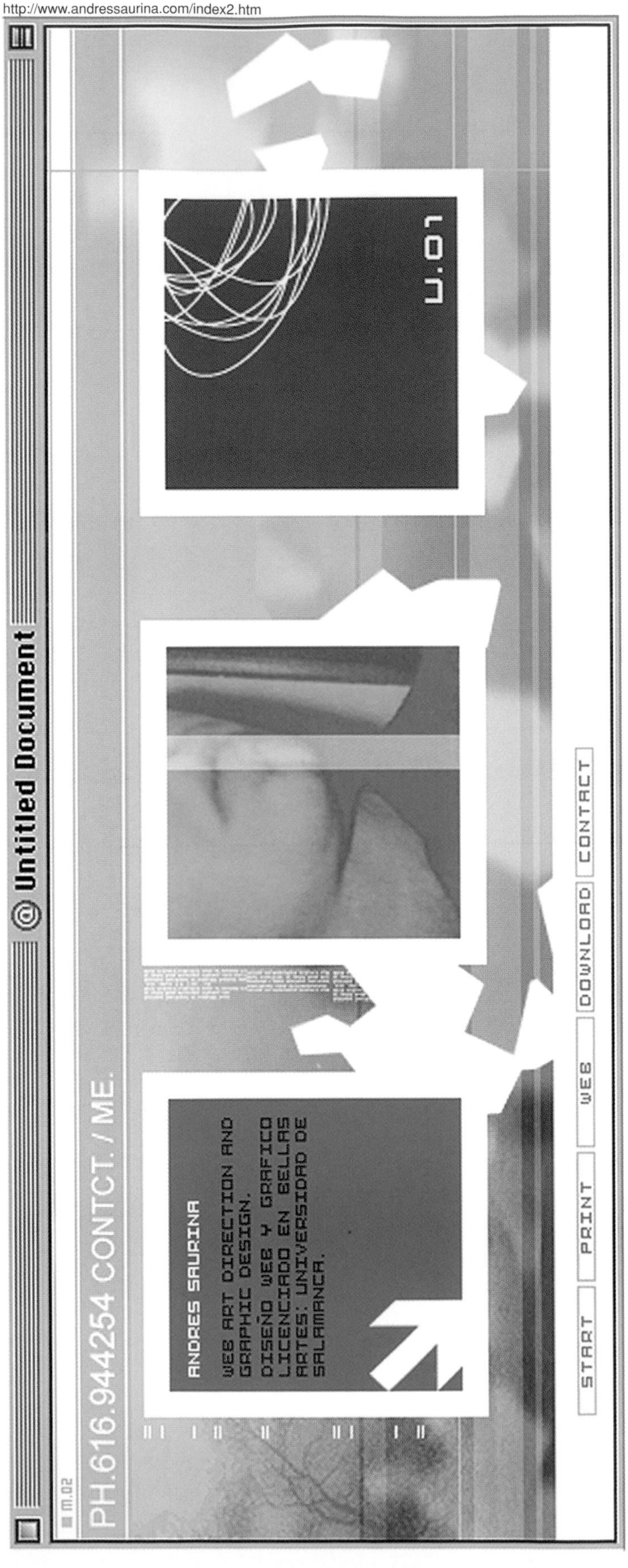
Untitled Document
PH.616.944254 CONTCT. / ME.
m.02
ANDRES SAURINA
WEB ART DIRECTION AND GRAPHIC DESIGN.
DISEÑO WEB Y GRAFICO LICENCIADO EN BELLAS ARTES: UNIVERSIDAD DE SALAMANCA.
U.01
START
PRINT
WEB
DOWNLOAD
CONTACT

@ WYSIWYG* Software Design GmbH

WYSIWYG* Software Design GmbH, Düsseldorf
WYSIWYG ist ein Betriebssystem zum Ausdenken, Finden und
Machen von Multimedia Lösungen. *What You See Is What You Get*

Gute Zahlen:
Die Website der NRW
Medien GmbH glänzt mit
einem monatlichen
Magazin. Resultat: Mehr
Besucher und weniger
Kosten als vorher.

>> mehr

Die beste Idee der Welt:
Total Recall – das
Festival des
nacherzählten Films.
Jetzt mit noch mehr
Filmen im Netz.

>> zur Website

Wie im Fernsehen:
Die neue Website des
Mineralwassers Volvic.
Unter anderem mit einem
sehenswerten Finger-
Kick Spiel

>> mehr

Ganz schön schlau:
Das neue
Geschäftskunden-portal
der Deutschen Telekom
AG. Sieht gut aus. Und
kann auch richtig was.

>> mehr

>> impressum

DE F C

www.lunapod.com

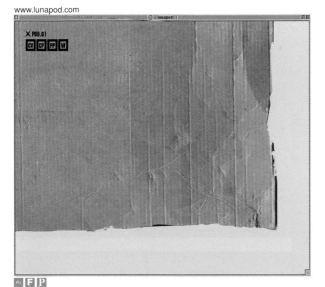

AU F P

www.brainworks.com.mx/me

USA F « P

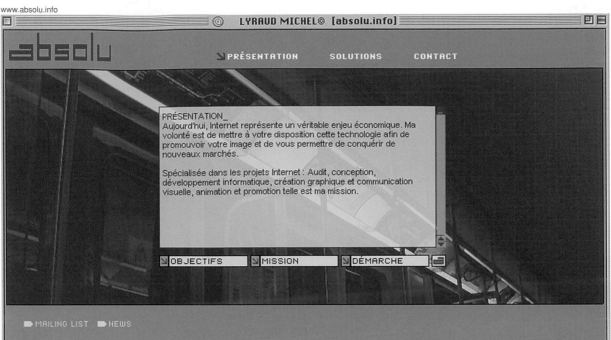

PRÉSENTATION_
Aujourd'hui, Internet représente un véritable enjeu économique. Ma volonté est de mettre à votre disposition cette technologie afin de promouvoir votre image et de vous permettre de conquérir de nouveaux marchés.

Spécialisée dans les projets Internet : Audit, conception, développement informatique, création graphique et communication visuelle, animation et promotion telle est ma mission.

OBJECTIFS   MISSION   DÉMARCHE

MAILING LIST   NEWS

www.wheelhousecreative.co.uk

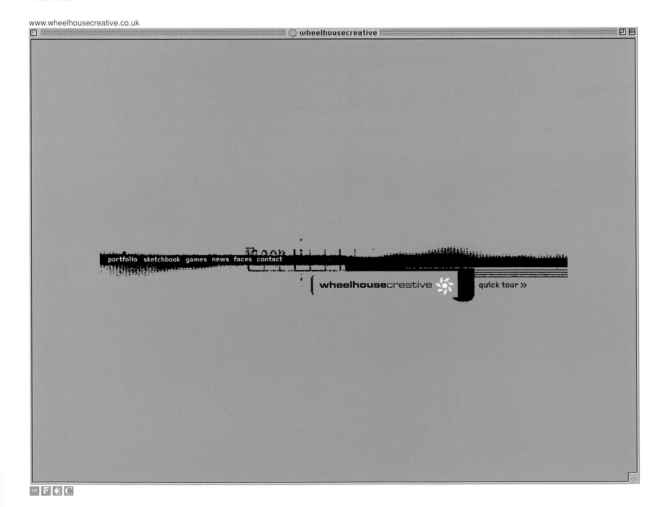

portfolio sketchbook games news faces contact

wheelhousecreative   quick tour »

www.evagarde.it

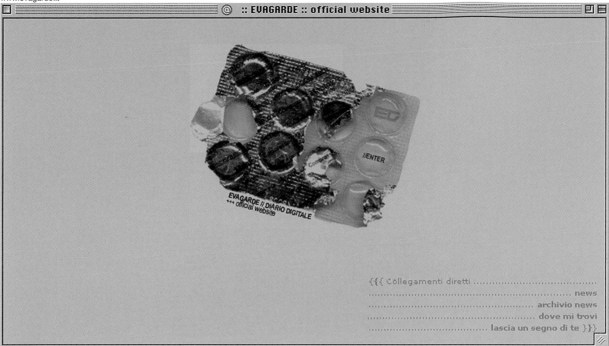

IT F K P

http://T4XI.de

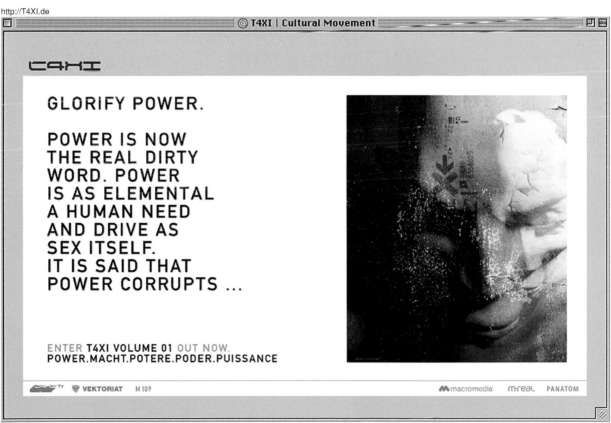

DE F K C

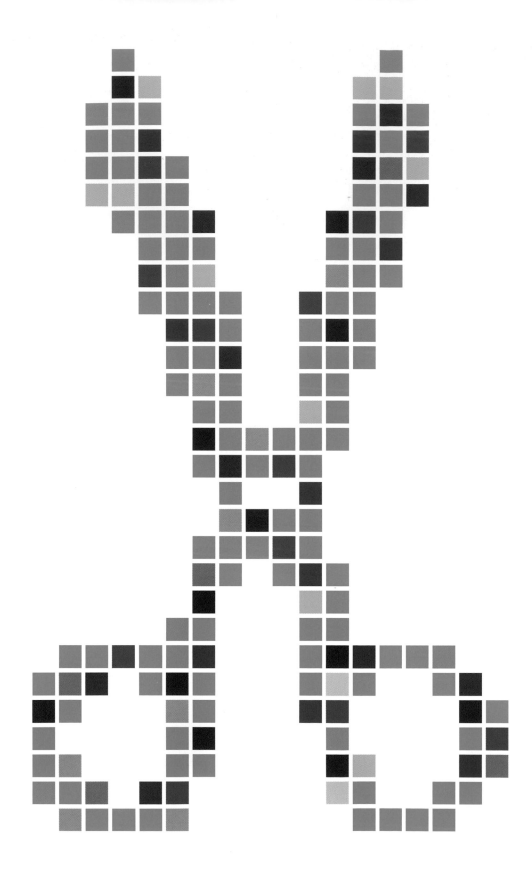

www.zoomp.com.br

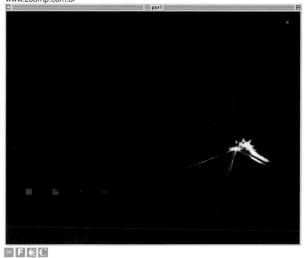

BR F K C

www.hektik.com.au

Explosionszeichnungen

AU C

www.binoche.be

binôche®
elgian Sunglasses

nederlands | français | english

Music: Daydreaming by Rollercone
concept and design by BoulevArt | created with Macromedia FlashMX

BE F K C

www.bugatti.de

Collection Partners Group Press Jobs Contact Impressum   bugatti

...im guten Fachhandel

DE C

www.stellamccartney.com

WELCOME TO
STELLAMcCARTNEY

YOU NEED TO HAVE FLASH 5 INSTALLED TO ENTER THIS SITE.
IF YOU HAVE IT ALREADY CLICK TO ENTER

IF YOU NEED FLASH 5 CLICK HERE TO DOWNLOAD IT...

UK F C

www.bcbg.com

BCBGMAXAZRIA   COMPANY   STORE LOCATOR   KEEP IN TOUCH   SWEEPSTAKES   INTERACTIVE

BCBGMAXAZRIA
COLLECTION   BCBGMAXAZRIA

USA F C

agnès b.

SIAÒNAAᖵ | HSIꞀ⅁NƎ | SIANOᕉAꓶ

ASU ƎNIꞀNO ꓒOHS

www.apc.fr

A.P.C.

ACCÉDER AU SITE EN FRANÇAIS
TO VIEW THIS WEB SITE IN ENGLISH   USA / OTHER
日本語ウェブサイトへのアクセス

Ce site nécessite le plug-in Flash5.
Vous pouvez le télécharger en cliquant içi.

You need Flash5 plug-in to surf on this website.
To download it, click here.

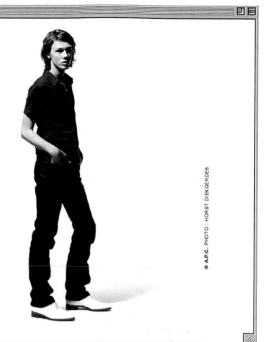

© A.P.C. PHOTO : HORST DIEKGERDES

FR F █ « C

---

www.alicialawhon.com

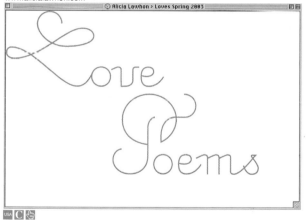

USA C ▣

---

www.carmelasutera.com

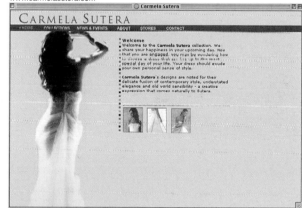

CARMELA SUTERA

HOME   COLLECTIONS   NEWS & EVENTS   ABOUT   STORES   CONTACT

Welcome
Welcome to the **Carmela Sutera** collection. We
share your happiness in your upcoming day. Now
that you are engaged, you may be wondering how
to choose a dress that can live up to this most
special day of your life. Your dress should exude
your own personal sense of style.

Carmela Sutera's designs are noted for their
delicate fusion of contemporary style, understated
elegance and old world sensibility - a creative
expression that comes naturally to Sutera.

USA F « C

antonio bernardo

galeria   oficina   antonio   espaço ab   notícias   orquidário   contato

---

Antonio Bernardo

galeria oficina antonio espaço ab notícias orquidário contato

GALERIA

Aqui você terá uma mostra do trabalho de Antonio Bernardo. Algumas peças estão reproduzidas em tamanho diferente do original para melhor visualização. Se você deseja mais informações sobre estas jóias ou ainda conhecer outras peças, clique aqui e fale conosco.

- Anéis / Alianças
- Brincos
- Colares
- Pingentes
- Pulseiras

Antonio Bernardo

galeria **oficina** antonio espaço ab notícias orquidário contato

OFICINA

Em nossas oficinas, Antonio Bernardo e uma equipe de ourives com sólida formação técnica e artística compõem uma rica parceria. O ouro, a principal matéria-prima, vai sendo transformado pelas mãos de nossos habilidosos profissionais. Da fundição do metal ao acabamento, com equipamentos de avançada tecnologia, o rigor e a fidelidade ao projeto inicial são mantidos, certificando a qualidade destas valiosas peças assinadas por Antonio Bernardo.

- Clique aqui para conhecer mais o Ouro, metal principal de nossas jóias.

Antonio Bernardo

galeria oficina antonio espaço ab notícias **orquidário** contato

antonio bernardo

ORQUIDÁRIO

Em 1997, consolidando uma antiga paixão pela flor, Antonio Bernardo adotou o Orquidário do Jardim Botânico do Rio de Janeiro, ajudando a recuperar e a divulgar uma das mais significativas e ricas coleções de orquídeas do Brasil.

- Dicas
- Veja as orquídeas que estão florindo agora

Antonio Bernardo

galeria oficina antonio **espaço ab** notícias orquidário contato

ESPAÇO ANTONIO BERNARDO

Exposições
- Leveza - Fabiana Santos, Leila Franco, Lia do Rio, Luiz Cesar Monken e Suely Farhi / outubro e novembro de 2002
- Fertilidade - Celeida Tostes / abril e maio de 2002

O que é o Espaço AB?

A arte toma conta do Espaço AB: exposições individuais e coletivas, palestras, mostras que

BR C

www.adidas.com

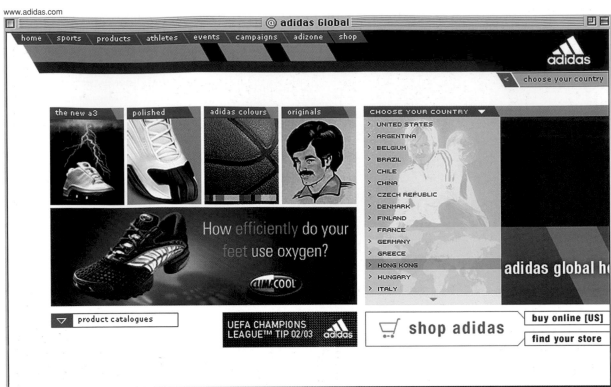

DE F C

www.benediktemai.dk

USA F C

www.BlundstoneUSA.COM

USA C

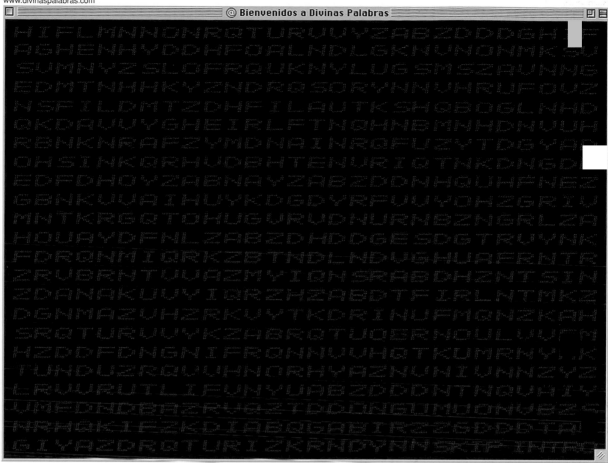

www.alexandermcqueen.net

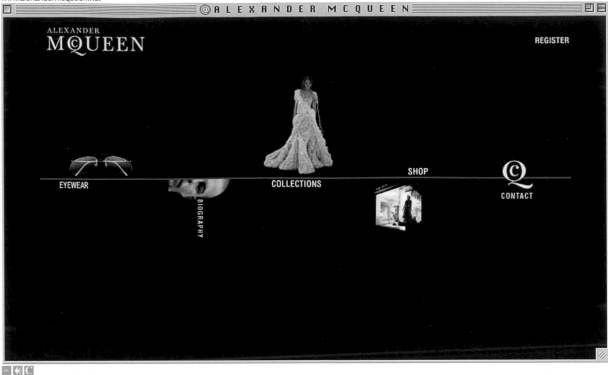

ALEXANDER
MCQUEEN

REGISTER

EYEWEAR

BIOGRAPHY

COLLECTIONS

SHOP

CONTACT

www.loewe.com

LOEWE

Por el olivar venían
bronce y sueño, los gitanos.

Spanish   Japanese

The Latest   Collections   The world of Loewe   The Loewe Club   Loewe Foundation   Loewe Vision   Map

www.bulgari.com

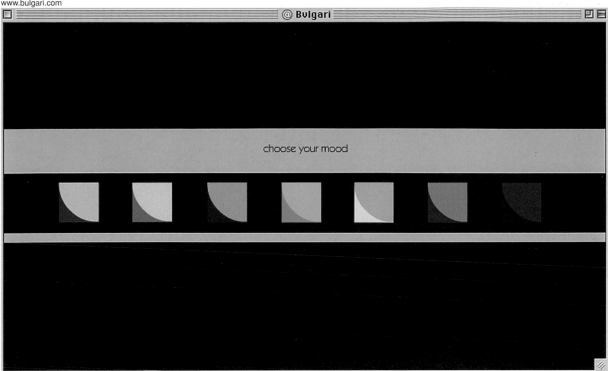

choose your mood

www.chanel.com

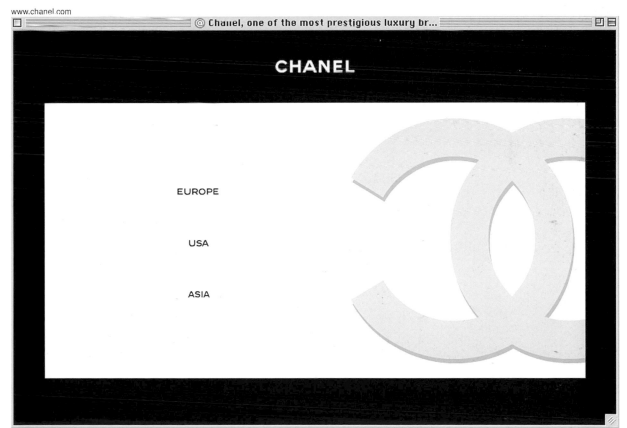

CHANEL

EUROPE

USA

ASIA

CAMPAIGN

COLLECTIONS

MOVIES

HISTORY

LOCATIONS

DIALOGUE

BRUUNS BAZAAR

www.cartier.com

@ Cartier - The famous french watchmaker-jeweler

BIENVENUE . WELCOME . ようこそ . 歡迎 . 환영합니다

Cartier

FR F C

www.chantelle.com

@ CHANTELLE : LIGNE LINGERIE ET SOUS-VETEMENT F...

Chantelle habille les femmes du monde

Chantelle

FRANCE | DEUTSCHLAND | ESPAÑA | ITALIA | UK | INTERNATIONAL (ENGLISH) | USA | 中文 (臺灣) | 日本語 | РОССИЯ

FR F C

@ colette : paris

colette

❶ ❷ ❸ ❹ ❺

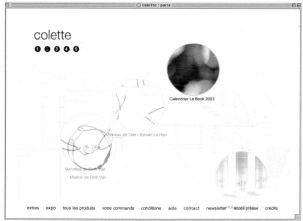

Calendrier Le Book 2003

Anneau de Tête - Sylvain Le Hen

Menottes de Dinh Van

Maillon de Dinh Van

extras   expo   tous les produits   votre commande   conditions   aide   contact   newsletter   accès presse   crédits

colette

❶ ❷ ❸ ❹ ❺

COLETTE N° 4

CD - COLETTE N°4

NY FAT de Michael Lau

CD - COLETTE N°5

Housse iPod Pucci

extras   expo   tous les produits   votre commande   conditions   aide   contact   newsletter   accès presse   crédits

produit

Porte-couverts Heinze

€ 22

envoyer à un(e) ami(e)   acheter ce produit

Porte-couverts Heinze

Simplissime, élégant et de forme épurée, pour une table parfaitement arrangée, ce porte-couverts en métal poli inoxydable sera du meilleur effet pour recevoir vos amis... et fini les taches sur les nappes!
Design Heinze.

Fourni sans couverts.
90 mm. de diamètre, 2 mm. d'épaisseur. Livré par set de 2.

www.h1e.com

produit

L'Ours Charles

€ 143

beige / ecru (photo)

envoyer à un(e) ami(e)   acheter ce produit

L'Ours Charles

Cet ours a été réalisé à partir du tissu "Small Dot" (représentant une structure moléculaire fictive) créé en 1947 par Charles & Ray Eames. Il aura fallu attendre 55 ans avant que cet imprimé soit édité pour la première fois par Kvadrat. L'Ours Charles est une exclusivité colette imaginé par Rodolphe Simon.

Édition numérotée et limitée à 50 exemplaires.
230 mm. x 160 mm. Poids: 250 g

FR F K C

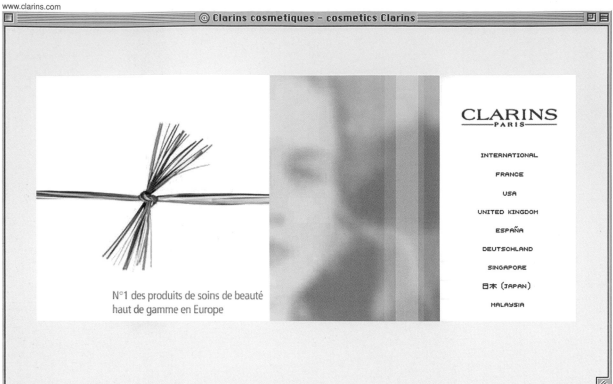

Clarins cosmetiques – cosmetics Clarins

N°1 des produits de soins de beauté haut de gamme en Europe

CLARINS
PARIS

INTERNATIONAL

FRANCE

USA

UNITED KINGDOM

ESPAÑA

DEUTSCHLAND

SINGAPORE

日本 (JAPAN)

MALAYSIA

Complementos CM – Complementos Nupciales

cm

Complementos Nupciales
Nuptial Complements

www.closed.com

◻ @ CLOSED ◻

CLOSED (c)

ENTER / GET FLASH 6

DE ⊦ ⟨ C

www.celine.com

CELINE: the French fashion brand of luxury re...

C E L I N E

FRANÇAIS
ENGLISH
日本語

FR F ⟨ C

www.donnakaran.com

Donna Karan New York

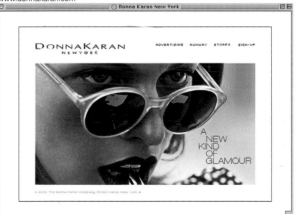

DONNAKARAN
NEWYORK

ADVERTISING   RUNWAY   STORES   SIGN-UP

A
NEW
KIND
OF
GLAMOUR

USA F C

DOLCE & GABBANA

ITALIANO   ENGLISH

IT F C

☰ ellusjeansdeluxe

ellusjeansdeluxe
entre versão português
enter english version

ČANATIBA   by.grafikonstruct

BR F C

@ FASHCAT [Moda - Internet - Diseño - Paginas ...

□□ << CONCEPTOS   □ << PACK 10

▓▓ CARGANDO

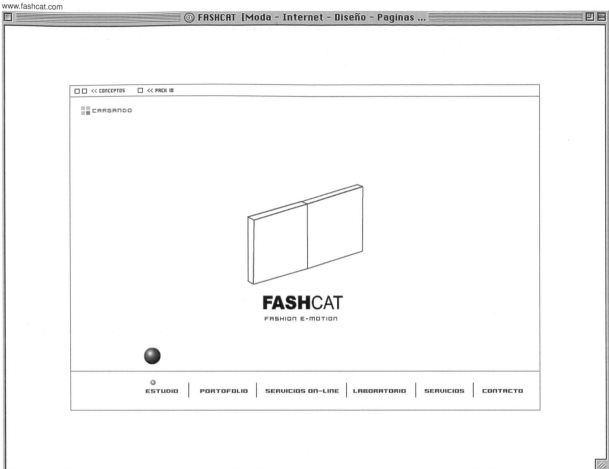

FASHCAT

FASHION E-MOTION

ESTUDIO | PORTOFOLIO | SERVICIOS ON-LINE | LABORATORIO | SERVICIOS | CONTACTO

ES F K C

www.eckounltd.com

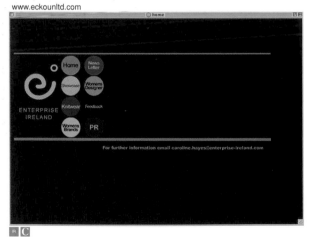

www.fabricfrontline.ch

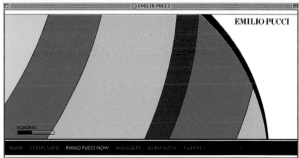

women

Wenn du Dich entschieden hast auf welchen flip*flops®
Du in Zukunft durchs Leben laufen willst, klick Deine
Favoriten einfach an und zieh Dir die Minis mit der Maus
in den Shop.

B-Colour   **Block**   **Flower Power**

Originals

Wome
sun
Größe
16.00

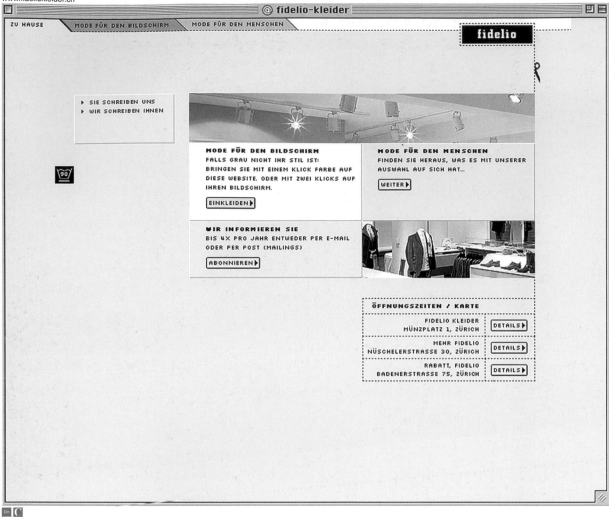

ZU HAUSE · MODE FÜR DEN BILDSCHIRM · MODE FÜR DEN MENSCHEN

fidelio

▶ SIE SCHREIBEN UNS
▶ WIR SCHREIBEN IHNEN

MODE FÜR DEN BILDSCHIRM
FALLS GRAU NICHT IHR STIL IST:
BRINGEN SIE MIT EINEM KLICK FARBE AUF
DIESE WEBSITE. ODER MIT ZWEI KLICKS AUF
IHREN BILDSCHIRM.

EINKLEIDEN ▶

MODE FÜR DEN MENSCHEN
FINDEN SIE HERAUS, WAS ES MIT UNSERER
AUSWAHL AUF SICH HAT...

WEITER ▶

WIR INFORMIEREN SIE
BIS 4X PRO JAHR ENTWEDER PER E-MAIL
ODER PER POST (MAILINGS)

ABONNIEREN ▶

ÖFFNUNGSZEITEN / KARTE

FIDELIO KLEIDER
MÜNZPLATZ 1, ZÜRICH — DETAILS ▶

MEHR FIDELIO
NÜSCHELERSTRASSE 30, ZÜRICH — DETAILS ▶

RABATT, FIDELIO
BADENERSTRASSE 75, ZÜRICH — DETAILS ▶

CH C

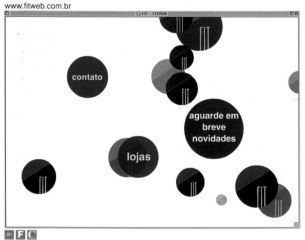

FIT - FITWEB

contato

aguarde em
breve
novidades

lojas

BR F C

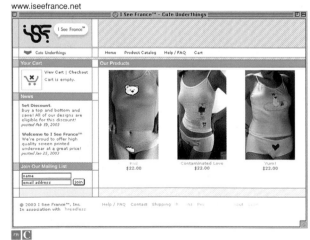

I See France™ - Cute Underthings

iSF I See France™

Cute Underthings   Home   Product Catalog   Help / FAQ   Cart

Your Cart
View Cart | Checkout
Cart is empty.

News
Set Discount.
Buy a top and bottom and
save! All of our designs are
eligible for this discount!
posted Feb 19, 2003

Welcome to I See France™
We're proud to offer high
quality screen printed
underwear at a great price!
posted Jan 25, 2003

Join Our Mailing List
name
email address   join

Our Products

Phil
$22.00

Contaminated Love
$22.00

Yum!
$22.00

© 2003 I See France™, Inc.
In association with threadless

Help / FAQ Contact Shipping R   ns Pr   out

FR C

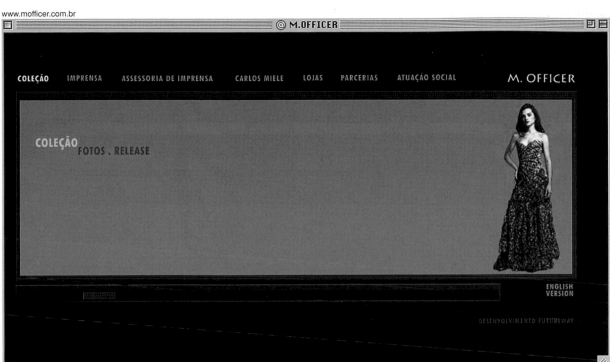

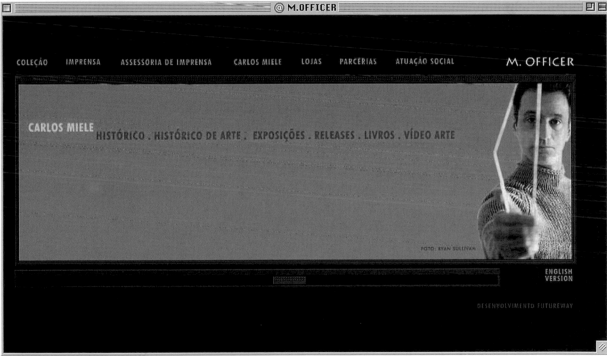

@ GIANFRANCOFERRE'

GIANFRANCO FERRE

ITALIANO
per la navigazione di questo sito
è necessario il plug_in di Flash 5

NOTIZIE LEGALI   INFO

ENGLISH
to view this website
you need Flash 5 plug_in

LEGAL NOTICES   INFO

IT F C

@ Giorgio Armani

I READ / SPEAK ENGLISH

LEGGO / PARLO ITALIANO

日本語

IT F C

www.givenchy.com

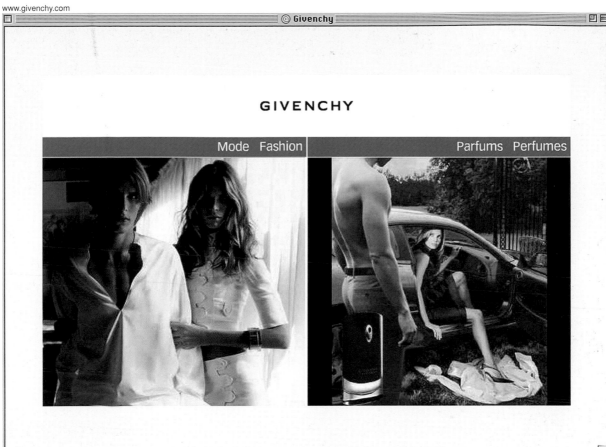

www.gucci.com

www.guerlain.fr

www.yohjiyamamoto.co.jp

@ YOHJIYAMAMOTO

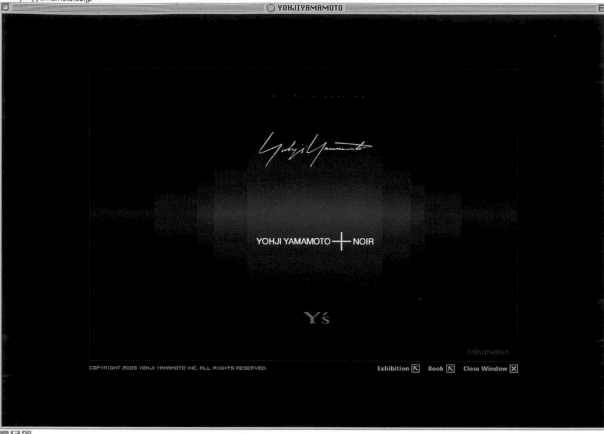

YOHJI YAMAMOTO ✚ NOIR

Y's

Information

Exhibition ↖   Book ↖   Close Window ✕

JP F C

www.hugoboss.com

HUGO BOSS

HUGO BOSS

English

Deutsch

DE F ‹ C

www.kenzo.com

© kOzen : cool web site, net culture, urban cha...

KENZO KOZEN

Découvrir le site Kozen
[kao] [zen] de Kenzo
en français

> Entrée

Discover Kozen
[kao] [zen] by Kenzo
in English

Enter ‹

copyright © 2002 KENZO

F ‹ C

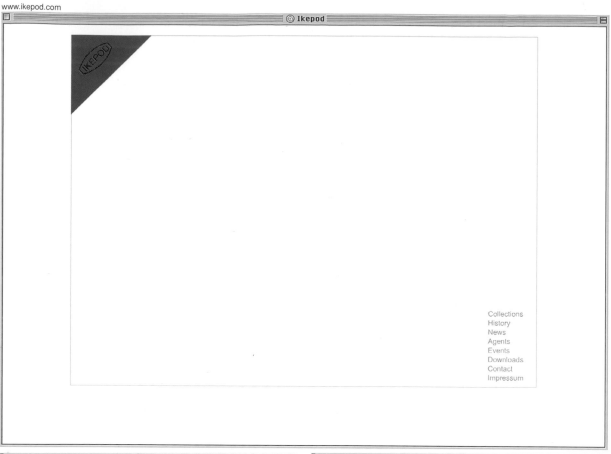

Collections
History
News
Agents
Events
Downloads
Contact
Impressum

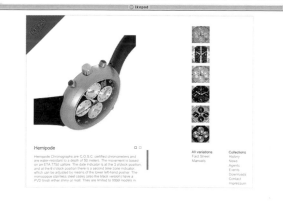

Hemipode

Hemipode Chronographs are C.O.S.C. certified chronometers and are water-resistant to a depth of 50 meters. The movement is based on an ETA 7750 calibre. The date indicator is at the 3 o'clock position, and at the 8 o'clock position there is a second time zone indicator, which can be adjusted by means of the lower left-hand pusher. The monocoque stainless steel cases (also the black version) have a PVD finish either shiny or matt. There are limited to 9999 models in

All variations
Fact Sheet
Manuals

Collections
History
News
Agents
Events
Downloads
Contact
Impressum

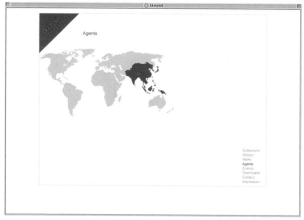

Agents

Collections
History
News
Agents
Events
Downloads
Contact
Impressum

Case
Strap

ISO-0501
Yellow Gold
Yellow Gold Matt Diamonds
White

Isopode Dual Time

The Isopode Dual Time is equipped with an ETA 2892-A2 movement. This C.O.S.C. certified chronometer displays a second time zone on a counter at 12 o'clock and the date at 6 o'clock. The case has the same monocoque style and dimensions as the Isopode Chronograph and is water-resistant to a depth of 50 meters. The monocoque stainless steel case has a PVD coating. Each version of the dial is being produced in a limited series of 9999 in stainless steel. 999 in

All variations
Fact Sheet
Manuals

Collections
History
News
Agents
Events
Downloads
Contact
Impressum

@ NaCo.

NaCo.

En NaCo. creemos que de alguna manera, en los ojos de otra gente todos somos nacos, acogemos la idea de celebrar quienes somos con seguridad y estilo.

NaCo. ofrece una gran variedad de productos inovadores y de calidad para saciar los gustos de nacos alrededor del mundo.

Lo invitamos a encontrar al naco que vive su interior!

NaCo.

NaCo. is a company dedicated to designing and producing innovative, quality products that reflect and celebrate the folklore and humor behind its concept.

We believe that in some way, through somebody else's eyes we are all nacos and we endorse the idea of stating who you are with confidence and style.

NaCo. offers a wide variety of designs and products to fit the wide spectrum of Nacos all over the world.

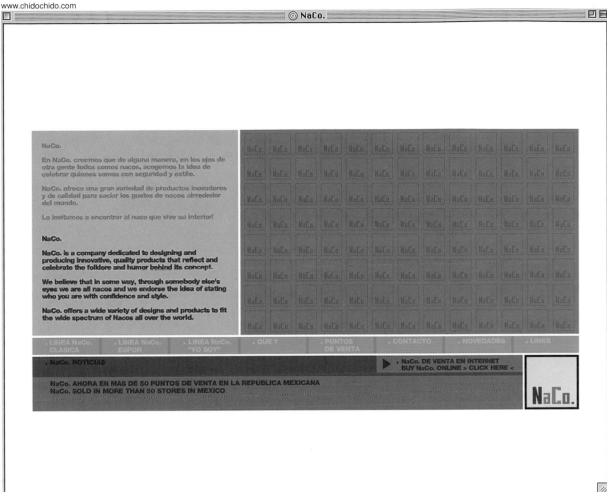

- LINEA NaCo. CLASICA   - LINEA NaCo. ESPOR   - LINEA NaCo. "YO SOY"   - QUE ?   - PUNTOS DE VENTA   - CONTACTO   - NOVEDADES   - LINKS

- NaCo. NOTICIAS   ▶ NaCo. DE VENTA EN INTERNET
                                      BUY NaCo. ONLINE > CLICK HERE <

NaCo. AHORA EN MAS DE 50 PUNTOS DE VENTA EN LA REPUBLICA MEXICANA
NaCo. SOLD IN MORE THAN 50 STORES IN MEXICO

NaCo.

www.bmf.es

index

B.M.F.
SPORT WOMAN

Oficina Central
Telf. 91 870 14 29
Fax 91 870 27 53

HOME   ENPRESA   CATALOGO   EMAIL

www.michikokoshino.co.uk

Michiko Koshino

MICHIKO KOSHINO

SKIP INTRO ▶

AVAILABLE SOON - OUR SPRING / SUMMER 2003 COLLECTION WILL BE IN STORE FROM THE END OF FEBRUARY. PLEASE VIEW SOME OF THE NEW DESIGNS ONLINE

PLEASE ENSURE TO BOOKMARK THIS PAGE AND COME BACK AND VISIT US

PLEASE ENTER OUR SITE ▶

@ **JeanPaulGaultier.com – Haute-Cout**

HAUTE COUTURE | PRÊT à PORTER | ACCESSOIRES | PARFUMS | UNIVERSE | GAULTIERLAND | BOUTIQU

Jean Paul GAULTIER

passer l'intro...

PRINTEMPS-ETE
2003

LA PERLA

NEWS   CATWALK   MUSIC   PRESS REV   FOR YOU   SUBSCRIBE   COMPANY   WHERE   E-SHOP

UNDERWEAR
SWIMWEAR
NIGHTWEAR
OUTWEAR
SPORTWEAR
TIGHTS
SHOES
EYEWEAR
BEAUTY

LA PERLA   OTHER BRANDS   MAN COLLECTION   JUNIOR COLLECTION

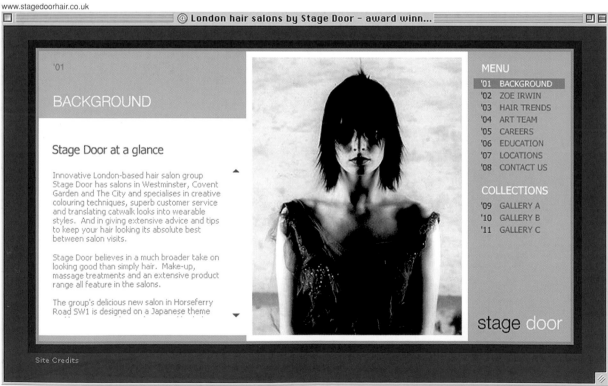

'01

BACKGROUND

Stage Door at a glance

Innovative London-based hair salon group
Stage Door has salons in Westminster, Covent
Garden and The City and specialises in creative
colouring techniques, superb customer service
and translating catwalk looks into wearable
styles. And in giving extensive advice and tips
to keep your hair looking its absolute best
between salon visits.

Stage Door believes in a much broader take on
looking good than simply hair. Make-up,
massage treatments and an extensive product
range all feature in the salons.

The group's delicious new salon in Horseferry
Road SW1 is designed on a Japanese theme

MENU

'01 BACKGROUND
'02 ZOE IRWIN
'03 HAIR TRENDS
'04 ART TEAM
'05 CAREERS
'06 EDUCATION
'07 LOCATIONS
'08 CONTACT US

COLLECTIONS

'09 GALLERY A
'10 GALLERY B
'11 GALLERY C

stage door

Site Credits

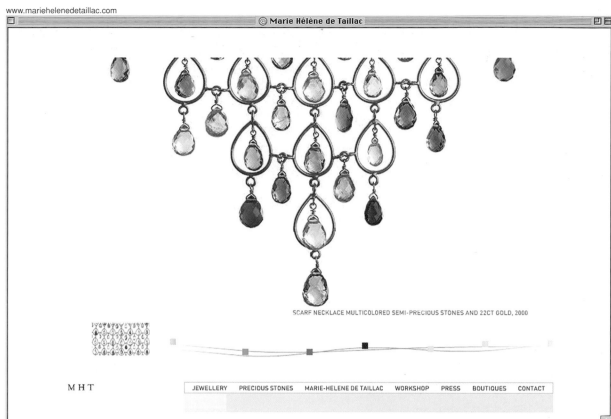

@ Marie Hélène de Taillac

SCARF NECKLACE MULTICOLORED SEMI-PRECIOUS STONES AND 22CT GOLD, 2000

M H T

JEWELLERY   PRECIOUS STONES   MARIE-HELENE DE TAILLAC   WORKSHOP   PRESS   BOUTIQUES   CONTACT

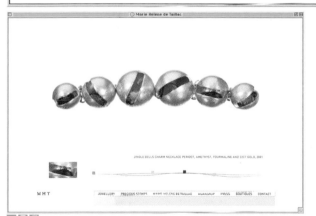

Marie Hélène de Taillac

JINGLE BELLS CHARM NECKLACE PERIDOT, AMETHYST, TOURMALINE AND 22CT GOLD, 2001

M H T   JEWELLERY   PRECIOUS STONES   MARIE-HELENE DE TAILLAC   WORKSHOP   PRESS   BOUTIQUES   CONTACT

Marie Hélène de Taillac

Stones specially cut for rings

L'ATELIER

It was in 1996 in Jaipur, or more precisely at the Gem Palace in Jaipur, that Marie-Hélène de Taillac discovered great ancient jewelry tradition of Indian artisans. The Gem Palace has been the court jeweller of the Maharajas the past eight generations and is home to one of the largest collections of stones in the world.
Spellbound, Marie Hélène de Taillac decided to live and work at the Gem Palace 6 months per year to create he range of jewelry. Indulging in the exceptionally rich variety of the stones and having access to the best stone ro in the world, de Taillac let free her passion for stones, colours and cuts which helped rediscover the historic "briolette" as well as creating new styles.

Jacques Brunel, Air France Madame.

M H T   JEWELLERY   PRECIOUS STONES   MARIE-HELENE DE TAILLAC   WORKSHOP   PRESS   BOUTIQUES   CONTACT

www.lucienpellat-finet.com

The Finest,
Most Luxurious and Unique
Cashmere and Apparel
In The World

lucien
pellat-finet

women   men   jeans   retail   press   history   contact

copyright LPF 2002

FR F C

www.melka.com

MELKA
COLLECTION | STORES | CATALOGUE | NEWS | PRESSROOM | COMPANY | PARTNE

Welcome to Spring 2003 with
MELKA
scandinavian menswear | since 1946

>>

SIE F C

www.modefabriek.nl

modefabriek

NL F C

www.merrellboot.com

OUR SHOES
SEARCH AND ENJOY
OUR WORLD

x PRIVACY POLICY   x TERMS + CONDITIONS   x COPYRIGHT INFO   x REGISTER   x MERRELLCANADA.COM

contact us

USA F C

www.microtiegroup.com

home
about us
brands
products
corporate neckwear
e-commerce
contact

MICRO-TIE GROUP

A KEEN EYE FOR FASHION
home

NL C

www.nudor.com

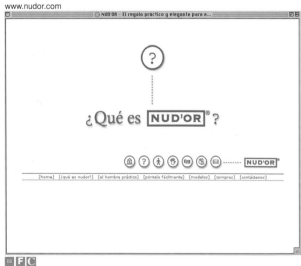

?

¿Qué es NUD'OR ?

NUD'OR

[home] [¿qué es nudor?] [el hombre práctico] [póntelo fácilmente] [modelos] [compras] [contáctenos]

ES F C

www.madelineshoes.com

www.ministryofhairsalon.com

www.nike.com

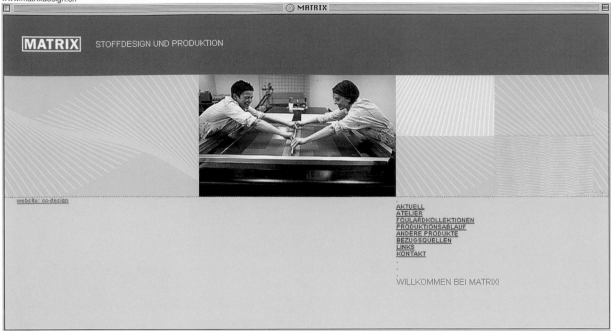

www.shoppingpong.ch

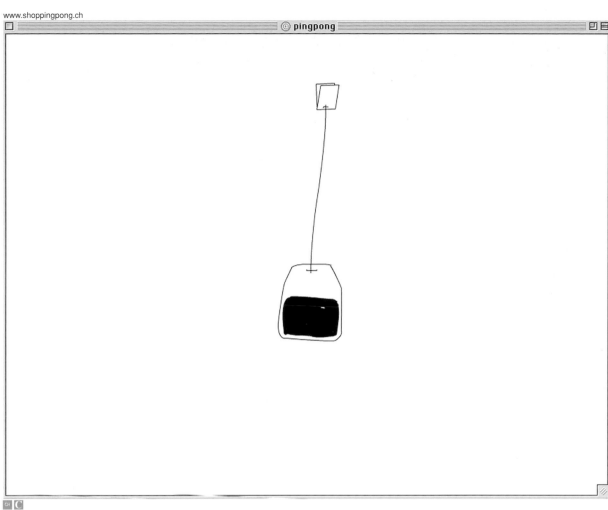

www.prognose.ch

PROGNOSE taschendesign:

www.versace.com

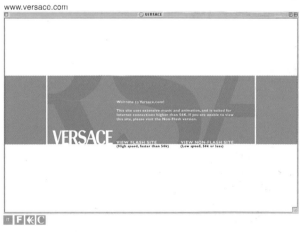

VERSACE

Welcome to Versace.com!

This site uses extensive music and animation, and is suited for
Internet connections higher than 56K. If you are unable to view
this site, please visit the Non-Flash version.

VIEW FLASH SITE
(High speed, faster than 56k)

VIEW NON-FLASH SITE
(Low speed, 56k or less)

www.rockport.com

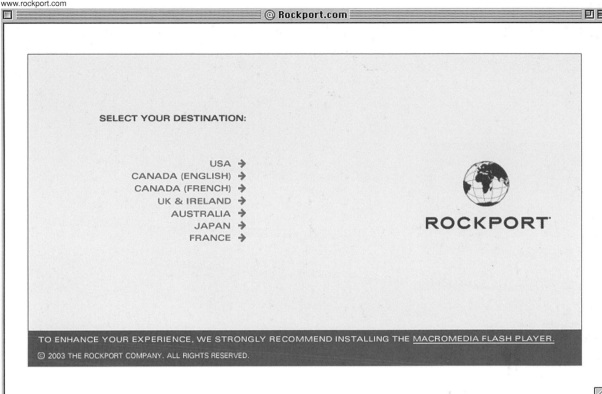

www.thebodyshop.com

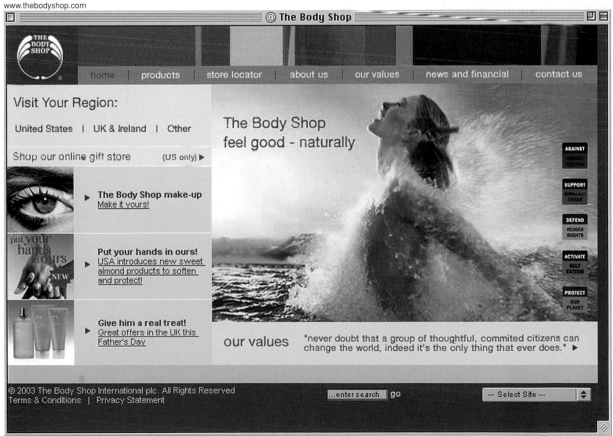

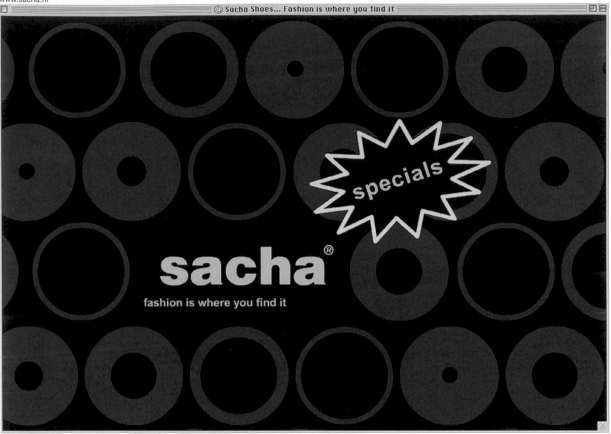

www.shiseido.co.jp/com/

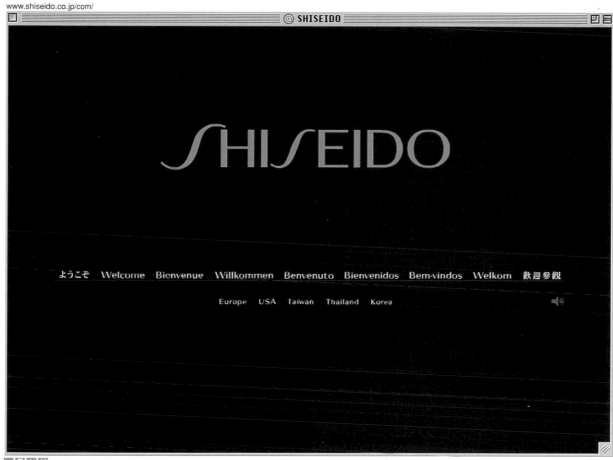

www.soniarykiel.com

www.isseymiyake.com

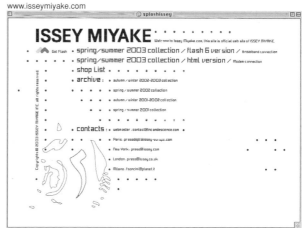

@ Camper

The Shoe | e-Shop | Origins | Customer Service | The Voice | Home | Español | CAMPER

e-Shop

drag&drop

Create your own and unique Camper Menu:

News

Catalogue

TWS

© Camper

The Shoe | e-Shop | Origins | Customer Service | The Voice | News | Home | CAMPER

camper catalogue   100% Camper   100% Fresh

© Camper

The Shoe | e-Shop | Origins | Customer Service | The Voice | News | Home | CAMPER

Camper International

At the beginning of the nineties, after 15 years of commercializing its designs in Spain, Camper was strong enough on the national market to be able to look outwards. Its management began to think about how to undertake an export policy, as they were aware that the Spanish product was discredited on international markets.

The 1992 Olympic games brought about a radical change in the perception that the whole world had of Spain and Spanish things, and Camper took advantage of this trend by launching itself on the European market.

It began simultaneously with the most difficult points –London, Paris, and Milan– cities in which groups with very influential

The Med the Net

ES F C

www.triton.com.br

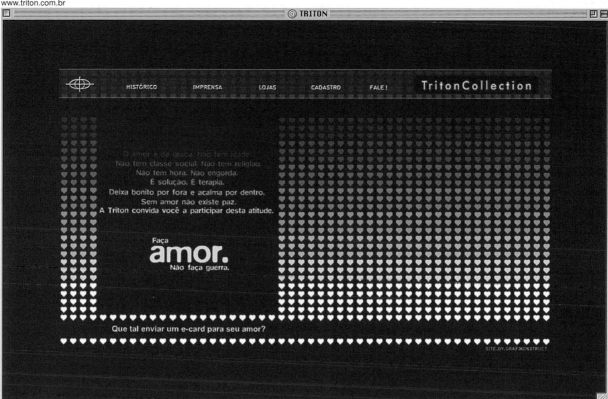

O amor é de graça. Não tem idade.
Não tem classe social. Não tem religião.
Não tem hora. Não engorda.
É solução. É terapia.
Deixa bonito por fora e acalma por dentro.
Sem amor não existe paz.
A Triton convida você a participar desta atitude.

Faça
amor.
Não faça guerra.

Que tal enviar um e-card para seu amor?

SITE.BY.GRAFIKONSTRUCT

BR F C

www.miashoes.com

USA F C

www.redley.com.br

USA F C

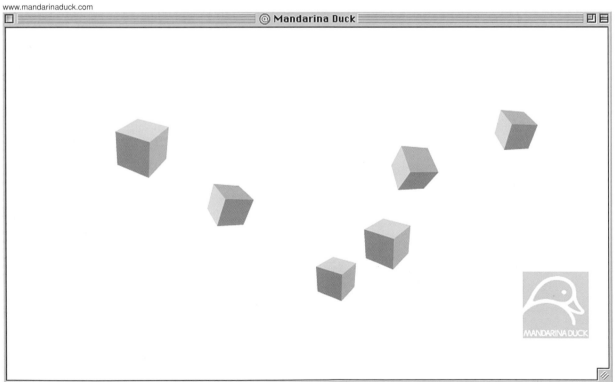

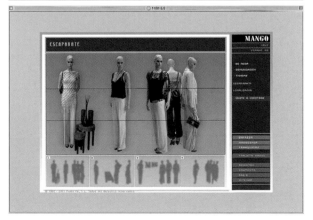

HOME | PRODUCTS | CAFES & EMPORIUMS | STORE LOCATOR | PARADISE NATION | ABOUT US

FAQ | Contact Us | Site Map

Terms of Use | Privacy Policy

www.ysl.com

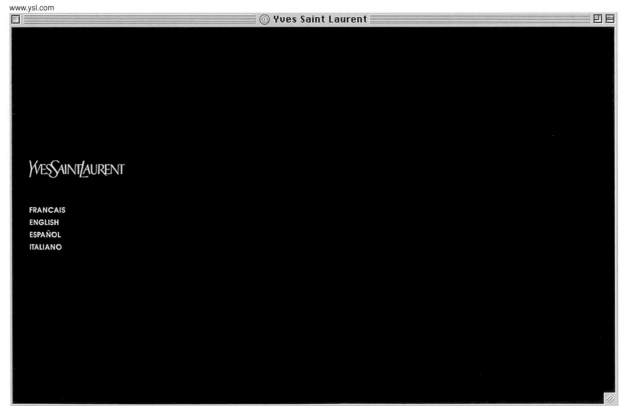

YVES SAINT LAURENT

FRANCAIS
ENGLISH
ESPAÑOL
ITALIANO

www.zara.com

www.zemcalcados.com.br

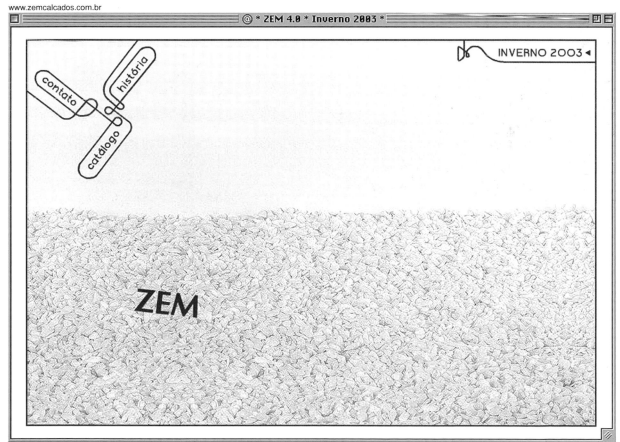

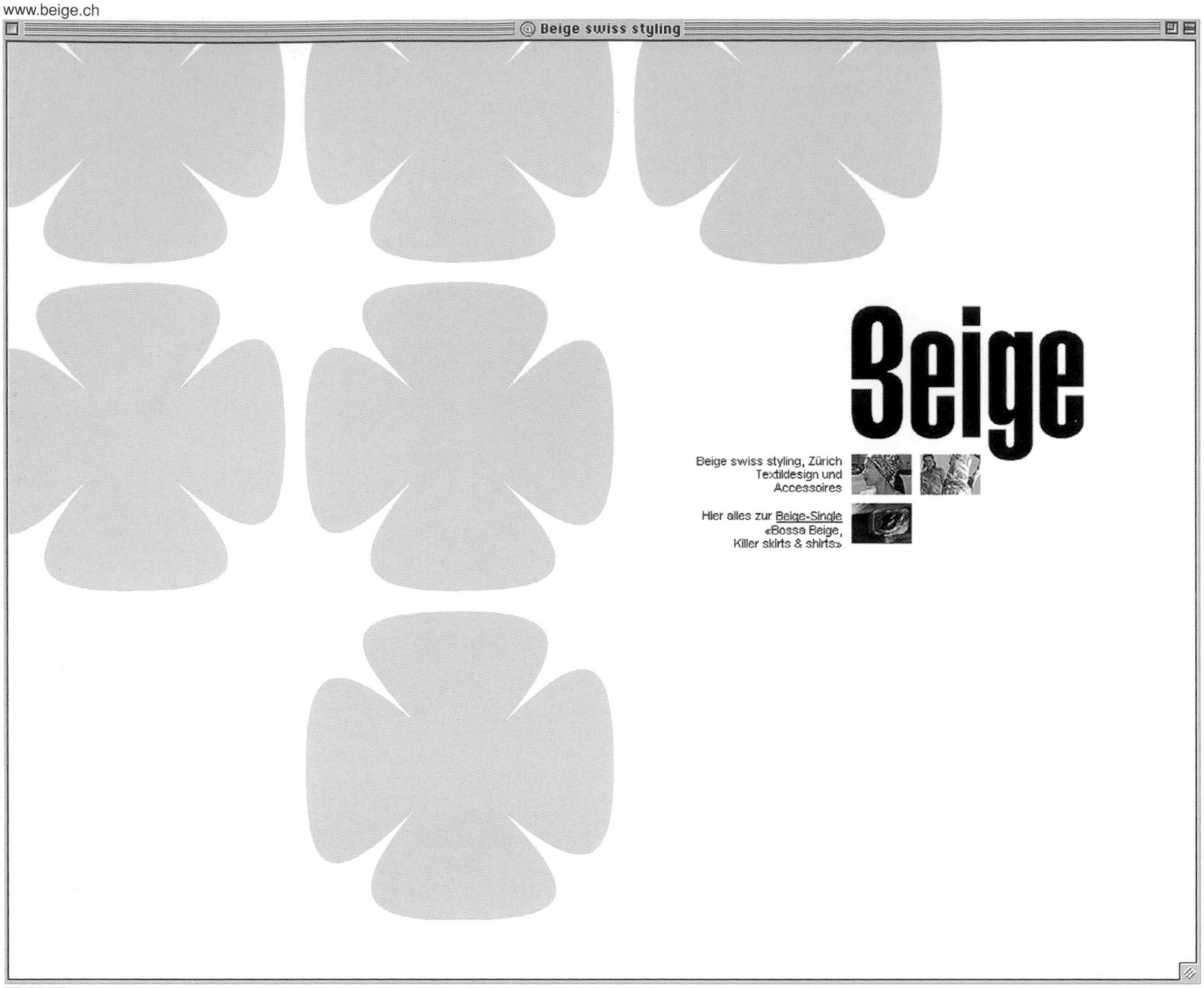
Beige swiss styling
Beige
Beige swiss styling, Zürich
Textildesign und
Accessoires
Hier alles zur Beige-Single
«Bossa Beige,
Killer skirts & shirts»

USA C

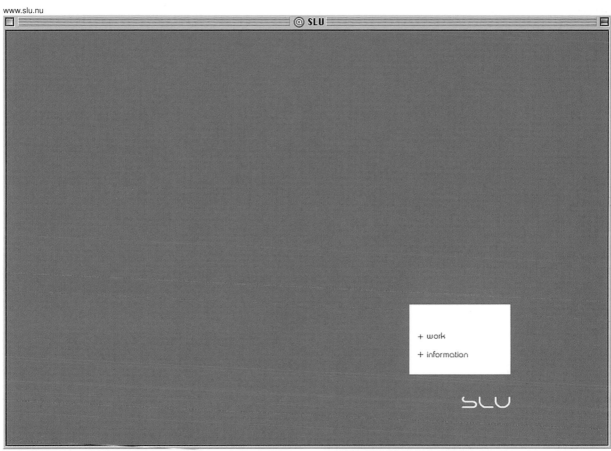

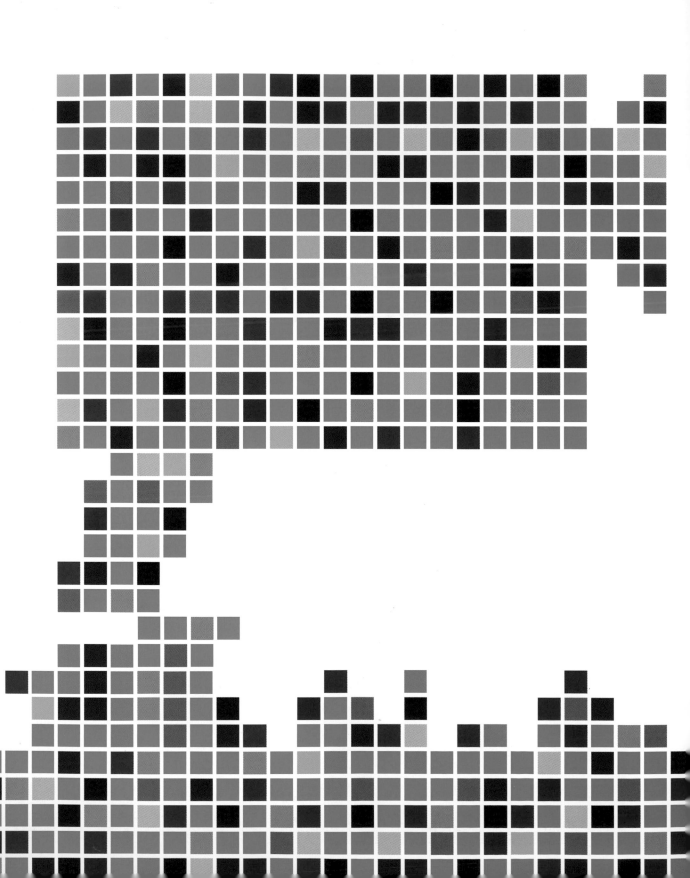

www.blur.com

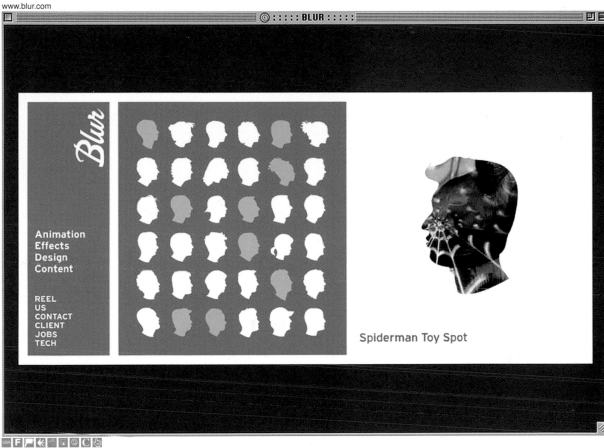

Spiderman Toy Spot

www.sights.com

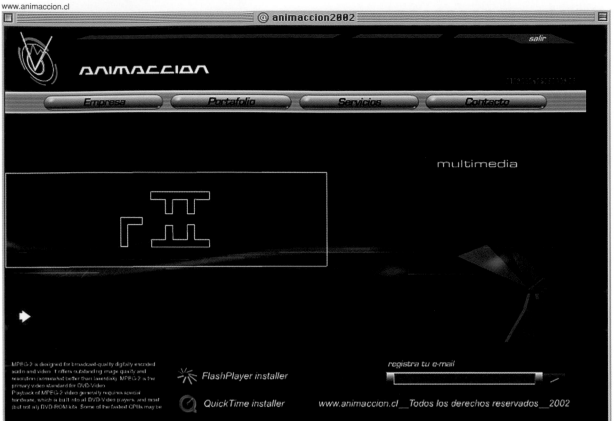

www.3dmercenary.dk

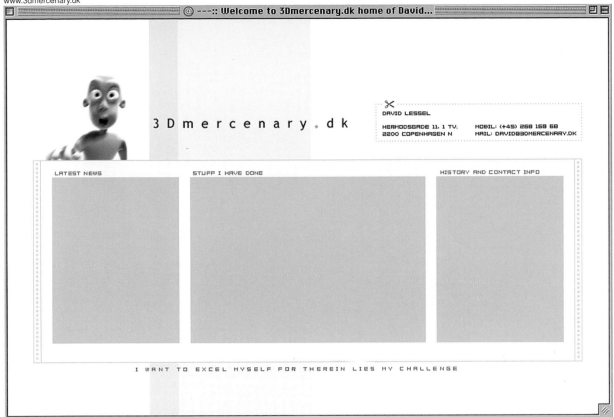

www.zedfilmes.com

www.assortednuts.se

@ .:: Welcome to official WebSite of the Movie ...

THE TALE AWAKENING THE BEST OUT OF YOU

L'uovo (THE EGG)

Sound Off

INTRODUCTION | SYNOPSIS | TEASER TRAILER | IMAGES | CHARACTERS | TECH SPECS/CONTACTS

IT F K I

www.pixelgrind.com

USA F K C

www.artmedia.qc.ca

USA F K C

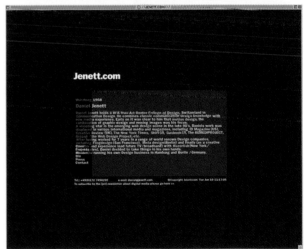

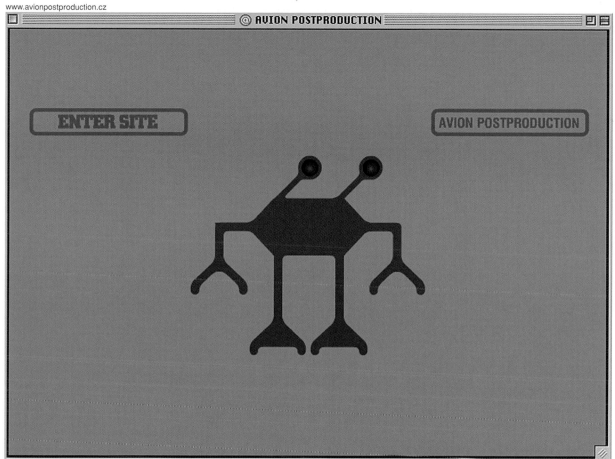

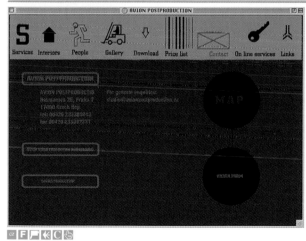

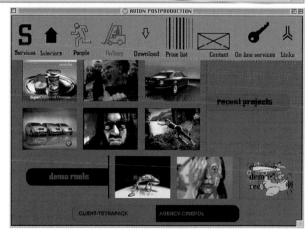

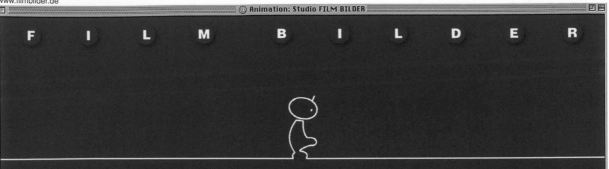

ANIMATION ONLINE

Welcome to the Website that can move mountains – or people, or vegetables, or tools, or umbrellas, or anything else. Meet the people who animated singer Gigi, pop group Tic Tac Toe, hit song "Zehn kleine Jägermeister", feature film "Run Lola Run" and television show "Celebrity Deathmatch". Get to know the FILM BILDER animation studio, order videos, and contact us direct! – Get moving!

Willkommen im Reich der schnellen Bilder! Lassen Sie sich animieren von Trickfilm im Netz, lernen Sie die Animatoren von Gigi, Tic Tac Toe, den zehn kleinen Jägermeistern, "Lola rennt" und "Celebrity Deathmatch" kennen, erfahren Sie alles Wissenswerte über das Studio FILM BILDER, bestellen Sie Videos und treten Sie mit uns in Kontakt! – Auf gehts!

This Site requires the Macromedia Flash 4 and the Apple Quick Time 5 Plug-In

www.a-film.dk

www.amberwoodanimation.com

www.attitude-studio.com

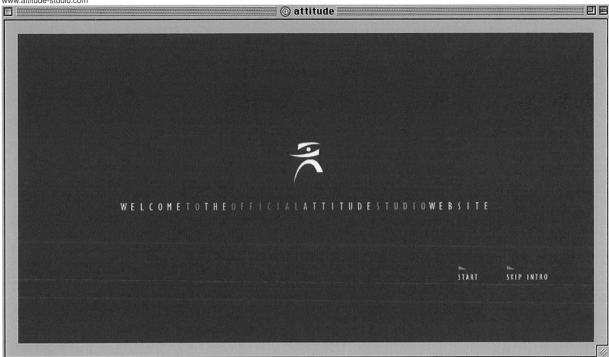

www.augenblickstudios.com

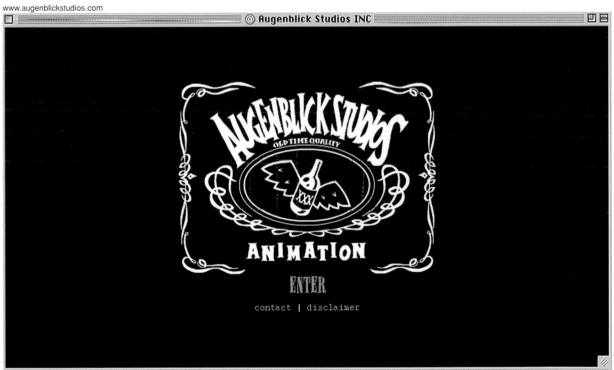

www.dominostudio.com

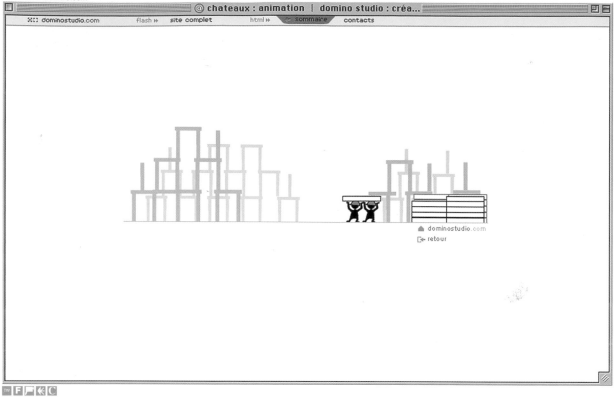

www.atomiccartoons.com

www.baasch.com

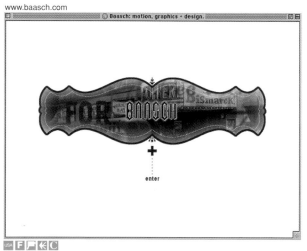

www.barrandov.cz

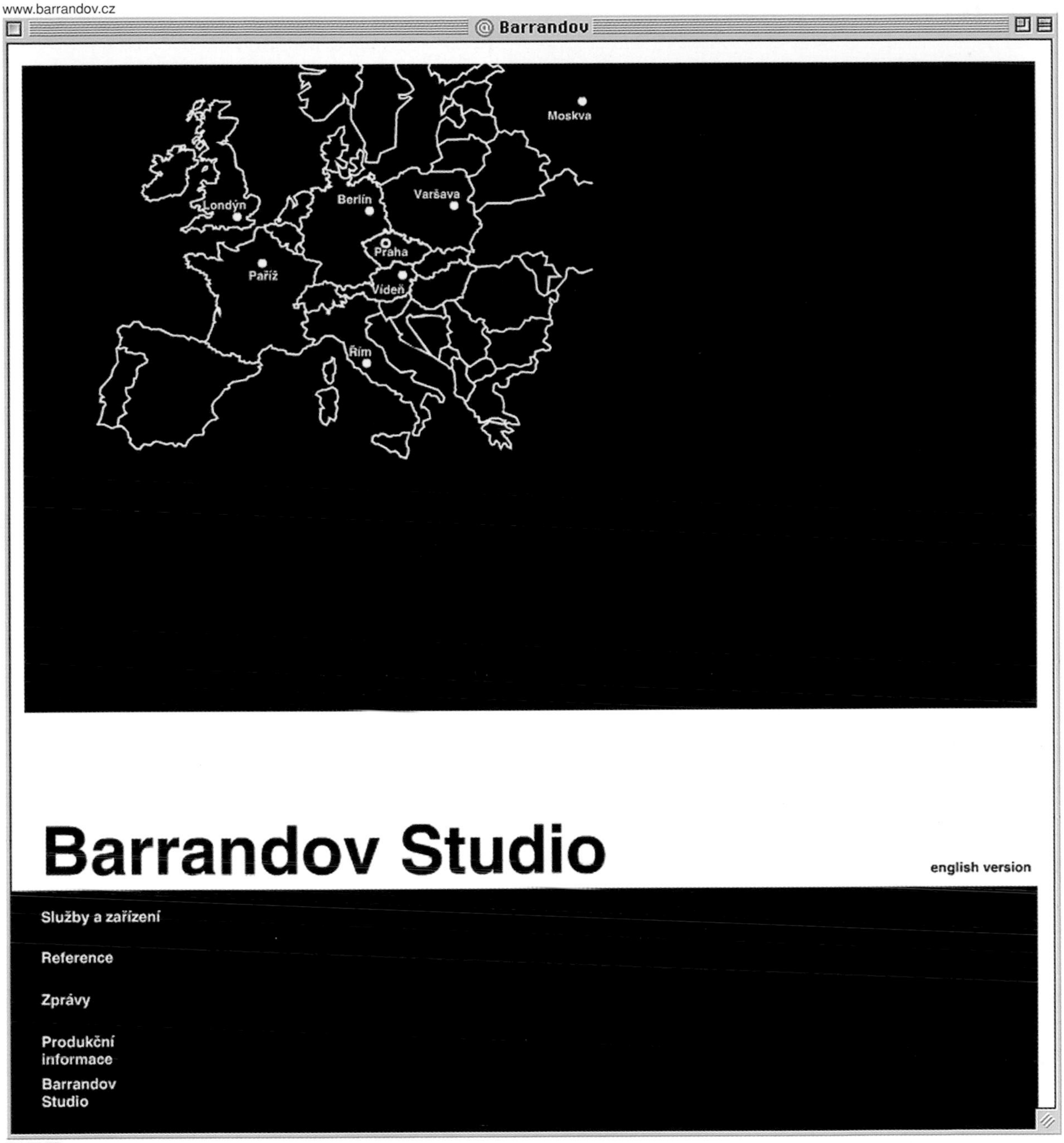

@ Barrandov

Moskva

Londýn Berlín Varšava

Praha

Paříž Vídeň

Řím

Barrandov Studio

english version

Služby a zařízení

Reference

Zprávy

Produkční
informace

Barrandov
Studio

www.cameronmiyasaki.com

cameron miyasaki

news   animation   artwork   about me   links   contact me

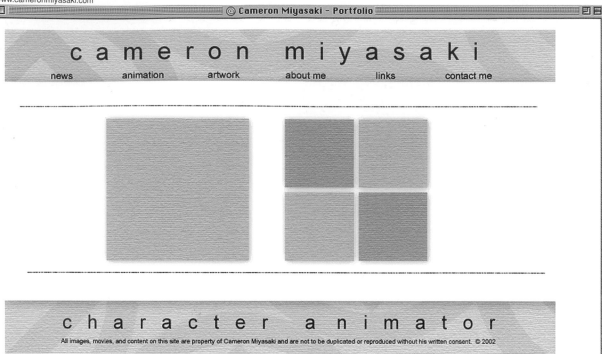

character animator

www.conduitfest.com

www.danceswithfilms.com

@ danceswithfilms 2003 [welcome]

danceswithfilms 6.0

about dwf   films   tickets/venues   schedules   sponsors/partners   press releases   contact

July 25-31, 2003

CALL FOR ENTRIES!
danceswithfilms is now accepting submissions for 2003!
Click Here!

© 1998-2003 danceswithfilms. Site Powered by Griffopolis

USA

www.computeranimation.dk/ck/

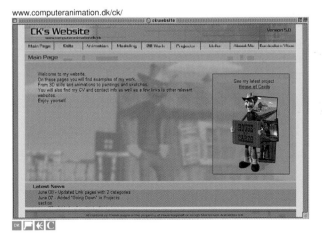

ckwebsite

CK's Website
www.computeranimation.dk

| Main Page | Stills | Animation | Modelling | 3D Work | Projects | Links | About Me | Curriculum Vitae |

Main Page

Welcome to my website.
On these pages you will find examples of my work.
From 3D stills and animations to paintings and sketches.
You will also find my CV and contact info as well as a few links to other relevant websites.
Enjoy yourself.

See my latest project
House of Cards

Latest News
June 08 - Updated Link pages with 2 categories
June 07 - Added "Going Down" in Projects section

DK

www.dsanimations.com

digitalsculpture

CONTACT US   DEMO REEL   DS TRAINING CENTER

USA F

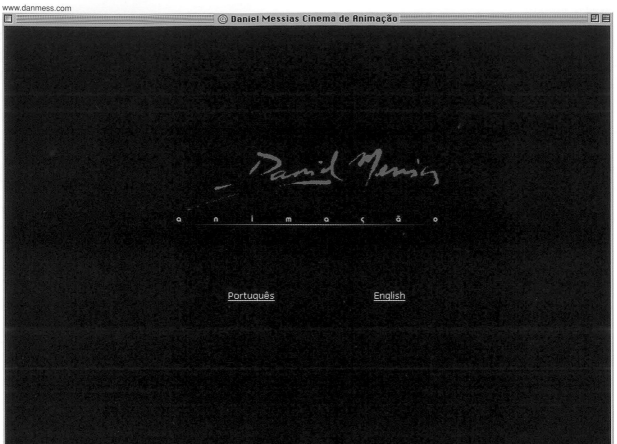

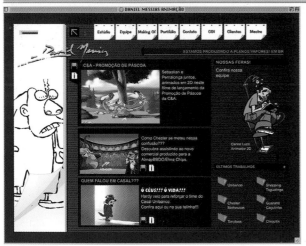

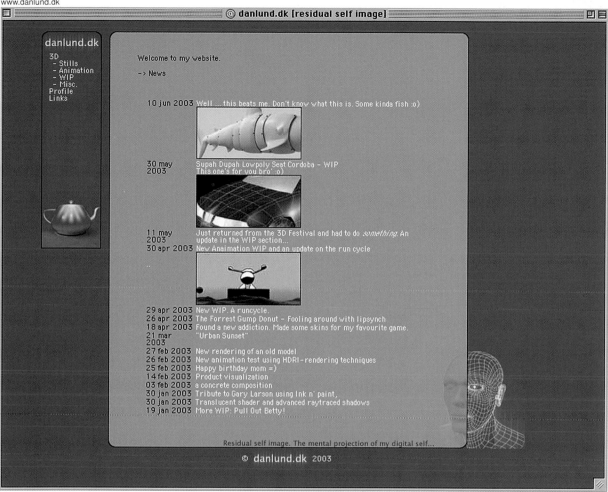

danlund.dk

3D
- Stills
- Animation
- WIP
- Misc.
Profile
Links

Welcome to my website.

-> News

10 jun 2003 Well ... this beats me. Don't know what this is. Some kinda fish :o)

30 may 2003 Supah Dupah Lowpoly Seat Cordoba – WIP
This one's for you bro' :o)

11 may 2003 Just returned from the 3D Festival and had to do *something*. An update in the WIP section...

30 apr 2003 New Anaimation WIP and an update on the run cycle

29 apr 2003 New WIP. A runcycle.
26 apr 2003 The Forrest Gump Donut – Fooling around with lipsynch
18 apr 2003 Found a new addiction. Made some skins for my favourite game.
21 mar 2003 "Urban Sunset"
27 feb 2003 New rendering of an old model
26 feb 2003 New animation test using HDRI-rendering techniques
25 feb 2003 Happy birthday mom =)
14 feb 2003 Product visualization
03 feb 2003 a concrete composition
30 jan 2003 Tribute to Gary Larson using Ink n' paint,
30 jan 2003 Translucent shader and advanced raytraced shadows
19 jan 2003 More WIP: Pull Out Betty!

Residual self image. The mental projection of my digital self...

© **danlund.dk** 2003

www.filmakademie.de

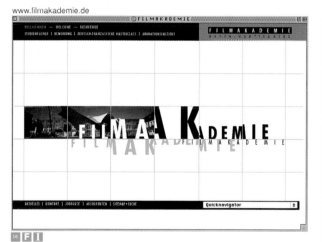

http://archive.essential-dreams.com/virginie/

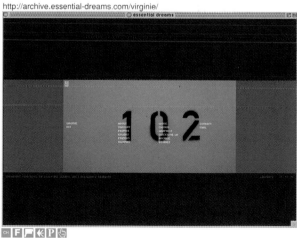

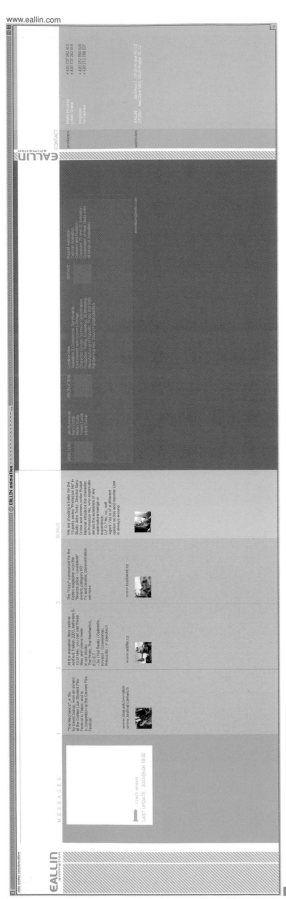

 conseqüência

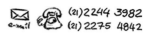 e-mail   (21) 2244 3982
(21) 2275 4842

THREE LITTLE BIRDS   SEGREDOS   BARRASHOPPING   ANIMA MUNDI

3 HERÓIS   ROUBADA!   HEIN?!

ANIM   MAQUETES   BIO   COMO FAZ?   PRÊMIOS   LINKS

NEWS:

[05-05-2003] - "Segredos" é indicado ao 10º Prêmio Multishow de Música Brasileira na categoria "Melhor Videoclipe".

[20-03-2003] - A vinheta de abertura do Anima Mundi 2002 é selecionada para competição oficial do Festival de Annecy, na categoria "Advertising or Promotional Film".

[17-02-2003] - Nosso site novo entrou no ar!

[06-02-2003] - Leo Santos, que dirigiu conosco "Segredos" e "Natal Barrashopping" embarca para Los Angeles. Ele será o representante brasileiro na equipe 3d da Blur Studios.

[05-01-2003] - Tem início a parceria Conseqüência / Draft para a produção de maquetes 3d.

[20-12-2002] - Sucesso total na promoção "Natal Barrashopping". Camisetas esgotadas!

[13-12-2002] - "Segredos" é exibido no Festival de Cinema Latinoamericano de Havana.

[01-12-2002] - Terminamos o segundo filme de Natal do Barrashopping.

[08-11-2002] - "Segredos" e "Roubada!" são exibidos no Cinanima, um dos mais importantes festivais de animação da Europa.

anim | maquetes | bio | como faz? | prêmios | links

www.eye-animation.com

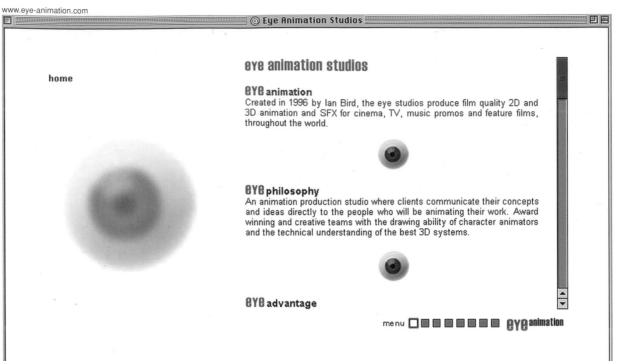

eye animation studios

eye animation
Created in 1996 by Ian Bird, the eye studios produce film quality 2D and 3D animation and SFX for cinema, TV, music promos and feature films, throughout the world.

eye philosophy
An animation production studio where clients communicate their concepts and ideas directly to the people who will be animating their work. Award winning and creative teams with the drawing ability of character animators and the technical understanding of the best 3D systems.

eye advantage

menu   eye animation

home

www.vectorlounge.com

http://www.vectorlounge.com/...gapour/index.html

WATCH THE REEL CONTACT CLOSE

WHAT'S NEW

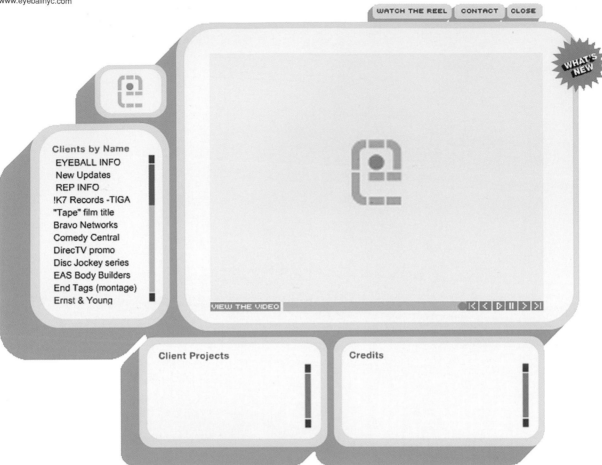

Clients by Name

EYEBALL INFO
New Updates
REP INFO
!K7 Records -TIGA
"Tape" film title
Bravo Networks
Comedy Central
DirecTV promo
Disc Jockey series
EAS Body Builders
End Tags (montage)
Ernst & Young

VIEW THE VIDEO

Client Projects

Credits

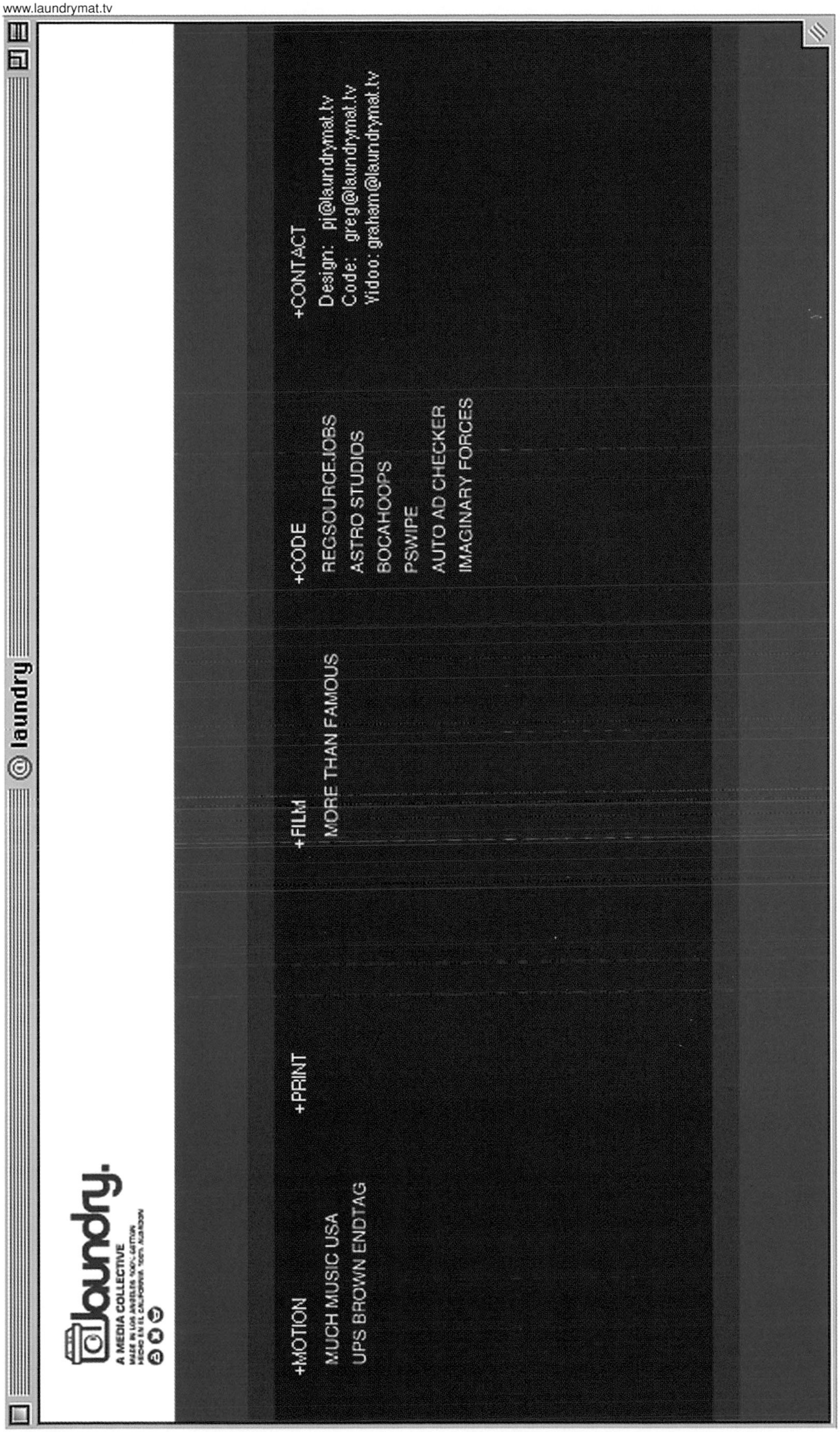

laundry.
A MEDIA COLLECTIVE
MADE IN LOS ANGELES 100% CAFFEINE
HECHO EN EE.CALIFORNIA 100% AGRADON

@ laundry

+MOTION
MUCH MUSIC USA
UPS BROWN ENDTAG

+PRINT

+FILM
MORE THAN FAMOUS

+CODE
REGSOURCE.JOBS
ASTRO STUDIOS
BOCAHOOPS
PSWIPE
AUTO AD CHECKER
IMAGINARY FORCES

+CONTACT
Design: pj@laundrymat.tv
Code: greg@laundrymat.tv
Video: graham@laundrymat.tv

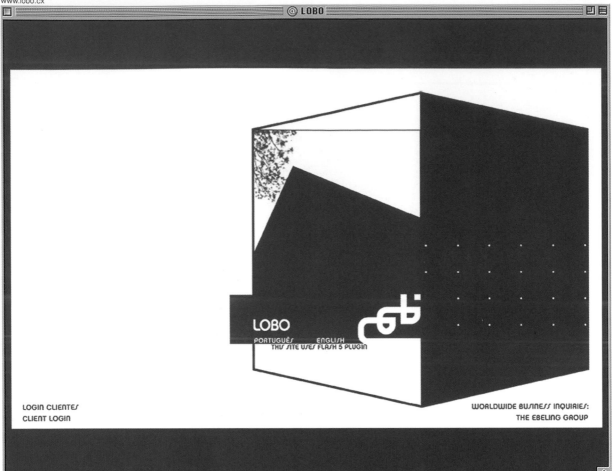

LOGIN CLIENTES
CLIENT LOGIN

WORLDWIDE BUSINESS INQUIRIES:
THE EBELING GROUP

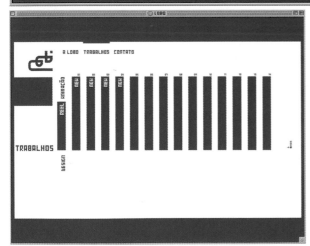

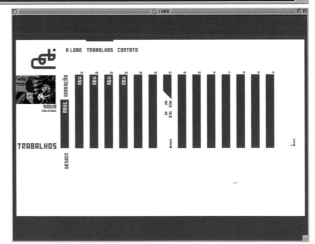

www.iloura.com.au

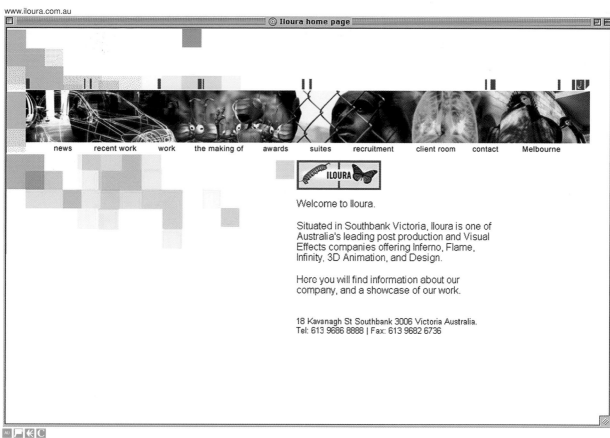

www.belief.com/exp/un02/main.html

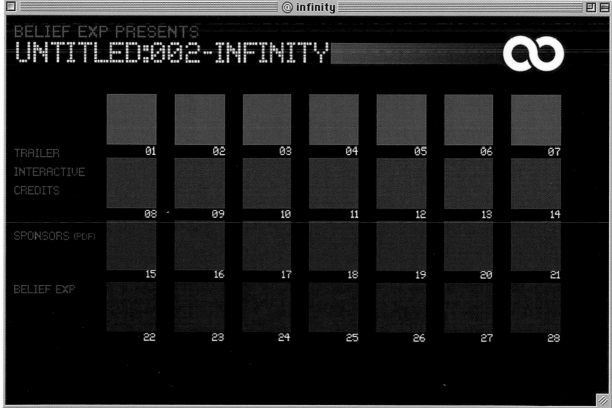

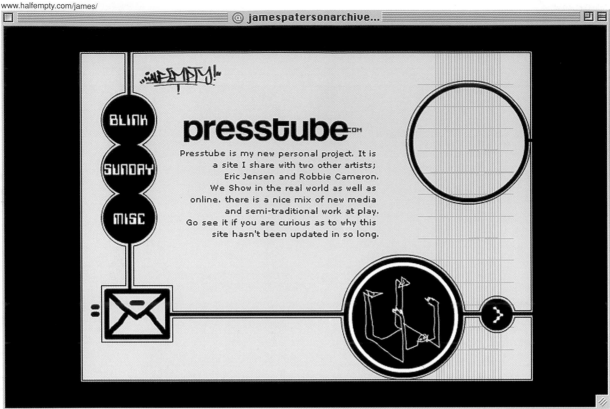

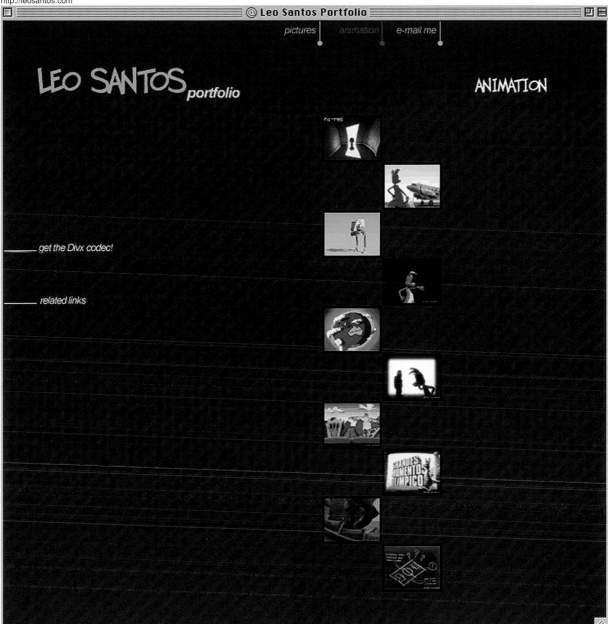

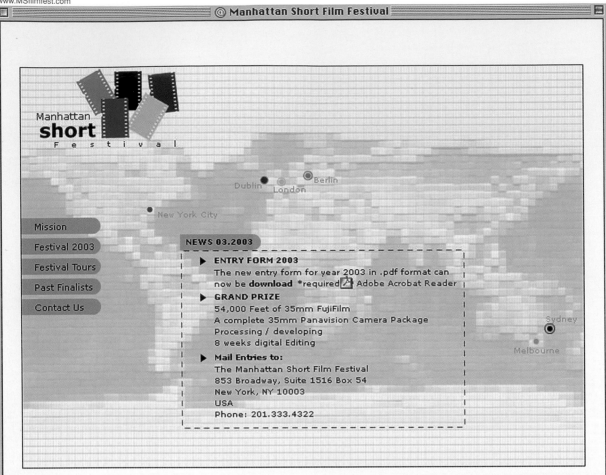

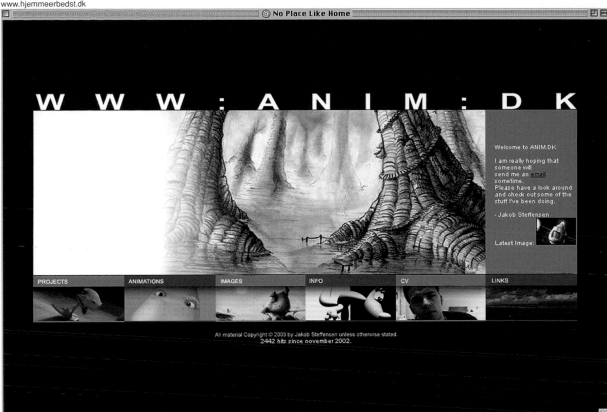

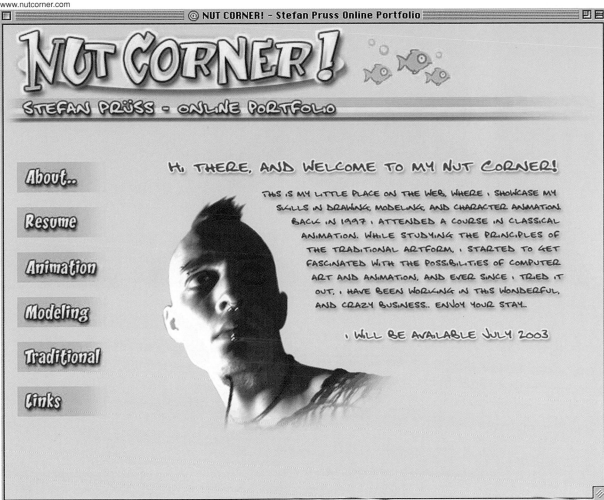

@ NUT CORNER! - Stefan Pruss Online Portfolio

NUT CORNER!

STEFAN PRÜSS - ONLINE PORTFOLIO

About..

Resume

Animation

Modeling

Traditional

Links

HI THERE, AND WELCOME TO MY NUT CORNER!

THIS IS MY LITTLE PLACE ON THE WEB, WHERE I SHOWCASE MY SKILLS IN DRAWING, MODELING, AND CHARACTER ANIMATION. BACK IN 1997 I ATTENDED A COURSE IN CLASSICAL ANIMATION. WHILE STUDYING THE PRINCIPLES OF THE TRADITIONAL ARTFORM, I STARTED TO GET FASCINATED WITH THE POSSIBILITIES OF COMPUTER ART AND ANIMATION, AND EVER SINCE I TRIED IT OUT, I HAVE BEEN WORKING IN THIS WONDERFUL, AND CRAZY BUSINESS.. ENJOY YOUR STAY..

I WILL BE AVAILABLE JULY 2003

www.powerhouseanimation.com

www.renegadeanimation.com

@ polygonhelvede.dk

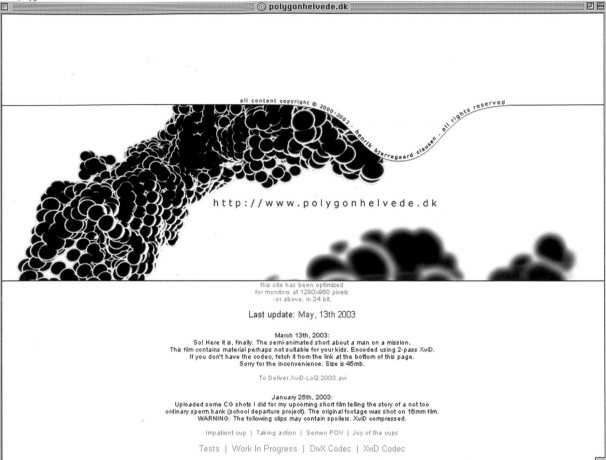

http://www.polygonhelvede.dk

this site has been optimized
for monitors at 1280x960 pixels
-or above, in 24 bit.

Last update: May, 13th 2003

March 13th, 2003:
So! Here it is, finally. The semi-animated short about a man on a mission.
This film contains material perhaps not suitable for your kids. Encoded using 2-pass XviD.
If you don't have the codec, fetch it from the link at the bottom of this page.
Sorry for the inconvenience. Size is 45mb.

To.Deliver.XviD-LoQ.2003.avi

January 25th, 2003:
Uploaded some CG shots I did for my upcoming short film telling the story of a not too
ordinary sperm bank (school departure project). The original footage was shot on 16mm film.
WARNING: The following clips may contain spoilers. XviD compressed.

Impatient cup | Taking action | Semen POV | Joy of the cups

Tests | Work In Progress | DivX Codec | XviD Codec

www.redrover.net

Red Rover Animation Studio

www.KlaskyCsupo.com

The Klasky Csupo Home Page

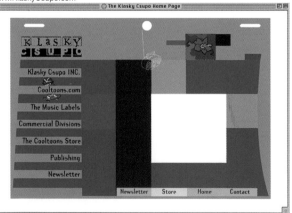

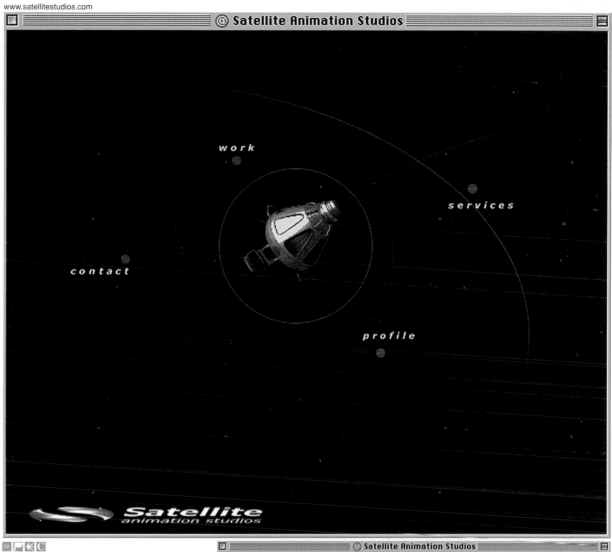

@ SCENE 360 -- [Film. Art. Music. Literature.]

SCENE 360'
FILM . ART . MUSIC . LITERATURE.

ART DIRECTION | DIRECTORS CHAIR | EDITING ROOM | T-SHOP | ABOUT | CONTACT

10-06-2003
dvGarage offers software and tutorials for 3D development (camera mapping, multipass rendering, creating 3D environments from 2D photos), compositing, surfacing (terrain, reflections, water damage), morphing, and much more. Register and check out their amazing tutorials.
—*Stuart Balcomb*

09-06-2003
Wellvetted has updated once again, and I found another design portal on it that I wasn't familiar with, called Cross Mind. Then on Cross Mind, I read a Flash Transition article by Maurice Wright (from Moluv) — which led me to a great design structured site, Fantasmagoria Interactive.
—*Adriana de Barros*

07-06-2003
Nervousroom has a new interview with photographer Steve Carty. There are some funny quotes in the interview from Carty, such as "I'm a pro. Been doing it from time. I got to be chill in order to get the moments I get from people. I do my best shit when I'm relaxed. I'm a rasta. And rastafari is love. I approach every session with love and my portraits have been the result." And also related with celebrity photo shoots, Carty says "I hung with DMX for 6 hours before I made a picture. We smoked a lot of draw. Funny. I got jarule pretty

DAILY NEWS | NEWS ARCHIVE | SUBMIT YOUR SITE

+ JOIN OUR NEWSLETTER
TO KEEP UPDATED   enter your email   SUBMIT >>
● Subscribe | UnSubscribe ○

CRÈME DE LA CRÈME
+ the best gourmet sites   [archive]

 Paul Yanez - a very clean site, with fast loading work.

 F.T.F. - Graf art on canvases; "Faking The Funk" exhibition.

SCENE 360 *presents*
debut digital book
"Love Within Us"
In Flash (file size 4.3MB)

View Now!

AARON JASINSKI
He draws, paints, mixes music, and lives in Seattle with his wife Whitney.

P4: JSP
The 4th part of the Server-Side Scripting with "JSP." An exclusive web series at Scene 360.

LOVE WITHIN US - EDITORS' PICKS
We would like to highlight works which we feel have extraordinary merit, and to celebrate the vision...

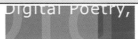

DIGITAL POETRY, VISUAL MEDIA
This article offers a perspective on how the Internet as a medium has affected the poetry genre.

+ FIND WHAT YOU ARE LOOKING FOR
THROUGH OUR DATABASE SEARCH   [   ] [>>]

EXTRA GOODIES
+ sweet as candy from our columns

THE BUSINESS OF STRANGERS
Feature Review: Hell hath no fury like a woman scorned. How about two pissed off women together?

QUICK TAKES: 10 FILMS
From big-screen Broadway to haunted websites, here are our most recent thrills and disappointments.

THE RACK AND RUIN PROJECT
A photo shoot by M. Shaefer. The man who built this installation has left a message on it, "Do not touch."

RINTOUL'S PHOTO SERIES
Visit the dark showcase to see strangely fascinating models photographed by Aaron Rintoul.

WHERE I BELONG
Pick your poison in this tale of crime and punishment by Julia Dudnik-Ptasznik.

[Short cut to column sections: ↕]

every **day** life
April May June **2003**
a competition by
nervousroom and scene360

30% OFF SPRING T-SHIRT SALE AT 360!
Discount available on exclusive designs by DIK, Mike Cina, NextDesignLife, and 360. Buy yours now!

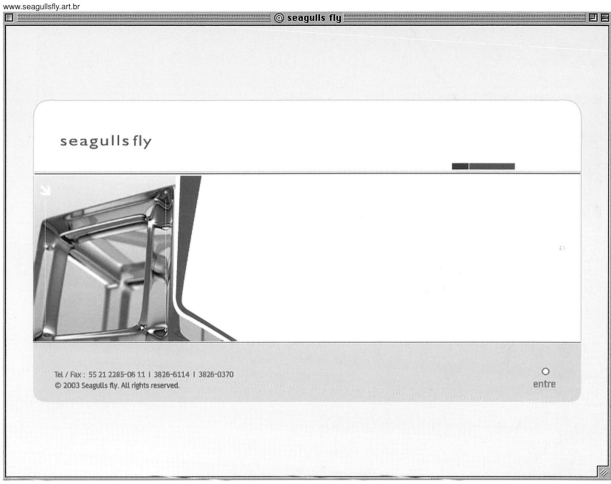

seagulls fly

Tel / Fax : 55 21 2285-06 11 I 3826-6114 I 3826-0370

entre

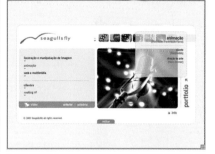

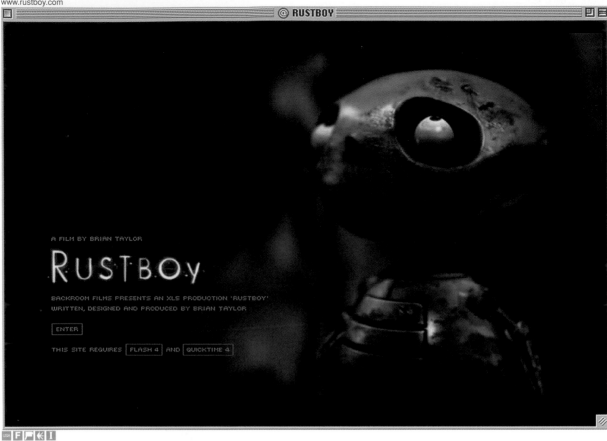

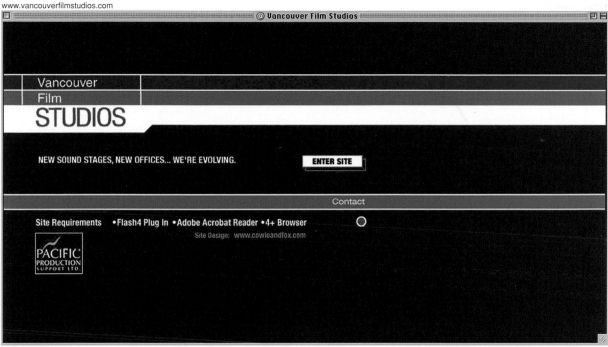

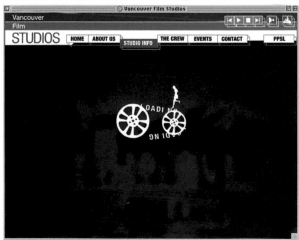

@ VCC Perfect Pictures AG

➜ Kontakt
➜ Sitemap
➜ English Version

| Über uns | Leistungen | Projekte | Jobs | Presse |

Creation of VCC **Perfect Pictures**

Technik kann nur so gut sein wie der Mensch, der sie bedient. Schließlich kann auch nur er Ihnen zuhören, Sie verstehen und Lösungen anbieten.

➜ Über uns
Die klassischen W-Fragen: Wer? Was? Wohin? Und Warum? Hier die Antworten. mehr...

➜ Leistungen
Wir beschäftigen uns mit bewegten Bildern aller Art. Dabei verfolgen wir in jedem Bereich unseres Leistungsspektrums nur ein Ziel: Creation of Perfect Pictures. mehr...

➜ Projekte
Werfen Sie einen Blick auf unsere Showreels und Projekte. mehr...

➜ Jobs
Werden Sie glücklich bei VCC. Hier finden Sie aktuelle Jobs und Bewerbungsformulare. mehr...

➜ Presse
Alles, was Journalisten das Leben erleichtert: aktuelle News, Presse-Kontakt, etc. mehr...

➜ **Workshop zum Thema "Motion Capture und 3D-Animation" in Frankfurt**
Am 6. Juni 2003 veranstaltet die Frankfurter Niederlassung des Postproduktionshauses VCC Perfect Pictures in Zusammenarbeit einen kostenlosen Workshop für Mitarbeiter aus Werbeagenturen, Marketingabteilungen und Filmproduktionen. Thema des Workshops (15.00 - 18.00 Uhr) ist die "Anwendung und Integration von Motion Capture-Aufnahmen und 3D-Animationen im Werbeumfeld".
weiter...

➜ **VCC Perfect Pictures gewinnt Animago-Award 2003**
VCC Perfect Pictures hat bei den diesjährigen Animago-Awards in der Kategorie "Professional / Compositing / Kurzfilm" den 1. Platz belegt.
weiter...

➜ **VCC Perfect Pictures-Gruppe bietet Ex-"das werk"-Mitarbeitern eine neue Heimat**
Die VCC Perfect Pictures-Unternehmensgruppe stellt einige ehemalige Mitarbeiter und Auszubildende des Wettbewerbers ,das werk' ein.
weiter...

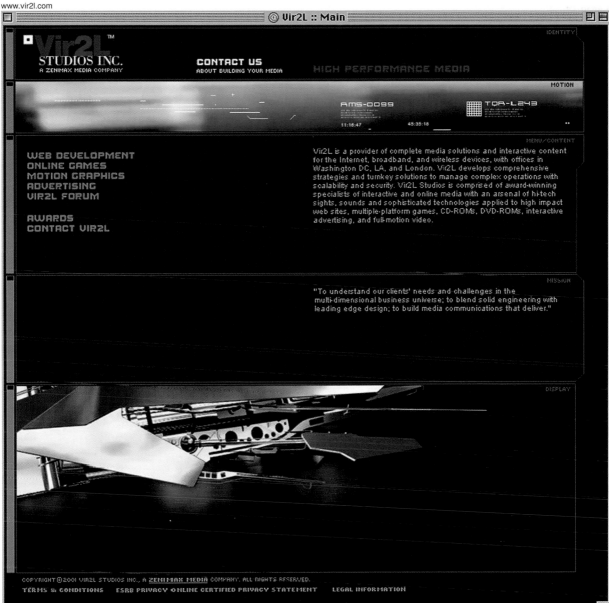

@ Vir2L :: Main

IDENTITY

Vir2L ™
STUDIOS INC.
A ZENIMAX MEDIA COMPANY

CONTACT US
ABOUT BUILDING YOUR MEDIA

HIGH PERFORMANCE MEDIA

MOTION

AMS-0099   TOA-L243

11:16:47   45:35:18

MENU/CONTENT

WEB DEVELOPMENT
ONLINE GAMES
MOTION GRAPHICS
ADVERTISING
VIR2L FORUM

AWARDS
CONTACT VIR2L

Vir2L is a provider of complete media solutions and interactive content for the Internet, broadband, and wireless devices, with offices in Washington DC, LA, and London. Vir2L develops comprehensive strategies and turnkey solutions to manage complex operations with scalability and security. Vir2L Studios is comprised of award-winning specialists of interactive and online media with an arsenal of hi-tech sights, sounds and sophisticated technologies applied to high impact web sites, multiple-platform games, CD-ROMs, DVD-ROMs, interactive advertising, and full-motion video.

MISSION

"To understand our clients' needs and challenges in the multi-dimensional business universe; to blend solid engineering with leading edge design; to build media communications that deliver."

DISPLAY

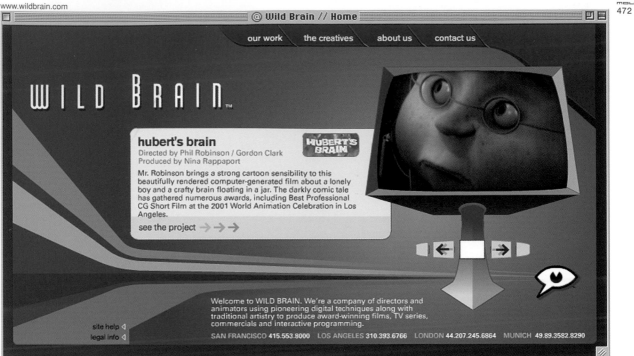

@ Wild Brain // Home

our work   the creatives   about us   contact us

WILD BRAIN™

hubert's brain
Directed by Phil Robinson / Gordon Clark
Produced by Nina Rappaport

Mr. Robinson brings a strong cartoon sensibility to this
beautifully rendered computer-generated film about a lonely
boy and a crafty brain floating in a jar. The darkly comic tale
has gathered numerous awards, including Best Professional
CG Short Film at the 2001 World Animation Celebration in Los
Angeles.

see the project → → →

site help ◁
legal info ◁

Welcome to WILD BRAIN. We're a company of directors and
animators using pioneering digital techniques along with
traditional artistry to produce award-winning films, TV series,
commercials and interactive programming.

SAN FRANCISCO 415.553.8000   LOS ANGELES 310.393.6766   LONDON 44.207.245.6864   MUNICH 49.89.3582.8290

USA F ⌐ « C

---

www.alkay.cz

@ www.alkay.cz\cz-or-en.html

LABORATORE ALKAY s r.o.

english ▶ **ALKAY** laboratore ◀ czech

The Prague studio of virtual puppets animation films and classic cartoon films.

Last updating 4.6.2003, Web design by Petra Neugebauerová

Internet Explorer 5.0 + Flash 5.0

✉

CZ F ⌐ « C

www.rhythm.com

http://sergioyamasaki.com

www.xilam.com

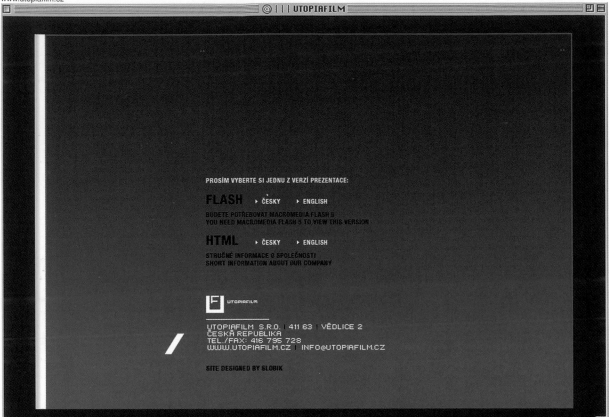

PROSÍM VYBERTE SI JEDNU Z VERZÍ PREZENTACE:

FLASH ▸ ČESKY ▸ ENGLISH

BUDETE POTŘEBOVAT MACROMEDIA FLASH 5
YOU NEED MACROMEDIA FLASH 5 TO VIEW THIS VERSION

HTML ▸ ČESKY ▸ ENGLISH

STRUČNÉ INFORMACE O SPOLEČNOSTI
SHORT INFORMATION ABOUT OUR COMPANY

UTOPIAFILM

UTOPIAFILM S.R.O. | 411 63 | VĚDLICE 2
ČESKÁ REPUBLIKA
TEL./FAX: 416 795 728
WWW.UTOPIAFILM.CZ | INFO@UTOPIAFILM.CZ

SITE DESIGNED BY SLOBIK

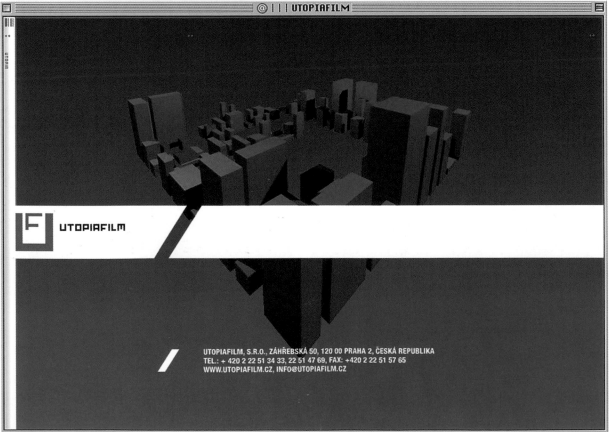

UTOPIAFILM

UTOPIAFILM, S.R.O., ZÁHŘEBSKÁ 50, 120 00 PRAHA 2, ČESKÁ REPUBLIKA
TEL.: + 420 2 22 51 34 33, 22 51 47 69, FAX: +420 2 22 51 57 65
WWW.UTOPIAFILM.CZ, INFO@UTOPIAFILM.CZ

TOTAL ЯƎƆALL
INT. FESTIVAL DES NACHERZÄHLTEN FILMS

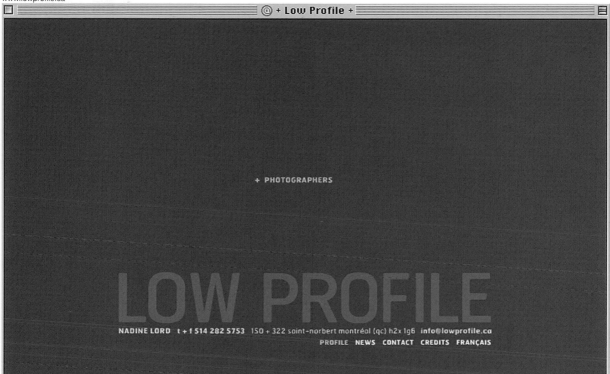

+ PHOTOGRAPHERS

LOW PROFILE

NADINE LORD t +1 514 282 5753   150 + 322 saint-norbert montréal (qc) h2x 1g6 info@lowprofile.ca

PROFILE NEWS CONTACT CREDITS FRANÇAIS

commissioned by
AUSTRALIAN STYLE MAGAZINE

PORTE-FOLIO

[–]

[+]

1 / 15

+ MAUDE ARSENAULT [PORTFOLIO] BIOGRAPHY CLIENTS AWARDS + EXHIBITS VISIT SITE

FRANÇAIS HOME PROFILE NEWS CONTACT CREDITS

LOW PROFILE

commissioned by
PASSIONATA - CHANTELLE

PORTE-FOLIO

[–]

[+]

1 / 15

+ PIERRE CHOINIÈRE [PORTFOLIO] BIOGRAPHY CLIENTS AWARDS + EXHIBITS VISIT SITE

FRANÇAIS HOME PROFILE NEWS CONTACT CREDITS

LOW PROFILE

commissioned by
LE CHATEAU
HOLIDAY 2000–2001

PORTFOLIO

[–]

[+]

1 / 17

+ DANIEL CIANFARRA [PORTFOLIO] BIOGRAPHY CLIENTS AWARDS + EXHIBITS STUDIO VISIT SITE

FRANÇAIS HOME PROFILE NEWS CONTACT CREDITS

LOW PROFILE

PERSONAL PROJECT

PORTFOLIO

[–]

[+]

1 / 15

+ ALAIN DESJEAN [PORTFOLIO] BIOGRAPHY CLIENTS AWARDS + EXHIBITS STUDIO VISIT SITE

FRANÇAIS HOME PROFILE NEWS CONTACT CREDITS

LOW PROFILE

www.minutiaeimages.com

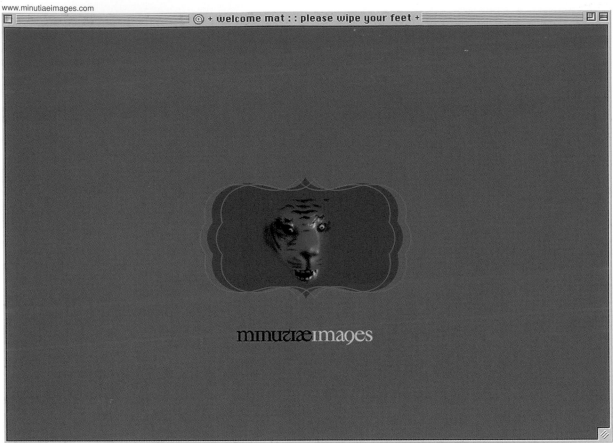

www.maloman.com

WELCOME TO MALOMAN PHOTO STUDIO
A DIGITAL PORTFOLIO OF PHOTOGRAPHER STEPHAN F. MALOMAN

OPEN PORTFOLIO | PROFILE / CONTACT / ◁ OFF

www.away.pl

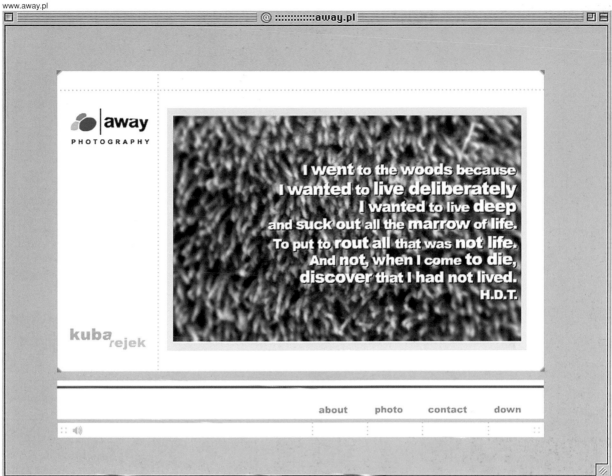

about   photo   contact   down

www.bellston.com

www.clickfactor.nl/photo/

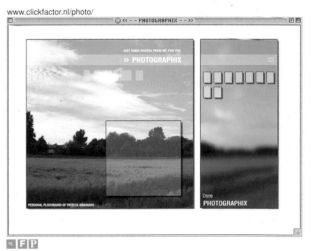

@ © **Kimm Saatvedt**

KIMM V.7 <
PORTFOLIO
INFO
CONTACT
CLIENTS
FRIEND OF THE MONTH
NICE SITES
OPINIONS

@ .thosegreeneyes............................

the sections

Photographs
Information
Music Control

thosegreeneyes

MO F P

.thosegreeneyes............

photographs

Landscape: 1 2 3 4 5 6 7 8 9 10 11 12 13 14 15 16 17 18 19 20 21
Compositional: 1 2 3 4 5 6 7 8
Portrait: 1 2 3 4 5 6 7 8 9 10 11 12

thosegreeneyes

.thosegreeneyes............

photographs

Landscape: 1 2 3 4 5 6 7 8 9 10 11 12 13 14 15 16 17 18 19 20 21
Compositional: 1 2 3 4 5 6 7 8
Portrait: 1 2 3 4 5 6 7 8 9 10 11 12

thosegreeneyes

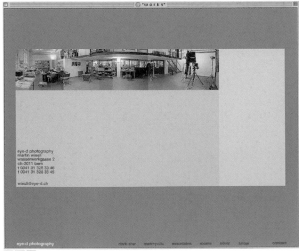

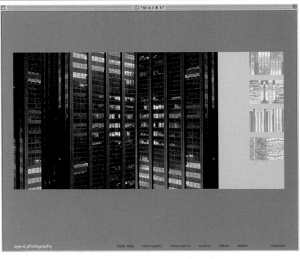

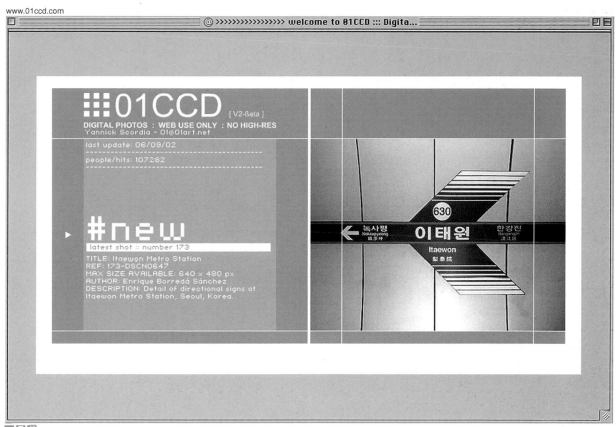

www.michelelaurita.com

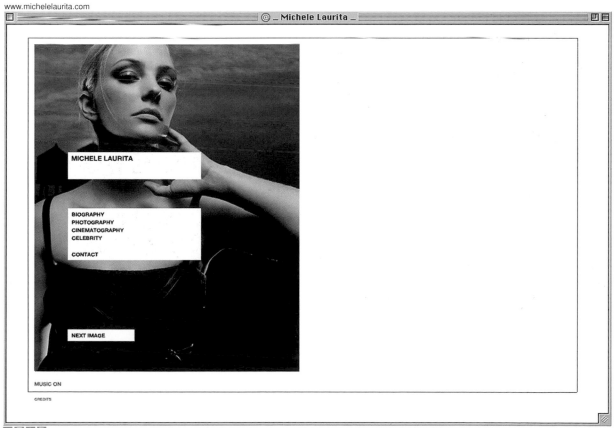

http://makrokosmos.xo.pl

@ makrokosmos art pl

ENTER
MAKROKOSMOS

PL C

http://acte3.com/

FR F P

www.alabama.art.pl

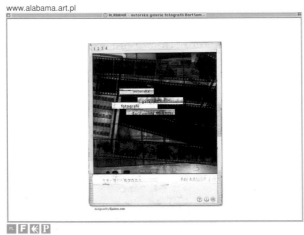

PL F P

>> Français   >> English

@ albert

FOTO: ALBERT

www.pierdomenico.com

close

ALESSIA PIERDOMENICO
PHOTOGRAPHER

Latest Reportages
Features
News
Politics
Entertainment
Fashion
World

Bio
Portfolio
Contact

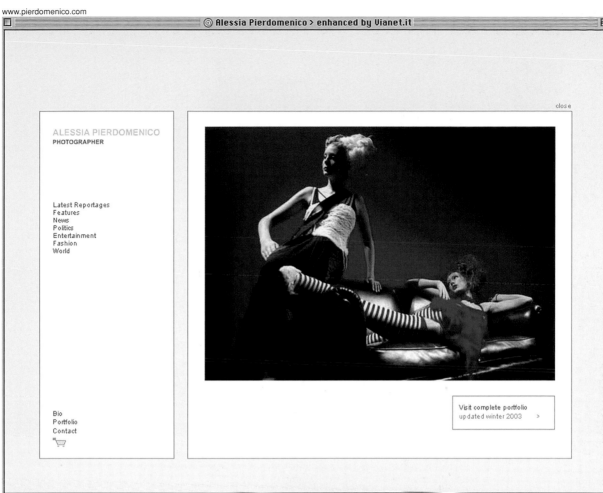

Visit complete portfolio
updated winter 2003   >

IT **F** **P**

www.austinyoung.com

INFO-
LINKS *mail* PRINTED **portraits** BEAUTY FILM news

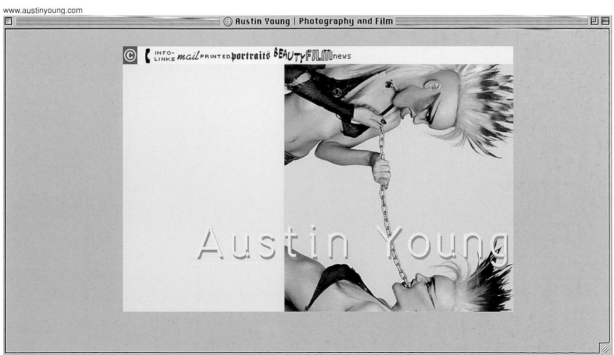

Austin Young

USA **P**

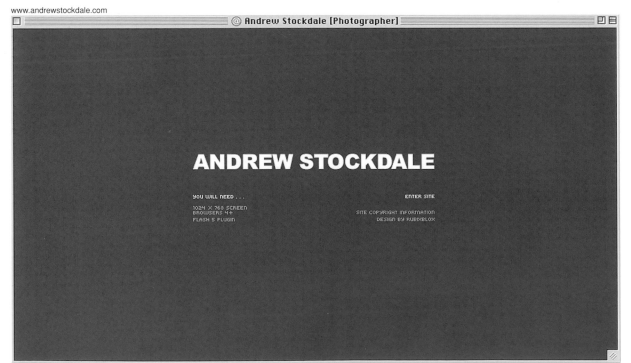

www.anatolyivanov.com

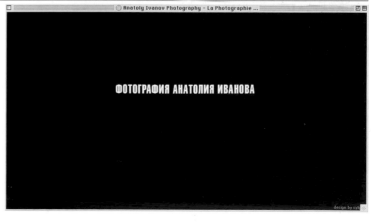

@ Antony Morgan | Professional Photographer

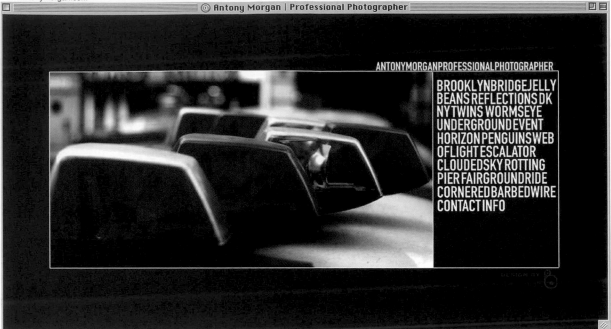

ANTONYMORGANPROFESSIONALPHOTOGRAPHER

BROOKLYNBRIDGEJELLY
BEANSREFLECTIONSDK
NYTWINS WORMSEYE
UNDERGROUNDEVENT
HORIZONPENGUINSWEB
OFLIGHTESCALATOR
CLOUDEDSKYROTTING
PIERFAIRGROUNDRIDE
CORNEREDBARBEDWIRE
CONTACTINFO

@ Bernd Spauke .... Photographie

"Jahr der 1. Küsse" ab 3.Oktober in den Kinos.

bernd **spauke** photography

stillphotography filmography backstage actors free works news contact

www.meeksphoto.com

www.brodylomorrow.com

@ B-man Artworks | v7/light

DK P

Chris Hall Photography

Chris Hall
Photography

people places studio

Need Help?

USA F P

© Christian Houge

NO F P

Please Help

I've created some T-shirts designs at Threadless.com. If enough people vote for them, the shirts will be printed out and i'll get 3 of them for free. So please if you like my site and don't know how to tell it to me, go there, and vote for mine. You won't get anything in return, except my sympathy. Thanks to all the people who already voted.

>> I WANT TO HELP YOU AND VOTE

© Dan Turner Art Gallery

<< End

01 | Straight shot, slightly cropped, no manipulation. © 2003 by Dan Turner

Next >>

Email Comments / Inquiries | Commercial Site

http://zillwood.co.nz

▶ the photographer

?

▷ the photographer
non-commissioned
commissioned

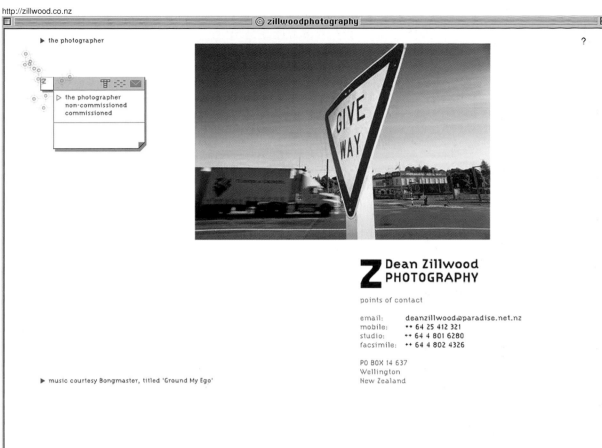

**Z Dean Zillwood
PHOTOGRAPHY**

points of contact

email: deanzillwood@paradise.net.nz
mobile: ++ 64 25 412 321
studio: ++ 64 4 801 6280
facsimile: ++ 64 4 802 4326

PO BOX 14 637
Wellington
New Zealand

▶ music courtesy Bongmaster, titled 'Ground My Ego'

NZ F K P

www.digitalvisiononline.com

UK F K P

www.sachabiyan.com

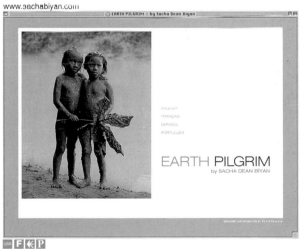

USA F K P

ASGER CARLSEN
PHOTOGRAPHY

PORTFOLIO   ABOUT A.   CONTACT

SITE DESIGN BY adopt:

www.emilianorodriguez.com.ar

EMILIANO
RODRIGUEZ
RUIZ
DE
GAUNA
PORTFOLIO V1.0

ESPAÑOL   ENGLISH

PARA LA CORRECTA VISUALIZACIÓN
DEL SITIO DEBERÁ TENER INSTALADO
EL PLUG-IN DE SHOCKWAVE FLASH

www.holzschuherstrasse.de

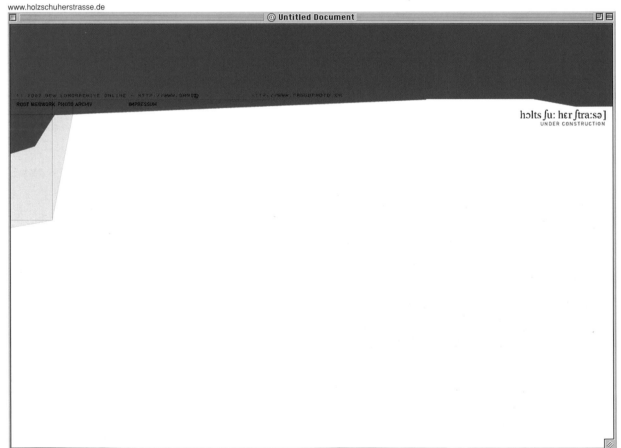

hɔlts ʃuː hɛr ʃtraːsə]
UNDER CONSTRUCTION

www.foundonline.org

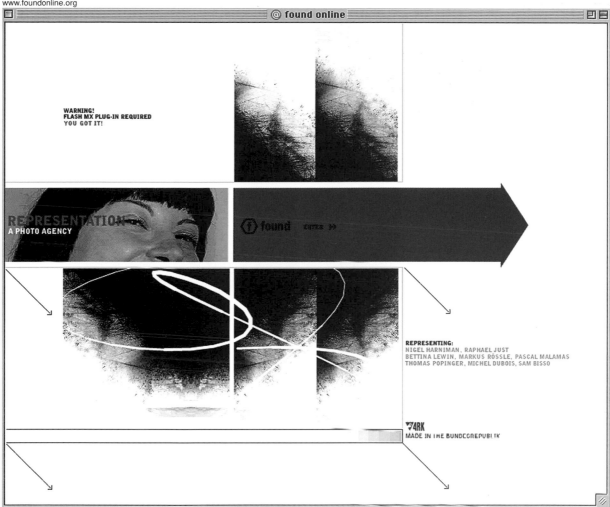

@ found online

WARNING!
FLASH MX PLUG-IN REQUIRED
YOU GOT IT!

REPRESENTATION
A PHOTO AGENCY

found

REPRESENTING:
NIGEL HARNIMAN, RAPHAEL JUST
BETTINA LEWIN, MARKUS RÖSSLE, PASCAL MALAMAS
THOMAS POPINGER, MICHEL DUBOIS, SAM BISSO

4RK
MADE IN THE BUNDESREPUBLIK

DE F C

www.garymoger.com

Gary Moger Photographer

UK F P

www.hillpeppard.com

Hill Peppard | Photography

hill peppard

IMAGE COLLECTIONS
PORTFOLIO BOOKS
THREE DIMENSIONAL
INFORMATION

HILL PEPPARD | PHOTOGRAPHY

CA F P

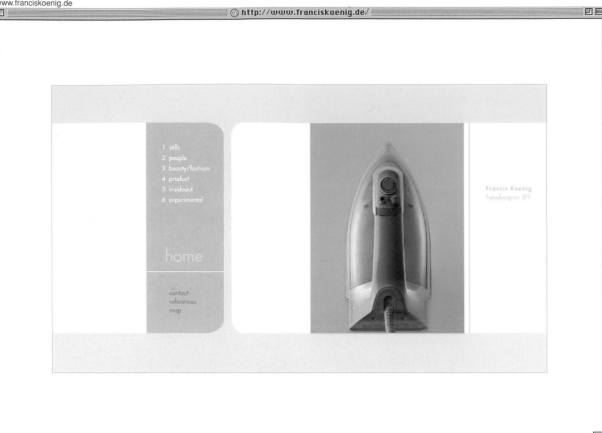

1 stills
2 people
3 beauty/fashion
4 product
5 insideout
6 experimental

home

contact
references
map

Francis Koenig
Fotodesigner BFF

DE F P

@ IAIN CLARIDGE / Photography. Design. New Medi...

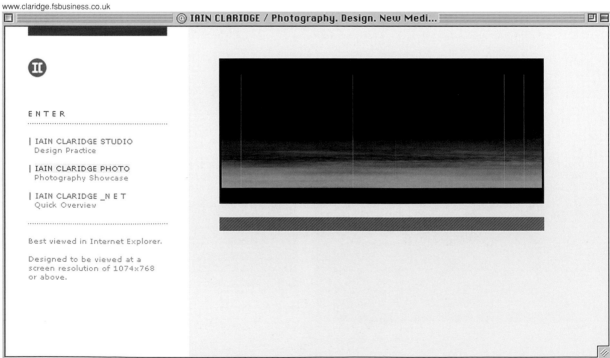

ENTER

| IAIN CLARIDGE STUDIO
Design Practice

| IAIN CLARIDGE PHOTO
Photography Showcase

| IAIN CLARIDGE _ N E T
Quick Overview

Best viewed in Internet Explorer.

Designed to be viewed at a
screen resolution of 1074x768
or above.

UK F C

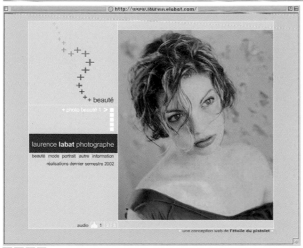

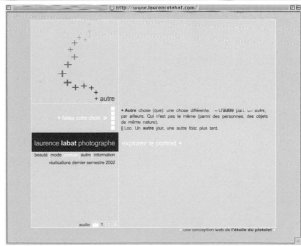

www.imageafter.com

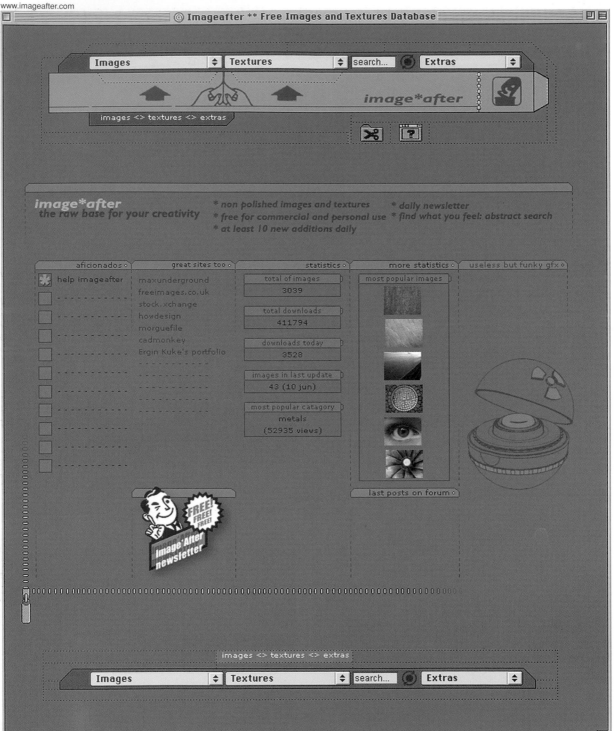

www.huskycz.cz

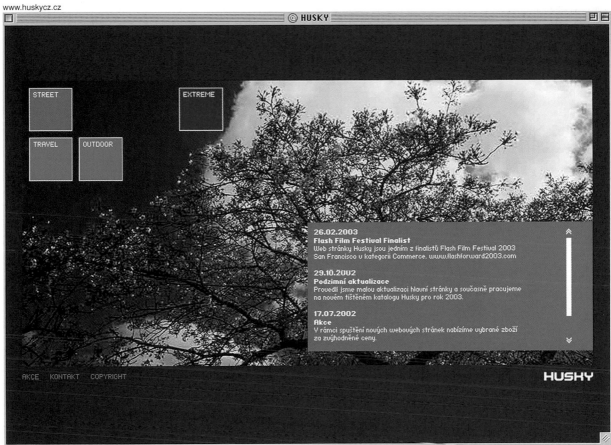

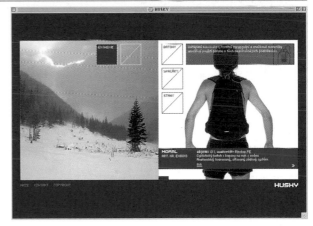

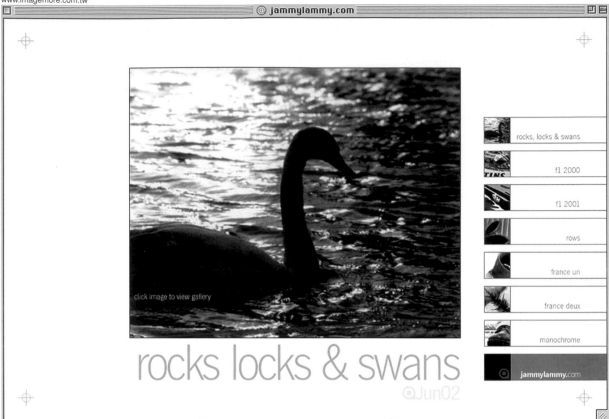

@ jammylammy.com

rocks, locks & swans

fl 2000

fl 2001

rows

france un

france deux

monochrome

jammylammy.com

click image to view gallery

rocks locks & swans
@Jun02

@ johanna thompson: mental/photography

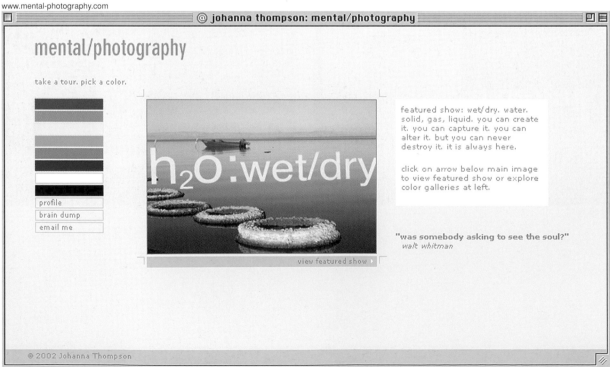

mental/photography

take a tour. pick a color.

profile
brain dump
email me

h₂o:wet/dry

view featured show ▶

featured show: wet/dry. water.
solid, gas, liquid. you can create
it. you can capture it. you can
alter it. but you can never
destroy it. it is always here.

click on arrow below main image
to view featured show or explore
color galleries at left.

"was somebody asking to see the soul?"
walt whitman

© 2002 Johanna Thompson

www.jasonmolyneaux.com

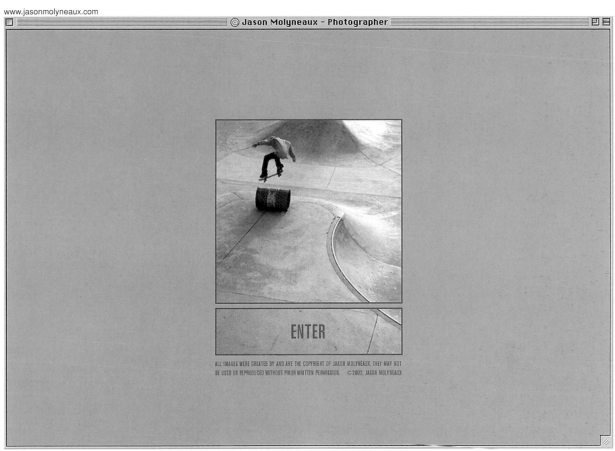

ENTER

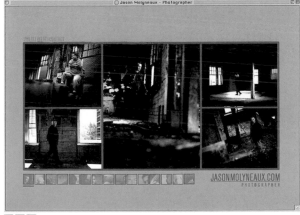

JEZEBEL, A SITE FOR SORE EYES, IS THE PERSONAL WEBSITE OF HEATHER CHAMP   ABOUT   COMMENT   COPYRIGHT 1994 - 2003

UPDATED FREQUENTLY
» harrumph!
» The Mirror Project

UPDATED INFREQUENTLY
» LomoHome
» harrumph! moho
» Jezebel's Mirror
» Postcards

NEWS

Oh-my-god-I'm-forty!
How did that happen? Many thanks to Melanie, and all those who helped, for making my birthday wish come true.
04/29/03

The Mirror Project garners two inaugural *Photobloggies* for "Best Photo Meme" and "Best Group/ Community." There's also a brief mention in The New York Times.
02/27/03

How much do I love my new Lomo?
01/28/03

SEND A JEZEBEL POSTCARD

A MIRROR FAVOURITE

» Are you looking for **Peter Pan?**
» Terms of use

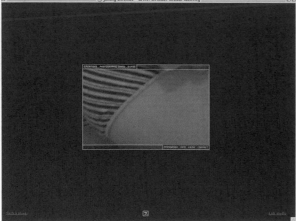

Lomo LC-A, **LomoHome**

---

www.blackeyed.com

@ jimmy owenns - artist without sexual identity

---

www.jordisarra.com

@ jordisarra

JORDI SARRÀ

http://dasvegas.com/phooto/

www.photoalto.com

www.petrihaggren.com

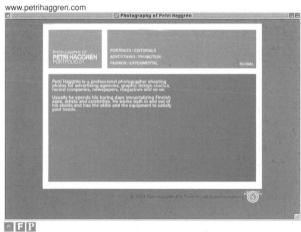

www.katinkabukh.com

@ katinka bukh photography

KATINKA BUKH

TRAVELS / LINZ / THAI 02   CONTACT

SITE DESIGN BY adopt: COPYRIGHT 2002 KATINKA BUKH. KBU@EUROMAN.DK

DK F P

www.kenmayerstudios.com

Ken Mayer Studios | Commercial and Advertisin...

KENMAYERSTUDIOS

people   art + artists   architecture   food   drink

COMMERCIAL AND ADVERTISING PHOTOGRAPHY

KEN MAYER STUDIOS   VANCOUVER   T 604 874 2259
SUITE 111   BRITISH COLUMBIA   F 604 974 6659
1000 PARKER STREET   V6A 2H2 CANADA   E KEN@KENMAYERSTUDIOS.COM

CA P

www.lareovazquez.com

LAREO-VAZQUEZ Photography™

Move your mouse to the squares

LAREO-VAZQUEZ
PHOTOGRAPHY

Skip to menu   Info

USA F K P

www.lackadaisical.com

www.lelandphoto.com

@ **markwinwood | photography**

mark winwood
photography

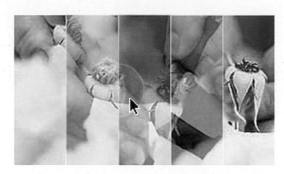

LATEST FLASH PLUG-IN

get flash | enter site

design and implementation : kit suman : contact@kitsuman.com

UK F C

@ Michael Prince Photography

Michael Prince Photography Home

USA F P

@ modelplus - welcome!   ple...

PL F C

INTRANSIENT
イントランジェント

PHOTO JOURNAL

HOMEBASE: SEKI CITY • JAPAN
POWERED BY MOVERABLE TYPE

Previous |

Photo Home
May
April
March
February
January
December
November
October
September

The Girls
Thursday, June 05

Please say hello to Haruka and Ayaka. Spring bar-b-q.

Thank you for visiting, kemp@intransient.com

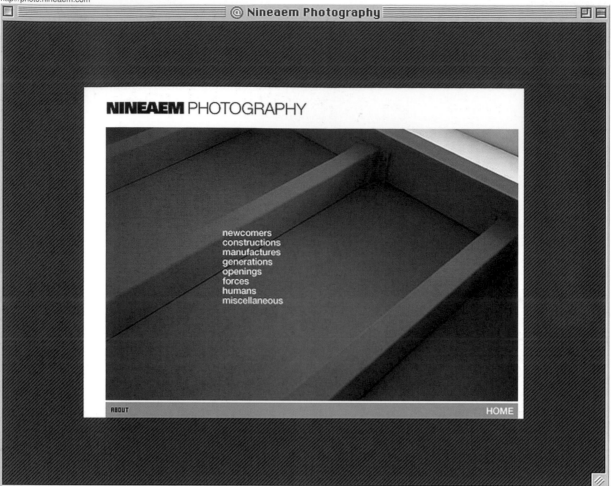

www.rootylicious.com/pastimater/splash.htm

www.ondreabarbe.com

ENTER SITE

FLASH PLUG-IN REQUIRED
CLICK HERE TO DOWNLOAD

www.earthy.co.uk

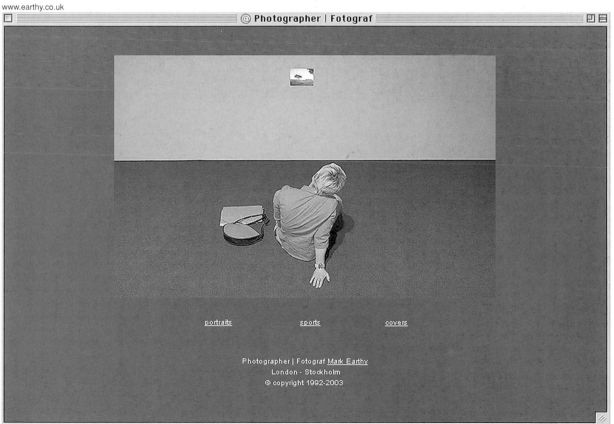

portraits   sports   covers

Photographer | Fotograf Mark Earthy
London - Stockholm
© copyright 1992-2003

PHOTO

the

o
24b

001

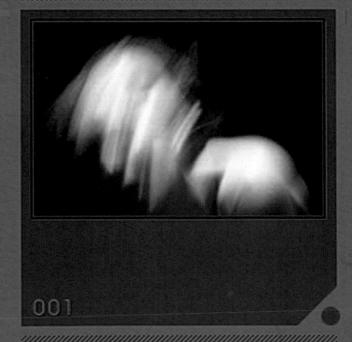

001

FE IN FRAMES

graphic portfolio,
omasz Jankowski

DU WILL NEED

with IE 6 or NN 6
& 1024 x 768 res
c speaker system
flash plug-in

ENTER
update: 22.04.03

002-2003 mondo

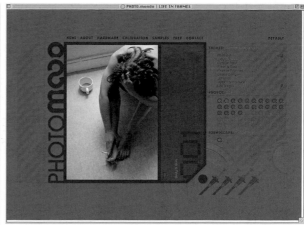

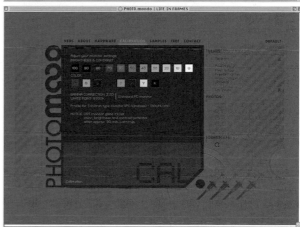

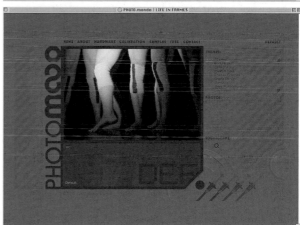

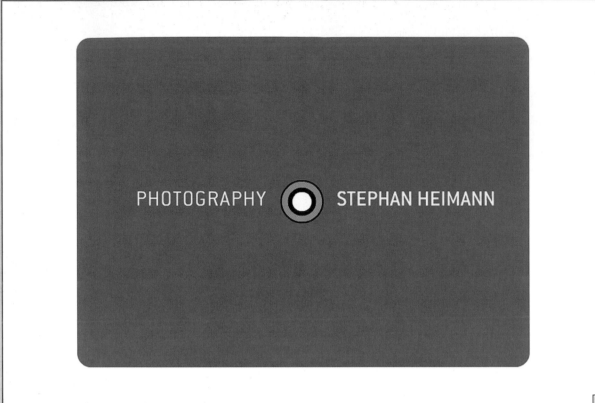

www.republikization.com

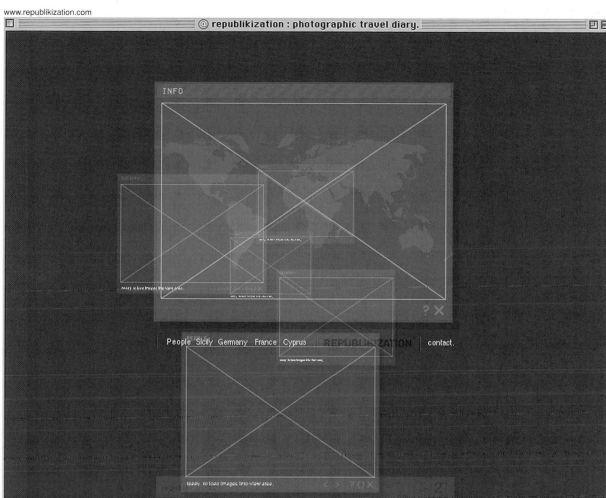

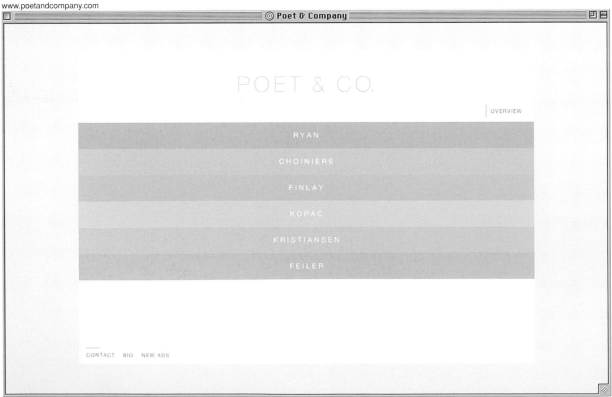

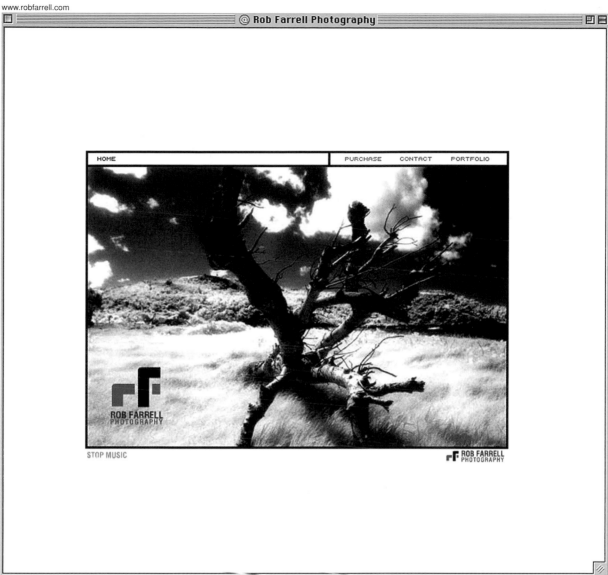

RICKY MOLLOY photography

> PARLAMENT 01   > TOKEI
> PARLAMENT 02   > TENERIFE
> PARLAMENT 03   > BEACH CULTURE

> PORTRAITS

CONTACT INFO

SITE DESIGN BY adopt

RICKY MOLLOY photography

> PARLAMENT 01   > TOKEI
> PARLAMENT 02   > TENERIFE
> PARLAMENT 03   > BEACH CULTURE

> PORTRAITS

CONTACT INFO

SITE DESIGN BY adopt

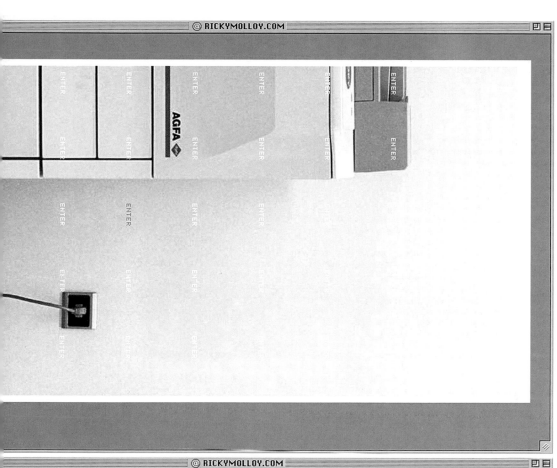

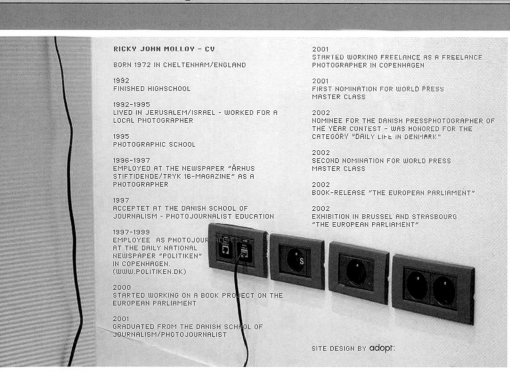

RICKY JOHN MOLLOY – CV

BORN 1972 IN CHELTENHAM/ENGLAND

1992
FINISHED HIGHSCHOOL

1992-1995
LIVED IN JERUSALEM/ISRAEL - WORKED FOR A
LOCAL PHOTOGRAPHER

1995
PHOTOGRAPHIC SCHOOL

1996-1997
EMPLOYED AT THE NEWSPAPER "ÅRHUS
STIFTIDENDE/TRYK 16-MAGAZINE" AS A
PHOTOGRAPHER

1997
ACCEPTET AT THE DANISH SCHOOL OF
JOURNALISM - PHOTOJOURNALIST EDUCATION

1997-1999
EMPLOYEE AS PHOTOJOUR
AT THE DAILY NATIONAL
NEWSPAPER "POLITIKEN"
IN COPENHAGEN.
(WWW.POLITIKEN.DK)

2000
STARTED WORKING ON A BOOK PROJECT ON THE
EUROPEAN PARLIAMENT

2001
GRADUATED FROM THE DANISH SCHOOL OF
JOURNALISM/PHOTOJOURNALIST

2001
STARTED WORKING FREELANCE AS A FREELANCE
PHOTOGRAPHER IN COPENHAGEN

2001
FIRST NOMINATION FOR WORLD PRESS
MASTER CLASS

2002
NOMINEE FOR THE DANISH PRESSPHOTOGRAPHER OF
THE YEAR CONTEST - WAS HONORED FOR THE
CATEGORY "DAILY LIFE IN DENMARK"

2002
SECOND NOMINATION FOR WORLD PRESS
MASTER CLASS

2002
BOOK-RELEASE "THE EUROPEAN PARLIAMENT"

2002
EXHIBITION IN BRUSSEL AND STRASBOURG
"THE EUROPEAN PARLIAMENT"

SITE DESIGN BY adopt:

www.robbycyron.de

www.schmidtfoto.de

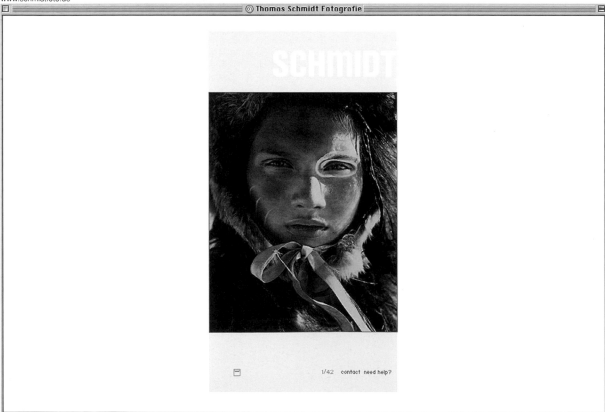

www.spektrumstudios.dk

@ Spektrum Studios

SPEKTRUM STUDIOS

STRANDGADE 70
1401 COPENHAGEN K
DENMARK

T (+45) 32 64 80 80
F (+45) 32 64 80 81
INFO@SPEKTRUMSTUDIOS.DK

CHRISTIAN GEISNÆS
PHOTOGRAPHER

DRASKO PETRIC
DIGITAL IMAGING

RENÉ RIIS
PHOTOGRAPHER

THOMAS IBSEN
PHOTOGRAPHER

TUE SCHIØRRING
PHOTOGRAPHER

CREDIT

DK F C

---

www.studio-braun.com

@ Studio Jan B. Braun

START

b
studio jan b. braun
DIGITALE PHOTOGRAPHIE

DE F C

www.simonhoegsberg.com

PRIVATE AND PUBLIC

PORTRAITS OF PEDESTRIANS AT MARBLE ARCH, LONDON
PHOTOGRAPHED BY SIMON HØGSBERG

SUMMER   AUTUMN   WINTER   SPRING

PRIVATE AND PUBLIC
–INTRO

PRIVATE AND PUBLIC
–NOTES

ABOUT SIMON

CONTACT

COMMERCIAL

The photographs on this site are taken within a 30 meters long strip of sidewalk on Edgeware Road, Marble Arch, London.

All images are taken over a period of one year – from early Summer, 2001 to late Spring, 2002 – and apart from the portraits taken during the Summer period, all pictures are taken from the same spot – 3 meters from the corner of Edgware Road and Oxford Street. None of the photographs have been set up but are all snapshots of pedestrians who happened to walk into the frame of the camera.

SITE DESIGN BY adopt.

www.stephenstickler.com

Stephen Stickler | Photographer

FASHION & AD
MUSIC
PORTRAIT
BUY
INDEX
CONTACT

STEPHEN STICKLER

www.artcoup.com

artcoup.com

ARTCOUP / 20 photos by BOOGIE
powered by dead by design

supported by

1 2 3 4 5 6 7 8 9 10 11 12 13 14 15 16 17 18 19 20   next ▶

Central Saint Martins College of Art & Design

Pushing the boundaries of arts, design and performance

- Central Saint Martins
- Fashion & Textiles
- Media Arts
- Fine Art
- Graphics
- Theatre & Performance
- 3D Design
- Interdisciplinary

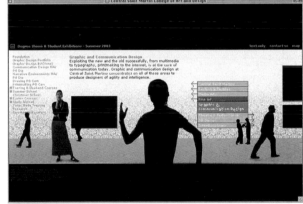

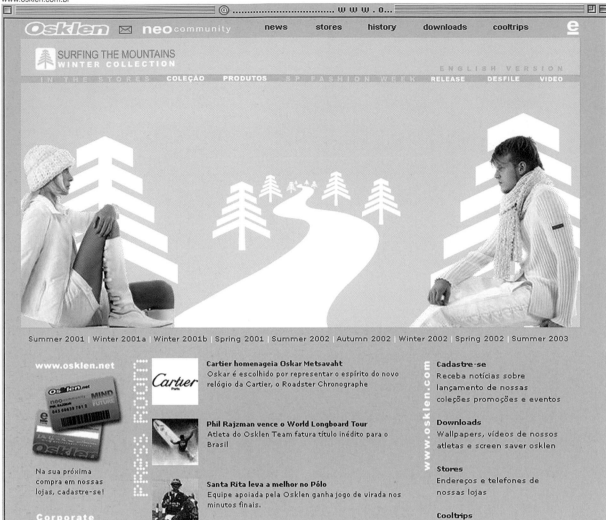

Summer 2001 | Winter 2001a | Winter 2001b | Spring 2001 | Summer 2002 | Autumn 2002 | Winter 2002 | Spring 2002 | Summer 2003

www.osklen.net

Na sua próxima compra em nossas lojas, cadastre-se!

Corporate
História
Sobre a empresa
Franquias
Recursos Humanos

Cartier homenageia Oskar Metsavaht
Oskar é escolhido por representar o espírito do novo relógio da Cartier, o Roadster Chronographe

Phil Rajzman vence o World Longboard Tour
Atleta do Osklen Team fatura título inédito para o Brasil

Santa Rita leva a melhor no Pólo
Equipe apoiada pela Osklen ganha jogo de virada nos minutos finais.

Cadastre-se
Receba notícias sobre lançamento de nossas coleções promoções e eventos

Downloads
Wallpapers, vídeos de nossos atletas e screen saver osklen

Stores
Endereços e telefones de nossas lojas

Cooltrips
Viagens, aventuras e expedições

www.bazpringle.com

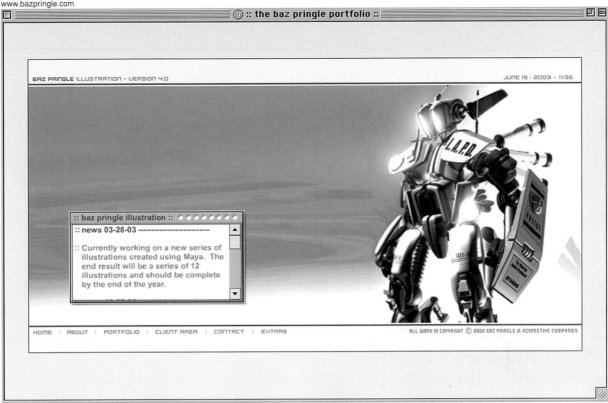

http://washingmachine.free.fr

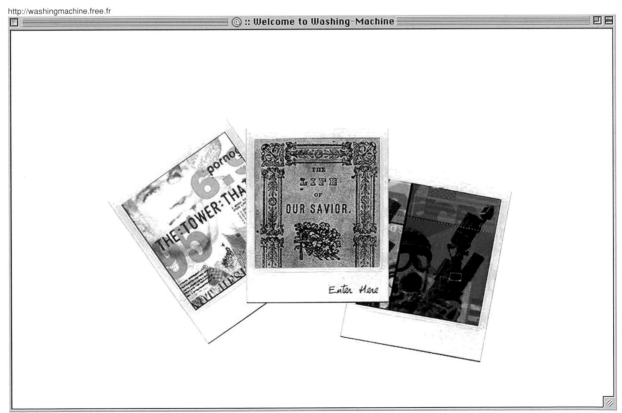

www.spectre7.org

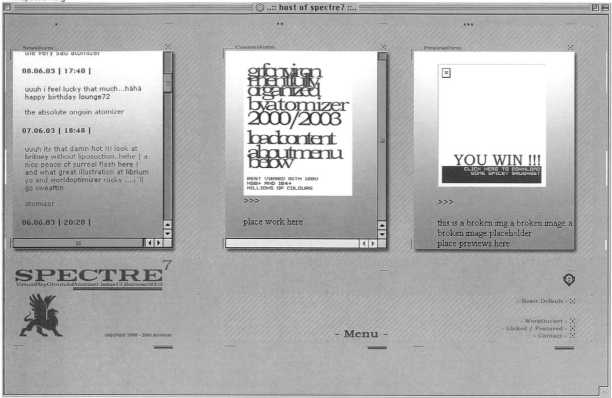

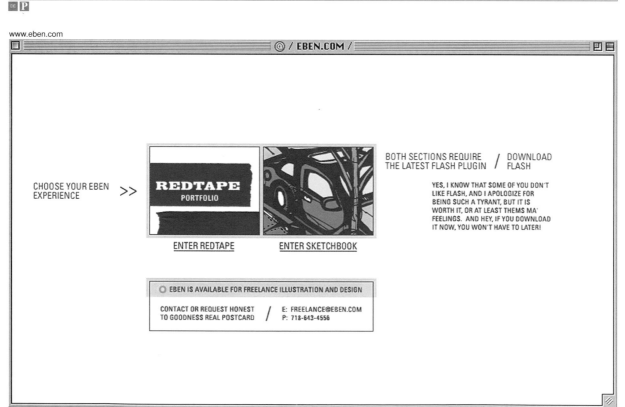

www.eben.com

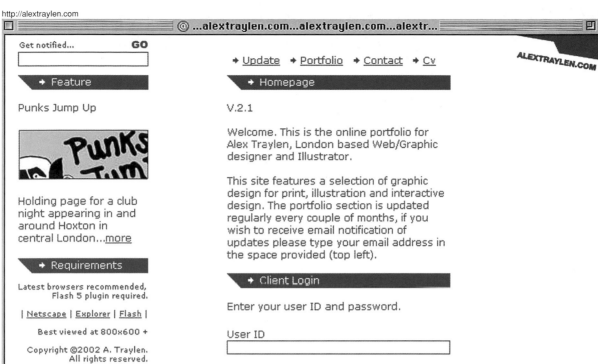

http://alextraylen.com

@ ...alextraylen.com...alextraylen.com...alextr...

Get notified...   **GO**

→ **Feature**

Punks Jump Up

Holding page for a club
night appearing in and
around Hoxton in
central London...more

→ **Requirements**

Latest browsers recommended,
Flash 5 plugin required.

| Netscape | Explorer | Flash |

Best viewed at 800x600 +

Copyright ©2002 A. Traylen.
All rights reserved.

→ Update   → Portfolio   → Contact   → Cv

→ **Homepage**

V.2.1

Welcome. This is the online portfolio for
Alex Traylen, London based Web/Graphic
designer and Illustrator.

This site features a selection of graphic
design for print, illustration and interactive
design. The portfolio section is updated
regularly every couple of months, if you
wish to receive email notification of
updates please type your email address in
the space provided (top left).

→ **Client Login**

Enter your user ID and password.

User ID

Password

Login

UK F P

A GET TOGETHER TO
TEAR IT APART

A SWEDEZINE PROJECT

AGETTOGETHER.NET

TURN PAGE BELOW
VÄND BLAD NEDAN

A GET TO
TEAR IT

A Get Together To
samlar ett gäng tr
fylla ett par sidor

Varje månad kor
designers. Konto

A Get Togethe
containing art
Contact: mail

1

Anthony Yankovic
http://www.junkdrawww.junkdrawer.s5.com

2

3

5

Anna Åsa A
http://www.quikanddirty.s/w

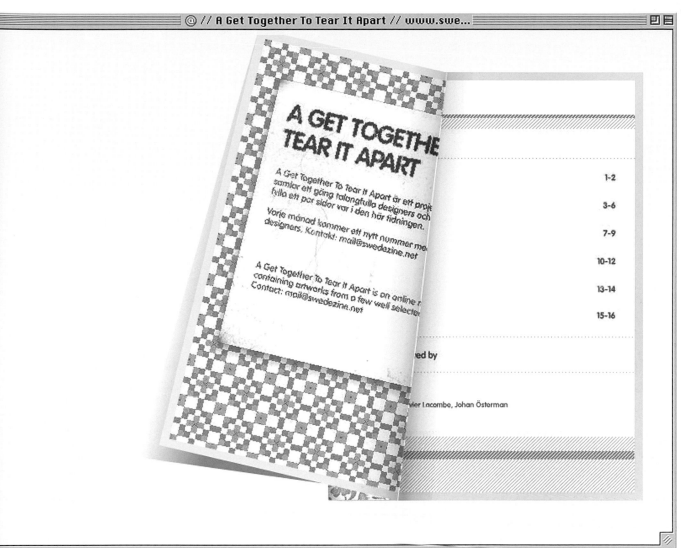

A GET TOGETHE
TEAR IT APART

A Get Together To Tear It Apart är ett projt
samlar ett gäng talangfulla designers och
fylla ett par sidor var i den här tidningen.

Varje månad kommer ett nytt nummer me
designers. Kontakt: mail@swedezine.net

A Get Together To Tear It Apart is an online
containing artworks from a few well selecte
Contact: mail@swedezine.net

...ed by

...vier Lacombe, Johan Österman

6

3

Anna Augul
http://www.quikanddirty.com

Anna Augul
http://www.quikanddirty.com

4

@ [The Best of What's Around]   The Dave Matthew...

The Best of What's Around A Dave Matthews Band Website

what's new • cover art • biographies • lyrics • photos • davespeak • tabs • links • tour • about

Best if viewed with a 1024 by 768 resolution. Gobowa.com © 1999-2002

1559

USA P

www.bacardidj.com

www.olgatanon.com

www.anemptyflight.com

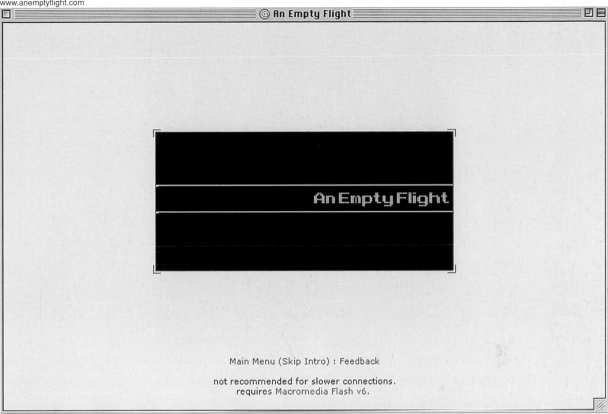

Main Menu (Skip Intro) : Feedback

not recommended for slower connections.
requires Macromedia Flash v6.

www.andy-potts.com

@ APAKSTUDIO©2003

APAK STUDIO

ENTER

FLASH 5.0 PLUGIN REQUIRED >>

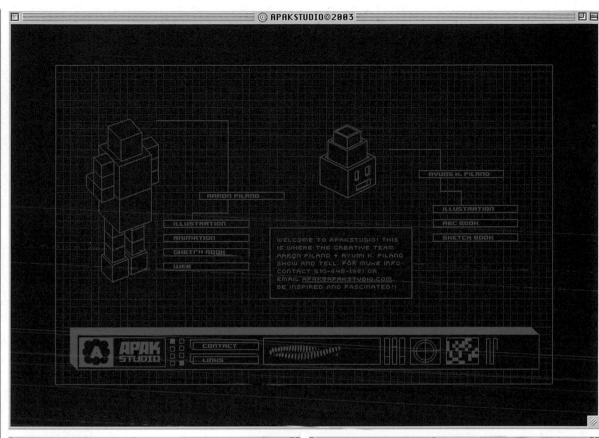

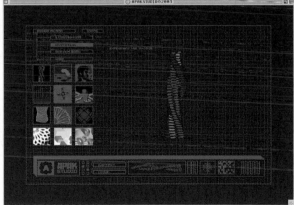

Character Design

Creature Design

Vehicle / Prop Design

Environment Design (Game)

Set Design (Film)

Rough Sketches

How I Work

- Main -

Freelance Info

Online Store

FAQ

Links

Contact Info

Hosted By
Fourbucks.net

All contents copyright (c)
Feng Zhu unless specified
Term Of Use

Feng Zhu - *Concept Artist*

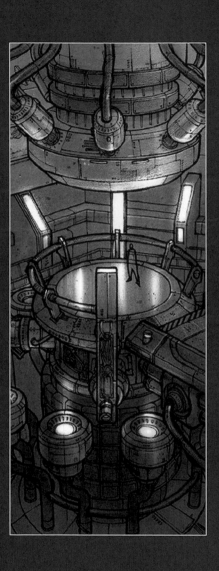

UPDATES:

May 1st, 2003

- Finally some updates! I've added a few sketches here and there. Look in the character and set design (films) sections. I've started to replace some of my older work with the new sketches.

Feb. 07th, 2003

- Article on the **Star Wars: Episode 3** Art Department. Click HERE to check it out.

-feng

Please note that the images displayed on this website are NOT related to Star Wars. For any SW related news, please refer to the official website at **www.starwars.com**. Thank you.

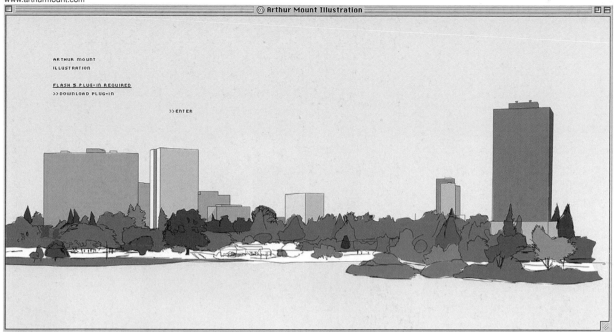

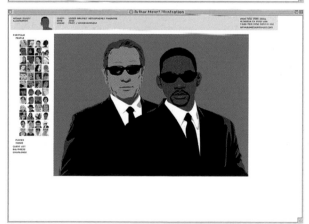

@ ashleywood.com/PRAXIS 2

01. General
/Regular

- **Newsfeed**
  01.A
- **Gallery**
  01.B

02. Informative
/Static

- **Press**
  02.A
- **About**
  02.B
- **Contact**
  02.C

- **Affiliates**
  02.D
- **Bio**
  02.E
- Credits
  02.F

03. DeLuxe
/Extra

- **Store**
  03.A
- **Archives**
  03.B
- **Display**
  03.C

Newsfeed

≡ **05/06/03**

POPBOT 4
is in stores NOW!
Go grab yourself a copy.

[AdminBot]

≡ **01/06/03**

Put some promo pics for LORE inthe gallery..Tomm is
working on a LORE website, so Im holding of on
dumping art in the gallery...

The LORE prologue will come out in November this
year, it will be 60 pages lone, color, 8.5x11..from
IDWpublishing..

You should be able to get Popbot 4 this week, or so im
told...ask for it by name!!! or they wont know what your
talking about....

ash wood

Gallery

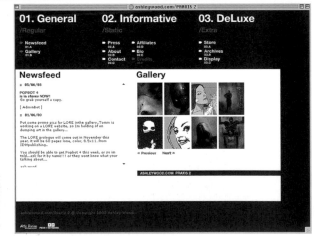

« Previous   Next »

ASHLEYWOOD.COM PRAXIS 2

Acte Divine   PEER 1 NETWORK

@ ashleywood.com/PRAXIS 2

01. General
/Regular

- **Newsfeed**
  01.A
- **Gallery**
  01.B

02. Informative
/Static

- **Press**
  02.A
- **About**
  02.B
- **Contact**
  02.C

- **Affiliates**
  02.D
- **Bio**
  02.E
- Credits
  02.F

03. DeLuxe
/Extra

- **Store**
  03.A
- **Archives**
  03.B
- **Display**
  03.C

Newsfeed

≡ 05/06/03

POPBOT 4
is in stores NOW!
Go grab yourself a copy.

[AdminBot]

≡ 01/06/03

Put some promo pics for LORE inthe gallery..Tomm is
working on a LORE website, so Im holding of on
dumping art in the gallery...

The LORE prologue will come out in November this
year, it will be 60 pages lone, color, 8.5x11..from
IDWpublishing..

You should be able to get Popbot 4 this week, or so im
told...ask for it by name!!! or they wont know what your
talking about....

ash wood

Display

▸ **Display case 1: Uno Fanta.**

› The Book.
› The Prints.

▸ **Display case 2: Illustration.**

› 7 Deadly sine CD art.

▸ **Display case 3: Comics.**

› Hellspawn Cover art.
› Sam & Twitch Cover art.
› Spawn: The dark ages Cover art.
› Spawn: Trade paperbacks Cover art.
› Kiss Cover art.
› THP Assorted Cover art.

ASHLEYWOOD.COM PRAXIS 2

ashleywood.com/Praxis 2 © Copyright 2002 Ashley Wood.

Acte Divine   PEER 1 NETWORK

USA F ← P

@ ashleywood.com/PRAXIS 2

01. General
/Regular

- **Newsfeed**
  01.A
- **Gallery**
  01.B

02. Informative
/Static

- **Press**
  03.A
- **About**
  02.B
- **Contact**
  02.C

- **Affiliates**
  02.D
- **Bio**
  02.E
- Credits
  02.F

03. DeLuxe
/Extra

- **Store**
  03.A
- **Archives**
  03.B
- **Display**
  03.C

Newsfeed

≡ 05/06/03

POPBOT 4
is in stores NOW!
Go grab yourself a copy.

[AdminBot]

≡ 01/06/03

Put some promo pics for LORE inthe gallery..Tomm is
working on a LORE website, so Im holding of on
dumping art in the gallery...

The LORE prologue will come out in November this
year, it will be 60 pages lone, color, 8.5x11..from
IDWpublishing..

You should be able to get Popbot 4 this week, or so im
told...ask for it by name!!! or they wont know what your
talking about....

ash wood

Gallery

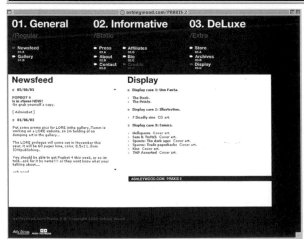

« Previous   Next »

ASHLEYWOOD.COM PRAXIS 2

Acte Divine   PEER 1 NETWORK

www.mdodesign.com/carlos

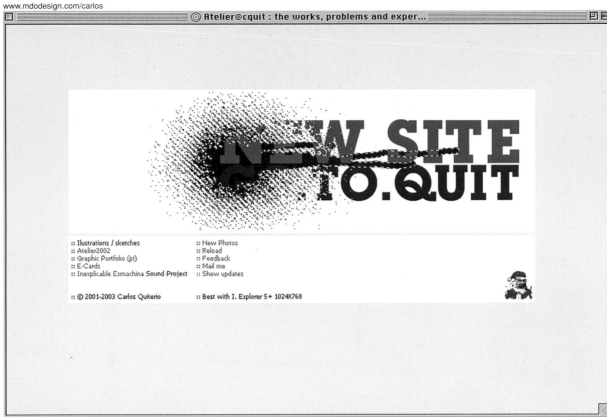

:: Ilustrations / sketches   :: New Photos
:: Atelier2002   :: Reload
:: Graphic Portfolio (pt)   :: Feedback
:: E-Cards   :: Mail me
:: Inexplicable Exmachina **Sound Project**   :: Show updates

:: © 2001-2003 Carlos Quiterio   :: Best with I. Explorer 5+ 1024X768

www.marisamonte.com.br

UOL | BATE-PAPO | BUSCA | CENTRAL DO ASSINANTE | DISCADOR | E-MAIL | ÍNDICE | SHOPPING | PERSONALIDADES

MARISA MONTE

RÁDIO MM | 0-35 | E+ | JOGO | PHONOMOTOR | MAPA

english version

○ Conheça "Tribalistas", projeto de Marisa com Carlinhos Brown e Arnaldo Antunes

○ Registre-se agora e ganhe um screensaver exclusivo!

<<<Enter
The Blimp

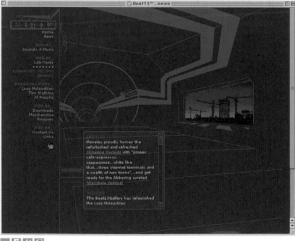

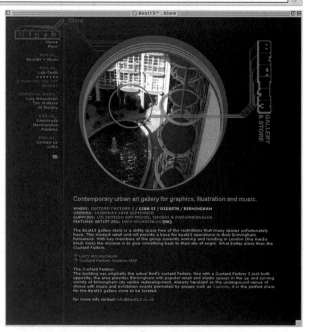

Contemporary urban art gallery for graphics, illustration and music.

WHERE: CUSTARD FACTORY 2 / GIBB ST / DIGBETH / BIRMINGHAM
OPENING: SATURDAY 28TH SEPTEMBER
SUPPLYING: LTD EDITION ART PRINTS, TSHIRTS & PARAPHERNALIA
FEATURED ARTIST 001: LUCY MCLAUCHLAN (UK)

The Beat13 gallery store is a utility space free of the restrictions that many spaces unfortunately have. This modest retail unit will provide a base for Beat13 operations in their Birmingham homeland. With key members of the group currently working and residing in London (the media black hole) the mission is to give something back to their city of origin. What better place than the Custard Factory.

LUCY MCLAUCHLAN
Custard Factory location MAP

The Custard Factory:
The building was originally the actual Bird's custard factory. Now with a Custard Factory 2 just built opposite, the area provides Birmingham with popular retail and studio spaces in the up and coming vicinity of Birmingham city centre redevelopment. Already heralded as the underground venue of choice with music and exhibition events promoted by groups such as Capsule, it is the perfect place for the Beat13 gallery store to be located.

for more info contact info@beat13.co.uk

www.boxstepmusic.com

@ Boxstep

www.boxstepmusic.com

show dates

boxstuff

enter
flash
site

timeline

contact

site design by: re\\ ripple effects interactive

@ Boxstep

boxstep — show dates · timeline · boxstuff · contact · volume

I'll weave cotton this year... at 25 die for pearls... we reach so together

about

@ Boxstep

boxstep — show dates · timeline · boxstuff · contact · volume

close ✕

about we are no test run

Formed in winter of 2000, boxstep is an eight-piece band that orchestrates love songs for lonely hearts.

press coverage

Choose an article ▼

"Concert Review: From Boxstep to Nelson, Farm Aid satisfies"
Pittsburgh Post-Gazette, Sunday, September 22, 2002
By Ed Masley, Pittsburgh Post-Gazette Music Critic

To get the full effect of Farm Aid at the Post-Gazette Pavilion yesterday, you really had to be there. If you watched it live on CMT, you missed out on two of the more inspired artists of the day -- Pittsburgh's Boxstep and the Drive-By Truckers.

As the only artist representing local interests, Boxstep occupied a second stage and got the whole thing rolling with the melancholy strings and slide guitar of "Ryan's Glacier," an impassioned performance of "Airport Arrivals," followed as the band reconstructed the towering wall of sound its fans have come to know and love while adding yet another brick in Deliberate Stranger Tom Moran, who brought a mandolin and banjo to the table. Eric Graf was screaming like a man possessed by old-school Detroit rock 'n' roll on "Route 1," trading lines with Sarah Siplak on a song that peaked with Erin "Scratchy" Hutter gearing up to take on Charlie Daniels' devil down in Georgia.

about
we are

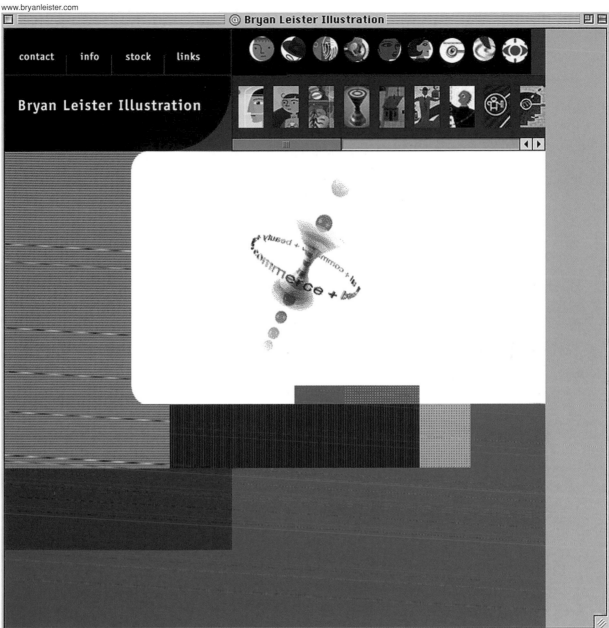

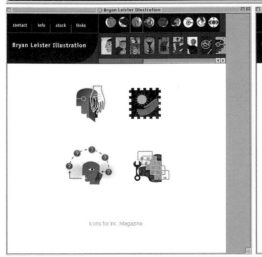

Icons for Inc. Magazine

Cover for a Thompson Financial identity brochure. Thompson was combining several companies under a single name based on input they had received from customers.

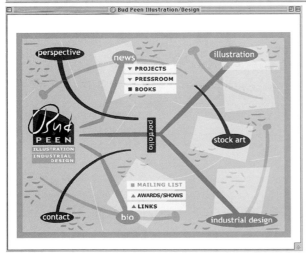

USA P

CA F K C

USA P

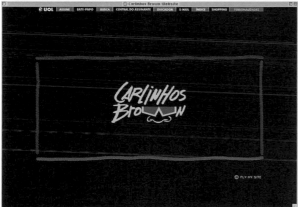

EXPERIENCE DESIGN: LIVEAREA ◇ PHOTO: KEN SHUNG

SLIDE SHOW >>>

FEATURED WORK: POSTERS

CocoMasuda

PORTFOLIO « > / ■ »   SELECT AN IMAGE TO DISPLAY IT. USE THE
CONTROLS TO SHUTTLE BACK AND FORTH.

COCO MASUDA STUDIO / 212■732■2599■NYC | CONTACT | BIO & CLIENTS | FEATURED ART | COCOSTOCK | HOME

This is the portfolio site of illustrator Coco Masuda. None of the images shown are "royalty free", "clip art" or "freeware". Most are available for paid, licensed usage through "CocoStock". Please contact Coco's studio for pricing information if you are interested in using any images on the site or would like to commission an original. All images on this site are Copyright © 2001 Coco Masuda, and may not be used for reproduction in print, on-line or in any other manner whatsoever, without the written permission of Coco Masuda. Unauthorized use is a violation of the Federal Copyright Law and International Copyright Agreement.

Faux Fur Coats
Commissioned by Dayton's

Included in:
Society of Illustrators 2001 Annual
Communication Arts Illustration Annual 2001

Back | Next | Home

PORTFOLIO « > / ■ »   SELECT AN IMAGE TO DISPLAY IT. USE THE
CONTROLS TO SHUTTLE BACK AND FORTH.

COCO MASUDA STUDIO / 212■732■2599■NYC | CONTACT | BIO & CLIENTS | FEATURED ART | COCOSTOCK | HOME

This is the portfolio site of illustrator Coco Masuda. None of the images shown are "royalty free", "clip art" or "freeware". Most are available for paid, licensed usage through "CocoStock". Please contact Coco's studio for pricing information if you are interested in using any images on the site or would like to commission an original. All images on this site are Copyright © 2001 Coco Masuda, and may not be used for reproduction in print, on-line or in any other manner whatsoever, without the written permission of Coco Masuda. Unauthorized use is a violation of the Federal Copyright Law and International Copyright Agreement.

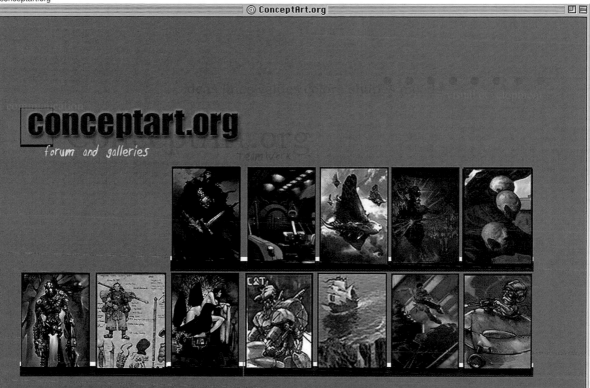

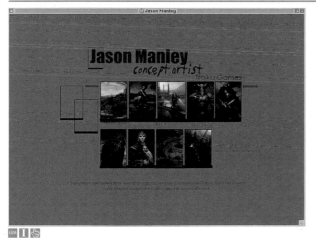

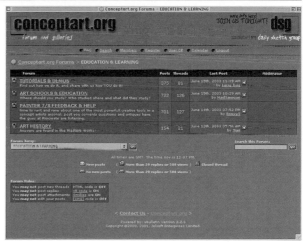

@ GIGER.COM – H.R. Giger's official US Site

GIGER.COM

The H.R. Giger designs, paintings, and sculptures on this site are the copyrighted works of the artist.

© GIGER.COM – H.R. Giger's official US Site

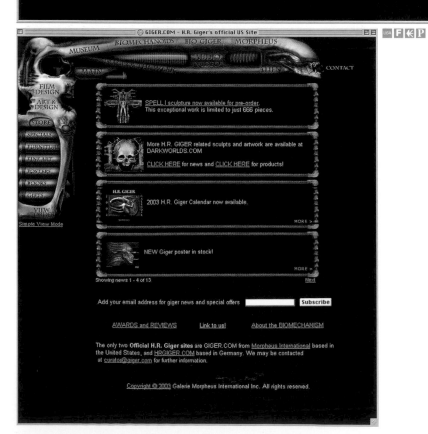

MUSEUM   BIOMECHANOIDS   BIO GIGER   MORPHEUS
AUDIO
VIDEO
MAIN   ALIEN   CONTACT

FILM
DESIGN
ART &
DESIGN
STORE
SPECIALS
FURNITURE
FINE ART
POSTERS
BOOKS
GIFTS
VIEW
ORDER
Simple View Mode

SPELL I sculpture now available for pre-order.
This exceptional work is limited to just 666 pieces.

More H.R. GIGER related sculpts and artwork are available at
DARKWORLDS.COM
CLICK HERE for news and CLICK HERE for products!

H.R. GIGER
2003 H.R. Giger Calendar now available.
MORE >

NEW Giger poster in stock!
MORE >

Showing news 1 - 4 of 13   Next

Add your email address for giger news and special offers   Subscribe

AWARDS and REVIEWS   Link to us!   About the BIOMECHANISM

INTRODUCTION

YOU HAVE REACHED THE GRAPHIC PORTFOLIO
OF DENNIS GLORIE ILLUSTRATION AND DESIGN.

THIS SITE SHOWS THE DIVERSITY OF PROJECTS
I HAVE VISUALIZED OVER THE LAST FEW YEARS.

SIT BACK, LISTEN TO THE BEAT, SCROLL DOWN
THE CONTENT AND ENJOY YOUR STAY.

CREDITS FOR THE MEDIAMONKS FOR PUTTING IN
AN EXCELLENT CONCEPT OF MOTION, BIG IT UP.

[CORPORATE IDENTITY DESIGN]

[GRAPHIC DESIGN]

[PERSONAL ART DESIGN]

[CONTACT INFO]

CONCEPT VISUALIZING

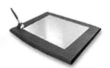

DIGITAL ARTWORK

PRODUCT STICKERING

PRINT ACCOMPANIMENT

DTP & GRAPHIC DESIGN

PRESENTATIONS

♫ [▶] [1] [2] [3] [4] [−] |▇▇▇▇▇▇▇ | [+] [75]

[▶] WELCOME   [01/01]
[−] | | [+]

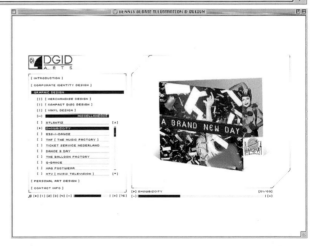

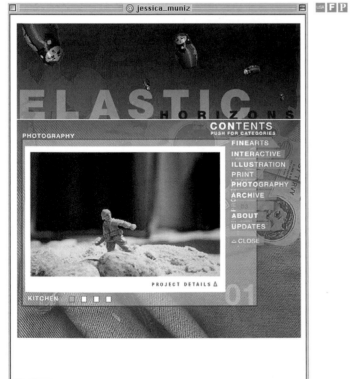

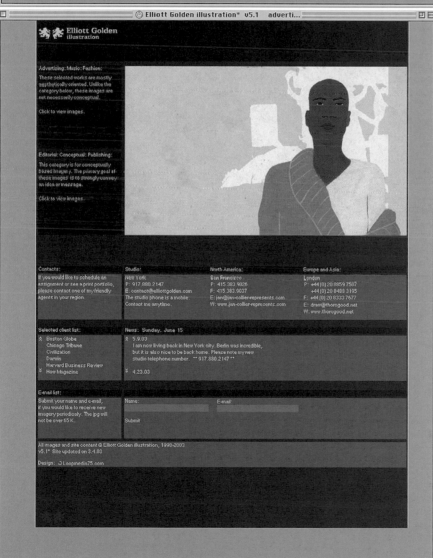

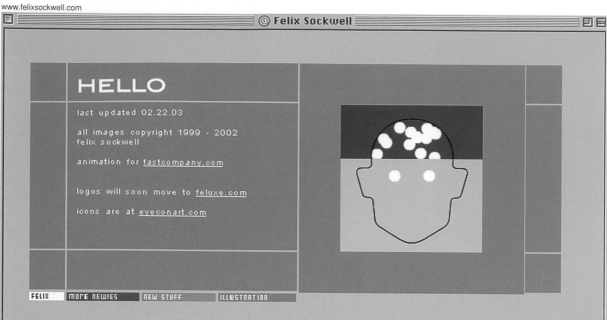

@ Felix Sockwell

HELLO

last updated 02.22.03

all images copyright 1999 - 2002
felix sockwell

animation for fastcompany.com

logos will soon move to feluxe.com

icons are at eyeconart.com

FELIX   MORE NEWIES   NEW STUFF   ILLUSTRATION

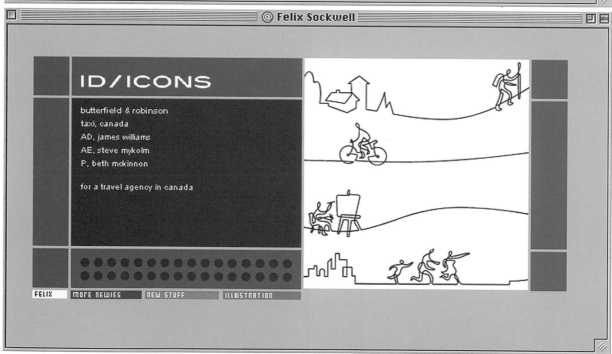

@ Felix Sockwell

ID/ICONS

butterfield & robinson

taxi, canada

AD, james williams

AE, steve mykolm

P, beth mckinnon

for a travel agency in canada

FELIX   MORE NEWIES   NEW STUFF   ILLUSTRATION

@ Felix Sockwell

FELIX

contact

felix sockwell
241 sixth avenue
suite #1g
new york, ny 10014

tel 212 579 5617

felix@felixsockwell.com

FELIX   MORE NEWIES   NEW STUFF   ILLUSTRATION

@ Felix Sockwell

NEW

ford motors
agency, the valentine group
art director, robert valentine

for a print piece that tells the story of
ford's blue oval - in progress

FELIX   MORE NEWIES   NEW STUFF   ILLUSTRATION

@ Fischerspooner

PROFILE | NEWS | SHOWS & EVENTS | MUSIC | PHOTO | VIDEO | SHOP

FISCHERSPOONER

Contact   Sign-Up   Links   Credits & Thanks

This site requires the Flash plug-in. If you can't see the animation above, you need to get it.

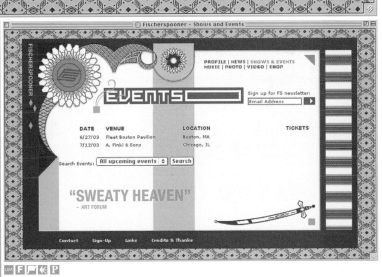

"SWEATY HEAVEN"
— ART FORUM

FRANCISCO.LEMOS
ILLUSTRATION.ONLINE.PORTFOLIO

ILUSTRACION

PINTURAS

PERSONAJES

KONTACTO

FRONT

7   6   5

4   3   2   1

clandestina

la vertical
:: studio

SONRÍE
EL FIN DEL MUNDO HA LLEGADO

@ Francisco Lemos - Online Portfolio

FRANCISCO.LEMOS
ILLUSTRATION.ONLINE.PORTFOLIO

ILUSTRACION

PINTURAS

PERSONAJES

KONTACTO

FRONT

ILUSTRACION

SUBBA.1
SUBBA.3
BRAIN
TINTA
JUNIO
JULIO
COMIC
SOUL

clandestina

la vertical
:: studio

SUBBA.1

Los trabajos de esta serie
fueron desarrollados
digitalmente. El soft
utilizado fue el Painter 8, en
una PC con una Intuos
Wacom.

ES P

@ Francisco Lemos - Online Portfolio

FRANCISCO.LEMOS
ILLUSTRATION.ONLINE.PORTFOLIO

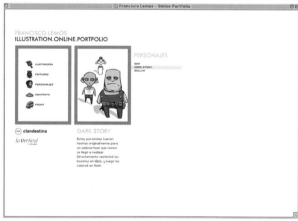

ILUSTRACION

PINTURAS

PERSONAJES

KONTACTO

FRONT

PERSONAJES

SSA
DARK STORY
GOLLUM

clandestina

la vertical
:: studio

DARK STORY

Estos personajes fueron
hechos originalmente para
un webcartoon que nunca
se llegó a realizar.
Directamente vectoricé los
bocetos en Illpiz, y luego los
coloreé en flash.

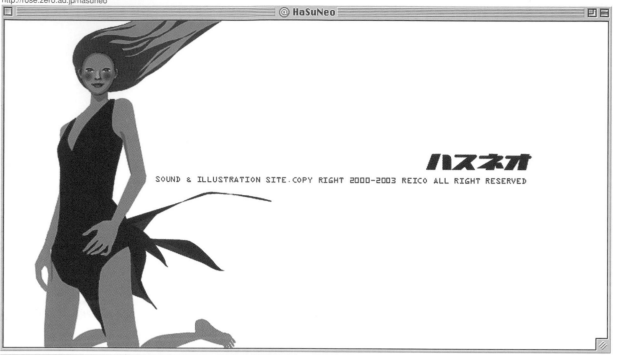

@ HaSuNeo

ハスネオ

SOUND & ILLUSTRATION SITE.COPY RIGHT 2000-2003 REICO ALL RIGHT RESERVED

@ :::::HaSuNeo:::::

ハスネオ HaSuNeo
GRAPHICS & ILLUSTRATION SITE
COPY RIGHT 2000-2002
REICO ALL RIGHT RESERVED.

@ :::::HaSuNeo:::::

マシンシステム
PowerMacG3
Pen III ＋Windows98
WacomTablet
mi2.1.0
TepaEditor
FFFTP
Illustlator9
Photoshop5
Paint Shop Pro6

セイサクシャ
レイコ／Reico
TOKYO JAPAN
デザイン学校卒業後
グラフィックデザイナー
として会社勤務。
現在はフリーでIllustを。
曲作りと音楽と宇宙と
ガーデニングをこよなく愛する。
好きな作家：リチャード・バック，
ジェームズ・レッドフィールド，
エンリケ・バリオス，etc…。

ハスネオインフォメーション
お仕事募集中です
イラストやWEBデザインなど随時お仕事受け付けております
メールフォームからお気軽にお問い合わせ下さい

HaSuNeoとは造語で、漢字での表記は「蓮新」としています

著作権により作成した画像等の無断使用を禁じます
転載の場合はメールにて事前にお問い合わせお願いします
サイトの感想等BBSやメールにてお聞かせ頂けると嬉しいです
動作確認：WIN＋IE6．NN6．2／MAC＋IE5．NN6．1のみ

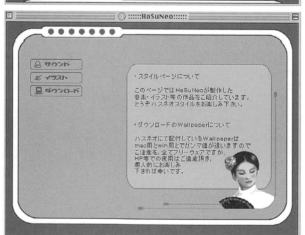

@ :::::HaSuNeo:::::

🔊 サウンド
🖼 イラスト
💻 ダウンロード

・スタイルページについて

このページではHaSuNeoが制作した
音楽・イラスト等の作品をご紹介しています。
どうぞハスネオスタイルをお楽しみ下さい。

・ダウンロードのWallpaperについて

ハスネオにて配付しているWallpaperは
mac用とwin用とでガンマ値が違いますので
ご注意を。全てフリーウェアですが、
HP等での使用はご遠慮頂き、
個人的にお楽しみ
下されば幸いです。

hell-o-rama

home > intro

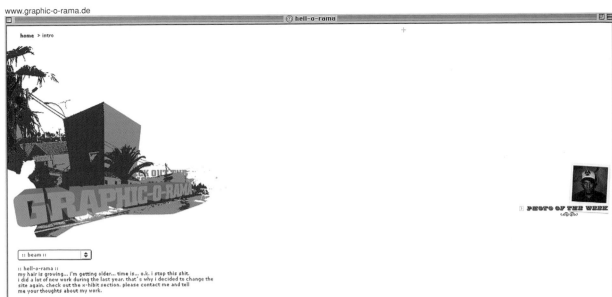

:: beam ::

:: hell-o-rama ::
my hair is growing... i'm getting older... time is... o.k. i stop this shit.
i did a lot of new work during the last year. that's why i decided to change the
site again. check out the x-hibit section. please contact me and tell
me your thoughts about my work.

© 2002 graphic-o-rama | impressum | last update 6 March, 2003 15:04

design-o-rama

home > intro > portfolio > design

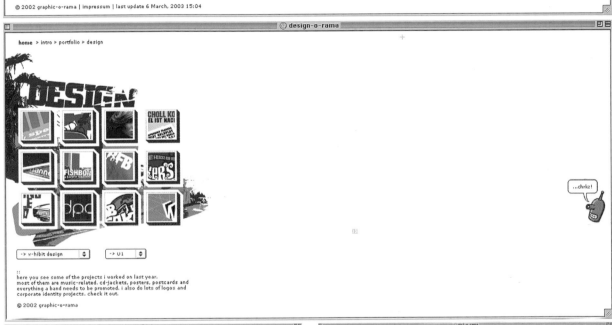

...chrkz!

-> x-hibit design   -> U1

::
here you see some of the projects i worked on last year.
most of them are music-related. cd-jackets, posters, postcards and
everything a band needs to be promoted. i also do lots of logos and
corporate identity projects. check it out.

© 2002 graphic-o-rama

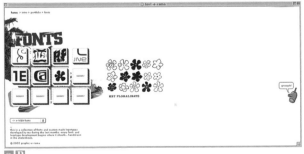

DE P

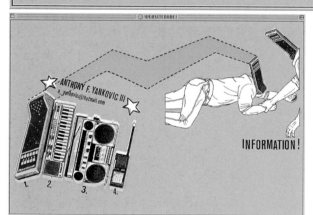

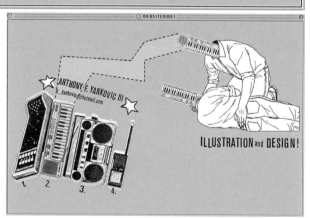

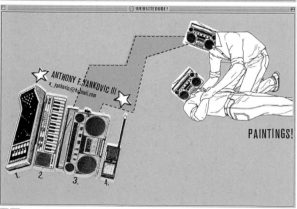

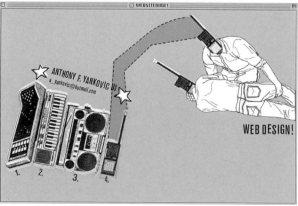

www.peterhoey.com

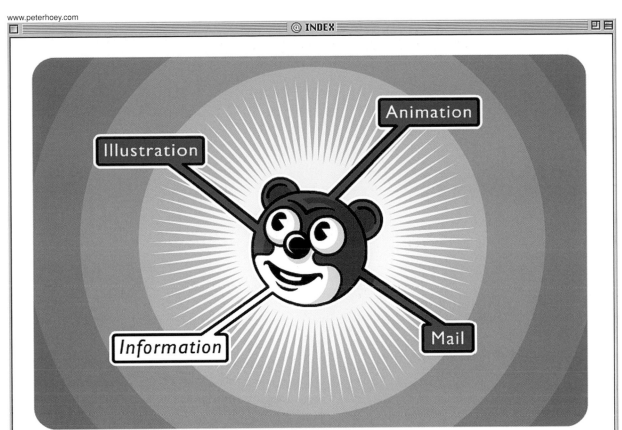

www.jferguson.com

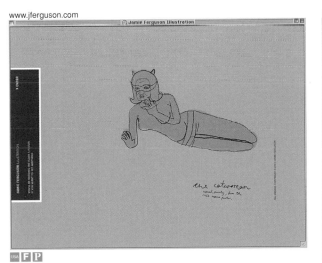

www.lavertical.com/juan

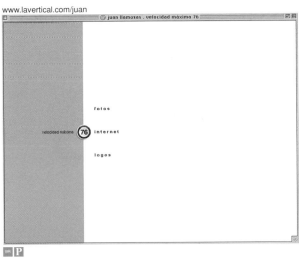

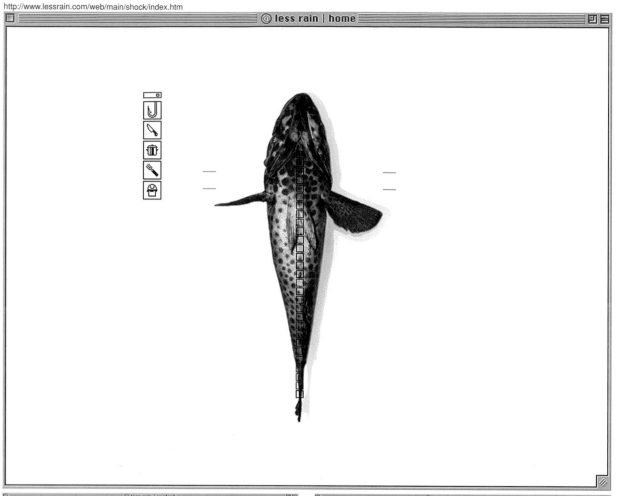

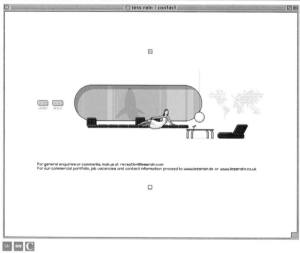

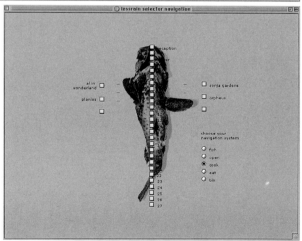

MASTERSOFT UNIVERSE
Easy to buy

CV ⇕	Kola ⇕	PERSONAL ⇕

Toilet doors for a bar. Mens door under development...

Tell me something good
Phone: (+358) 40 725 4775
E-mail: leo@mastersoftuniverse.com

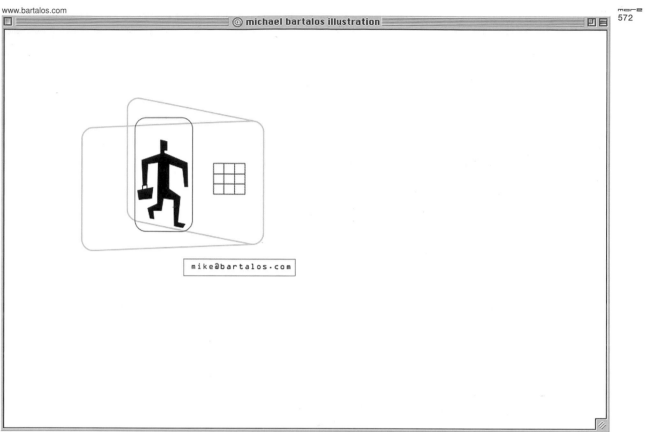

michael bartalos illustration

mike@bartalos.com

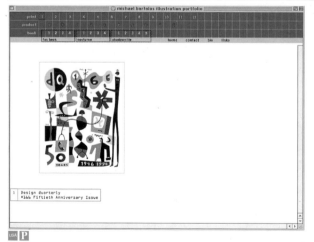

1 | Design Quarterly
    #166 Fiftieth Anniversary Issue

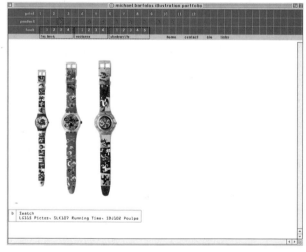

b | Swatch
    LG115 Pictos, SLK107 Running Time, SDJ102 Poulpe

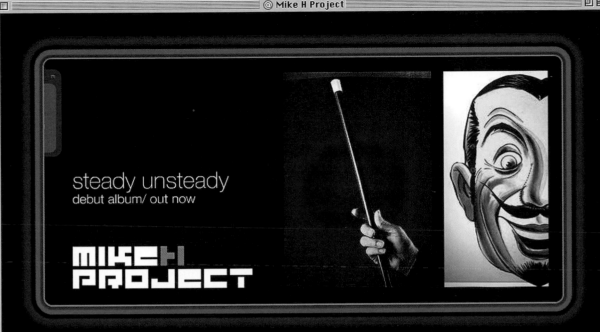

* Critics are raving about NERD...click here to read 'em

N·E·R·D

MAIN·PREVIEW ALBUM·NEWS·BIO·GALLERY·TOUR·JOIN NERD·FORUM·STORE

ALBUM IN SEARCH OF NERD IN STORES NOW

> PREVIEW THE CD

The Neptunes

...reign as today's most successful hip-hop production team. Over the last five years, they have helped propel the talents of a number of artists, their punctuating beats and syncopated rhythms fueling a unique sonic aesthetic.

Now they introduce N*E*R*D and the album IN SEARCH OF....Mixing everything from hard hip-hop beats to black psychedelic pop to classic rock to new wave, the album brings a beguiling new sound to the pop landscape.

SOCIETY MAKING YOU ILL?

POLITICIANS SOUNDING LIKE STRIPPERS TO YOU?

OH BABY YOU WANT ME?"

OH BABY YOU WANT ME?"

:: FREE LAPDANCE | CLICK HERE

:: GO TO THE FORUM

New ROCK STAR Video

PARENTAL ADVISORY EXPLICIT CONTENT

:: PARENTAL GUIDE.ORG

VIRGIN RECORDS AMERICA | STARTRAK MUSIC | WWW.KELIS.COM

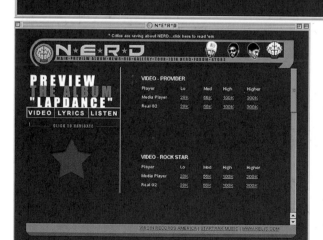

N·E·R·D
MAIN·PREVIEW ALBUM·NEWS·BIO·GALLERY·TOUR·JOIN NERD·FORUM·STORE

PREVIEW THE ALBUM "LAPDANCE"

VIDEO | LYRICS | LISTEN

CLICK TO NAVIGATE

VIDEO - PROVIDER

Player	Lo	Med	High	Higher
Media Player	28K	55K	100K	200K
Real G2	28K	55K	100K	300K

VIDEO - ROCK STAR

Player	Lo	Med	High	Higher
Media Player	28K	55K	100K	200K
Real G2	28K	55K	100K	300K

VIRGIN RECORDS AMERICA | STARTRAK MUSIC | WWW.KELIS.COM

N·E·R·D
MAIN·PREVIEW ALBUM·NEWS·BIO·GALLERY·TOUR·JOIN NERD·FORUM·STORE

GALLERY

VIRGIN RECORDS AMERICA | STARTRAK MUSIC | WWW.KELIS.COM

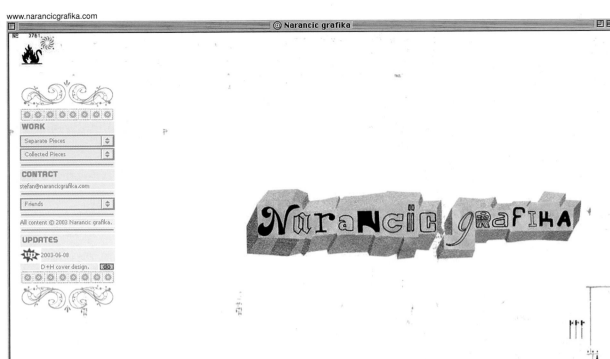

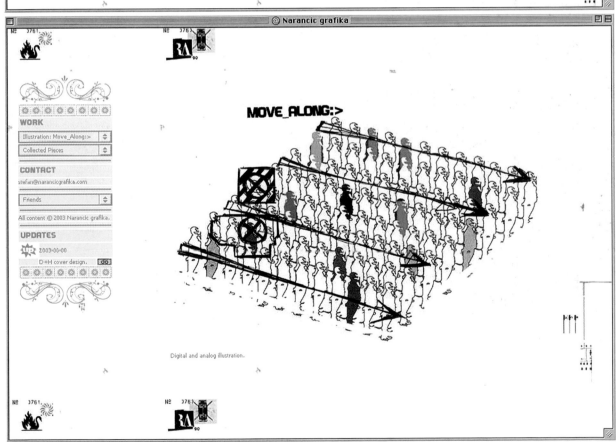

Digital and analog illustration.

noiselab.com
(flash 5 requerido y una conexión rápida es recomendada)

■ cale

■ **foros de discusión**

■ noti

> resi

■ **espacio tres**   ■ **contacto**

■ **memory full**   *next*   ■ **be a robot**

■ **downloads**   ■ **links**

◆ **noise**lab *radio*   *conéctate* ⠿

escucha

■ **mailing**/list/

suscríbete para recibir noticias y
notificaciones via email:

| escribe tu email | | Enviar » |

dj's

 noiselab
listening station

pause
■ ■

noiselab
noiselab.com

programas en vivo desde 11.00 am méxico
los angeles 10.00 am

noiselab *radio*
música continua 24h/7d

conéctate >

ºsmo
1505

mpilaciones

04 **005**

006

007

@ pamela

links • contact • about pam

welcome to pamorama.com

Pamela Hobbs: Digital Artist 2000
order your copy today

Play Pamcentration

click above to skip intro

UK F P

www.dobi.nu

www.bearskinrug.co.uk/sketchbook/

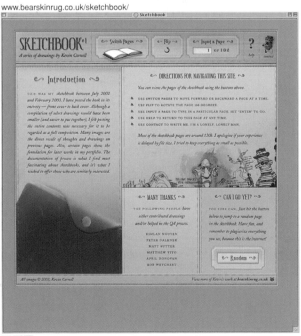

UK F P

@ STS

SOAK THE SIN

- NEWS
- AUDIO
- PICTURES
- FUNNY
- TOUR / INFO
- DIARY
- GUESTBOOK

@ STS

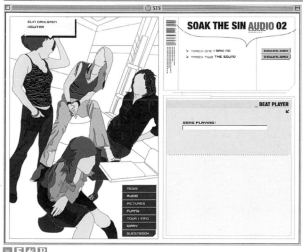

ELIN DAHLGREN
//GUITAR

SOAK THE SIN AUDIO 02

- ↘ TRACK ONE | SAID NO
- ↘ TRACK TWO THE SOUND

DOWNLOAD
DOWNLOAD

_ BEAT PLAYER ↖

SONG PLAYING:

- NEWS
- AUDIO
- PICTURES
- FUNNY
- TOUR / INFO
- DIARY
- GUESTBOOK

@ STS

SOAK THE SIN PIX 03

LOAD SET 13
// RECORDING SESSION AT
STUDIO ROOM 5/ SPRING 2003

LOAD SET 12
// GIG AT 5H/ ARLIGSJAUA
10/4 2003

LOAD SET 11
// STS ON TOUR WITH THE REEFERS
14/2 - 23/2 2003 (PART ONE)

LOAD SET 10
// ON TOUR (PART TWO)

LOAD SET 09
// ON TOUR (PART THREE)
PHOTOS BY TOMAS AHANE

LOAD SET 08
// STS PREFORMING A BEATLES
SONG AT UNDERBAR 5/10-02

LOAD SET 07
// SHOWCASE AT PINKERTON
18/10-02

LOAD SET 06
// TRÅSTOCKFESTIVALEN 19/7-02

MORE PICTURE SETS HERE >>

- NEWS
- AUDIO
- PICTURES
- FUNNY
- TOUR / INFO
- DIARY
- GUESTBOOK

SE F K P

GRUPO CORPO

Patrocínio

BR
PETROBRAS

histórico   obras   sala de imprensa   ficha técnica   agenda   corpo ltda   patrocinador   contato | english

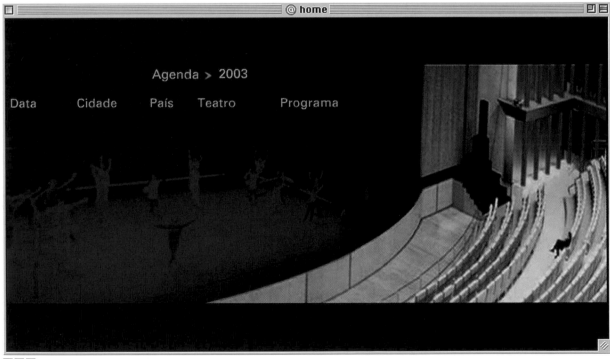

Agenda > 2003

Data   Cidade   País   Teatro   Programa

tshirts

1 sneakerbuilder	atat
3 tie fighter	4 headphones	5 stereo
6 plug	7 stupid humans	8 bleedin edgy	9 skull

UK P

vegas 01
1 2 3 4 5 6 7

cut Place

suma

@ WWW.FIONAHEWITT.COM

★ WELCOME ★

Greetings!

from Fiona Hewitt

BIOGRAPHY · View Work · CONTACT

@ WWW.FIONAHEWITT.COM

Back ◄ 1 2 3 4 5 6 7 8 9 10 11 ► Next

2 : click to enlarge image

Client: Financial Times Magazine
Brief: for article on profits and skiing.

BIOGRAPHY · View Work · CONTACT

@ WWW.FIONAHEWITT.COM

Fiona graduated with a
b.a. honours in drawing and
painting from edinburgh college
of art in 1990. She then went
on to receive a masters degree
from the royal college of art
in july 2000.

··· next ···

BIOGRAPHY · View Work · CONTACT

@ WWW.FIONAHEWITT.COM

Close ○

Click and hold to magnify

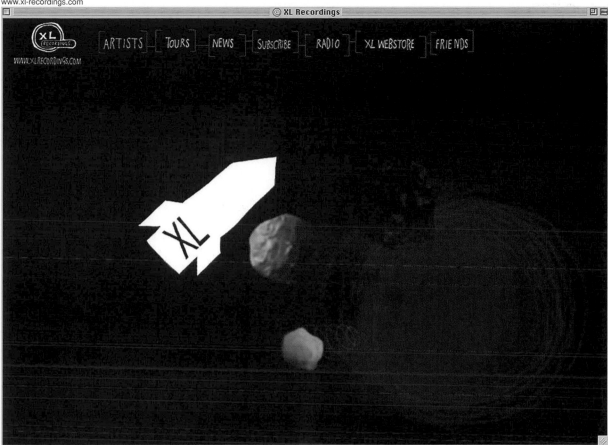

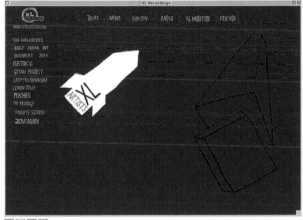

[rinoa.nu]

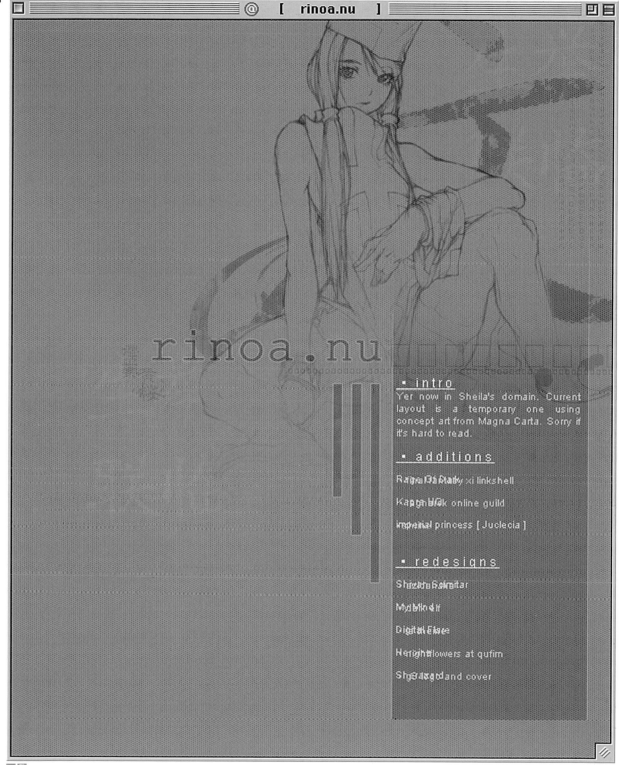

rinoa.nu

- **intro**

Yer now in Sheila's domain. Current layout is a temporary one using concept art from Magna Carta. Sorry if it's hard to read.

- **additions**

Ragnarok Party xi linkshell

Kapph Klok online guild

Imperial princess [Juclecia]

- **redesigns**

Shazza Scimitar

My blond ir

Digital Eaze

Height flowers at qufim

Shg land cover

@ ROOTYLICIOUS.Studios>T>Y>O>E>

ROOTYLICIOUS.STUDIOS/02

REQUIREMENTS: FLASH.5 PLUGIN

ENTER THE SITE

+ + +

USA F C

www.asroma-addict.com

@ Welcome to the Un-Offical AS Roma Italian Ser...

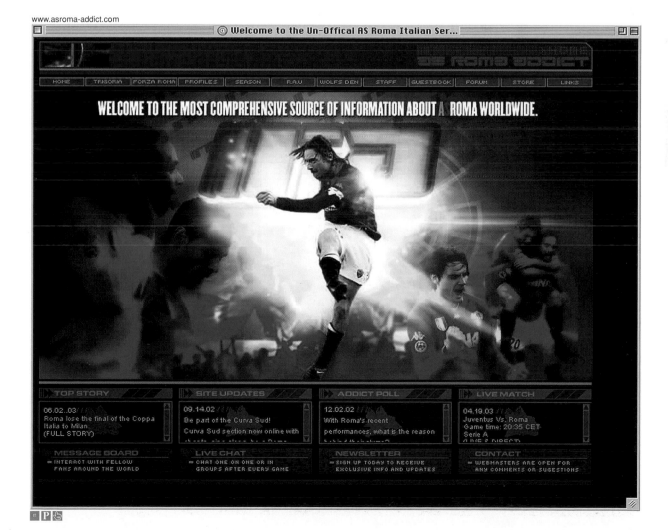

AS ROMA ADDICT

| HOME | TRIGORIA | FORZA ROMA | PROFILES | SEASON | R.A.U | WOLFS DEN | STAFF | GUESTBOOK | FORUM | STORE | LINKS |

WELCOME TO THE MOST COMPREHENSIVE SOURCE OF INFORMATION ABOUT AS ROMA WORLDWIDE.

TOP STORY

06.02..03
Roma lose the final of the Coppa Italia to Milan.
(FULL STORY)

SITE UPDATES

09.14.02
Be part of the Curva Sud!
Curva Sud section now online with

ADDICT POLL

12.02.02
With Roma's recent performances, what is the reason

LIVE MATCH

04.19.03
Juventus Vs. Roma
Game time: 20:35 CET
Serie A

MESSAGE BOARD
■ INTERACT WITH FELLOW FANS AROUND THE WORLD

LIVE CHAT
■ CHAT ONE ON ONE OR IN GROUPS AFTER EVERY GAME

NEWSLETTER
■ SIGN UP TODAY TO RECEIVE EXCLUSIVE INFO AND UPDATES

CONTACT
■ WEBMASTERS ARE OPEN FOR ANY COMMENTS OR SUGESTIONS

IT P

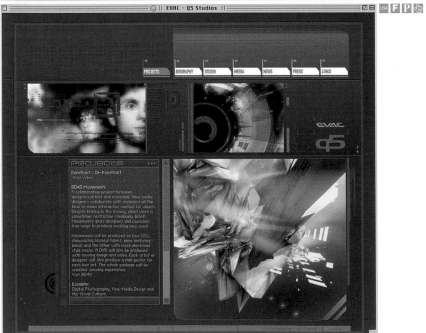

www.gregbenz.com

@ Welcome | Greg Benz.com

GREG|BENZ
WWW.GREGBENZ.COM

▶ NEWS **26.5.03**

Greg and production partner
Marco Di Carlo have been busy in
the studio finishing up a remix of
John Acquaviva's "Metal Detector"
and a remix of the Flash Bros.
"Release Time". Both remix's will
be out soon.... "Release Time" will
be coming out on Release Records
in the upcoming months.

Greg and Marco[Benz and MD]

NEWS BIO AUDIO GUESTBOOK LINKS CONTACT
PLAYLIST
CALENDAR

SITE DESIGN | VELOCITY STUDIO

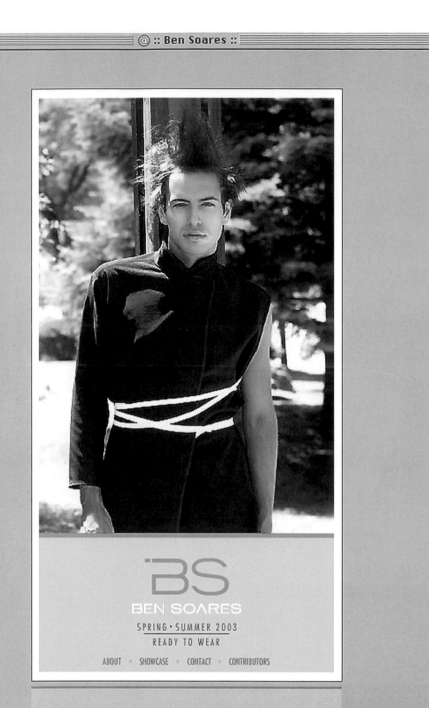

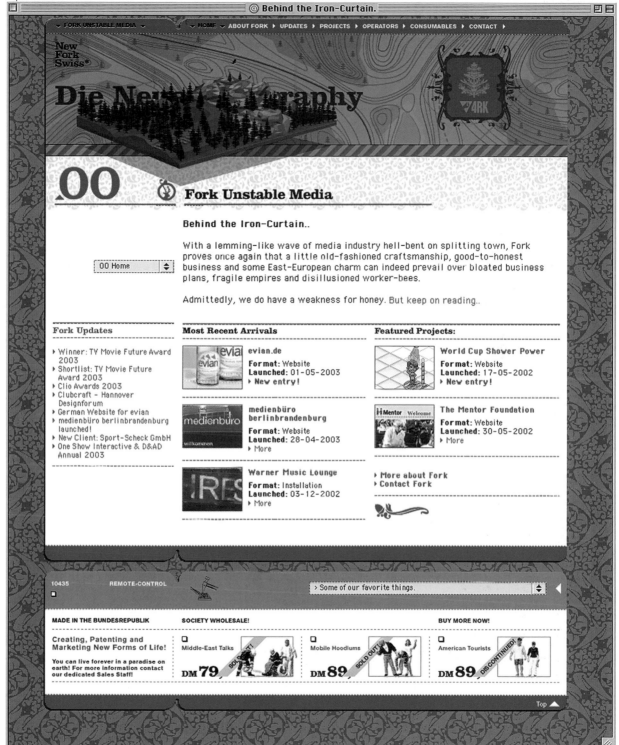

@ Behind the Iron-Curtain.

FORK UNSTABLE MEDIA | HOME | ABOUT FORK | UPDATES | PROJECTS | OPERATORS | CONSUMABLES | CONTACT

New Fork Swiss®

Die Neue ...raphy

.OO Fork Unstable Media

Behind the Iron-Curtain..

With a lemming-like wave of media industry hell-bent on splitting town, Fork proves once again that a little old-fashioned craftsmanship, good-to-honest business and some East-European charm can indeed prevail over bloated business plans, fragile empires and disillusioned worker-bees.

Admittedly, we do have a weakness for honey. But keep on reading..

OO Home

Fork Updates

▸ Winner: TV Movie Future Award 2003
▸ Shortlist: TV Movie Future Award 2003
▸ Clio Awards 2003
▸ Clubcraft – Hannover Designforum
▸ German Website for evian
▸ medienbüro berlinbrandenburg launched!
▸ New Client: Sport-Scheck GmbH
▸ One Show Interactive & D&AD Annual 2003

Most Recent Arrivals

evian.de
Format: Website
Launched: 01-05-2003
▸ New entry!

medienbüro berlinbrandenburg
Format: Website
Launched: 28-04-2003
▸ More

Warner Music Lounge
Format: Installation
Launched: 03-12-2002
▸ More

Featured Projects:

World Cup Shower Power
Format: Website
Launched: 17-05-2002
▸ New entry!

The Mentor Foundation
Format: Website
Launched: 30-05-2002
▸ More

▸ More about Fork
▸ Contact Fork

10435 REMOTE-CONTROL

> Some of our favorite things.

MADE IN THE BUNDESREPUBLIK

Creating, Patenting and Marketing New Forms of Life!

You can live forever in a paradise on earth! For more information contact our dedicated Sales Staff!

SOCIETY WHOLESALE!

Middle-East Talks   SOLD OUT!
DM 79

Mobile Hoodlums   SOLD OUT!
DM 89

BUY MORE NOW!

American Tourists   DISCONTINUED!
DM 89

Top ▲

DE F P

A BROKEN
BEAUTY

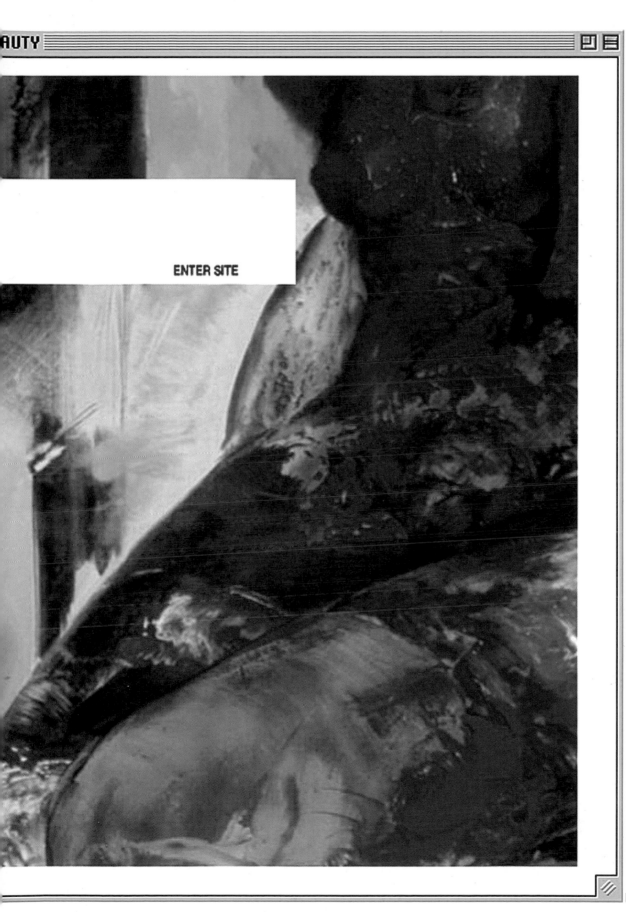

ENTER SITE

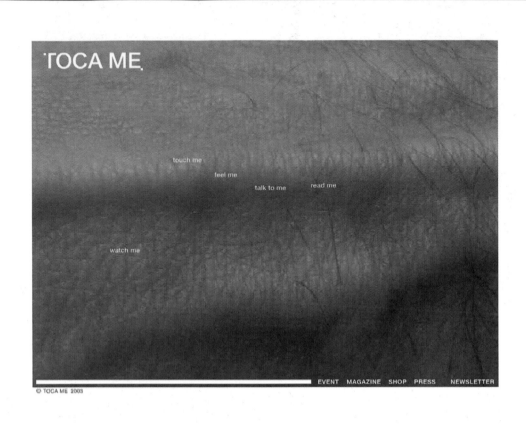

TOCA ME.

touch me

feel me

talk to me   read me

watch me

EVENT   MAGAZINE   SHOP   PRESS   NEWSLETTER

© TOCA ME 2003

ES F ‹ P

www.noodlebox.com

Noodlebox was an experimental web experience made at the
Amaze company by Daniel Brown between 1997-2001. There
are two pieces on this site, the older noodlebox, and the later
bits and pieces.

Shockwave plugin from Macromedia is required to view both
pieces.

New works by Daniel will in the future be found at play/create,
at www.play-create.com

Daniel Brown can be contacted at daniel@danielbrown.com

His commercial site is at www.danielbrown.com

To be on the mailing list and be informed of updates and new
projects, subscribe your email address here (this is the same
list as the play-create list):

your email address   Submit

UK F SW P

www.play-create.com

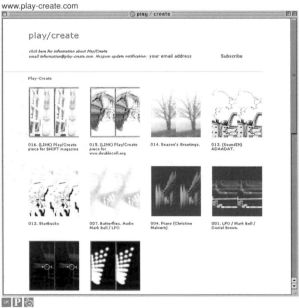

play/create

click here for information about Play/Create.
email information@play-create.com. No spam update notification: your email address   Subscribe

Play-Create

016. (LINK) Play/Create   015. (LINK) Play/Create   014. Season's Greetings.   013. (SoundIN)
piece for SHIFT magazine   piece for   ADAADAT.
                           www.doublecell.org

012. StarBucks   007. Butterflies. Audio   004. Piano (Christine   001. LFO / Mark Bell /
                          Mark Bell / LFO   Malvern)   Daniel Brown.

UK P

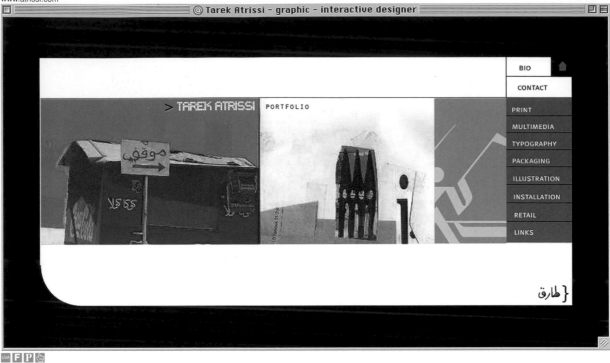

> TAREK ATRISSI   PORTFOLIO

BIO
CONTACT
PRINT
MULTIMEDIA
TYPOGRAPHY
PACKAGING
ILLUSTRATION
INSTALLATION
RETAIL
LINKS

USA F P

http://andreaskoller.com

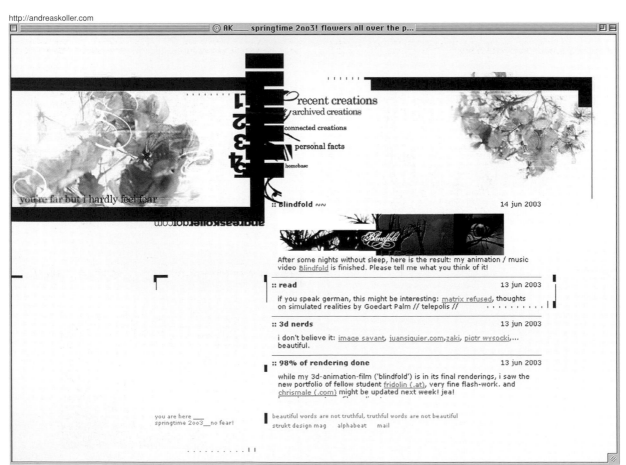

@ AK____ springtime 2oo3! flowers all over the p...

recent creations
archived creations
connected creations
personal facts
homebase

you're far but i hardly feel fear

:: blindfold ~~   14 jun 2003

After some nights without sleep, here is the result: my animation / music video Blindfold is finished. Please tell me what you think of it!

:: read   13 jun 2003

if you speak german, this might be interesting: matrix refused, thoughts on simulated realities by Goedart Palm // telepolis //

:: 3d nerds   13 jun 2003

i don't believe it: image savant, juansiquier.com, zaki, piotr wysocki,... beautiful.

:: 98% of rendering done   13 jun 2003

while my 3d-animation-film ('blindfold') is in its final renderings, i saw the new portfolio of fellow student fridolin (.at), very fine flash-work. and chrismale (.com) might be updated next week! jea!

you are here ____   beautiful words are not truthful, truthful words are not beautiful
springtime 2oo3__no fear! strukt design mag   alphabeat   mail

AT P

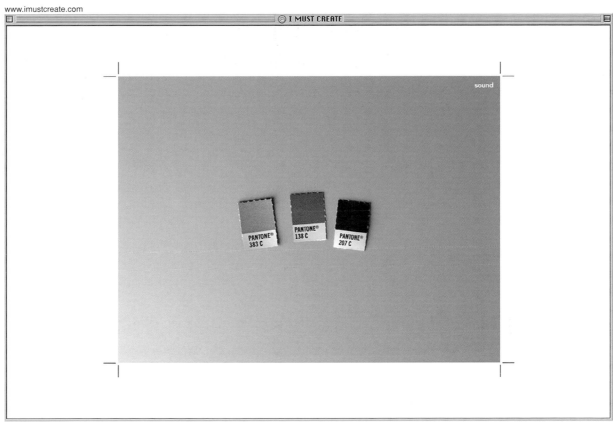

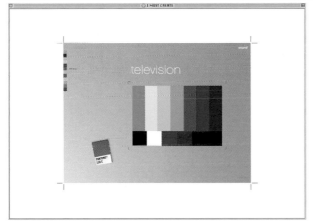

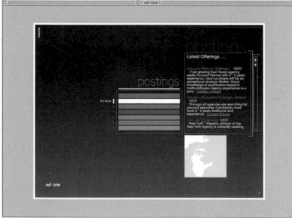

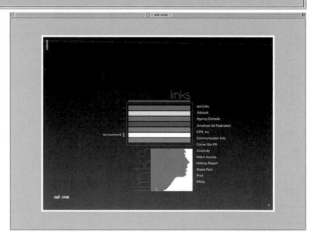

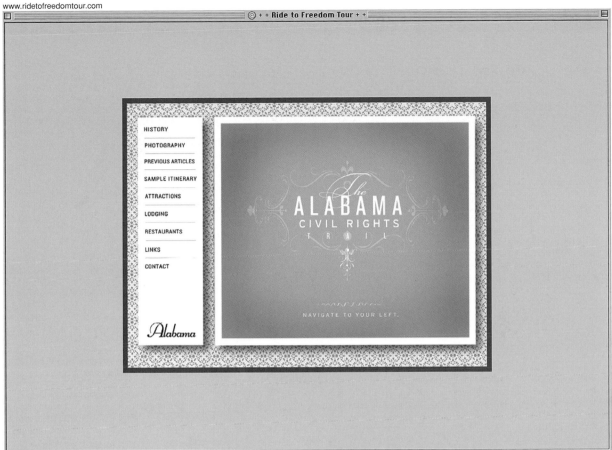

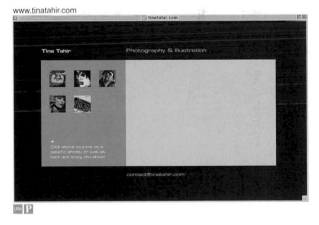

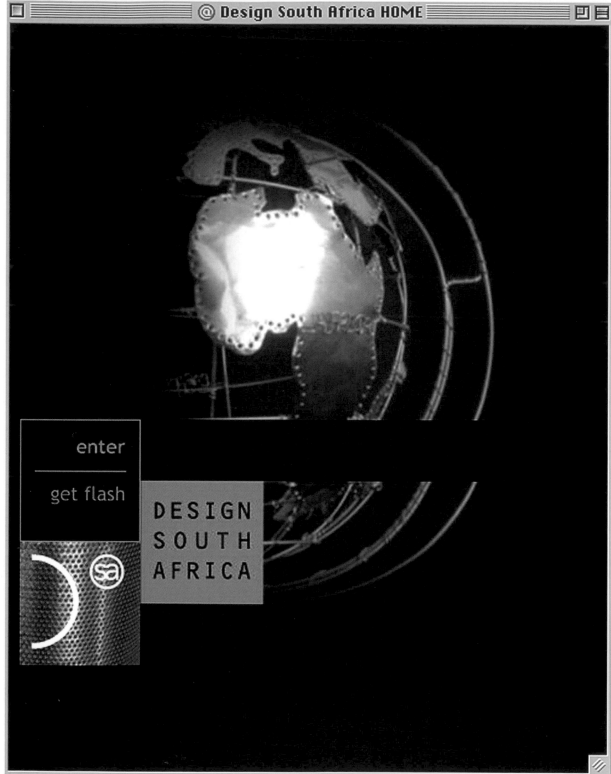

enter

get flash

DESIGN
SOUTH
AFRICA

@ antoniocosta.com

antonio costa

email   resume

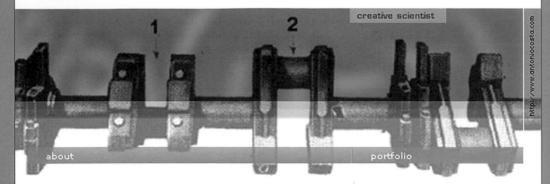

creative scientist

http://www.antoniocosta.com

about   portfolio

A combination of

design, technology and creativity

incredible...

Whether it is design, technology or both - multimedia design demands a person who can be a creative scientist.

web

multimedia

print

concept

resume   PDF

---

news

04.09.2003
Incredible record label - Guidance - check them out and play some tunes at: 33rpm.com

03.24.2003
If you have some time check out http://www.massiveattack.com/ - awesome web experience - site done by hi-res

03.23.2003
New site... just added a new look to the site - more of a portal feel, easier access to portfolio and featured projects. Look around and drop me a line with any feedback - thanks.

02.12.2003
Designed this record sleeve for the new label Bachelor - new release coming out soon.

01.10.2003

featured work

http://www.maryduffymorris.com

http://www.brianataylor.net

http://www.growroomrecords.com

N.e.w. - experimental site

Credits

All rights of the Internet pages and respective brands featured belong to the respective companies and web site holders. www.groupe-e2.com - © Groupe-e2 / Jacques CADILHAC-Architecte EPFL/Cédric CORNU-Architecte EPFL/Antoine SANTIARD-Architecte EPFL/Christophe POUSSIELGUE-Architecte DPLG, Urbaniste ENPC / www.icon-town.de - Bernd Holzhausen www.be-e.de / AllesWirdGut: www.alleswirdgut.cc - designed by www.knallgrau / www.secession.at - design by Christina Goestl / www.simon-robinsonsculptor.com - designed by www.clusta.com / www.designmuseum.org - Copyright Design Museum / www.bludot.com - designed by www.visualade.com / www.enterexit.co.uk - design & art direction: Andy Cole & Imran Younis / www.experimental.ro - Cover photography copyright Antoine Verglas / www.benediktemai.dk - designed by Anders Hornstrup from STUKA www.stuka.dk / www.slu.nu - designed by Rade Milicevic - www.beautifulinformation.com / www.katinkabukh.com - designed by Rune Hoegsberg, from Adopt design: http://adoptdesign.com / www.kenmayerstudios.com - designed by Maria Roth of Maria Roth Design / www.richardmeier.com photograph on the first page by Michael Rutchik / www.grimshaw-architects.com - designed by www.Smoothe.com / www.egidemeertens.be - designed by www.purecommunication.be / DVD credits: narration in English: Malcolm Greene, Germany; Japanese interview translation:Tamami Sanbonmatsu, French interview translation Marc Combes, France; interview in japanese and interpreting: Kazue Imasato, Japan.

Acknowledgements

This publication would never have been completed without the help of many people from all around the world. I would like to thank all designers and companies, who have been creating the face of this new world for their support and generosity. I would like to thank also the production team, specially Thomas Grell and Ricardo Gimenes, whose tireless work have lead to this beautiful book. My many thanks go also to our colaborators in the DVD, Janet Galore, Wim, Boulevart in Belgium, Nicholas Mir Chaikin, Alex Koch, Wysiwyg.de in Germany, Shin Kawakami, Artless Co. in Japan, Malcolm Greene, Tamami Sanbonmatsu, Marc Combes and Kazue Imasato.

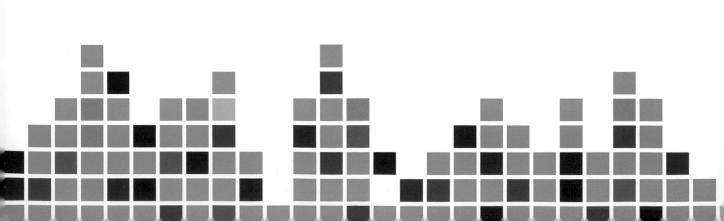

imprint

© 2002 TASCHEN GmbH Hohenzollernring 53, D-50672 Köln
www.taschen.com

Design & layout: Julius Wiedemann, Cologne
Production: Thomas Grell
Editor: Julius Wiedemann
DVD Design, Edition and Production: Ricardo Gimenes
German Translation: Karin Hirschmann
French Translation: Marc Combes
Japanese Translation: Masaaki Takahashi
Chinese Translation: Lay Ya-ching
korean Translation: Moonzoo Yeo
Spanish Translation: Gemma Deza Guil for LocTeam S.L., Barcelona
Portuguese Translation: Miguel Cabelo for LocTeam S.L., Barcelona
Italian translation: Quirino di Zitti for LocTeam S.L., Barcelona
Dutch Translation: Michiel Postema

ISBN: 3-8228-2586-7
ISBN: 4-88783-252-4 (Japanese edition)
Printed in Germany